Innovations in Urban Climate Governance

Building on unique data, this book analyzes the efficacy of a prominent climate change mitigation strategy: voluntary programs for low-carbon buildings and cities. It evaluates the performance of thirty-five voluntary programs from the global North and South, including certification programs, knowledge networks, and novel forms of financing. The author examines them through the lens of club theory, urban transformation theory, and diffusion of innovations theory. Using qualitative comparative analysis (QCA) the book points out the opportunities and constraints of voluntary programs for decarbonizing the built environment, and argues for a transformation of their use in climate change mitigation. The book will appeal to readers interested in sustainable city planning, climate change mitigation, and voluntarism as an alternative governance mechanism for achieving socially and environmentally desirable outcomes. The wide diversity of cases from the global North and South generates new insights, and offers practical guidelines for designing effective programs.

JEROEN VAN DER HEIJDEN is an associate professor of urban climate governance at the Australian National University. He aims to improve local, national, and international outcomes of urban governance on some of the most pressing challenges of our time: climate change and urbanization.

Business and Public Policy

Series Editor

Aseem Prakash, University of Washington

Series Board

Vinod K. Aggarwal, University of California, Berkeley

Tanja A. Börzel, Freie Universität Berlin

David Coen, University College London

Peter Gourevitch, University of California, San Diego

Neil Gunningham, The Australian National University

Witold J. Henisz, University of Pennsylvania

Adrienne Héritier, European University Institute

Chung-in Moon, Yonsei University

Sarah A. Soule, Stanford University

David Vogel, University of California, Berkeley

This series aims to play a pioneering role in shaping the emerging field of business and public policy. *Business and Public Policy* focuses on two central questions. First, how does public policy influence business strategy, operations, organization, and governance, and with what consequences for both business and society? Second, how do businesses themselves influence policy institutions, policy processes, and other policy actors and with what outcomes?

Other Books in the Series

Innovations in Urban Climate Governance

Voluntary Programs for Low-Carbon Buildings and Cities

Jeroen van der Heijden

Australian National University

CAMBRIDGE
UNIVERSITY PRESS

CAMBRIDGE
UNIVERSITY PRESS

University Printing House, Cambridge CB2 8BS, United Kingdom

One Liberty Plaza, 20th Floor, New York, NY 10006, USA

477 Williamstown Road, Port Melbourne, VIC 3207, Australia

4843/24, 2nd Floor, Ansari Road, Daryaganj, Delhi – 110002, India

79 Anson Road, #06–04/06, Singapore 079906

Cambridge University Press is part of the University of Cambridge.

It furthers the University's mission by disseminating knowledge in the pursuit of education, learning, and research at the highest international levels of excellence.

www.cambridge.org
Information on this title: www.cambridge.org/9781108415361
DOI: 10.1017/9781108233293

© Jeroen van der Heijden 2017

First published 2017

Printed in the United Kingdom by Clays, St Ives plc

A catalog record for this publication is available from the British Library.

Library of Congress Cataloging-in-Publication Data
Names: Heijden, Jeroen van der, 1977- author.
Title: Innovations in urban climate governance : voluntary programs for low-carbon buildings and cities / Jeroen van der Heijden, Australian National University.
Description: New York, NY : Cambridge University Press, 2017. | Series: Business and public policy | Includes bibliographical references and index.
Identifiers: LCCN 2017006427 | ISBN 9781108415361 (Hardback)
Subjects: LCSH: Urban ecology (Sociology) | Sustainable urban development–Citizen participation. | City planning–Environmental aspects–Citizen participation. | Social action. | Voluntarism. | BISAC: POLITICAL SCIENCE / General.
Classification: LCC HT241 .H443 2017 | DDC 304.2/091732–dc23
LC record available at https://lccn.loc.gov/2017006427

ISBN 978-1-108-41536-1 Hardback

Contents

Tables

Moving Forward, Moving Sideways
Understanding Voluntary Programs and Their Role in Sustainable City Development and Transformation

I am like the crawfish and advance sideways   Michel Foucault (2009, 78)

No book on governance and governmentality appears to be complete without a quotation from Foucault — and this is one of my personal favorites. Although unenlightening about governance and governmentality, the notion of sideways advancement perfectly captures the four-year cross-border research project that lies at the foundation of this book (2012–2015).[1]

This work explores innovative forms of governance for low-carbon building, city development, and transformation. It studies a series of voluntary programs that incentivize individuals and organizations to improve the performance of their cities and buildings well beyond the requirements of statutory building codes and planning legislation. It is of interest to readers engaged in the issues surrounding resource-efficient and environmentally sustainable city planning, climate change mitigation, and voluntarism as an alternative governance mechanism for achieving societal and environmentally desirable outcomes. The book comprises insight derived from thirty-five voluntary programs from nations including Australia, India, Malaysia, the Netherlands, Singapore, and the United States.

Let me offer some insight regarding the sideways advancement mentioned. As a trained architect with a PhD in public administration, I have a curiosity in buildings and cities, governance, and climate change that has led to the conjunction of these aspects in the research project underlying this book. The research project was generously funded by the Netherlands Organisation for Scientific Research through a competitive grant scheme. My initial research proposal for this grant sought to use the "club theory perspective" (Potoski & Prakash, 2009) as a point of departure in explaining and studying the performance of voluntary programs throughout Europe.

Life being the way it is, by the time I was awarded the grant, circumstances had already begun to move sideways. My relocation to Australia to take up a position at the Australian National University resulted in changes to the project: it now made sense not only to look at programs in European countries, but also to include examples from Australia. Similarly, regular stopovers in Asia on my travel between Australia and the Netherlands deepened my interest in Asian cities and urbanization, suggesting the benefit of including examples from Asia also. In addition to this first sidewise move from the original research plan, I expanded the research project to include a number of further voluntary programs in the United States that I could study while attending conferences — in Chapter 1 I explain the theoretical and practical motivations of their inclusion.

An additional set of changes to this research project have been theoretical. In seeking to explain the performance of the thirty-five voluntary programs, I quickly realized that the club theory perspective could not fully account for the observed variance in program performance. The club theory perspective holds that the stringency of rules underlying a voluntary program, the stringency of their enforcement, and the rewards to program participants explain program performance. Seeking to understand better what explained the variance in program performance in my study, I had to make another sidewise change. This occurred through a broad exploration of related literature: urban transformation literature directed me to examine the role of local governments in voluntary programs, and diffusion of innovation literature suggested the need to analyze the network of prospective participants a voluntary program is designed to reach. By adding theoretical perspectives from these literatures to the club theory perspective — those of local government and diffusion of innovation networks — I am able to delineate the full scope of observed variance in program performance of the thirty-five examples studied. Chapter 1 further explains this iterative and sidewise-moving process of research development.

By the time I had effected these reorientations — from a Eurocentric research project reliant on the club theory to a more global six-nation study amalgamating three theoretical perspectives — and collected my data, I anticipated that outlining and discussing the results in monograph format would be relatively easy. However, the process of writing has constituted the most challenging, most significant component of the research. This has been a process of considerable retrospection, particularly in view of the difficulties of reporting an in-depth medium-n study, which necessitates balancing a wealth of unique understandings with a confined number of general patterns. Which unique insights should be included and which omitted? How often should findings be repeated to demonstrate a general pattern? While the methodological literature is highly positive about the possibilities of in-depth medium-n studies like this one, it is reticent on how to report on such studies (see, e.g., Brady &

Collier, 2004; Della Porta & Keating, 2008; Engeli & Rothmayr, 2014; Goertz & Mahony, 2012).[2] In addition to this, not many examples of in-depth medium-n governance studies were available at the commencement of writing.[3] This necessitated the most radical sidewise redirection at the time of beginning the book: establishing a monograph structure that captures both the breadth and the depth of the research parameters. I began by applying a number of different models. The first model was fairly conventional and grouped the examples by clusters according to country, dedicating a chapter to each — for example, considering the causes for adoption of voluntary programs, and their performance, in each country. This resulted in much repetition regarding findings on roughly similarly designed programs across the chapters. The second model clustered the examples qualitatively according to the programs' design characteristics and dedicated a chapter to each cluster. Again this resulted in much repetition. The third model relied heavily on the logic and tools of qualitative comparative analysis (QCA — extensively explained in Appendix C) to develop an evidence-based typology at the start of the book, and then dedicated a chapter to each type. This model required a readership with considerable knowledge of QCA to be able to follow the narrative, which I felt asked too much.

The final sidewise step is a deviation from the conventional book models mentioned (clustering by country, clustering by design, evidence-based clustering) to the model used in this book. I first discuss programs aligning with three dominant designs from roughly similar country contexts (Australia, the Netherlands, and the United States) as a means of developing an understanding of the unique details of these programs. I then apply QCA to the full set of programs from these countries in order to discern general patterns in program performance. I conclude the empirical part of the book by discussing a set of similarly designed programs that are implemented in different country contexts (India, Malaysia, and Singapore) to gain an understanding of the reach of the findings and the conclusion drawn from the general patterns of performance in the previous section.

Looking back at the book-writing process, it is the final sidewise development of the research analysis — and of the structure and emphasis of that analysis for the reader — that has enabled a particularly valuable step forward. It has allowed me to present a narrative that does justice to the theoretical and empirical nuance of the study as well as the breadth and depth of the data, propelling forward our understanding of voluntary programs and their role in resource efficient, low-carbon, and environmentally sustainable city development and transformation.

xii   Moving Forward, Moving Sideways

About the Author

Dr Jeroen van der Heijden (1977) is an Associate Professor holding a joint position at the Australian National University (RegNet: School of Regulation and Global Governance) and the University of Amsterdam (Amsterdam Law School). He received his PhD in public administration (highest honors) in 2009, and his MSc in architecture (high distinction) in 2002, both from the Delft University of Technology, the Netherlands.

Jeroen works at the intersections of regulation and governance, policy change, and urban development and transformation. His research aims to improve local, national, and international outcomes of urban governance on some of the most pressing challenges of our time: climate change, energy and water use, and a growing and increasingly urbanizing world population. Through his work Jeroen seeks to inform ongoing academic debates on these challenges, as well as to provide hands-on lessons to policy makers and practitioners on how to govern urban sustainability and resilience on a day-to-day basis.

He has a track record of outstanding publications. Over the last decade he has published four books (including *Governance for Urban Sustainability and Resilience*, Edward Elgar, 2014) and more than forty articles in peer-reviewed journals. He has also published a series of more than sixty articles, book chapters, and positioning papers for a policy and practitioner audience. Jeroen maintains an urban sustainability and resilience blog on which he regularly discusses his research findings (www.urban sustainabilityresilience.wordpress.com).

Acknowledgments

No part of a book is more enjoyable to write than the acknowledgments. While this book is a sole-authored monograph, I prefer to look on it as a collaborative project involving many people. I was in the fortunate position to meet them, to learn from them, to be guided and corrected by them, and to draw all their insights on voluntary programs, environmentally sustainable buildings and cities, and responses to climate change together in this book.

First and foremost, I am grateful for the more than two hundred individuals — voluntary program administrators, policy makers, bureaucrats, property developers, contractors, property owners and managers, architects, engineers, and building end-users — who have given me some of their time to answer questions I had about voluntary programs in which they were involved or had experience. I have interviewed most of them in the period 2012–2014, and a small number in follow-up interviews in 2015. You have provided me with much more than just answers to my questions. The research underlying this book has been a life-changing experience. I fondly recall a CEO of a major corporation who bred butterflies in his office, locals from Delhi who introduced me to the region's fabulous cuisine, government officials in the United States who have gone out of their way to introduce me to informants, and all the other unique experiences that have come with each and every interview conducted. The narrative that unfolds in this book does not look favorably on some of the voluntary programs in which you are or have been involved. I hope you understand this is not intended as personal critique, but rather as empirical observation. Without people such as you placing so much time and effort into trying to improve the environmental sustainability of buildings and cities, the world would be even worse off.

I am also grateful to Aseem Prakash and John Haslam, who have supported me in seeing this book published with Cambridge University Press — thanks also to all other Cambridge University Press staff in processing the book manuscript, and to two anonymous reviewers for excellent comments on an earlier draft version. Andrew Watts has done an amazing job in cutting out all redundant words and sentences from an earlier version of this book, and in making the text more accessible. Particular thanks go to Veronica Taylor, Sharon Friel, Adrienne de Moor-van Vugt, Edgar du Perron, and Leonard Besselink for making possible the joint position I held at the Australian National University and the University of Amsterdam while carrying out the research underlying this book. The Dutch Organisation for Scientific Research provided me with a generous VENI grant in the period 2012–2015 to conduct this research (grant number 451-11-015), and the Australian Research Council awarded a generous DECRA fellowship that I have partly used to tie up loose ends for this book in 2016 (grant number DE15100511). Thanks to both organizations for trusting me with the time and funds provided.

As always I like to thank Peter May for his ongoing support — reading draft chapters, providing book-writing advice, and checking in every now and then about how I am doing personally. Thanks to Ben Cashore for challenging my initial research design at the very start of the project, and for making me think more critically about voluntary programs. Many thanks to my colleagues at RegNet (now the School of Regulation and Global Governance) for listening to my ramblings about this book, and specific thanks to Peter Drahos, Neil Gunningham, and Peter Grabosky for commenting on draft chapters and offering sage advice about the ups and downs of writing scholarly books (and to Peter D. for playing a game of chess that has taken longer, so far, than writing this book — that keeps matters in perspective). Thanks to Andy Jordan, Ricky Burdett, and Gundre Jayachandra Reddy for hosting me for extensive periods at, respectively, the Tyndall Centre for Climate Change Research (University of East Anglia), LSE Cities (London School of Economics), and the Centre for Southeast Asian & Pacific Studies (Sri Venkateswara University). Thanks to Mike Howlett for inviting me to a workshop at the Lee Kuan Yew School of Public Policy (National University of Singapore). And special thanks to Andy and Mike for reading and commenting on draft sections of this book.

I am particularly grateful to Joost and Joachim for ongoing friendship and support in my academic (ad)ventures — friendship and support that are growing stronger even while we are some sixteen thousand kilometers apart these days. Thanks to my parents and brother for understanding that I put my academic curiosity in front of being close to them, and for supporting me in this decision.

Some aspects of Chapter 1 advance ideas that I introduced in Van der Heijden (2013a, 2013b, 2013c, 2013e). Chapter 2 builds on and incorporates ideas that I have explored and developed in van der Heijden (2012, 2014a, 2015c), and Chapter 3 on van der Heijden (2012, 2013d, 2015f, 2015g). Chapter 4 is inspired by and builds on work that I began to explore in van der Heijden (2015b), Chapter 5 on van der Heijden (2016a), Chapter 6 on van der Heijden (2017), and Chapter 8 on van der Heijden (2016b).

1 Why Focus on Voluntary Programs for Sustainable Buildings and Cities?

This book is about an essential part of our lives — buildings and cities. At their most basic level they provide shelter from the elements, but they do much more than that. Buildings and cities are where we spend most of our time; they are crucial to wealth accumulation, and they are an important part of our cultural identity. They are essential also in the transition toward a resource-efficient, low-carbon, environmentally sustainable way of living.

Buildings and cities are a significant source of local and global environmental problems, including water and air pollution, resource depletion, loss of biodiversity and, last but not least, climate change. Their construction, maintenance, and use require unsustainable levels of nonrenewable resources and result in unsustainable levels of waste. The wastes resulting from these activities are problematic, in particular their carbon emissions, which make the built environment an area where rapid action is necessary: already 35 percent of global carbon emissions are related to the construction, maintenance, and use of buildings. To make matters worse, today's built environment has to grow rapidly over the next decades to accommodate an increasing and further urbanizing world population. If a business-as-usual development scenario persists, this will only add to today's global environmental problems.

Paradoxically, the answer to these problems lies in the further and future (re)development of the built environment. The technology and knowledge of behavioral change are widely available to construct buildings and cities that use fewer resources and emit less carbon than conventional ones, or none at all. Even more, significant cuts in building-related carbon emissions can be made at net cost benefit — reduction estimations range from 30 to 80 percent. But to achieve these goals this technology and knowledge need timely application, and on a large scale.

Governing this transition is complicated, and traditional governance instruments, such as mandatory building codes and planning legislation, have not been able to incentivize quick and comprehensive implementation. In response governments, firms, and other organizations have been trialing and experimenting innovative governance instruments for some decades now. Often these instruments do not mandate compliance by individuals and organizations, but instead incentivize them through monetary, informational, reputational, and other benefits to commit voluntarily to them. This book seeks to understand this trend of voluntary programs for resource-efficient, environmentally friendly, and low-carbon buildings and cities, and questions whether it helps in accelerating and enlarging decarbonization of the built environment.

Main Questions

Between 2005 and 2010 Australia's three largest cities were in healthy competition to become the nation's leading city in terms of carbon emission reductions — similar "competitions" were under way in other countries (van der Heijden, 2014a). Sydney, Melbourne, and Brisbane were outbidding each other's anticipated reductions, and set ambitions that reached well beyond those prescribed by the Australian Commonwealth Government. In all cities it was expected that retrofitting the existing building stock, in particular, would considerably add to the cost of meeting these ambitions. Yet, the cities lacked the governance instruments to achieve these goals, and faced resistance from local property owners when they proposed mandatory retrofits (Beatley, 2009; Cork, 2010).

Inspired by examples in London and Toronto, the city of Sydney set up a voluntary program — the Better Buildings Partnership — that joins the City Council and the city's fourteen major commercial property owners that together claim title to more than 50 percent of the city's office space. This space is responsible for 25 percent of the city's carbon emissions — predominantly as a result of the energy needed to heat, cool, and otherwise operate these buildings. In the partnership the property owners have committed to reduce their property's carbon emissions voluntarily by 70 percent of 2006 emission levels by 2030. Through the partnership they share their experiences to learn from each other, and the city supports them by reducing regulatory barriers for building retrofits, involves them in future city development policies so they can plan their property portfolios accordingly, and highlights their leading performance in national and international media outlets. At the time of writing this book, in 2015, they had already achieved half of their reduction target — well ahead of their initial planning: a truly extraordinary performance (see Chapter 5).

The voluntary programs this book is concerned with are, specifically, innovative forms of financing such as revolving loan funds, property owner—government networks like the Better Buildings Partnership, and the certification and classification of urban sustainability credentials of buildings and city districts (the term "urban sustainability" is used throughout the book to refer to resource-efficient, low-carbon, and environmentally sustainable buildings and cities). Normally they are introduced as complements or substitutes for traditional governance instruments such as mandatory building codes and planning legislation. Voluntary programs for sustainable building and city development have been trialed around the globe for some decades now. However, very little in the way of analysis exists as to their performance. This book therefore asks: *To what extent and how do voluntary programs contribute to the construction, maintenance, and use of resource-efficient, low-carbon, environmentally sustainable buildings and cities? What future application of these voluntary programs may help in accelerating decarbonization of the built environment?* It seeks to answer these questions by systematically analyzing the performance of thirty-five voluntary programs in Australia, India, Malaysia, the Netherlands, Singapore, and the United States.

Answering these questions is theoretically relevant for at least two related reasons. First is the commitment to these voluntary programs by governments (B. Evans, Joas, Sundback, & Thobald, 2005; Global Cities Covenant on Climate, 2013; ICLEI, 2012; Mazmanian & Blanco, 2014): why are they considered improvements on mandatory governance instruments? Their uptake is a considerable institutional break from centuries of urban governance practice that likely comes at substantial cost and loss of power for governments (Pierre, 2011; van der Heijden, 2014a). Second is the adoption of these voluntary programs by actors other than governments, such as citizens, civil society organizations, and firms (IPCC, 2014; UN, 2012a). Why would they subject themselves voluntarily to governance instruments that require them to change their behavior? This is contrary to what would be expected of business entities, as they will likely incur financial and other costs with no immediate dividend (a comparable argument is made by Dashwood, 2012).

Pivotal Message: A Leadership Delusion

Assessing the performance of voluntary programs can be challenging, a topic further discussed in Chapter 3. This book follows current practice in related studies and assesses this performance by addressing three direct program outcomes (de Vries, Nentjes, & Odam, 2012; Gunningham, 2009; Potoski & Prakash, 2009): (i) their ability to incentivize participation and attract participants; (ii) their ability to improve participant behavior in terms of sustainable buildings constructed or retrofitted, or improved building use performance; and (iii) their relative performance when contrasted with the behavior of the full pool of prospective participants. Yet, merely focusing on direct outcomes might overlook other important outcomes, such as policy lessons learned, spillover effects on nonparticipants, or longer-term outcomes (Auld, 2014). In order to glimpse behind the statistics and understand their broader implications, the empirical chapters single out a number of programs for in-depth analysis.

This book argues that considering their direct outcomes, the voluntary programs for low-carbon buildings and cities studied should not be overly relied on — or at least, not in the ways they are currently applied. In absolute numbers their performance is sometimes mind-bogglingly effective, with some programs attracting thousands of participants and billions of square meters of built-up space. Yet, in relative numbers they often indicate little overall improvement of reduced resource consumption and carbon emissions. As is often the case with innovative governance instruments, voluntary programs for low-carbon buildings and cities are replete with almost as many constraints as opportunities.

The opportunities of these programs are readily apparent: they allow trials of innovative governance approaches to decarbonize the built environment; they incentivize the construction and property sectors to move beyond compliance with mandatory building codes and planning legislation; and they reward leading practice by property developers, owners, and occupants. Throughout the book it becomes clear that these programs have generated a wealth of lessons learned about how — and how not — to govern building and city decarbonization, and have resulted in an uncountable number of best practices for low-carbon building, city development, and use. The opportunities of these programs should, however, not be overestimated: although they have set standards for best practice and revealed important lessons, their relative impact is marginal at best — and includes a number of caveats.

I argue that what is most problematic for these programs is that they have resulted in a leadership delusion. That is, those involved in the development, administration, and implementation of voluntary programs — as well as those who voluntarily commit to them — have strong incentives to present a narrative of successful performance even where there is none. This leadership delusion operates at different levels. To begin, the programs predominantly focus on the leaders in the construction and property sectors (in the sense of pioneers or "front-runners"; see Teisman, van Buuren, & Gerrits, 2009) and not on the majority of property developers, owners, and occupants. Solutions to the environmental problems of buildings are, however, nonscalable — the built environment is not characterized by "winner takes all" processes but by a "long tail" — which requires the inclusion of both leaders and the majority. Program administrators and participants also tend to market the marginal performance of these programs as outstanding, and the popular media echo this narrative by concentrating attention on the few instances of positive performance rather than on the negative aspects of the challenges faced. This may direct political and societal attention away from this challenge, giving rise to the false impression that sustainable buildings are "the new norm" in the construction and property sectors (Yudelson & Meyer, 2013, 17). Finally, many programs marketed as leaders in performance actually lack ambition and set relatively easy targets for resource efficiency improvements and carbon emission reductions — the ambitious Better Buildings Partnership in Sydney is an exception in this regard. Although low targets make programs attractive to prospective participants because they are easy to meet, the buildings included under such programs can become locked into suboptimal levels of performance while their owners and users mistakenly feel that participation in a "leading" voluntary program establishes their environmental credentials.

Notwithstanding my critique of voluntary programs for sustainable buildings and cities, I see prospective value in their use in relation to mandatory programs. In Chapter 9 I argue that their position in the larger urban governance framework needs rethinking: hybrid mandatory/voluntary governance instruments may be created that require participation but leave the level of compliance voluntary; instead of opting into voluntary programs one could think of programs that allow for opting out, or voluntary programs may be part of a rolling-rule regime that makes today's leading practice in a voluntary program tomorrow's mandatory bottom line.

Main Theoretical, Empirical, and Methodological Contributions

This book is relevant to a range of scholarly audiences, as well as to policy makers and practitioners concerned with low-carbon city development and transformation. More precisely, the book will be relevant to those seeking long-term responses to climate change, those focused on sustainable cities, and those seeking information on the efficacy of voluntary programs and other novel governance approaches as policy tools in modifying societal behavior toward desirable ends. The core focus of the book is on voluntary programs for low-carbon building and city development and transformation, but the lessons drawn from the empirical study in all likelihood apply to voluntary programs and other innovative or experimental governance approaches well beyond those addressing the construction and property sectors. The book makes major theoretical and empirical contributions, as follows.

Theoretical Contributions

The book's major theoretical contribution is the introduction of a "diffusion network perspective" to studies of voluntary programs. The diffusion network perspective helps to better understanding of how a voluntary program spreads throughout the pool of participants it targets, or fails to do so. This perspective acknowledges that if the pool of participants is heterogeneous — as is often the case with voluntary programs for sustainable building and city development — a voluntary program may face considerable difficulties in attracting specific sub-groups of targeted participants. Earlier theoretical perspectives of voluntary programs have not accounted for the possibility of both homogeneous and heterogeneous participant pools occurring in voluntary programs. The diffusion network perspective considers both options, thereby advancing an understanding of the conditions that affect the performance of voluntary programs in terms of uptake and goal achievement.

A second major theoretical contribution of the book is the introduction of a template suitable for the study of voluntary programs that specifically target low-carbon building and city development. This template combines an established theoretical perspective in voluntary program literature — Matthew Potoski and Aseem Prakash's (2009) "club theory" perspective — with theoretical perspectives from the urban governance literature — that local government is ideally situated to address complex urban governance issues such as environmental sustainability (cf. B. Evans et al., 2005) — and the diffusion network perspective mentioned previously. As illustrated in this book, this theoretical template advances understanding of variance in the use of governance instruments in different urban settings and countries, the role of government and other actors in contemporary urban governance, and variance in urban governance failure and success. In doing so it bridges and contributes to debates on novel forms of environmental governance, specifically voluntary programs (Backstrand, Khan, Kronsell, & Lovbrand, 2010; Holley, Gunningham, & Shearing, 2012; Prakash & Potoski, 2012; Wurzel, Zito, & Jordan, 2013), and governance for urban sustainability

(Fiorino, 2014; Kjaer, 2009; Mossberger & Stoker, 2001; Peters & Pierre, 2012; Pierre, 2011; Tao, 2009).

Empirical Contributions

The book's major empirical contribution is observed behavior and responses indicating what I have termed here the "leadership delusion." It advances earlier observed instances of "greenwash" and "window dressing," as these often relate to situations where only the participants of voluntary programs and other novel governance instruments create an illusion of good performance (Lyon & Wren Montgomery, 2015). The leadership delusion may help to provide a partial answer to the oft-raised question why, in the face of a major environmental crisis, so many urban sustainability solutions are merely symptomatic and not fundamental (Blanco & Mazmanian, 2014; Bulkeley & Betsill, 2003; P. James, 2015; P. Taylor, 2013). With reputations at stake, money and time invested in the development of voluntary programs, and an eagerness to be perceived as leading city — or not-for-profit — ventures in the area of urban sustainability, the program administrators' self-interest easily outweighs the public interest.

A second major empirical contribution of the book is the focus on voluntary programs that align with the currently popular policy paradigms of ecological modernization and green growth. These paradigms build on a win–win narrative that new technologies designed to improve resource efficiency and reduce carbon emissions are a sufficient response to climate change risks and help to stimulate the economy (Dryzek, 2005; Hayden, 2014; Matthews, 2015). This narrow view of urban sustainability as a form of ecoefficiency is often censured. Critical scholars duly ask: How can the paradigm of economic growth and the ongoing development that it builds be sustainable in a finite world? How does a narrow understanding of urban sustainability address inequalities between populations in the Global North and South? Why does this narrow understanding of urban sustainability only address "doing less harm" as opposed to improving unsustainable circumstances (B. Evans et al., 2005; Hayden, 2014; Krueger & Gibbs, 2007; Robinson & Cole, 2015)? While the scholarly community is increasingly critical of these policy paradigms, albeit often on normative grounds, the idea of ecoefficiency is infiltrating urban policies at the national and city levels. This book provides empirical support for growing scholarly critique. It determines that the win–win narrative attached to many of the voluntary programs studied is not realized in practice, and ought not to be considered attractive enough for individuals and organizations to participate in them.

Methodological Contributions

The book combines rigorous in-depth analyses of voluntary programs for low-carbon buildings and cities with qualitative comparative analysis (further discussed in the following section). This has resulted in two main contributions to the comparative method (Goertz & Mahony, 2012; Peters, 1998; van der Heijden, 2014b). First is the insight that qualitative comparative analysis is ideally suited to make visible and analyze asymmetry between factors related to a single phenomenon (condition, independent variable, explanans) and to that phenomenon itself (outcome, dependent variable, explanandum).[1] We humans are biased toward symmetry and easily assume that if X is somehow involved in the occurrence of Y, then Y will not occur when X is not involved (Kahneman, 2011). There is often, however, no theoretical reason to assume symmetry between these factors and that phenomenon. This observation goes back to Karl Popper's (2002 [1935]) insight that the empirical sciences are concerned with one-sided falsification of statements, and that no symmetrical relationships can be assumed from one-sided falsification. This book makes visible a number of such asymmetrical relationships between voluntary program design conditions and their outcomes. One of these relates to the role of financial rewards that accrue to participants in voluntary programs. In line with the literature on voluntary programs, this study finds that such rewards are vital in explaining why individuals and organizations participate in voluntary programs. The absence of such rewards, however, is not crucial to explaining why they do not participate, and flags the asymmetrical relationship between financial rewards and program outcomes.

The second methodological contribution is the inclusion of both successful voluntary programs in the study and programs that are less successful in attracting participants and changing their behavior. In Chapter 7 it becomes clear that the less-successful programs provide a much richer understanding of voluntary program performance than do the successful ones. While this is partly a result of the dominance of less successful programs in this study, the finding indicates that a bias toward studying successful examples in evaluation studies of the type presented in this book, as is sometimes observed (Taleb, 2007), will only provide a limited understanding of why programs perform as they do.

It was not my initial aim to make this a book about the comparative method, and these findings should be considered as a fortunate but unplanned direction of the study. They may, however, be of inspiration to others interested in theorizing on and applying the comparative method.

Research Approach: Adaptive Theory, Realist Evaluation Practice, and a Configurational Comparative Research Design

To answer the two main research questions introduced earlier, as well as the broader questions they address, this book examines a series of voluntary programs in six countries. The set of programs studied in this book is by no means representative of all possible program designs and contexts; I feel, however, that this set does provide a broad enough knowledge base and open up a sufficient window on their opportunities and constraints to provide answers to these questions. Furthermore, the limitation of breadth is balanced against the depth and rigor of the programs systematically studied in the empirical chapters (a comparable approach to studying voluntary programs is followed by, among others, Hoffmann, 2011; Morgenstern & Pizer, 2007). The study reported on in this book commenced in 2012 and was completed in 2015, but it is also informed by work carried out for the book *Governance for Urban Sustainability and Resilience,* which collects together a series of research projects I was involved in from 2005 to 2013. These projects offered background insight into the global rise of innovative and experimental governance instruments for urban sustainability, including voluntary programs (van der Heijden, 2014a).

Adaptive Theory: Moving Backward and Forward between Theory and Data

In this project I followed an "adaptive theory" approach. Adaptive theory seeks to connect existing theory with insight from empirical research to understand best the topic of inquiry, here the ability of voluntary programs to accelerate the transition to low-carbon building and city development and transformation (cf. Layder, 2006). Adaptive theory helps to develop bounded generalizations and propositions about the basic performance patterns and mechanisms of voluntary programs that will likely be found in diverse settings — this is known as "moderatum generalization" (Payne & Williams, 2005). This approach aligns with what others refer to as "abductive research" — a means to bridge inductive and deductive approaches to generalize study findings (Paavola, 2004; Van Eijk, 2010), and it aligns with the development of "middle-range theory," which allows for the production of propositions about the common threads of, for instance, voluntary programs, while acknowledging that the wide diversity in individual program designs and contexts makes a comprehensive explanatory framework unlikely (Merton, 1957; Pawson, 2013).

In the process of moving backward and forward between theory and data — which I believe is the easiest way to explain the adaptive theory approach to research — I started with an extensive review of the state of the art in voluntary program literature to understand what program conditions are expected to affect program performance (van der Heijden, 2012, see further Chapter 3). This review pointed to a number of program design conditions (their rules, the enforcement of these rules, and the rewards to those participating in the program) and context conditions (existing legal and regulatory requirements, economic circumstances, and societal pressures) as being relevant in influencing voluntary program performance, including their ability to attract participants, and their capacity to change the behavior of participants. These conditions and program outcomes (independent and dependent variables; explanans and explanandums) are central in Matthew Potoski's and Aseem Prakash's (2009) "club theory perspective" of voluntary programs. This perspective was prominent in the initial phase of the research project. I later found, however, that these conditions are insufficient to explain variance in the performance of the programs studied.

Realist Evaluation Practice and a Configurational Comparative Research Design

In explaining program performance I followed realist evaluation practice — a form of theory-driven evaluation (Pawson & Tilley, 1997). This evaluation practice sits well with the adaptive theory approach because it acknowledges the role of context and provides explanation according to the precise circumstances under which a theory holds (Pawson, 2013). In realist evaluation the core question is whether and how differences in program outcomes can be explained by differences in program contexts and program designs.[2] Context here should be understood as having a broader meaning than differences in country or sector characteristics of voluntary programs, and may also relate to, for instance, differences between groups of participants involved in these programs. As becomes clear later in the book, differences between various groups of participants indeed help to explain the differences in program performance. What makes realist evaluation of further relevance is that it acknowledges that outcomes are likely explained by configurations of conditions and mechanisms — as opposed to evaluative practices that seek to find the single condition or small number of conditions that explain these outcomes best. That voluntary program performance is a result of a range of interacting design and context conditions is, indeed, a key finding of the review of the voluntary program literature. Over the years scholars have pointed out, often through small-n case studies, that differently designed voluntary programs may yield similar outcomes — known as "equifinality" — and have highlighted that there likely is no single condition that explains the performance of voluntary programs best. This work points out that program performance is best explained by focusing on interacting conditions — known as "conjunctural causation" (further discussed in Chapter 3).

The book sets out a project that seeks to understand the performance of voluntary programs through comparative analysis of real-world examples. In studying these it follows a condition-oriented approach to gain insight into the performance of the programs studied, and combines this with a case-oriented approach — known as a configurational comparative research design (Rihoux & Ragin, 2009). This design is ideally suited to accommodate conjunctural causation (interacting conditions) and equifinality (different sets of interacting conditions that may yield similar outcomes). The design is also ideally suited to explore the explanatory reach of existing theorizing — following realist evaluation I carried out this research, in part, as a means to assess the club theory perspective, and made this one of the study's topics of inquiry (cf. Pawson, 2013). Following realist evaluation practice, I have combined quantitative and qualitative data sources throughout the study.

Adaptive Theory in This Book

I shall describe how, and why, I combined the adaptive theory approach, realist evaluation practice, and configurational comparative research design. The study began with a strict application of Potoski and Prakash's (2009) club theory perspective for voluntary programs. This perspective holds that three core voluntary program design conditions explain program performance — the rules they set for participants, the enforcement of these rules, and the rewards that accrue to participants. In my study these three conditions explain the variance in program performance of only a small number of the programs studied (fewer than 10 percent), and leave the variance of program performance of the majority of programs unexplained. Strictly speaking, the explanatory value of this perspective in absolute terms is limited to the programs studied in this book. Potoski and Prakash emphasize, however, that program participants may receive different rewards. Therefore, I unpacked the broad condition "rewards" in the three dominant rewards characterizing the programs studied: financial, leadership, and other nonfinancial rewards. These five conditions (rules, monitoring and enforcement, and the three rewards) explain the variance in performance of fewer than half of the programs studied (46 percent), but still leave the majority unexplained. This still does not constitute satisfactory coverage.

To understand what may explain the remaining variance in performance I then turned to urban transition literature. This literature looks favorably on voluntary programs and other innovative and experimental governance interventions that seek to scale up and speed up decarbonization of the built environment. This literature is decidedly hopeful about the involvement of local governments in this process, and building on this literature I added the condition "local government involvement" to the theoretical framework (B. Evans et al., 2005). The full set of now six conditions explained the variance in the performance of a little more than half of the voluntary programs studied (59 percent), but still left a considerable part of the variance unexplained. From here on I returned to the data collected to understand what might explain the remaining variance. In closely studying my data and through follow-up interviews I realized that the experts I had interviewed repeatedly discussed the problem of reaching out to prospective participants. The diffusion of innovation literature is interested in the communication of novel ideas (e.g., new governance instruments such as voluntary programs) within a social system (for instance, a pool of prospective participants), and from this literature I took the condition "type of diffusion network" as an additional condition that may explain voluntary program performance (E. M. Rogers, 1995). The full set of seven conditions finally enabled me to explain all variance in the voluntary programs studied and their performance outcomes.

In sum, the theoretical template that I built for this research is more precise in explaining the observed variance in the voluntary programs studied than any of the individual theoretical perspectives from which it draws. The template reflects ongoing dialogue between theory and data in studying these programs, following the adaptive theory approach that emphasizes the dual influence of prior theoretical ideas and models and the generation of concepts and theory from the ongoing generation of data (see also Levy, 2008; Ragin, 1987).

Program Context and Program Design Selection

The full research project this book reports on includes close to seventy voluntary programs for sustainable building and city development and transformation.[3] The book discusses twenty-six of these programs (in Australia, the Netherlands, and the United States) in detail in the empirical

Chapters 4 to 6, and in Chapter 8 includes findings from another nine programs (in India, Malaysia, and Singapore) to broaden the findings to other country contexts. The choice for this staged release of research findings throughout the book is largely methodological, as explained before, and partly inspired by Steven Vogel's (1996) *Freer Markets, More Rules*. Programs were selected to include sufficient variety and similarity in country contexts and program designs.

Country Selection: Homogeneity and Heterogeneity

The literature considers a number of contextual conditions of relevance when seeking to explain the performance of voluntary programs. Dominant among these are existing and possible future state-led regulation and legislation, economic circumstances, and societal pressure in the area these programs address (Chapter 3). These conditions already allow for considerable variety in how they and their interactions relate to program performance. Combined with the other conditions this book is concerned with — the rules of a program, their enforcement, the rewards to participants, the role of local governments, and the type of diffusion network — I quickly ran out of cases to explain variance in all these conditions and the performance of the programs studied; this is what Arend Lijphart famously referred to as the problem of "many variables, small number of cases" (Lijphart, 1971, 685; see also, van der Heijden, 2014b).

To reduce the complexity of the large number of conditions the research deals with, the empirical chapters (Chapters 4–6) and the comparative synthesis chapter (Chapter 7) study a set of programs in countries that are relatively homogeneous in context conditions and representative of industrialized and comparatively wealthy countries in the Global North: Australia, the Netherlands, and the United States. These countries show considerable similarity in their statutory building code regimes (Liu, Meyer, & Hogan, 2010), and particularly their focus on resource sustainability and energy consumption of their built environments (IEA, 2013). The countries rank comparably in terms of economic development and citizens' standards of living (UNDP, 2013b), and in terms of environmental awareness of citizens and businesses (OECD, 2013) and their concerns about climate change (Nielsen, 2011; WVS, 2014) — see also Appendix A. For the purpose of this analysis these contextual conditions are considered homogeneous enough to exclude their impact on the individual programs studied.[4] The impact of these contextual conditions is, however, considered as explanatory for the relatively poor performance of the full set of programs studied in these countries. In other words, the findings from these empirical chapters need to be considered in the light of these contextual conditions. Selecting cases from relatively similar contexts to the extent possible in a study like this allows me to concentrate on the set of design conditions in these empirical chapters. Thus, while I aim to keep the context conditions constant in discussions in Chapters 4–7, by no means do I exclude the influence of context on program performance.

The three countries were chosen for both theoretical reasons and what Richard Rose calls "opportunistic happenings" (2014, 142). In terms of theoretical motivations: all these countries have a history of voluntary programs in general and sustainable buildings in particular, and these are to some extent documented in the literature (Backstrand et al., 2010; Hoffmann, 2011; Wurzel et al., 2013). In addition, the contextual conditions that are considered of relevance in explaining program performance are fairly similar in these countries (see previous discussion). In terms of opportunistic happenings: when carrying out the research project I held academic positions at the Australian National University and the University of Amsterdam and visited a number of conferences in the United States. This circumstance enabled me to conduct fieldwork in these countries. This choice implies, however, that the empirical chapters only focus on the opportunities and constraints of voluntary programs for sustainable buildings in a set of highly developed and wealthy economies. Yet, voluntary programs are also gaining prominence in other national contexts, including rapidly developing economies and other non-OECD countries.

To gain insight into the opportunities and constraints of voluntary programs in other, non—Global North country contexts I have studied a set of these in India, Malaysia, and Singapore — again chosen for theoretical reasons (all countries have a history of voluntary programs in the area of research) and as a result of opportunistic happenings (when traveling from Australia to the Netherlands my stopovers are often in India, Malaysia, or Singapore). Chapter 8 draws on a number of these cases in seeking to understand how differences in the contextual conditions between the first set of countries and the second set affect program performance. In other words, I change the research design here from "similar contexts, different program designs" to "different contexts, similar program designs." Chapter 8 emphasizes that constraints of voluntary programs experienced in Australia, the Netherlands, and the United States are even more problematic for voluntary programs in, particularly, India and Malaysia. This may have considerable impact on how policy makers, practitioners, and scholars wish to think about voluntary programs in the Global South.

Case Selection: Theory Guided Idiographic Case Studies

The units of analysis in this book are the real-world voluntary programs for low-carbon building and city development and transformation — I refer to each instance as a case. Cases were selected from a larger pool of sixty-eight potential cases to study that was derived from an extensive Internet search using keywords such as "sustainable development AND [country]," "sustainable building AND [country]," "green building AND [country]," "sustainable construction AND [country]," and "green construction AND [country]." Cases were selected when they explicitly focused on increasing the environmental and resource sustainability of new and existing buildings through new development or the retrofitting of existing buildings beyond state-led regulation. This helped to place some boundaries around all the possible actions governments, citizens, and firms can take in voluntarily decreasing the resource and carbon intensity of cities, for example, carpooling initiatives, waste collection initiatives, water reuse initiatives. Other selection criteria for including cases in this larger pool were the information available on their rule structure, the enforcement of these rules, and the incentives for participants: this is sometimes referred to as "information-oriented selection" (Flyvbjerg, 2015, 79).

From this larger pool I have selected cases for inclusion in the research discussed in this book when they met a number of criteria. First, cases were selected that have matured to at least three years of implementation. I expected that some time would be needed for cases to achieve measurable outcomes. Second, I selected cases to include a variety of approaches to goal achievement in order to gain an understanding of how the design of a voluntary program affects its performance. In collating the pool of cases I realized that there are, broadly, three dominant approaches to goal achievement — certification and classification programs, information generation and sharing programs, and programs that provide funds — and I have clustered the programs accordingly throughout the book. These dominant approaches provide for enough heterogeneity in program design to gain insight into the role of program rules, enforcement, participant rewards, and how they affect program performance (Rihoux & Ragin, 2009). In other words, these approaches can be typified as theory guided idiographic case studies following conditions deemed relevant for program performance, as discussed in Chapter 3 (Levy, 2008). Third, I have selected cases to ensure a variety of actor constellations in the cases studied, as well as a variety of urban settings and differing scales. This allows for assessment of expectations of the role of local governments in developing and implementing

Table 1.1 *From Full Pool of Potential Cases to Those Studied in This Book*

Approach to Goal Achievement	Brief Description*	Full Pool	Studied in This Book
Certification and classification	Programs that allow participants to market their buildings and cities as more sustainable than those of nonparticipants	19	16**
Information generation and sharing	Programs that reward participants with information on how to achieve low-carbon buildings and cities	18	8
Providing funds	Programs that provide participants with financial support to develop low-carbon buildings and cities	20	11
Other	Programs that seek to improve participant behavior in other ways	11	-
Total		68	35

Notes: See Chapter 3 for extensive descriptions
** These include nine programs in India, Malaysia, and Singapore, discussed in Chapter 8

voluntary programs, and the impact of the diffusion network on voluntary program performance. Table 1.1 provides an overview of the variety of cases in the larger pool of potential cases to study, and the subset of cases considered in this book.

The voluntary programs I have chosen to study are usually the larger programs in a city or country, and for which there is some publicly shared information available. There usually is more information available on public than on private voluntary programs, and this has skewed the programs studied in favor of those developed or administered by governments. I prefer to discuss these programs over wholly private ones, because doing so allows interested readers to follow up on the examples studied through the publicly accessible sources I provide. Appendix B provides brief descriptions of all voluntary programs discussed in this book as well as Web links to them.

In selecting programs I was not aware of program performance. That being said — based anecdotally on information availability, such as website accessibility, indicating sufficient resourcing and organization, and in many cases government backing, indicating the expectation of greater commitment to environmental ideals than corporate interests — I would assume the programs studied in this book are the more "successful" ones, making my finding that the vast majority of the programs studied have not achieved meaningful performance all the more concerning. Less successful programs are unlikely to appear in a sampling approach that largely relies on Internet searches (Taleb, 2007). To overcome this potential selection bias for "success" I also used social media — predominantly, sustainable and "green" building groups on LinkedIn — and my network of policy makers, administrators, architects, engineers, constructors, developers, investors, and so on, in Australia, India, Malaysia, the Netherlands, Singapore, and the United States to identify potential cases. I organised a half-day seminar in the Netherlands during the 2012 Green Building Week to discuss voluntary programs for urban sustainability and participated in two sustainable city development conferences in India in March 2013. At these meetings I was directed to voluntary programs that I had not yet uncovered in Internet searches. Finally, when interviewing stakeholders I employed chain-referral sampling, asking whether there were any other voluntary programs that would be of interest for this study, and following up on suggestions. In particular it is through my Singaporean interviews that I was directed to the Malaysian cases studied.

Data Collection and Analysis

Relevant data for analysis of the programs were obtained from websites, existing reports, and other sources. Novel data were acquired through a series of in-depth face-to-face elite interviews conducted between 2012 and 2014, with some follow-up interviews in 2015. The 2015 interviews sought to fill in gaps and resolve conflicts in the data from other sources, thereby hoping to gain additional insight into the programs under scrutiny. Interviewees were traced through Internet searches and through social network websites, particularly LinkedIn. This resulted in a pool of 116 interviewees of various backgrounds in Australia, the Netherlands, and the United States; as well as a pool of 97 interviewees with diverse backgrounds in India, Malaysia, and Singapore (see further Appendix D).

The data were processed by means of a systematic coding scheme and qualitative data analysis software (Atlas.ti). By using this approach the data were systematically explored and insight gained as to the "repetitiveness" and "rarity" of experiences shared by the interviewees, and those reported in the existing information studied (see further Appendix D). For discussion of comparative synthesis in Chapter 7, the data were further analyzed using qualitative comparative analysis (QCA) logic, techniques, and FS/QCA software (version 2.5; www.compasss.org; Ragin & Davey, 2014).

QCA differs from other data analysis methods in its focus. It is a typical configurational comparative method:

The key issue [for QCA] is not which variable is the strongest (i.e., has the biggest net effect) but how different conditions [for example, participant rewards] combine and whether there is only one combination or several different combinations of conditions (causal recipes) of generating the same outcome (Ragin, 2008, 114).[5]

QCA is grounded in set theory, a branch of mathematical logic that allows studying in detail how causal conditions derived from the theory contribute to a particular program performance outcome (see preceding discussion). The fundamentals and background of QCA are well explained and documented in a series of conventional textbooks (Goertz & Mahony, 2012; Ragin, 2008; Rihoux & Ragin, 2009; Schneider & Wagemann, 2012). This book applies crisp set QCA (csQCA). More sophisticated applications of QCA are available — multivalue and fuzzy set qualitative comparative analysis (mvQCA and fsQCA). Although there is no fixed rule for choosing one version of QCA over the other, some scholars express a default preference for the more complex versions, mvQCA and fsQCA (Schneider & Wagemann, 2012). In my opinion this choice should be based on careful consideration of the research project, the data obtained, the theory applied, and the objective of QCA in that project. The more complex versions of QCA readily become academic endeavors for the sake of the endeavor when chosen as the default option, and not for the sake of increased understanding of the phenomenon of interest — this resonates with Bent Flyvbjerg's critique that too often the "subjective" social sciences desire to imitate the "objective" natural sciences to no advantage (Flyvbjerg, 2015).

My choice for csQCA is in part theory driven and in part determined by the limitations of the method. In terms of theoretical motivations, csQCA is sufficient to assess the explanatory power of the club theory perspective for voluntary programs (Potoski & Prakash, 2009), as well as the explanatory power of the more complex theoretical template underlying this research project. In terms of methodological limitations, one of the analyses in the synthesis chapter builds on fourteen voluntary programs studied. This limits the added value of using more complex forms of QCA and makes csQCA the obvious choice for this specific analysis (Berg-Schlosser, 2012). While I have applied fsQCA to the data obtained for this research project elsewhere (van der Heijden, 2015d, 2015e), I have decided to keep the application of QCA constant throughout this book, and I have therefore chosen csQCA for all analyses. Although csQCA may be critiqued for unduly reducing the richness of qualitative data — it is a binary technique, after all — I maintain that the extensive program descriptions in Chapters 4–6 overcome this problem. Appendix C provides more extensive discussion of my application of QCA, as well as data collection and coding, and interviewee selection. Appendix C also applies fsQCA to part of the data set: this is a brief "robustness test" of the QCA findings presented in the main text (cf. Skaaning, 2011).

Outline of the Book

The outline of the book is straightforward: Chapter 2 provides a background to the sustainable building challenge faced, which boils down to the following: the construction, maintenance, and use of buildings account for approximately 40 percent of global energy use and approximately 35 percent of global carbon emissions. As a result of rapid urbanization, improvement in wealth, and access to modern energy services in the Global South, current building-related energy demand is expected to double over the next few decades, and as of 2010 building-related carbon emissions were expected to rise by 50–150 percent by midcentury. The built environment holds huge potential for improvement: with matured and widely applied technology and with behavioral and lifestyle changes, cost-effective energy consumption and carbon emission reductions can be achieved, ranging from 30 to 80 percent. The built environment holds the largest potential for a rapid and cost-effective transition toward a resource-efficient and low-carbon way of living (IPCC, 2014; UNEP, 2009). There is, however, a major complication: dominant governance instruments have not yet been able to accelerate the transition to a resource efficient and low-carbon built environment, and a series of market barriers further hampers this transition. Dominant governance tools, building codes, and planning legislation are often slow to develop and implement, and face considerable enforcement shortfalls. This is a major complication for rapidly developing economies in the Global South: every year of delayed implementation of effective codes and legislation will likely lock in a component of new development to suboptimal performance. Another problem of these dominant instruments is that they often only address new buildings and not existing ones. This is a major complication, particularly for developed economies in the Global North: about 75 percent of the anticipated building stock in use in 2050 there has already been built. A third problem of these tools is that they address objects and not building users' behavior and lifestyles. This leaves considerable potential for improvements as yet unaddressed. Finally, these tools set minimum requirements and often do not challenge the construction and property sectors to construct and retrofit buildings to achieve optimal performance (Eames, Dixon, May, & Hunt, 2013; World Bank, 2011a).

Market barriers to low-carbon development are numerous. These include the high fragmentation of the construction and property sectors, split incentives between those bearing the cost of improvements and those receiving the benefits, and an unwillingness of banks and other finance providers to supply funds for sustainable buildings. Seeking to overcome problems with dominant governance instruments as well as seeking to overcome the many market barriers that hamper rapid and large-scale transition to low-carbon building and city development, governments, firms, citizens, and civil society groups have begun to implement voluntary programs. Chapter 3 introduces the theoretical template used throughout this book, namely, combining the club theory perspective with two advanced perspectives: local government involvement in voluntary programs, and the role of diffusion networks. It also introduces the three clusters of voluntary programs that form the topic of the empirical chapters, situating them and the larger trend of voluntary programs for sustainable buildings in the larger literature on voluntary programs (e.g., Croci, 2005; DeLeon & Rivera, 2010; Morgenstern & Pizer, 2007; Potoski & Prakash, 2009; Ronit, 2012). The chapter further discusses the specific program performance outcomes this book is concerned with, and the complications of assessing these, and develops a number of propositions about what performance may be expected from the programs studied.

The empirical Chapters 4, 5, and 6 each discuss one of a dominant category of voluntary programs for sustainable buildings in Australia, the Netherlands, and the United States: certification and classification programs (Chapter 4), knowledge generation and sharing programs (Chapter 5), and programs that provide funds for sustainable building development and retrofits (Chapter 6). Each chapter begins by introducing the individual programs studied in that chapter and provides theoretical background where required to understand their performance. These three chapters consider the twenty-six voluntary programs that compose the core of the book, but to prevent excessive overlap in the descriptive analysis I have singled out ten programs for in-depth discussion. These are selected because they are the best or worst performing examples of programs studied, or because they provide an extreme illustration of another issue related to the full set of voluntary programs studied, for example, the tendency of program administrators to oversell the rather poor performance of their programs. Chapter 7 comparatively studies the twenty-six programs discussed throughout the earlier empirical chapters using csQCA.

Chapter 8 opens up the research findings to rapidly developing and other non-OECD countries. Here I introduce nine certification and classification programs in India, Malaysia, and Singapore. Again, the majority of the programs studied in these countries have only achieved marginal performance when contrasted to the sustainable building challenges faced. These findings nevertheless add relevant insight to earlier conclusions. Particularly considering the cases in India and Malaysia, it becomes clear that voluntary programs may face even more constraints in rapidly developing economies in the Global South.

To conclude, Chapter 9 argues that most of the voluntary programs studied are subject to a leadership delusion, a term I use to indicate three factors: that they focus on a small segment of the "market" for sustainable buildings (the early market, and not the majority market); that their program administrators and participants depict an unjustifiably positive narrative of their performance; and that over-all the programs set non-ambitious requirements. That being said, I see potential in voluntary programs, arguing that their position in the larger governance regime for sustainable building development and use needs rethinking. The the last section of Chapter 9 discusses a number of alternative uses for voluntary programs and answers the broader and the specific research questions raised in this introductory chapter.

2   The Sustainable Building Challenge
Contextualizing the Problem

This chapter seeks to improve our understanding of how the built environment contributes to environmental problems — climate change included — and discusses its potential for improvement in terms of reduced resource consumption and carbon emissions. It explores the dominant governance instruments currently in place that seek to achieve such reductions, and why these instruments have not yet secured large-scale and rapid transition to resource-efficient, low-carbon, environmentally sustainable buildings and cities. The chapter concludes by discussing why governments, firms, citizens, and civil society organizations have turned to voluntary programs.

The Built Environment and Environmental Problems

Globally, the construction, maintenance, and use of buildings require 40 per ent of all energy produced and 45 percent of all raw materials extracted — many of which are nonrenewable resources such as fossil fuels, or only slowly renewable ones such as old-growth timber (IEA, 2008; Kibert, 2008; Pérez-Lombard, Ortiz, & Pout, 2008).[1] These activities account for 35 percent of global carbon emissions[2] and 40 percent of global solid wastes, many of which take a long time to degrade, such as concrete, asphalt, and plastic (Dodman, 2009; IPCC, 2014; UNEP, 2003). They also require large volumes of potable water, and groundwater and other potable water sources are commonly overabstracted to operate the built environment (UN, 2012a; World Water Council, 2007). In particular, energy consumption is related to the high carbon intensity of the built environment. Most building-related energy is consumed during the operational phase for heating, cooling, and ventilating buildings as well as for operating appliances; as a result, most building-related carbon is emitted during this phase — approximately 80 percent for both energy consumption and carbon emissions. Building-related energy consumption is split roughly evenly between the residential and nonresidential property sectors (U.S. Energy Information Administration, 2013).

Current levels of building-related resource consumption and carbon emissions are already unsustainable, and under a business-as-usual development scenario this problem is expected to worsen over the next few decades. The year 2008 is marked as the threshold point at which the world's urban population had outgrown rural population. Modest forecasts by the United Nations indicate that by 2050 the vast majority of people will live in cities: 66 percent globally, or 6.4 billion people — representing almost a doubling of the number of people living in cities in 2008 (UN, 2014)[3]—partly as a result of ongoing urbanization and partly as a result of population growth. Obviously, more buildings will be sought to accommodate these people — and more buildings will only increase the resource consumption and carbon emission problems of today.

The largest share of urban growth will occur in rapidly developing countries in the Global South, and it is also here where rapid industrialization and economic development are expected over the next several decades (Hong & Laurenzi, 2007; Martine, 2011). Continuance of existing building methods will provide urban inhabitants of the Global South access to the current unsustainable levels of consumption practiced by citizens in the Global North, among others in the form of large houses and offices (Cheshire, Nathan, & Overman, 2014; Grimm et al., 2008; Satterthwaite, 2009; Sen, 2013). As a result of rapid urbanization, improvement in wealth, and access to modern energy services in the Global South, current building-related energy demand is expected to double globally over the next few decades, particularly in the nonresidential sector, and by midcentury current building-related carbon emissions are anticipated to rise by 50–150 percent of 2010 rates (Hall & Pfeiffer, 2013; IPCC, 2014). Current levels of building-related energy demand and carbon emissions in the Global North are expected to remain stable in the residential sector, and increase by less than 1 percent per year in the nonresidential sector (U.S. Energy Information Administration, 2013). That being said, current and expected future per capita building-related energy use and carbon emissions in the Global North are three to seven times those in the Global South (see Appendix A). This raises considerable questions regarding environmental inequalities and environmental justice at a global level (cf., Bulkeley, Carmin, Castan Broto, Edwards, & Fuller, 2013; Redclift & Sage, 1998).

In sum, current levels of resource consumption, particularly energy derived from fossil fuels employed for the construction, maintenance, and use of buildings and cities, and the carbon emissions resulting from these activities, are unsustainable. Under a business-as-usual development scenario with a projected expansion of building stock, particularly in the Global South, resultant resource consumption and carbon emissions are projected to grow exponentially rather than linearly.

Solutions to These Problems

Although these expectations are undeniably gloomy, there is much potential for change and improvement. Technologies and design solutions are available that allow for cost-effective reductions of building resources and carbon emissions of 30–80 percent (IPCC, 2014; Mumovic & Santamouris, 2013). They include now-conventional approaches for generation of renewable energy at building level, widely available building materials that reduce significantly the energy required for heating or cooling buildings, and well-trialed designs that require less material use (Mazmanian & Blanco, 2014; Wheeler & Beatley, 2009). A large number of reductions are possible at net-cost benefit: in the United States, for example, possible energy savings of up to 23 percent are worth double the costs of up-front investments, with a return rate of ten years — an astonishing $1.2 trillion can be saved if $520 billion is invested (McKinsey, 2009a). Some studies even go so far as to forecast fully carbon-neutral built environments for the United States and China at net economic gain if currently available technology is widely applied (Lovins 2013; Rocky Mountain Institute, 2016). This unique combination and potential for mitigation (mature technology and reductions at reduced life-cycle costs) are not present in any other anthropogenic area, including agriculture, industry, and transport — these all hold the potential for significant reductions also, but lack available mature technology, require considerable financial investment that would not be returned, or both (Harvey, 2006; IPCC, 2007, 2014; Mumovic & Santamouris, 2013).

Unfortunately, this Promethean scenario— full reliance on technological solutions to achieve high levels of built environment sustainability — faces a number of complications. The initial costs needed may simply be too high to bear for citizens, firms, governments, and other organizations — particularly those in developing economies in the Global South (M. A. Brown & Sovacool, 2011; Kaygusuz, 2012). But also under favorable economic circumstances individuals and firms may prefer the short-term gain of not investing in this technology over the long-term gain of doing so — often termed hyperbolic discounting (Greene, 2011; Wada, Akimotot, Sano, Oda, & Homma, 2012). In addition, banks and other finance suppliers are still unwilling to issue funds for buildings and city developments that move beyond business-as-usual practice, as they consider such projects too risky to finance (Junghans & Dorsch, 2015; Pivo, 2010; Xiadong Wang, Stern, Limaye, Mostert, & Zhang, 2013). Another complication is that new and alternative technologies for improved resource efficiency and reduced carbon emissions often face resistance from policy makers, businesses, practitioners, and citizens. Skepticism, vested interests, dedicated costs, and the habit of existing practice often favor business-as-usual technologies over innovative ones (Eames et al., 2013; Hoffman & Henn, 2009; Sengers, Raven, & Van Venrooij, 2010).

In addition, merely relying on technological innovation does nothing to alter the wasteful behavior and lifestyles of citizens and firms. Households waste at least 10 percent of their energy consumption by using default stand-by settings rather than switching off appliances, and an even larger percentage is lost through inefficient heating and cooling (Harvey, 2013; Rusk, Mahfouz, & Jones, 2011). Office users show even greater wasteful behavior: studies indicate that more than 50 percent of all office energy is consumed after working hours when hardly anyone uses office buildings (Greensense, 2013; Masoso & Grobler, 2010). Solely relying on technology may even be counterproductive if people increase consumption, feeling it is offset by energy savings where their residences are branded as purportedly highly sustainable — a problem known as the rebound effect (Sunikka-Blank & Galvin, 2012).

Scholars from the behavioral sciences have observed that changing societal norms on issues such as energy consumption, indoor temperature, or the use of particular construction materials may very well be as important in reducing the environmental problems that buildings and cities cause as creating ever more efficient technological solutions is (Cialdini, 2009; Goldstein, Cialdini, & Griskevicius, 2008; Heiskanen, Johnson, Robinson, Vadovics, & Saastamoinen, 2010; Osbaldiston & Schott, 2012; Timmer, 2012). Building on this finding, the United Kingdom government ran a large-scale experiment in 2010 that sought to reduce office energy use by 10 percent within a year (Cabinet Office, 2011). With 3,000 office buildings and 300,000 civil servants involved this may well be one of the largest trials thus far undertaken. The experiment achieved its goal by relying on unobtrusive interventions such as changing norms on heating and cooling, competition between building users, changed defaults (such as more optimal heating and cooling times, and slightly altered seasonal heating and cooling temperatures), and very practical changes to building management (such as eliminating unnecessary and redundant lighting).

Summing Up: The Sustainable Building Challenge

An increase in energy demand and related carbon emissions is projected for all energy end-use sectors (including transport and industry) over future decades, but the most rapid increase is expected in the building sector — the entire process of constructing, maintaining, and using buildings (U.S. Energy Information Administration, 2013). At the same time the building sector holds the largest potential for cost-effective reductions of resource consumption and carbon emissions: mature, trialed technology is available for improvements, as is knowledge on how to alter consumption behavior (IPCC, 2007, 2014). This technology and knowledge have been available for some decades now, however, raising the question as to why it has not been implemented on a large scale already — even if people and organizations do not wish to reduce their consumption and carbon emissions because of environmental concerns, one would expect they would be attracted by lower development and operational costs of their buildings. The answer is, as so often, that the market for sustainable buildings is not a perfect market. People and organizations may not have access to knowledge available (information asymmetries), they exhibit time-inconsistent preferences (hyperbolic discounting), they cannot make improvements to their property if others do not do likewise or may feel that their personal action adds little to global problems (collective action problems), or they may not suffer themselves from current unsustainable levels of resource consumption and carbon emissions of their property (negative externalities) — to mention a few typical market failures in this area. The sustainable building challenge this book is interested in therefore boils down to how to move from possessing technology and knowledge available for resource-efficient, low-carbon, environmentally sustainable buildings and cities to applying it on a large scale and in a timely manner.

Governing Sustainable Buildings through Mandatory Codes and Legislation

With such market failures in place the typical response is for governments to step in and introduce incentives to steer people and organizations toward desirable behavior. And so they do. The dominant instruments chosen by governments to improve the resource efficiency and reduce the carbon intensity of buildings and cities are direct regulatory interventions such as building codes and planning legislation — subsidies and other economic instruments are used as well, but to a much smaller extent (IEA, 2013; van der Heijden & De Jong, 2009). It is beyond the scope of this book to provide an extensive historical analysis of building codes and planning legislation, but a backward glance will still help to clarify where we are now.[4]

Some seven thousand years ago, the first citylike settlements in ancient Mesopotamia became centers of economic activity and attracted relatively large numbers of people — a process recorded throughout history and in our times faced by rapidly developing economies (Brunn, Hays-Mitchell, & Zeigler, 2012; UN, 2012b). They required forms of governance, particularly to ensure military defense and civil convenience. City walls were erected for protection, and rudimentary building codes and planning legislation were introduced by city rulers to ensure building safety and suitable urban development. Examples of these early urban governance instruments are found throughout Asia, Africa, the Americas, and Europe — with the oldest preserved building codes dating back four thousand years (Chiarella, 2005; Milburn, 2015; P. Taylor, 2013).

Building codes and planning legislation evolved when further development and growth of cities throughout the world set city governments the task of governing the risks that occur in densely populated areas. Directly after fires that almost devastated Amsterdam in 1452 and London in 1666, for example, both city governments introduced building codes stipulating that houses were to be built of stone and not wood, as was customary, and that roofs were to be thatched with tiles, and not straw, aiming to prevent a repetition of these major fires. These were unprecedented government interventions in the lives of citizens and organizations in those days (Breen, 1908; Charles II, 1667 [1819]) — and similar processes are documented in other parts of the world (Genest, 1924; Lechtman & Hobbs, 1986; Milburn, 2015; Qinghua, 1998; Wenren, 2012). Colonization, modernization, industrialization, and the development of new building materials and techniques steadily gave governments cause to become increasingly involved in the regulation of buildings and city development, and building codes and planning legislation became ever more detailed (A. King, 1976; Sen, 2013; P. Taylor, 2013; United Nations, 2013).

Up to the 1960s, governments around the globe predominantly governed health and safety issues in buildings and cities through building codes and planning legislation. Improving living standards in the 1960s gave rise to demands for better housing and other buildings, and the oil crises in the 1970s were the catalyst for governments around the globe to introduce the first building energy performance requirements — particularly in the Global North. With climate change concerns emerging in the 1990s the stringency of these requirements has been ever increasing — in the Global North and South (EC, 2010; IEA, 2008, 2013; Shui et al., 2009). For example, under the European Energy Performance Building Decree in Europe, by 2020 all new buildings are required to be nearly zero-energy — that is, they must produce as much energy as they consume — and similar requirements are in force in California (Garvin, 2014; van der Heijden & Van Bueren, 2013).

From the 1990s onward governments have also used subsidies and other economic instruments to stimulate improved urban sustainability, but their use is marginal compared to the employment of codes and legislation. Subsidies are often introduced to support property owners in improving the energy performance of their buildings. These are vulnerable to political and financial swings, however, and many were discontinued after new governments came to power or when financial circumstances changed — the 2008 global financial crisis was among the main reasons for termination of many subsidies (Frondel, Ritter, & Schmidt, 2008; Macnintosh & Wilkinson, 2011).[5] Some governments have introduced taxes or other economic instruments to put a price on the negative environmental externalities resulting from buildings and cities. In various European countries a tax applies, for example, to the extraction of sand, gravel, and rock for the cement industry. The environmental costs of these activities would otherwise not be included in the price of cement and other construction materials — and thus not in the development of buildings and cities (EEA, 2008). A more innovative economic instrument is Tokyo's mandatory carbon trading scheme for office buildings, introduced in 2010 (EDF & IETA, 2013). This form of carbon trading has, however, not seen a wide uptake globally — thus far only China has followed suit by introducing carbon trading markets for buildings in selected cities in 2013 (Environomist, 2014; Peters-Stanley & Hamilton, 2012).[6]

In sum, the development of and dominant reliance on mandatory building codes and planning legislation by governments to govern sustainable building and city development align with the notion of path dependency: because these were the prevailing instruments for governing structural safety, health, and amenity of buildings, governments have continued to rely on these for governing building-related resource consumption and carbon emissions (for path dependency, see Mahoney, 2000; Pierson, 2004). Table 2.1 provides a brief overview of the dominant governance instruments for urban sustainability presently in place in the six countries that provide contexts for this book, and Appendix A includes extensive discussion.

Assessing the performance of these dominant governance instruments in achieving resource-efficient and low-carbon building and cities is complicated: few comparative data are available, available data from local sources are noisy, and those reporting data may have incentives to present local circumstances as rosier or as darker than they are. The International Energy Agency is among the few organizations with a long

Table 2.1 *Dominant Governance Instruments for Urban Sustainability in the Six Target Countries (2015)*

Country	Dominant Governance Instruments
Australia	• Planning legislation: National Urban Policy • Building codes: Building Code of Australia, first mandatory building energy efficiency requirements introduced in 2003 • Other instruments: Marginal — several subsidies in force approximately 1990–2010, but have been terminated
India	• Planning legislation: National Housing and Habitat Policy; Jawaharlal Nehru National Urban Renewal Mission; National Mission on Sustainable Habitat • Building codes: Energy Conservation Building Code, voluntary standards for building energy efficiency introduced in 2007 • Other instruments: Nil
Malaysia	• Planning legislation: Malaysia Plan; National Physical Plan; State Structure Plans; Metropolitan Plans; Local Plans; National Green Technology Policy; Construction Industry Master Plan • Building codes: No mandatory building energy efficiency codes • Other instruments: Nil
Netherlands	• Planning legislation: Wet Ruimtelijke Ordening (National Planning Legislation) • Building Code: Bouwbesluit (Dutch Building Code), first mandatory building energy efficiency requirements introduced in early 1980s • Other instruments: Marginal — numerous subsidies approximately 1980–2010, but have been terminated
Singapore	• Planning legislation: Five Year Master Plan; Sustainable building Masterplan • Building Code: Green Mark, first mandatory building energy efficiency requirements introduced in 2008 • Other instruments: A series of subsidies to support the development and retrofitting of buildings with high urban sustainability performance
United States	• Planning legislation: Standard Zoning Enabling Act; Standard City Planning Enabling Act • Building codes: International Codes; ASHREA Standard 90.1; first model building energy efficiency requirements introduced in late 1970s • Other instruments: Much variety at state level, but no dominant application

Source: Appendix A (Country Snapshots).

history of comparatively studying the performance of different countries. It reports that building energy efficiency codes introduced since the early 1990s have resulted in a 22 percent reduction of energy consumption of the residential building stock in the Netherlands and Germany (IEA, 2013). At first glance these are impressive results, but it is likely that other causes have been at play, such as the high economic growth experienced in these countries during that period, resulting in demand for high-quality housing, high citizen awareness of environmental problems and a willingness to address these, the role of the Dutch government as commissioner of the vast majority of housing built in that period, and high subsidies provided to citizens and firms in that period to improve the energy efficiency of their property in Germany and the Netherlands (Beerepoot & Beerepoot, 2007; Frondel et al., 2008; Mikler, 2009). Southern European countries, for example, show only a 6 percent reduction. Moreover, building-related carbon emissions in the Netherlands are roughly similar to those in Australia when considered per capita (for 2014), and four times those of Singapore (see further Appendix A) — the International Energy Agency considers Australia a laggard country in terms of drafting building energy efficiency codes, and Singapore was very late in introducing them (IEA, 2013). Are mandatory building codes and planning legislation perhaps not very successful in achieving a resource-efficient and low-carbon built environment?

Obstacles Faced by Mandatory Codes and Legislation

The International Energy Agency data can also be interpreted in another light. Since the 1990s, the richest and most developed countries in the world have achieved building energy consumption reductions of at best 1 percent per year, and these reductions cannot be fully attributed to mandatory building codes and planning legislation. Cost-effective technology and knowledge on behavioral change for improved building performance have become widely available in this period, but have not been taken up on a large scale and in a timely manner. "We have all the technology and the knowledge; we know how to do it." a senior sustainable building consultant from the Netherlands observed in one of the many interviews I have undertaken. "The question is: how are we going to operationalize that technology and knowledge?" (int. 70).[7] In light of the sustainable building challenge faced, he and other interviewees concluded that building codes and planning legislation do not yet constitute an adequate response. A closer look at the six countries under consideration indicates that these principal instruments face considerable obstacles in achieving their goals. Table 2.2 gives an overview — Appendix A again presents more detailed discussion. In what follows these obstacles are clustered in four themes.

Slow to Develop, Slow to Implement, Slow to Cause Change

Governments take a long time to develop and implement mandatory building codes and planning legislation, and it takes even longer for these

Table 2.2 *Obstacles Faced by Dominant Governance Instruments in the Six Countries*

Country	Obstacles
Australia	• Complicated three-tier system of urban governance • Focus on new construction work, with little or no attention given to existing buildings and (parts of) cities • Lenient urban sustainability requirements and introduced comparatively recently; lenient enforcement of building energy efficiency codes • Conservative construction and property sectors; resistance to change
India	• Complicated three-tier system of urban governance; complicated patchwork of mandatory requirements, policy programs, and voluntary standards • Focus on new construction work, with limited or no focus on existing buildings and (parts of) cities • Building energy efficiency codes are voluntary, introduced relatively recently, set lenient requirements (compared to those of other countries), and face lenient or no enforcement • Many (parts of) cities without urban development plans • Low-tech, conservative construction and property sectors, resistance to change
Malaysia	• Complicated patchwork of mandatory requirements, policy programs, and voluntary standards • Main focus on new construction work; limited to no focus on existing buildings and (parts of) cities • Building energy efficiency codes are voluntary, introduced relatively recently, set lenient requirements (compared to other countries), and face lenient or no enforcement. • Low-tech, conservative construction and property sectors, resistance to change.
Netherlands	• Main focus on new construction work, limited to no focus on existing buildings and (parts of) cities • Lenient enforcement of building energy efficiency codes • Conservative construction and property sectors, resistance to change
Singapore	• Building energy efficiency codes introduced relatively recently; little experience with and knowledge of ambitious urban sustainable buildings in construction and property industries • Passive stance toward urban sustainability in construction and property sectors
United States	• Complicated three-tier system of urban governance • Main focus on new construction work, limited to no focus on existing buildings and (parts of) cities • Lenient enforcement of building energy efficiency codes • Conservative construction and property sectors, resistance to change

Source: Appendix A (Country Snapshots).

to effect change. Their development requires many checks and balances to ensure democratic accountability and transparency. Governments at different levels (national, regional, and local) are often involved in the development and implementation of these instruments, resulting in overlapping tasks and responsibilities — interviewees in Australia, India, Malaysia, and the United States were particularly critical of the three-tiered system of building code and planning legislation development and implementation in these countries (see Appendix A). While technology in the area of sustainable building development is fast-moving, government regulation is not and often cannot keep pace with the speed of technological development (Essig et al., 2015; van der Heijden, 2014a). What further complicates the governance of buildings and cities is that proposals for change readily become politicized: a proposal for mandatory retrofits affects all homeowners — and they represent a policy maker's electorate. Or, a proposal for changed construction practice affects property developers and construction material producers — and their interest groups often financially support a policy maker or its party. The construction and property sectors are found resistant to changes that require improved resource efficiency and reduced carbon intensity of buildings. Policy makers take high risks in proposing ambitious direct regulatory interventions or amendments for sustainable buildings, and if they do they often face a long process of lobbying and being lobbied (for a candid account from the United States, see Papadopoulos, 2015; see also W. L. Lee & Yik, 2004; Lillie & Greer, 2007; Moe, 2012).

This impeded development is particularly problematic in transition economies such as India and Malaysia. India is, for example, expected to witness an annual urban growth rate of 5 to 10 percent for several decades to come (IIHS, 2011; McKinsey, 2010). Such transition allows these countries to leapfrog the resource and carbon intensive technology lock-in of the built environment faced by developed economies (Murthy, 2010; Srinivasan, Ling, & Mori, 2012). Yet, governments in these transition economies often lack the capacity to develop and implement effective mandatory building codes and planning legislation — with each year of delay in implementation implying another 5–10 percent of poorly performing built-up space (Hong & Laurenzi, 2007; Nath & Behera, 2011). That said, even when developed, these instruments are no guarantee of improvement: time and again enforcement shortfalls are reported as a major complication in achieving sustainable buildings — in developed and transition economies alike — because inspectors prioritize classic regulated areas (such as structural safety and healthiness) over the relatively novel area of resource efficiency and carbon intensity

(M. Evans, Halverson, Delgado, & Yu, 2014; Healthy Environs, 2015; Iwaro & Mwasha, 2010; Pan & Garmston, 2012; van der Heijden, 2013a, 2015a).

Exempting Existing Buildings from New Interventions

Normally only buildings yet to be developed are subject to new and amended building codes and planning legislation. Grandfathering clauses normally exempt existing buildings from new and amended codes and legislation. Existing property rights of existing buildings restrict policy makers in proposing mandatory upgrades and retrofits. This is problematic because today's built environment already requires unsustainable levels of resources and already emits unsustainable levels of carbon emissions. Grandfathering clauses reduce the impact of amended and new mandatory instruments, a situation that is particularly challenging for developed economies. Here cities transform by at best 2 percent per year — it is estimated that in many OECD countries 70 percent of today's buildings will still be in use by 2050 (Ma, Shao, & Song, 2013). In other words, at any time the vast majority of buildings are exempted from new or amended mandatory instruments. Achieving a resource-efficient and low-carbon built environment is a battle on two fronts: the existing building stock and the future building stock — this is not always well understood (IEA, 2009; Shavell, 2007; Vinagre Diaz, Wilby, & Belén Rodríguez González, 2013).[8]

Obstacles to upgrading and retrofitting existing buildings are among the most important ones to overcome. Building owners tend to oppose proposals for building retrofits — irrespective of whether they are presented as mandatory or voluntary — even when retrofitting promises considerable gains: reduced operation costs, healthier buildings, more livable built environments. The transaction costs they face are high: it is difficult to obtain and understand the information required for making a choice on retrofits, and all the more so for homeowners; during a retrofit a building is temporarily unusable, a detriment that is particularly problematic for homeowners and small businesses; and gains do not always accrue to those paying the costs, making owners hesitant to carry out retrofits — a typical issue in tenant—landlord relationships. The initial cost to retrofit a building may be high as well, and people have a tendency to discount the future gains (Cabinet Office, 2011). Existing mandatory building codes and planning legislation are ill suited to deal with these specific issues (EC, 2013; IEA, 2009; Urban Green, 2013).

A Focus on Objects, Not Behavior

Building codes and planning legislation address objects — building components, buildings, city precincts — and not the behavior of people using buildings and cities. It would be unheard-of for a government to require its citizens to wear an extra sweater when they feel cold instead of turning up the heating.[9] User behavior is, as illustrated previously, a crucial aspect of the resource consumption and carbon emissions of the built environment. Even without upgrades and retrofits much improvement of energy use in existing buildings is possible — simply by pointing out to users that they consume more than their peers, for example, households and firms will likely reduce their energy consumption (Cabinet Office, 2011; De Almeida, Fonseca, Schlomann, & Feilberg, 2011; Solanki, Malella, & Zhou, 2013). Moreover, a sole focus on ecoefficiency — improved resource efficiency and reduced carbon emissions through technology — has the potential to cause unwanted outcomes when people and organizations increase their building-related resource consumption as a result of occupying sustainable buildings. As mentioned earlier, they may feel that their wasteful behavior is justified because of the sustainability credentials of their buildings.

Behavior is relevant also in the light of the rapid growth of the built environment globally. Ecoefficiency gains accrued through application of sustainable building technologies are likely outrun by an overall increase of built environment resource consumption and greenhouse gas emissions because of this rapid growth (Alcott, 2005). The problems resulting from grandfather clauses are a further argument to focus on building user behavior in the transition to resource-efficient environments (cf. Hayden, 2014; Matthews, 2015).

Requiring Minimal Performance, Not Optimal Performance

Building codes and planning legislation set minimal rather than optimal performance requirements. Interviewees generally argued that organizations in the construction and property sectors considered building codes as the absolute target they have to achieve for compliance, rather than a baseline to outperform. With the large variety of possible construction projects and buildings and the diversity of building locations — and their local climatological and geological characteristics — governments often seek a common denominator that building developers and owners can meet for many building types in a range of settings, and therefore tend to keep requirements simple and generic. This tendency logically results in building codes that often require less in terms of energy efficiency and carbon intensity than is possible in specific situations. To give an example: while a government could require that solar panels be installed on roofs on all future buildings, such as the government of France stipulated in 2015 (Guardian, 2015), this requirement would only make sense for buildings with enough sun exposure. In situations where a building does not receive sufficient exposure the solar panels are not an optimal solution — they could have been better used elsewhere and would be an unnecessary cost for the future building owner. "Sustainable building ... well, it has to sell itself," a policy maker in the Netherlands involved in the development of building codes stated. "What we, as the national government, aim to achieve is, in the end, the lowest common denominator. We will raise the bar, but it may not hamper development" (int. 59).

The construction and property sectors are, however, highly unlikely to construct or retrofit buildings with better levels of performance than are required by building codes and planning legislation because of the market barriers they face (Liu et al., 2010; UNEP, 2007). To mention the most dominant barriers: investment decisions are often made by building developers and investors, not by prospective occupants or tenants; developers and investors have little incentive to provide resource-efficient buildings (these situations are regarded as involving "split incentives"); building owners and users often do not include building resource efficiency or carbon intensity in their choice of a building — in part because this information is often not available for the buildings they seek to buy or rent ("information asymmetries"); they are further found to shy away from resource efficiency retrofits because they fear they will not own or occupy the building long enough to see the cost of the investment returned ("first cost barrier"); developers, investors, engineers, and other professionals in the construction and property sectors may simply not be aware of the technological solutions available ("information shortages"); and, last, the building sector and the process of constructing and retrofitting are highly fragmented, and the interests of all parties involved are often not aligned ("conflicting interests").

The Turn to Voluntary Programs for Sustainable Buildings

In sum, the dominant approach to govern sustainable buildings — government-led mandatory building codes coupled with planning legislation — faces considerable obstacles in achieving a speedy and large-scale transformation of today's buildings and cities, and in ensuring that those of the future are constructed and used as energy efficiently and low-carbon intensively as possible. These problems are acknowledged by governments, firms, and civil society organizations. Since the early 1990s they have been trialing and experimenting with innovative governance instruments, often as substitutes for or complements to traditional ones. As explained in Chapter 1, this book is concerned with a specific cluster of such innovative and experimental instruments — voluntary programs. These motivate building developers to construct buildings that are more resource-efficient and less carbon-intensive than is required by codes and legislation or, in absence of codes and legislation, than is considered conventional practice, but without the force of law; likewise they motivate building owners to retrofit their property voluntarily, and building users voluntarily to change their behavior.

The turn to voluntary programs can partially be explained as a response to the obstacles faced by government in governing sustainable building. However, governments, firms, and citizens and civil society organizations have additional motivations for turning to them. Chapters 4 to 6 will provide a better understanding of these motivations by explaining the variety of program designs, as well as the performance of these programs. Table 2.3 briefly summarizes the principal actors involved in the programs studied and their motivations for turning to these — Appendix A offers more extensive discussion.

Motivations for Governments

Interviewees explained that voluntary programs provide alternatives when governments anticipate implementation of new legislation to be costly or otherwise difficult to implement and enforce. They considered voluntary programs promising for investigating or promoting innovative policy ideas. Many of the programs studied in Chapters 4–6 align with and promote larger policy programs: some programs in the United States assist in achieving goals under the President Obama's Climate Action Plan, some in the Netherlands assist in complying with European legislation, and those developed by major cities in Australia assist in meeting policy requirements set at the national level (City of Sydney, 2008; Ministry of Infrastructure and the Environment, 2013; White House, 2013). Interviewees stressed, finally, that these voluntary programs may help in addressing political or societal resistance that hampers implementing mandatory instruments — such motivations underlie those identified in the literature on voluntary programs in other areas (e.g., Darnall & Carmin, 2005; Delmas & Terlaak, 2001; Esty & Chertow, 1997; Lyon & Maxwell, 2007; Segerson & Miceli, 1998; Sheehy, 2011; Short & Toffel, 2010).

Table 2.3 *Dominant Actors Involved and Their Motivations*

Country	Dominant Actors in Voluntary Programs and Their Motivations
Australia	• Major cities responding to national government's requirements, aiming to overcome shortfalls of dominant governance instruments, and seeking rewards from being progressive in terms of built environment sustainability (jobs, investments, increased populations) • Actors in the construction and property sectors tapping into a niche market, and seeking acknowledgment for their leading practice
India	• Government of India (and some regional and local governments) seeking to overcome shortfalls of dominant governance instruments and responding to international pressure • International organizations that support urban governance improvement projects and have experience with voluntary programs • Actors in the construction and property sectors tapping into a niche market and seeking acknowledgment for their leading practice
Malaysia	• Government of Malaysia (and related organizations) seeking to overcome shortfalls of dominant governance instruments and responding to international pressure • International organizations that support urban governance improvement projects and have experience with voluntary programs • Actors in the construction and property sectors tapping into a niche market and seeking acknowledgment for their leading practice
Netherlands	• Dutch Government aiming to overcome shortfalls of dominant governance instruments, and responding to European legislation on energy consumption and carbon emission reductions • Local and regional governments responding to national government's requirements • Actors in the construction and property sectors tapping into a niche market and seeking acknowledgment for their leading practice
Singapore	• Singapore government seeking to improve built environment sustainability within Singapore and to influence built environment sustainability in the Southeast Asian region and responding to international pressure • Actors in the construction and property sectors tapping into a niche market and seeking acknowledgment for their leading practice.
United States	• Environmental Protection Agency and Department of Energy aiming to overcome shortfalls of dominant governance instruments and seeking more influence in governing built environment sustainability • States and cities aiming to overcome shortfalls of dominant governance instruments, and seeking rewards from being progressive in terms of built environment sustainability (jobs, investments, increased populations) • Actors in the construction and property sectors tapping into a niche market,and seeking acknowledgment for their leading practice

Source: Appendix A (Country Snapshots).

A typical example from the countries studied in this book is the fierce opposition that New York's then-mayor Bloomberg faced from the local construction and property sectors when, in 2009, he proposed to introduce mandatory energy retrofits for existing buildings. In a time of global economic stress, so argued these sectors, his proposals carried financial risks that were simply too high (Cheatham, 2009). Seeking to address the problem of resistance to mandatory retrofitting, the City of New York is now working closely with the Urban Green Council, a sustainable building interest group, in a number of voluntary programs (UGC, 2014a). For instance, the city is active in voluntary training and certification programs for building professionals and property managers, seeking to raise awareness at the individual builder and manager level. This awareness is anticipated to permeate these builders' and managers' organizations through interactions they have with colleagues, superiors, clients, and suppliers (NYC Buildings, 2013; UGC, 2014b).

Interviewees also considered voluntary programs to be promising in enabling governments to bypass complicated institutional requirements for mandatory governance of built environment sustainability. The United States has instituted a three-tier governance structure for built environment sustainability, as have Australia, India, and Malaysia. It gives considerable power to state and local governments, and limited power to the federal government. Over many decades a system of building codes and planning legislation has emerged that can best be understood as a patchwork of local requirements, with major differences occurring between and even within states (Garvin, 2014). Nationwide voluntary programs developed and administered by the Federal Environmental Protection Agency and the Department of Energy, however, seek to ensure some national-level harmonization and the expansion of federal government influence in this area.

The reputational benefits of these programs were mentioned by respondents as a further motivation for governments to turn to them. An administrator in the Netherlands reflected on his long experience with a range of voluntary programs for sustainable buildings: "Look, they are also a bit of a parking lot for complicated policy problems. . . . Asking a government commission to research the problem means it drops off the agenda. Asking academics to research it means it's pushed into the future," he observed. "But these programs. It's a way for policymakers to . . . well, to show that you're trying to solve a problem in a policy area renowned for complex policy problems" (int. 80). Particularly in Australia and the United States, representatives of city and regional governments considered voluntary programs as a means to showcase their progressive built environment sustainability ambitions. "They help positioning Boston as a green hub," a Boston city administrator explained, "and that attracts people and businesses that are future-thinking" (int. 192).

Motivations for Firms

Seeking financial gain was mentioned most often as a motivation for firms to turn to voluntary programs. Many of the programs studied seek reduced energy consumption, making them attractive for firms because they result in direct cost savings, so explained interviewees. But firms may profit financially from participating in these programs in other ways as well. Some consumers are willing to pay higher market prices and rental rates for buildings with higher levels of resource efficiency and lower levels of carbon intensity than are required by mandatory governance instruments or conventional practice. Firms seeking to enter this market, however, face a problem: how can they highlight — and monetize — resource efficiency beyond compliance or beyond conventional practice credentials of the property they offer? Consumers face a related problem: how can they trust firms that offer such property in the absence of mandatory building codes? This information asymmetry has predominantly spurred the development of certification and classification instruments as a means to develop this market — further discussed in Chapter 4. Again such motivations confirm the broader literature on voluntary programs: seeking financial gain is often (expected) the primary motivator for firms to turn to voluntary programs in other areas as well (e.g., Arora & Cason, 1995; Florida & Davison, 2001; Heyes & Maxwell, 2004).

Preventing the anticipated introduction of government-led building codes or planning legislation was considered another motivation for firms to turn to voluntary programs. "They understand that if they do not act the government comes in with regulation that is not going to suit them as much as when they are more proactive," a representative of an international environmental consultancy firm observed; "that is a fear in the sector" (int. 29). Alternatively, in the absence of mandatory building codes for built environment sustainability, as in India and Malaysia, firms may see an opportunity to steer government in a certain direction by developing and implementing their own programs and committing to these. Again, such motivations are reported in other areas also (e.g., Baron & Diermeier, 2007; Maxwell, Lyon, & Hackett, 2000; Salop & Scheffman, 1991).

A final set of motivations mentioned by interviewees are reputational benefits to firms that subject themselves to voluntary programs. For some firms these programs may help to showcase that they are concerned with environmental and societal problems, and that they respond to these problems. "High-end tenants ask for sustainable buildings: they need them to meet their CSR [corporate social responsibility] targets," a manager of a Dutch voluntary program explained (int. 64). For other firms these programs may simply provide a means to call attention to their practice in the area of built environment sustainability. Once more, such impetus resonates with those identified in other areas (e.g., Albertini, 2013; Bekkers & Wiepking, 2010; Berliner & Prakash, 2014; Lyon & Wren Montgomery, 2015; Sheehy, 2011). However, there remains the perverse possibility that stakeholders might punish firms rather than reward them for taking voluntary action in the area of environmental sustainability (Kim & Lyon, 2015).

Motivations for Citizens and Civil Society Organizations

Interviewees considered that, broadly speaking, citizen and civil society organizations have similar motivations to firms to turn to voluntary programs: cost savings, showcasing their concern with societal or environmental problems, and a means of guiding governments in governing built environment sustainability — further confirming such motivations reported in other areas (e.g., Domask, 2003; Fransen & Burgoon, 2014a; Lane & Morrison, 2006). Voluntary programs may help them to overcome collective action problems and may provide a platform through which they can interact with governments. A typical example here is the international Transition Towns network, which invites communities to improve built environment sustainability and resilience (Connors & McDonald, 2010; Smith, 2011). It has set out sixteen criteria for participants to commit to, ranging from the sort of sustainability and goals to pursue to maintaining links with local government. Through a website and a handbook information is provided on how citizens participating in the network can improve built environment sustainability at street, neighborhood, and city levels. Around the globe close to five hundred Transition Town initiatives are in place, many of which collaborate with and receive financial or other support from local governments.[10]

Voluntary programs also offer citizens and civil society organizations a means to reward firms for positive environmental behavior, for instance, by purchasing products that have been labeled or certified as meeting certain voluntary requirements. Less obviously, but highly valuably, they may give citizens and civil society organizations a means of putting flesh on the bones of their activist campaigns (Fransen & Burgoon, 2014a). For example, in 1999, Greenpeace successfully campaigned against Home

Depot — then the largest supplier of do-it-yourself products in the United States — aiming to prevent the corporation from selling wood products from old-growth forests and otherwise unsustainable sources. This campaign resulted in Home Depot's voluntarily seeking certification from the Forest Stewardship Council[11] for all its timber products; this action had a cascading effect in the United States, with other do-it-yourself product suppliers voluntarily following Home Depot's lead (Domask, 2003).

High Expectations That Reach beyond Sustainable Buildings

This chapter has painted, in broad brushstrokes, the sustainable building challenge faced and the obstacles experienced by governments in addressing this challenge with dominant mandatory governance instruments — building codes and planning legislation. It has discussed the turn to voluntary programs as a logical response to these obstacles, and has also considered other motivations for governments, firms, citizens, and civil society organizations to turn to voluntary programs. Chapter 3 positions this turn to voluntary programs for sustainable buildings in the broader voluntary program literature and highlights that these are widely applied in related areas such as forestry, organic food production, and environmental management systems. Evaluations of voluntary programs from other areas do not present unequivocal stories of success, however: some studies indicate successful program performance in terms of improved behavior by those committing to voluntary programs, or an overall contribution to desired collective ends, but often studies find no or at best limited performance in such terms (Brouhle & Ramirez Harrington, 2014; Coglianese & Nash, 2014; Matisoff, 2013; Resolve, 2012; Zobel, 2013). In light of these findings from other areas, I asked my interviewees why such high hopes have persisted for these instruments in addressing the built environment.

They often stressed that financial gains from reduced building energy consumption and carbon emissions are expected to be so attractive that once property developers, owners, and users realize, experience, or are able to market these gains, they will voluntarily move toward sustainable buildings. In addition to this, so explained interviewees, these programs are expected to contribute not only to decarbonizing the built environment, but also to economic growth. "People often ask: Isn't this program about creating jobs for the construction industry?" an administrator of a program in the United States observed. "And that is indeed a huge policy goal. Our retrofitting program helps to create jobs" (int. 184).

This reflects typical "ecological modernization" and "green growth" narratives that underlie the sustainable development policies and agendas of many governments and firms around the globe (Dryzek, 2005; Hayden, 2014; Matthews, 2015; Mattoo & Subramanian, 2013) — the idea that through ecoefficiency not only can carbon emissions be reduced, but this can be done at net-cost benefit. "The [voluntary] program is a breath of fresh air for the nation's environmental health and economic growth," claims Green Lights, one of the first voluntary programs for sustainable building use in the United States (U.S. EPA, 1993). "By encouraging the widespread use of energy-efficient lighting [it] is providing that profitability and environmental protection can go hand in hand" (U.S. EPA, 1993, 1). Or similarly, as is argued for a program studied in this book, "If the Netherlands wishes to keep on track with sustainable development [elsewhere] in Europe we have to get our act together. . . . It is important to pick and support those innovations [including voluntary programs] that combine sustainability and economic growth. Those are the initiatives that serve Dutch society as a whole" (Green Deal Board, 2012, 2 — my translation).

Such win–win narratives sound appealing, but without reference to any of the likely obstacles or anticipated shortcomings they also seem a little too good to be true. As highlighted in the empirical Chapters 4 to 6, most of the voluntary programs studied do not yet live up to these high expectations. But before I move to discussing the individual programs studied in more depth, I first describe in Chapter 3 the broader global development of voluntary programs and the theoretical template employed to assess their performance.

3   A World of Voluntary Programs
Prevailing and Advanced Theoretical Perspectives

Voluntary programs are not unique to the area of sustainable building and city development and transformation. Over the last few decades they have become popular for governing societal and environmental problems in a wide variety of sectors ranging from apparel to forestry, from fisheries to energy supply (Marx & Wouters, 2014; van der Heijden, 2012). Following this development a rich empirical and theoretical literature has developed that seeks to understand whether and how voluntary programs help to achieve desired collective ends, and what conditions contribute to the outcomes of voluntary programs. This chapter explores the state of the art in this literature to develop a theoretical template for addressing the main questions of the research underpinning this book.

In the Chapter 1 I have explained the adaptive theory approach and realist evaluation practice applied in this project's research (Layder, 2006; Pawson, 2013; Pawson & Tilley, 1997). I began research using this approach by applying Matthew Potoski and Aseem Prakash's (2009) club theory perspective on voluntary programs to understand their performance. As discussed, this perspective was insufficient to explain fully the observed variance of performance in programs. Seeking to develop a comprehensive theoretical template that accounts for this variance I included theoretical developments from urban transformation literature and literature on the diffusion of innovations. Urban transformation theory added a local government perspective to this study (B. Evans et al., 2005); innovation diffusion research contributed a diffusion network perspective (E. M. Rogers, 1995). As becomes clear in the final chapters of this book, addition of the diffusion network perspective in particular is a major advance in understanding the performance of voluntary programs.

Before I outline this theoretical template I will first discuss voluntary programs as a logical step in the historical development of governance. From here on I introduce the voluntary program outcomes (dependent variables, explanans) that I seek to explain, followed by the conditions that may explain the described performance (independent variables, explanandums). These conditions are drawn from the three perspectives that together provide the theoretical template — club theory, local government, and diffusion network perspectives. Subsequently, the set of voluntary programs studied is introduced. The chapter concludes with expectations of their performance based on the state of the art literature discussed.

A Logical Step in the Ongoing Historical Development of Governance

Voluntary programs can be understood as a logical development in an ongoing philosophy of deregulation and government reform, both constituting a larger shift in rethinking the role of government in governing society (DeLeon, Rivera, & Manderino, 2010). Substantial change can be traced back to the late 1970s when command-and-control-style mandatory government intervention was questioned as too expensive for society and unworkable for government, and when the increasing political power of firms and markets began pressuring governments to deregulate (Baldwin, Cave, & Lodge, 2011; Hodge, 2000; Osborne & Gaebler, 1992; Vogel, 1996). Later global turns toward new public management and neoliberalism reinforced the search for innovative governance instruments (Barry, Osborne, & Rose, 1993; Hay, 2001; Osborne & Gaebler, 1992; Steger & Roy, 2010). A broader turn to governance[1] that began in the 1990s has further paved the way for voluntary programs — for sustainable buildings and other goods and services. This "shift from government to governance" is documented in almost all societal areas, including the governing of environmental problems and responses to climate change (Backstrand et al., 2010; Chhotray & Stoker, 2010; Pierre, 2011; Rhodes, 2007; Wurzel et al., 2013).

At least two related trends can be distinguished in this shift. First is a move away from exclusive state authority in governing societal and environmental problems toward the involvement of public and private sector stakeholders in doing so (Ansell & Gash, 2008; Armstrong & Kilpatrick, 2007; De Búrca & Scott, 2006; Trubek & Trubek, 2007); second is an interest in governance instruments that encourage self-organization, market solutions, or both as substitutes for or complements to mandatory command-and-control-style interventions (Gunningham, Kagan, & Thornton, 2003; Wurzel et al., 2013). Voluntary programs stand out in particular for moving away from a traditional governance approach of coercion through mandatory legal instruments toward incentivizing desired behavior through instruments that reward spontaneous behavioral change — for instance, the construction of buildings with higher levels of built environment sustainability than are required by law.

That having been said, while being a novel step in the evolution of governance, voluntary programs show remarkable similarities with traditional mandatory governance instruments: they are often rule regimes that consist of a set of requirements, a process for monitoring and enforcement of those subject to these requirements, and a system for rewarding compliant behavior. They are developed, implemented, and administered by one party (referred to as "rule-makers" in this book) and committed to by another (referred to as "rule-takers"). Rule-makers are often governments, collectives of firms, civil society organizations, or collaborations of these. Rule-takers include governments, citizens, firms, civil society organizations, and other organizations. Actors can be, and often are, rule-makers and rule-takers at the same time. As is clear from Chapter 2, both rule-takers and rule-makers have incentives for being involved in voluntary programs. A city government acting as rule-maker, for example, might seek to contribute to its overall built environment sustainability policy of reducing the city's carbon emissions; as a rule-taker it might see an opportunity to lead by example and show its progressive stance on addressing environmental problems.

Evaluating Voluntary Program Performance: Outcomes of Interest in This Book

The fundamental question asked of the voluntary programs discussed in the empirical chapters is whether and how they contribute to decarbonizing the built environment. Measuring voluntary program performance is, however, complicated: "Keep in mind there are many measures of success," a program administrator in Brisbane, Australia, emphasized. "You can look at participation [i.e., the number of rule-takers], but that does not say anything about square meters of buildings addressed, carbon emissions reduced, or simply knowledge generated. It's not easy" (int. 36). Her insights reflect the complexities discussed by scholars in earlier evaluations of voluntary programs (Biermann, 2008; Borck & Coglianese, 2009; Khanna, 2007; Morgenstern & Pizer, 2007; Prakash & Potoski, 2012).

Program Performance: Direct and Indirect Outcomes

All voluntary programs considered in this book require sustainable building performance beyond that required by traditional mandatory governance instruments, and beyond what is considered conventional

practice when mandatory instruments are not in place. This performance indicator guided the selection of voluntary programs and helps
in understanding how much they challenge rule-takers. To evaluate
the performance of the programs studied I question how many rule-
takers it has attracted from the complete pool of prospective rule-takers
it targets, how much these rule-takers improve their performance
(particularly reducing their building-related resource consumption or
carbon emissions), and the relative performance of a program in contributing to improved built environment sustainability — for example,
the overall building-related energy reductions achieved by a program's
rule-takers compared to all building-related energy consumption of the
prospective rule-takers the program targets (see further Appendix B).
These three performance indicators — the number of participating
rule-takers, the performance of these rule-takers, and the overall contribution to a desired collective end — follow related evaluative studies
of such voluntary programs (de Vries et al., 2012; Gunningham, 2009;
Potoski & Prakash, 2009).

Overall the voluntary programs studied do not achieve sweeping
results on these performance criteria, as becomes clear in the empirical
chapters. However, interviewees were often positive about programs
even when they had only attracted a small number of rule-takers, or only
resulted in development or retrofitting of a handful of buildings. They
specifically looked upon such performance as relevant best practices that
helped to change norms and conventions in the construction and property sectors: "These instruments create awareness," a policy maker in
Brisbane argued. "People look at their retrofitted clubhouse and think,
ah this is happening. The developer looks at the sustainable building
developed down the street and thinks, I've got to compete with that"
(int. 27). Again this reflects the larger literature on voluntary programs,
which points to possible program diffusion effects and suggests that
knowledge generated by a few rule-takers may gradually diffuse to non-
rule-takers and thus may ultimately alter norms and conventional
practice in a sector (Arimura, Hibiki, & Katayama, 2008; Darnall &
Sides, 2008; E. Rogers & Weber, 2010).

In a related vein, interviewees often considered these programs valuable for drawing lessons on how to achieve a timely and speedy transition toward resource-efficient, low-carbon buildings. By implementing
these programs, they argued, knowledge is gained regarding what type
of incentive is attractive to what type of actor and why, what type of
barriers a specific program design confronts when implemented, and
so on. This again confirms the literature in this area, which stresses that
indirect outcomes (spillover effects) of voluntary programs have a place

in evaluative studies (Carroll & Shabana, 2010; Lim & Prakash, 2014). Such indirect outcomes are, however, not the central focus of this study: first and foremost it seeks to understand how the various programs studied perform on the performance indicators mentioned. Yet acknowledging the importance of indirect outcomes, these are discussed to some extent in the empirical chapters — by scrutinizing how, for instance, rule-makers, rule-takers, and others use the knowledge and best practices generated.

Some Complication in Assessing Performance

Scholars point out various complications encountered in studying the performance of voluntary programs, some of which are likely to apply to the programs studied in this book. One of the main issues they highlight is the self-selection bias of rule-takers (Lenox & Nash, 2003). The sheer number of rule-takers or even an improvement in their behavior does not indicate whether they were perhaps more willing than others to change their behavior in the first instance: whether they were better equipped than others to do so, for instance, because they have more funds or were already performing at a high level before participating. Such selection problems might be overcome with econometric techniques, but these require considerable numbers of rule-takers in a program to be applicable (Berliner & Prakash, 2015; Frondel & Schmidt, 2005; Hartman, 1988; Imbens & Wooldridge, 2008). In the current study often only a small number of rule-takers participate in a program — the fourteen major property owners participating in the Better Building Partnership (introduced in Chapter 1, discussed in Chapter 5) resemble in number the entire pool of prospective rule-takers the program initially targeted. This makes the application of econometric techniques difficult in this study, but through the program histories in the empirical chapters some insight is gained about this self-selection bias and its consequences for the programs studied.

Another complication holds particularly for the performance indicators set: the performance of programs may change over time (Auld, 2014; Potoski & Prakash, 2009). The initial group of rule-makers, initial design choices, or initial contextual conditions may have a lasting impact on the performance of an instrument — rule-makers can lack legitimacy in the eyes of rule-takers (NeJaime, 2009; Trubek & Trubek, 2010; Wilkinson, 2010), or a program may lack flexibility to respond and adapt to changes in its environment (Gunningham, 2009; Scott & Sturm, 2006; Walker & de Búrca, 2007). Over time programs may also become subject to increased shirking behavior by their rule-takers — new rule-takers may be attracted to a program once it has achieved a good reputation, but they might only intend to free-ride on this reputation and not conform to its rules (Potoski & Prakash, 2009; Welch, Mazur, & Bretschneider, 2000). The program histories provided in the empirical chapters will go behind the descriptive statistics seeking to delineate performance indicators — for selected programs — and address relevant temporal issues that aid in understanding program performance (cf., Auld, 2014; Mosier & Fisk, 2013).

A Prevailing Perspective to Explain Voluntary Program Performance: Club Theory

Empirical research into the performance of voluntary programs has produced mixed results. Some studies find that programs have improved rule-takers' behavior in desired ways (Hsueh, 2013; Khanna & Damon, 1999; Potoski & Prakash, 2005), while others do not (Brouhle & Ramirez Harrington, 2014; Coglianese & Nash, 2014; Matisoff, 2013; Resolve, 2012; Zobel, 2013). Such studies often seek to identify which conditions matter most in explaining program performance, and can roughly be clustered into studies that are interested in program design and studies concerned predominantly with program context. Unfortunately cross-national or cross-program studies are rare, as are studies considering program designs and contexts as configurations of conditions. This limits the ability to draw expectations about what program design (the whole of design conditions that make up a program) may be most promising in which context (the entirety of context conditions a design is embedded in).

One of the most advanced perspectives that seek to explain voluntary programs as a configuration of design conditions is Matthew Potoski and Aseem Prakash's club theory perspective (Potoski & Prakash, 2009, 2013b; Prakash & Potoski, 2012). Under this perspective voluntary programs are considered as rule systems that prescribe desired behavior and exclusively reward compliant rule-takers. The club theory perspective builds on earlier insight into voluntary programs and has seen wide application. In what follows I discuss the core program design and context conditions considered relevant in affecting program performance from the perspective of club theory and related literature.

Design Conditions and Expectations

The literature consistently points out three design conditions as related to program performance: the strictness of a program's rules, the strictness of the monitoring and enforcement of these rules, and the rewards accruing to rule-takers when committing to a program (Borck & Coglianese, 2009; DeLeon & Rivera, 2010; Potoski & Prakash, 2009). These three conditions are at the foundation of the club theory perspective, which considers that the essential, defining aspect of voluntary programs is constituted by their rules. The rules prescribe the goals of the programs, their expected outcomes, and expected rule-taker behavior. Stipulating these rules is a complicated matter for rule-makers. Setting progressive rules (say, requiring a more than 30 percent improvement of building energy efficiency compared to conventional practice) will mean that a program responds adequately to the need to decarbonize the built environment. Progressive rules may also help to define a voluntary program in relation to mediocre programs and signal to consumers or other stakeholders that rule-takers in that program are highly concerned with the problem it seeks to address. This signaling function of progressive rules may make a program attractive to prospective rule-takers (Berliner & Prakash, 2014). Progressive rules may, however, also discourage prospective rule-takers — for instance, when they consider that the cost or effort of participating does not outweigh the rewards of doing so. In attracting rule-takers and improving their performance the strictness of these rules is thus ameliorated by program designers choosing to work within the frame of conventional expectations. Designers will do this by anticipating prospective rule-takers' cost—benefit calculations when determining whether or not to join a program (Coglianese & Nash, 2014; Potoski & Prakash, 2009; Prakash & Potoski, 2012). For voluntary program rule-makers it is germane to understand this trade-off and to choose a level of strictness that suits their ambition.

For voluntary programs to be effective these rules require compliance by rule-takers, and without some form of monitoring or enforcement they are unlikely to do so (Bailey, 2008; Lyon & Maxwell, 2007; Rivera & de Leon, 2004). It is repeatedly pointed out that programs relying on self-monitoring by rule-takers or even monitoring by rule-makers (administrator monitoring) run the risk of noncompliance, and instituting additional third-party or government monitoring is considered to be more effective (Bartle & Vass, 2007; Cashore, Auld, & Newsom, 2004; A. A. King & Lenox, 2000). Another approach is to seek compliant behavior through community building and peer pressure. A program may include processes that help rule-takers to support and correct each other in their behavior (Carraro & Leveque, 1999; Gibson, 1999c; Howes, Skea, & Whelan, 1997). Stringent monitoring and enforcement may also enhance the credibility of a program and make it more attractive to dedicated rule-takers, their clients, and stakeholders, because it would demonstrably ostracize free-riders and shirking behavior. Yet, this aspect of voluntary programs also entails a trade-off: while stringent monitoring might help in identifying noncomplying rule-takers, it may also discourage rule-takers from committing to the instrument when they regard it as too stringent in limiting a rule-taker's options for demurral or lessening of standards (for instance, in response to unforeseen circumstances), or too bureaucratically difficult to work with (Marx & Wouters, 2014; OECD, 2003; Prakash & Potoski, 2012).

For programs to be attractive to prospective rule-takers their rewards must be exclusive and what they consider worthwhile (Berghoef & Dodds, 2013; A. A. King & Lenox, 2000; Turaga, Howarth, & Borsuk, 2010). The voluntary programs for sustainable buildings studied are often marketed by rule-makers as helping rule-takers to reduce operational costs, as highlighted in Chapter 2 and further discussed in the empirical chapters (for discussion of other areas see Croci, 2005; Moon & Ko, 2013). Programs may also help them in distinguishing their goods or services from those of competitors through an instrument-brand that helps them to attract a specific client base or to charge higher prices for their products or services (Feddersen & Gilligan, 2001; Li, Clarck, Jensen, & Yen, 2014; Moon & Ko, 2013; Prakash & Potoski, 2012). Interviewees often considered such monetary gains as the most important reward for rule-takers: "For companies the key objective is to make profit," an academic in Singapore insisted: "There are very few companies that would go more sustainable if they cannot make profit out of it" (int. 95). Yet, other rewards are available as well, and — as becomes clear from the empirical chapters — a voluntary program can provide different rewards at the same time. Voluntary programs may, for instance, provide rule-takers with knowledge of how to improve the resource efficiency or reduce the carbon intensity of their future buildings that is otherwise costly or difficult for them to acquire, or may help them in generating such knowledge (Darnall & Carmin, 2005; Delmas & Terlaak, 2001; Videras & Alberini, 2000). Yet another form of rewarding rule-takers is reputational, namely, that of recognition of their leading roles in a sector. Being recognized as a leader may yield marketing benefits for rule-takers (Borck, Coglianese, & Nash, 2008; Khanna & Anton, 2002; Rivera & de Leon, 2004). For the rewards discussed it is expected that the higher the rewards the more willing rule-takers are to join voluntary programs (Berghoef & Dodds, 2013; Moon & Ko, 2013; Turaga et al., 2010). In a related vein, since noncompliance with program rules might result in a penalty of being denied rewards, it is also expected that the higher the rewards the more willing rule-takers are to honor commitments — but only if enforcement is adequate (A. A. King & Lenox, 2000).

Context Conditions and Expectations

The literature on voluntary programs has become increasingly aware that similarly designed programs may perform differently in dissimilar contexts. Voluntary programs, such as organic food labeling or pay-per-plastic-bag fees, have been found to achieve positive outcomes in one country or region but not in another, even when implemented by a similar set of actors (Ackerman, 1997; Thøgersen, 2010). The literature consistently points out three context conditions as related to program performance: existing environmental legislation, economic circumstances, and societal pressure.

Scholars are particularly interested in the interaction between voluntary programs and existing and potential future government-led regulation and legislation (Bernstein & Hannah, 2008; Dibden & Cocklin, 2010; Thatcher & Coen, 2008). Existing regulation and legislation can be considered the baseline from which prospective rule-takers view voluntary programs. If that baseline is already high they might find it difficult to commit to a program, but if the baseline is low an instrument may provide them with the opportunity to obtain commitment rewards with relatively little cost (De Búrca & Scott, 2006; Héritier & Eckert, 2008; Hertier & Lehmkuhl, 2008). Existing regulation and legislation may also harness a culture of rule-taking and committing to such instruments, thereby helping capable rule-makers to implement voluntary programs effectively (Hettige, Huq, Pargal, & Wheeler, 1996; C. Kirkpatrick & Parkers, 2004; Nath & Behera, 2011). Scholars discuss the importance of existing or expected future regulation and legislation as providing an incentive for rule-takers to commit to such programs in anticipation of, or in seeking to prevent the introduction of, government regulation (Darnall & Carmin, 2005; Reid & Toffel, 2009; Short & Toffel, 2010). Likewise, a voluntary program may fill a niche in regulation or legislation and provide participants with rewards they cannot obtain through compliance with mandatory governance instruments (NeJaime, 2009; Wilkinson, 2010). Even more, in a context of low or absent mandatory requirements a voluntary program might function as a signal, enabling rule-takers to indicate that they are concerned with societal or environmental problems (Berliner & Prakash, 2014).

Economic circumstance is often regarded as another contextual condition that affects program performance. While the direct relationship between economic wealth and environmental degradation is a topic of much debate,[2] there is some evidence indicating that the higher the disposable income of consumers (individuals and organizations alike), the more likely it is that they demand environmentally benign products and services (see the literature on "green consumers": Baron & Diermeier, 2007; Florida & Davison, 2001; Heyes & Maxwell, 2004). Programs seeking to incorporate such concerns may therefore be expected to achieve better outcomes in contexts where economic circumstances are favorable. Related, higher levels of wealth may also provide for more resources for rule-takers to free up the cost and time necessary to commit to these programs — for instance, acquiring handbooks or training staff (cf. Baughn, Bodie, & McIntosh, 2007; Croci, 2005; Howarth, Hadda, & Paton, 2000; Welford, 2005). It might further be expected that programs targeting wealthy consumers or rule-takers outperform those that target less affluent consumers (Gamerschlag, Möller, & Verbeeten, 2011). Distinguishing between the level of wealth of a program's context as a whole and that of its rule-takers and their customers is important in that it helps to overcome the simplistic perception that voluntary programs implemented in developed economies outperform those implemented in developing economies in terms of attracting participants and improving behavior (Biermann, 2008; Blackman, Uribe, van Hoof, & Lyon, 2013; Perkins & Neumayer, 2010). A program may fail to attract "poor" rule-takers in a context where economic circumstances are generally favorable, but succeed in attracting "rich" rule-takers in a context where economic circumstances are generally not favorable.

A final set of contextual conditions that the literature considers related to program performance can be captured under the term "societal pressure" (Briscoe & Safford, 2008; Den Hond & De Bakker, 2007; Fransen & Burgoon, 2014b; B. G. King, 2008; Mikler, 2009; Reid & Toffel, 2009). Seeking to respond to such pressure, individuals and organizations may be expected to commit to programs as a way of seeking public recognition for their products and services (Arora & Cason, 1995; Baron & Diermeier, 2007; Briscoe & Safford, 2008). It should be noted, however, that these three contextual conditions are related and likely mutually reinforce each other (cf., Biermann, 2008; Choumert, Combes Motel, & Dakpo, 2013). Higher levels of economic development are, for instance, often related to higher levels of literacy and education, which typically indicate greater awareness of environmental problems. Higher levels of economic development are often also related to higher levels of mandatory environmental legislation, and such legislation may make citizens further aware of environmental problems and the need to address these; in combination, these factors are likely to contribute to societal pressure (Dasgupta, Mody, Roy, & Wheeler, 2001; Hungerford, 1996; Özen & Küskü, 2009).

Advanced Perspectives: Local Government Involvement and Diffusion Networks

While the club theory perspective is one of the most advanced to date, it is incapable of explaining the full variance in the performance of the voluntary programs studied in this book. Seeking to explain this variance I have included two perspectives: a local governance perspective and a diffusion network perspective (the reasons for adding these have been explained previously in Chapter 1). In what follows I discuss the conditions pertaining to these perspectives that are relevant for explaining the performance of the programs studied here.

A Local Government Perspective

One of the many characteristics that make voluntary programs intriguing is that they can be developed and implemented by governments, firms, civil society organizations, and combinations of these. That different actors can be involved in voluntary programs as rule-makers or rule-takers is widely acknowledged in the literature, and it is assumed that their involvement is likely to affect the performance of these programs differently (Carraro & Leveque, 1999; DeLeon & Rivera, 2010; Gibson, 1999c; Morgenstern & Pizer, 2007; Ronit, 2012; US EPA, 1997). The literature points in particular to the involvement of governments as having a potentially positive effect on program performance in terms of attracting rule-takers, incentivizing them to improve their behavior, or doing both (Auld, 2014; Fiorino, 2009; Gibson, 1999b; Koehler, 2007; Morgenstern & Pizer, 2007). For instance, as third-party state-sanctioned actors with a "neutrality" born of relative corporate independence, governments have the capacity to confer legitimacy on such programs in the eyes of the public (Solomon, 2008); they may also be considered neutral actors by nonstate rule-takers, increasing their willingness to become involved (Kickbusch, Hein, & Silberschmidt, 2010). Governments are also most likely to be able to enforce program adherence, thereby contributing financial security for rule-takers when committing to programs, and to provide rule-takers with positive media exposure to recognize their efforts (Borck & Coglianese, 2009; Gunningham, 2009; Irvine, Lazarevski, & Dolnicar, 2012). For the research field of sustainable buildings, government involvement in voluntary programs is expected to be especially promising: governments are major consumers of office space and other building types. In their position as tenants or building commissioners they might demand goods and services that meet specific program criteria, or simply require their suppliers to join a particular program (cf. Van der Horst & Vergragt, 2006).

More specifically, the literature on urban transformation is hopeful about the involvement of local governments in voluntary programs for sustainable buildings and cities and their capacity to effect transformation to a low-carbon built environment (Athens, 2009; Aust, 2015; Betsill & Bulkeley, 2006; Bulkeley et al., 2013; B. Evans et al., 2005; T. Lee & Koski, 2012; Mosier & Fisk, 2013; Portney & Berry, 2013; R. Wang, 2012). It considers local government the level closest to citizens, most capable of understanding the area context of sustainable building problems, and best suited to collaborate with local stakeholders in developing solutions. This largely overlaps with the substantial role imagined for local governments in Agenda 21 — a resolution passed at the Earth Summit held in Rio de Janeiro in 1992 stating basic principles guiding nations toward more sustainable development in the twenty-first century (Lafferty & Eckerberg, 1998; UNCED, 1992).[3] As such, local governments may be most aware of what type of voluntary program is applicable to their context. Because they know the local pool of prospective rule-takers they may also be more capable of attracting these to a program than more distant regional or national organizations, including nonlocal government bodies and private sector or civil society interest groups. Furthermore, local governments may have a strong incentive to develop specific voluntary programs that attract investors, firms and employment, or citizens to their jurisdiction — or to prevent them from moving elsewhere (Cheshire et al., 2014).

A Diffusion Network Perspective

A specific condition that has had little attention, if any, in the voluntary programs literature to date is the role of diffusion networks in voluntary programs. Like any innovation— a product, a technology, a change in behavior, a governance instrument, or simply an idea — a voluntary program needs to be accepted and committed to by rule-takers to achieve its desired outcomes. Yet, not all prospective rule-takers are alike: the diffusion of innovations literature provides some means to distinguish varying types of prospective rule-takers and their willingness to commit to a voluntary program (MacVaugh & Schiavone, 2010; Nan, Zmud, & Yetgin, 2014; E. M. Rogers, 1995; E. M. Rogers, Medina, Rivera, & Wiley, 2005). This part of the literature understands diffusion as "the process by which an innovation is communicated through certain channels over time among the members of a social system" (E. M. Rogers, 1995, 6). As becomes clear in the empirical chapters, every voluntary program has a distinct diffusion network. Rule-makers can partly influence this network, but not entirely, as a voluntary program is subject to planned and unplanned spreading and uptake; also, within a similar context different voluntary programs face different diffusion networks.[4]

Four distinct aspects matter in the diffusion of an innovation: the type of innovation, the time of diffusion, the network of individuals and firms targeted, and the communication channels. The literature distinguishes between continuous and discontinuous innovations (Moore, 2002; Yu & Hang, 2010). A continuous innovation is merely an upgrading of current practice and does not require a significant change of behavior or acquisition of new knowledge or skills; for example, an increase of energy efficiency requirements in mandatory building codes is typically a continuation of existing instruments. A discontinuous innovation is, however, a break from current practice and often requires significant change of behavior or acquisition of new knowledge and skills — many of the voluntary programs studied require prospective rule-takers to become familiar with new rules, new rule structures, and new compliance mechanisms, and require them to weigh the cost and effort of committing to a voluntary program against the rewards of doing so. Therefore, ensuring uptake of a discontinuous innovation, such as a voluntary program for sustainable buildings discussed in this book, requires careful consideration of how an innovation is communicated throughout the diffusion network. Actions such as making their relative advantage clear to users, ensuring compatibility with existing practice, reducing the complexity of an innovation, allowing trials for prospective users, and making the results of the innovation observable are all measures expected to contribute to its uptake (E. M. Rogers, 1995).

But not only is the content of communication regarding innovation important in stimulating its uptake: the process of communication is also crucial. The literature considers peer-to-peer communication as more promising than mass-media channels and sees repetitive, rather than sporadic exposure of prospective adopters as more promising. It further stresses that prospective adopters are more likely to commit to an innovation when authoritative figures or organizations such as industry peak bodies support it. The main problem faced in communication is, however, that not all who ultimately commit to an innovation are similar in terms of networks and receptive capacities, which hampers diffusion through peer-to-peer communication. A useful distinction is made among five groups based on their motivation to adopt or reject an innovation: leaders,[5] early adopters, early majority, late majority, and laggards (E. M. Rogers, 1995). Leaders are eager to trial an innovation and possess the means to do so; for them the return of taking the risk of trialing an innovation is that it further cements their image as leader in a sector — however, they are a very small group, often estimated as approximately 2.5 percent of a given market. Early adopters are also willing to take the risk of being among the first to commit to an innovation, but more than leaders they do so because they see a competitive advantage. Early adopters are considered important in mainstreaming an innovation as they highlight the practical application of it, as well as its potential returns (Gladwell, 2000; E. M. Rogers, 1995). The early majority is considered more pragmatic in committing to an innovation than the first two groups. They look for an improvement of current practice that is demonstrated to function effectively and generate positive returns. They are willing to be early in adopting an innovation, but are not willing to take financial risks. Following from the early majority, the late majority is considered highly conservative and adopts an innovation only when it makes financial sense and when network pressures are considerable. Laggards, finally, are considered skeptical and prefer not to commit to an innovation until it no longer makes sense to avoid adoption. For instance, if a city government would no longer provide for communal electricity supply in new residential development areas because the technology is available for households to generate and store their own electricity, a laggard would commit to this technology. The first two groups are different from the latter three more generally in that they are more likely to communicate through vertical channels. They are the people who attend and speak at business conferences, who write in trade journals and give guest lectures at colleges and universities.[6] The latter groups communicate mostly through horizontal channels; that means that for them innovations diffuse predominantly through peer-to-peer communication (cf. Moore, 2002; E. M. Rogers, 1995).

Finally, earlier diffusion studies highlight that successful uptake of an innovation resembles an S-shaped curve: slow to commence, rapidly increasing for a period, and then decreasing again as program adoption numbers drop. Successful uptake of an innovation may be expected after 10–25 percent of market saturation (E. M. Rogers, 1995). This is the point at which an innovation makes the transition from the early market (dominated by leaders and early adopters) to the mainstream market (dominated by the early majority and the late majority). It is a critical juncture, as it demarcates the "chasm" between the two market segments (Moore, 2002): of these segments the latecomer majority groups may be inspired by the early adopting groups to accept and commit to an innovation, but at this stage very little communication occurs between the segments. That is, while early adopters may be inspired by leaders and the late majority by the early majority, it is unlikely that the early majority is inspired by insight and knowledge transferred by the early adopters. Those in the early market are willing to risk being the first in their industry to implement the innovation because they expect it to provide a competitive edge in the future; those in the mainstream market are more risk-averse and seek an improvement of existing practice that has guaranteed returns — as Geoffrey Moore (2002, 15) argues, "They want evolution, not revolution." Because of this specific difference early adopters are not often an inspiration for the early majority, and different communication strategies or simply different sales pitches are required for the different markets.

The Voluntary Programs Studied

The voluntary programs discussed in the empirical chapters exhibit a broad variety of designs, but are bound together by their primary characteristics: they are rule regimes that seek improved sustainable building development and use and that provide rewards to rule-takers who voluntarily commit to these. For comparative analysis the literature suggests various approaches to categorizing voluntary programs. Each category has its own strengths and weaknesses, and no categorization is perfect (e.g., DeLeon & Rivera, 2010; Ronit, 2012; Wood, 2007; Wurzel et al., 2013). These include conditions such as actors involved (public, private, something in between); voluntariness (negotiated agreements between governments and firms, public voluntary programs, business self-regulation, and so on); and "programness" (strictness of rules, monitoring, and enforcement). In this book the programs discussed are categorized according to the obstacles they seek to address: information asymmetry between suppliers and consumers; the lack of knowledge at developer, owner, and user levels; and the lack of funds made available by banks and other financial institutions.

Bridging Supply and Demand

The literature on green consumerism indicates that some consumers are willing to pay a premium for services or goods that are more environmentally sustainable than required by regulation, and firms are often willing to target this market by providing such goods and services (Brounen & Kok, 2011; Deng, Li, & Quigley, 2012; Eichholtz, Kok, & Quigley, 2010). At question are how consumers are satisfied that the product offered meets the "beyond compliance" credentials claimed by suppliers and how suppliers differentiate their legitimate "beyond compliance" product from competitors who make false product claims.

This is a typical example of information asymmetry between consumers and suppliers, and between honest and dishonest suppliers (for further discussion see Chapter 2).

But not only in the area of sustainable buildings do consumers and suppliers face such information asymmetries — it also holds for the provision of organic food, sustainably sourced forest products, and certain management practices. A prevalent governance innovation that seeks to overcome these information asymmetries is voluntary certification of products and services. Voluntary certification programs are often built on a set of requirements to be met by goods and services, and are typically developed by a group of firms, an industry peak body, a government agency, or a combination of these. Program compliance is normally monitored — by the rule-takers themselves, by program administrators, or by a third party — and if the product satisfies the rules a certificate is issued, often in the form of a label, acknowledging compliance. Suppliers can use this certificate for marketing purposes: it helps them to distinguish their goods and services from those of others, and it provides to consumers a measure of certainty that the credentials claimed are valid (Giddens, 2009; Lyon & Maxwell, 2006; Wood, 2003).

Although voluntary certification programs for sustainable buildings and city districts are generally built on this design, they involve a twist: buildings are highly technical goods and a wide range of compliance and beyond-compliance behavior is possible in terms of resource efficiency and carbon intensity. Early on in the development of these programs rule-makers realized that a certificate in itself has limited value if it lacks information concerning relative performance. Classification is therefore often part of these voluntary certification programs: it provides information on how a certified product or service performs compared to others (Pérez-Lombard, Ortiz, González, & Maestre, 2009). Certification and classification programs for sustainable buildings have been implemented by governments, firms, and civil society organizations since the early 1990s, and constitute the dominant category of voluntary programs in the field. Hundreds of them operate globally, varying in scope and scale — from highly local to international, and from certification of individual buildings to certification for cities as a whole (Cole & Valdebenito, 2013; K. M. Fowler & Rauch, 2006a; Mazmanian & Blanco, 2014). This category of voluntary programs is assessed in Chapter 4.

Generating and Sharing Knowledge

The second category of programs studied displays greater variety than certification and classification programs. These programs seek to generate and disseminate knowledge on how to construct and retrofit sustainable buildings, and how building users' behavior can be modified to achieve reduced resource consumption. Chapter 2 discussed the circumstances in which developers, contractors, property owners and users, and governments often lack information on how to construct and use buildings sustainably — sometimes because this information is not available, but more often because they experience difficulties in obtaining that information.

Programs in this category create knowledge in the process of design and construction, either while developing or retrofitting sustainable buildings or by reconstructing user behavior (B. Evans et al., 2005; Gollagher & Hartz-Karp, 2013). "Urban sustainability is so complex you cannot solve this in a lab. You have to get out there and do it," stated an administrator in the Netherlands after discussing a number of programs that fit this category (int. 81). By lifting restrictive building codes to allow knowledge generation in a "regulation light" situation, for example, or by pooling resources so that the risks of losing time and money invested are not carried by a single rule-taker, they create secure and supportive rule-taker environments.

The programs in this category can roughly be divided into two subsets. Programs in the first subset focus on individual rule-takers, in which the flow of information is often from rule-maker to rule-taker. A classic example is Green Lights in the United States, one of the Environmental Protection Agency's (EPA's) first voluntary programs implemented in the early 1990s (EPA, 1994).[7] Through Green Lights the EPA sought to overcome initial resistance to and unfamiliarity with energy efficient lighting. It made visible to building users the ease of reducing energy consumption and supported them in generating knowledge relevant for running their business. Green Lights participants committed to installing energy efficient lighting in 90 percent of their facilities — but only where this was profitable to do so. In return the EPA provided participants with tools (predominantly software) to conduct assessments and monitor energy savings, helped them to connect with lighting retrofitting services, and advised them of potential funding opportunities. Green Lights operated from the early to mid-1990s, and experiences with it lie at the basis of the development and implementation of the later certification and classification program Energy Star for Buildings (Moon & Ko, 2013).

Programs in the second subset focus on a collective of rule-takers and rule-makers. Often the flow of information is from rule-takers to other rule-takers, with rule-makers acting as intermediaries for knowledge dissemination. The Better Building Partnership in Sydney is a typical example of a program fitting this subtype. It draws together Sydney's major property owners and the city government and aims for significant building-related carbon emission reductions through, among others, building energy retrofits. By working together and sharing knowledge on how they have upgraded their individual property, all participating property owners gain from each other's experiences. This category of voluntary programs for sustainable buildings is assessed in Chapter 5.

Providing Funds

The third and final category of voluntary programs discussed seek to create sustainable buildings by providing property developers and owners with funding earmarked for achieving such ends: recipients agree to improve resource efficiency or reduce the carbon intensity of future buildings. Such "ecofinance" is gaining popularity as a means to address built environment sustainability (Chou, Hammer, & Levine, 2014; Matthews, 2012; XiaoHu Wang, Hawkings, & Berman, 2014).[8] The programs within this category strongly build on a win–win narrative: improved resource efficiency and reduced carbon emissions go hand in hand with financial gains for participants — this narrative also underlies many programs in the two earlier categories. In other words, so the developers of these programs argue, sustainable buildings require fewer resources to operate, entailing fewer costs for their owners and users. This enables owners to pay back loans and mortgages (Kats, Menkin, Dommu, & DeBold, 2012; J. Kirkpatrick & Bennear, 2014). Being aware of possible mandatory interventions that place prices on carbon emissions — such as cap and trade schemes — investors also become receptive to the financial prospects of sustainable buildings.

Banks and other funds providers, however, do not argue this way. They are concerned that the additional cost of improving resource efficiency and reducing carbon intensity of existing and future buildings will not be reflected in these buildings' market value. They perceive a risk that lenders will not be able to pay back the additional funds provided (Pivo, 2010; Xiadong Wang et al., 2013). The idea that future gains of sustainable buildings — lower operation costs, among others — improve building owners' ability to pay back loans and mortgages does not fit a traditional financing business model, which seeks improved profit on investment with minimized risk — such business models are based on cash flows from production and economic growth (Bals, Warner, & Butzengeiger, 2006; World Bank, 2011a). They are also concerned that building owners show "rebound effect"—type behavior and increase their resource consumption after building improvements— thereby dampening the expected savings — because they no longer feel morally restrained by the poor performance of their building (Sunikka-Blank & Galvin, 2012). The global financial crisis (2008–2011) only worsened the risk aversion of banks and financial institutions (Coiacetto & Bryant, 2014; Venugopal, Srivastava, & Polycarp, 2012). Property owners typically follow the lead of the banks. They might be concerned that they would not own a property long enough to recoup investment through reduced operational costs; they might not value the long-term gains over the short-term costs (hyperbolic discounting); or they may face a situation of split incentives, whereby the owner has invested the capital but their tenants receive the gains in terms of reduced operational costs (Ameli & Brandt, 2015; Swan & Brown, 2013).

The voluntary programs that were researched in this cluster strikingly illustrate the different perspectives with which diverse people and organizations assess the opportunities and constraints when responding to the issues of carbon and resource efficiency: some perceive a financial win–win opportunity that they happily take; others see a financial risk they rather avoid (cf., Hoffman, 2015). Like the information generation and sharing programs, the researched financing programs can be further clustered within two subsets: programs that address the risks experienced by third-party funds providers and programs that directly fund sustainable building development. This category of voluntary programs for sustainable building is assessed in Chapter 6.

Expectations and Propositions on Voluntary Program Performance

This chapter has systematically reviewed the literature on voluntary programs. It has outlined the development of a theoretical template for studying a set of voluntary programs for sustainable buildings, to be discussed in the remainder of this book. The review has adapted Potoski and Prakash's (2009) club theory perspective to the field of voluntary programs for low-carbon building and city development and transformation, unpacking the various types of rewards accruing to rule-takers in these programs. To this perspective it has added two specific perspectives seen to affect the performance of voluntary program: a local government perspective and a diffusion network perspective. These three perspectives compose the theoretical template used.

This then leaves one final task: clarifying propositions on what it is "about the [programs] that is [expected to work], for whom and in what circumstances" (Pawson, 2013, 22). The propositions are particularly useful in terms of evaluating the explanatory reach of the club theory perspective.[9] I refrain from stating propositions regarding the two other perspectives, however, because these were supplemental to the original theoretical structure of the study and were included to account for program performance that the club theory did not explain. To begin, it may be expected that potential differences in stringency of program rules and the monitoring and enforcement of these, combined with differences in rewards accruing to rule-takers, affect a program's performance in terms of attracting participants, improving their behavior, or doing both.

Two configurations of these conditions (program designs) are promising. In the first model, voluntary programs combining relatively lenient rules with relatively high rewards are expected to be successful for attracting relatively large numbers of participants. In this specific design strict monitoring and enforcement are not necessary conditions for improving rule-taker performance because the rules are lenient and easy to obey. They are not expected to challenge rule-takers to improve their behavior substantially. The advantage of this program design — lenient rules and enforcement, and high rewards — is expected to lie in indirect outcomes: it might change rule-takers' mind-set by exposing them to the advantages and opportunities of sustainable building, city development, and transformation. Stated formally:

H1.1   *Voluntary programs for sustainable buildings and cities that combine relatively lenient rules with relatively high rewards attract relatively large numbers of rule-takers,* but

H1.2   *these programs fail to improve the behavior of these rule-takers substantially in terms of reducing their building-related resource consumption or carbon emissions,* and

H1.3   *in this specific design stringent monitoring and enforcement are nonnecessary conditions for improving rule-taker performance.*

In the second model, voluntary programs combining stringent rules with high rewards are expected to attract small groups of dedicated rule-takers. In this design stringent monitoring and enforcement are necessary conditions: they increase the likelihood that noncompliant or free-riding behavior is discovered. This likely discourages those who merely seek to participate in a voluntary program to "greenwash" their reputation, while attracting those who are seeking an exclusive and credible program. It is anticipated that the combination of stringent rules with stringent monitoring and enforcement would result in the substantial improvement of rule-taker behavior. This is, however, a program design that is not expected to have a large-scale impact on decarbonizing the built environment unless it attracts the major organizations in an industry sector, for instance, large property owners. The aggregated performance of the small group of rule-takers will be limited compared to the sustainable building challenge faced. Again, stated formally:

H2.1   *Voluntary programs for sustainable buildings and cities that combine stringent rules with relatively high rewards attract small groups of dedicated rule-takers,* and

H2.2   *these programs succeed in improving the behavior of these rule-takers substantially in terms of reducing their building-related resource consumption or carbon emissions,* and

H2.3   *in this specific design stringent monitoring and enforcement are necessary conditiosn for improving rule-taker behavior.*

Other design types are not expected to perform successfully. Programs that combine stringent rules with low rewards would ask too much of prospective rule-takers and give too little in return — irrespective of whether they built on stringent or lenient monitoring and enforcement — and are expected to result in a too-small participant base to have meaningful impact. While the club theory perspective does not differentiate the type of rewards provided to rule-takers, building on the broader literature it can be expected that immediate, calculable returns on investment will be attractive to prospective rule-takers relative to nonmonetary reward (Alberini & Segerson, 2002; Arora & Cason, 1995; Gibson, 1999a; Howarth et al., 2000; Moon & Ko, 2013):

H3   *Voluntary programs that provide direct monetary gains outperform those providing other rewards in terms of attracting rule-takers and improving their behavior.*

These propositions point to the two main theoretical expectations underlying this study: that various program conditions combine and interact in causing their performance outcomes (conjunctural causation), and that different combinations of conditions (e.g., stringent rules with high financial rewards, or lenient rules with high leadership rewards) may result in similar outcomes (equifinality).

Finally, building on the literature discussed, it is expected that the causal direction of program conditions and program performance is positive for all conditions — those from the club theory perspective, as well as those from the local government perspective and the innovation network perspective. Thus, if a condition is present, it positively influences program performance; for instance, a diffusion network that ensures that prospective rule-takers are frequently exposed to the voluntary program and that has authoritative individuals or organizations supporting the program is capable of communicating the ease and advantages of committing to the program to prospective rule-takers in the early and majority markets, or is characterized by combinations of these traits, and is expected to be positively related to the number of rule-takers a program attracts. The exception to this rule of a positive relation between conditions and performance are the conditions "rules" and "monitoring and enforcement." Following on from the club theory perspective, it is expected that stringent rules and stringent monitoring and enforcement can be related both positively and negatively to program performance, as can lenient rules and lenient monitoring and enforcement.

4   Certification and Classification
Bridging Supply and Demand

In 1990, the United Kingdom—based Building Research Establishment (BRE) wrote history by launching the first version of BREEAM — the BRE Environmental Assessment Method. BREEAM allows property developers and property owners to obtain independent verification of how their buildings move beyond mandatory sustainability requirements. Under BREEAM an external evaluator assesses their buildings against a set of rules — including aspects such as energy use and carbon emissions — and awards credits for compliance with rules. The more rules that are met, the more credits are awarded. On the basis of this assessment a certificate is issued specifying the sustainability credentials of that building. When launched, BREEAM was among a range of novel voluntary programs in the United Kingdom that allowed businesses to showcase their environmentally responsible behavior (Beaufoy, 1993), but it was immediately considered as "perhaps the most interesting initiative" among those since it allowed property owners and users to determine "whether or not they are receiving value for money from their buildings" (Varcoe, 1991, 364).

Over the last twenty-five years or so, BREEAM has broadened its scope and has become more sophisticated. It now allows for the assessment of a wide range of building types — residential and commercial — and even city precincts, and has assessment protocols in place for both new and existing buildings. The scope of assessment has broadened also: a new commercial building is, for instance, assessed against close to fifty detailed rules specified in a 450-page manual (BRE, 2011). It is safe to say that in this period BREEAM has had a noticeable impact on the construction and property sectors: around the globe 425,000 buildings are BREEAM-certified and another 2 million have been registered for future certification. BREEAM is adopted in fifty countries, and has inspired many to implement their own certification programs.[1] It is estimated that hundreds of comparable programs are in place around the world that allow for the assessment of environmental credentials of buildings, building products, building users, city precincts, and cities — making this the most widely implemented type of voluntary program for sustainable building and city development (Cole & Valdebenito, 2013; K. M. Fowler & Rauch, 2006a; Mazmanian & Blanco, 2014; Pérez-Lombard et al., 2009).

Chapter 3 explained that voluntary certification programs help in bridging supply and demand of sustainable buildings that perform beyond the requirements of mandatory regulation. This situates programs like BREEAM in a larger trend of voluntary certification programs in areas such as environmental sustainability in forestry, in fisheries, and in environmental management programs (Auld, 2014; van der Ven, 2015). However, certification programs for sustainable buildings often have a specific complicating element: classification. Where certification helps to distinguish certified buildings from noncertified ones, classification helps to distinguish buildings within a program.

All programs do not have a similar approach to classification, and distinctions are made in benchmarking, rating, and labeling. Because differences in classification make this category as applied to sustainable buildings murkier than in other sectors, it is addressed first in what follows. The chapter then explores the trend of voluntary certification and classification programs by considering the roles of governments and others in them and the transfer of these programs from one context to the next. After addressing these issues, three programs are studied in depth to gain an understanding of the opportunities and constraints of this category of voluntary programs for decarbonizing the built environment.

Benchmarking, Rating, and Labeling

All certification and classification programs establish rules for rule-takers to follow, but different approaches to classification allow rule-makers to tailor these programs to specific problems or needs of distinct groups of rule-takers. Benchmarking is the simplest approach. Certification based on benchmarking communicates that a certified building performs better than the average building in a sample — the benchmark — but does not specify how much better it performs. The certification of forest products and the certification of a firm's environmental management system are examples from other fields. They indicate that a product or service meets the rules of a certification program (Bartley, 2003; Zobel, 2013). An example from the set of programs studied is EnviroDevelopment in Australia. The program allows for certification of buildings and development projects in different categories: energy efficiency, water efficiency, material use, consideration of ecosystems, reductions of waste sent to landfill, and community governance and engagement. For each category certification can be obtained by meeting specific criteria, resulting in a number of credits. If the number of credits required for a category is awarded, the building or development project is certified in that category. A leaf motif displayed in different colors is used to indicate the categories of certification achieved. Note, however, that these categories are not grades of performance. Within these categories the program does not distinguish among buildings or development projects that perform better or worse than others in the program — it is limited to specifying satisfaction of the minimum criteria required for that categorization.

Rating systems are more complex. They use performance data to certify the relative performance of a building within the set of buildings certified within a given program. Identifiers such as stars or colors are often used to indicate this relative performance — the higher its relative performance compared to that of other certified buildings, the higher the number of stars awarded — indicating the specific class of certification. Rating arrangements require a database and statistical analysis to derive such rating, whereas benchmarking only requires a baseline (Pérez-Lombard et al., 2009). Rating arrangements often certify individual performance indicators — for instance, energy efficiency, water consumption, or carbon emissions. Typical examples of other product types are the color-coded food labels that indicate how much saturated fat or sugar a food product contains and the energy star labels on many household appliances (Horne, 2009; IPSOS & LEC, 2013). An example from the set of programs studied is the National Australian Built Environment Rating System (NABERS). It assesses the energy performance or water performance of buildings and issues certificates in six classes using a star rating to highlight differences among certified buildings. If a building is certified for energy and water performance, two different certificates are issued.

Labeling is the most complex form of classification — and the most widely applied for sustainable building certification (K. M. Fowler & Rauch, 2006a; Pérez-Lombard et al., 2009). Like rating, it certifies a building in a performance class to indicate relative performance compared to that of other certified buildings within the program; however, a major difference stands out. Labeling often takes a comprehensive approach. It does not certify energy efficiency or water consumption or greenhouse gases emitted, but seeks to classify buildings on the basis of overall performance. Credits are normally awarded for sustainability credentials in different categories, including energy performance and carbon emissions, but also project management and transportation (incentivizing property developers and owners to reduce car transport to and from their buildings, for instance). Often different weights are attributed to the categories — for instance, credits for energy efficiency weigh more than credits for water efficiency — and the final score represents a summarized weighted outcome of all credits. This implies that a building with, for example, poor performance in terms of its water consumption but good performance in terms of its energy consumption might still achieve an overall high class of certification. As with rating, identifiers such as stars are used to indicate the class of certification. BREEAM awards certifications, for instance, in the classes "outstanding" (represented by five stars, corresponding with at least 85 percent of the maximum number of credits possible), "excellent" (four stars, at least 70 percent of credits), "very good" (three stars, at least 55 percent of credits), "good" (two stars, at least 45 percent of credits), and "pass" (one star, at least 30 percent of credits) (see further BRE, 2011).

Another major difference between sustainable building certification and certification in other areas is that building certification and classification do not consider achieved performance per se. Different forms of certification exist: "as designed," "as built," and "in operation" (Casals, 2006; Cole & Valdebenito, 2013; Newsham, Mancini, & Birt, 2009). The first form certifies expected performance of a building design, the second form the performance of a building built in compliance with that design, and the final form achieved performance often after a specified period of use — it is often subject to periodical renewal. The first two forms are dominant, and the latter form was developed in response to critique of the first two: buildings are often not built in compliance with their (certified) design, and during construction many flaws might occur that program administrators or their inspectors do not notice, or user behavior may undo the sustainability credentials of a building — all of which could prevent a certified design or completed building from meeting its expected performance.

Table 4.1 provides a summary of the programs studied (Appendix B provides further description of the programs). It illustrates a major complication of certification and classification programs for sustainable buildings: while all programs certify the sustainability credentials of buildings, from the outset it is often not directly clear what a certificate and a specific class of certification mean. Does the certificate relate to design, the building as it is constructed, or performance of the building when in use? Does a star classification specify rating or labeling? Does a high level of classification signify that the building achieved an overall high performance during the assessment process, or is the level of classification achieved by outstanding performance in some categories that could be traded off against low performance in others? Such ambiguity makes it complex for potential property owners and users to assess the

Table 4.1 *Overview of Certification and Classification Programs Studied*

Name	Brief Description	Classification	Indicators	Form		
				ad	ab	io
BREEAM-NL (Netherlands, 2009)	Adaptation of international BREEAM program. Dominant application in new commercial property market	Labeling	Stars (1–5)	X	X	X
Energy Star Building (United States, 1999)	Program for energy efficient commercial property. Applied in new and existing commercial property market	Rating	Stars (1–5)		X	X
Energy Star for Homes (United States, 1999)	Program for energy efficient residential property. Dominant application in new residential property market	Rating	Stars (1–5)		X	
EnviroDevelopment (Australia, 2006)	Program for resource-efficient buildings. Dominant application in large scale new commercial and residential development projects	Benchmarking	Colored leaves			X
Green Star (Australia, 2003)	Comprehensive sustainable building program (comparable to BREEAM). Dominant application in new commercial property market	Labeling	Stars (4–6)	X	X	X
LEED (United States, 2000)	Comprehensive sustainable building program (comparable to BREEAM). Dominant application in new commercial property market	Labeling	Certified, Silver, Gold, Platinum	X	X	X
NABERS (Australia, 1998)	Program for energy efficient buildings. Dominant application in new and existing commercial property market	Rating	Stars (1–6)			X

Note: ad = as designed certification; ab = as built certification; io = in operation certification
Program abbreviations: BREEAM = BRE Environmental Assessment Method; LEED = Leadership in Energy and Environmental Design; NABERS = National Australian Built Environment Rating System

value of a certificate — and, as becomes clear throughout the remainder of this chapter, it makes it very complicated to assess the performance of certification and classification programs.

Governance without Government?

At the outset governments appear to play a limited role or no role at all in many voluntary certification and classification programs for sustainable buildings (K. M. Fowler & Rauch, 2006a). The typical organizations involved as rule-maker in these programs are national green building councils — the Dutch Green Building Council administers BREEAM-NL; the Green Building Council of Australia administers Green Star; the United States Green Building Council administers Leadership in Environmental and Energy Design (LEED); and so on. They are typically nonprofit organizations, with constituencies including representatives of the construction and property sectors. "Look, the [Green Building Council of Australia] is basically a sub-branch of the Property Council," a policy maker in an Australian state capital city explained, "and the Property Council is the national advocacy and policy group that represents property owners and developers: think of it as little more than a lobby group" (int. 16). Such organizations were launched, so explained interviewees, because various stakeholders in the construction and property sectors were aware of a potential market for sustainable buildings. Building on existing examples, such as BREEAM, they expected to be able to access this market through a national or local certification and classification program.

On closer investigation of these green building councils and related organizations, however, a different picture emerges. Sometimes governments are acting in advisory roles or take up roles in the boards of these organizations, as is the case with the United States Green Building Council (USGBC, 2013d). Governments often also indirectly support programs administered by these organizations. State and local governments in the United States offer property developers and property owners tax breaks for having their building certified and classified under LEED (USGBC, 2013b). Governments in Australia, the Netherlands, and the United States have in place sustainable procurement criteria requiring government agencies to attain a high-level classification under these programs for their new buildings or leased office space (e.g., Australian Government, 2013; Pianoo, 2015). Interviewees stressed that this role of governments as launching customers has been essential for these "private" voluntary programs to achieve their outcomes to date — for example, close to 30 percent of all LEED certified projects in the United States are government owned or leased (USGBC, 2013b).

In this sense, it is worth briefly recounting the history of BREEAM. The BRE was originally a government-funded research laboratory. By the late 1980s the relationship between climate change and urbanization had become more evident, and the United Kingdom government was looking for innovative approaches to environmental protection (Bailey, 2007). This led to the development of BREEAM by the BRE. In the 1990s the BRE operated as an executive agency of the United Kingdom government, and in 1997 it was fully privatized. This mirrors the management and privatization of many government agencies in that era — in the United Kingdom and elsewhere (Hodge, 2000; McLaughlin, Osborne, & Ferlie, 2002). Now independent of the United Kingdom government, the BRE could more easily expand BREEAM and export it well beyond the borders of the United Kingdom (BRE, 2013). Comparable developments can be found around the globe. Voluntary certification and classification are gaining increasing attention from governments as a complement to existing mandatory requirements for sustainable buildings — and sometimes programs are designed as hybrids of mandatory and voluntary requirements (Corbett & Muthulingam, 2007; Schindler, 2010). But other motivations for governments to adopt a role as rule-maker in voluntary certification and classification programs were also identified.

NABERS was introduced by the New South Wales government in 1998 to rate and certify the energy performance of offices. It was initiated for reasons similar to those for BREEAM: to give building users knowledge of the performance of their buildings. "When NABERS was developed there were no tools that addressed the environmental performance of building design or performance in the Australian market," a senior NABERS administrator explained; "[however,] the question as to whether good environmental building design did actually equate to good environmental performance was missing" (int. 40). But it quickly became apparent that NABERS could serve other purposes. Shortly after its introduction the Australian Commonwealth government required Australian state and territory governments to develop long-term urban development plans — and to report periodically on goal achievement (COAG, 2012b). NABERS provided one of the means necessary to collect and report performance data. Other state governments showed interest in the program in the early 2000s and implemented it locally, and in 2005 the Australian government implemented the program nationally. In 2010, it took a further step, making NABERS certification compulsory for all office space greater than two thousand square meters on the market for sale or lease. The class of certification, however, is voluntary, making NABERS a unique example of a quasi-voluntary program for sustainable buildings (NABERS, 2013).

Finally, the Energy Star Buildings and Energy Star for Homes programs are illustrative of how governments might use voluntary programs to gain influence beyond their jurisdiction. Both programs were introduced in 1999 by the United States Environmental Protection Agency, building on the agency's earlier experiences with certification arrangements for computers and other office equipment. The agency historically relied on command-and-control-type regulation, but by the mid-1990s this approach was considered too slow and ineffective in response to climate change risks (EPA, 1997). The Energy Star programs are examples of alternative governance instruments the agency has since been using. They are also examples of a way to bypass the formal building regulation and planning legislation system in the United States: while the U.S. Constitution does not give the federal government or its agencies powers to regulate sustainable buildings, the Energy Star programs nevertheless provide a means by which to be involved in this area (EPA, 1994).

A Market for Certification and Classification Programs

NABERS and BREEAM illustrate another phenomenon: the development and exportation of certification and classification programs have become markets in themselves. But why would countries and organizations adopt an existing certification and classification program? The adaptation of BREEAM in the Netherlands gives some explanation.

BREEAM-NL, the Dutch national version of BREEAM, was implemented in 2009 by the Dutch Green Building Council. By then the Dutch Building Code already set stringent requirements for building sustainability. Firms in the construction and property sectors were, however, aware of consumer demand for office buildings with "beyond compliance" performance. As explained by a senior manager at the Council: "They realized that if you certify this beyond-compliance behavior you can monetize it. Certification will result in commerce" (int. 64). The specific driver for a certification and classification program in the Netherlands was a high-profile large-scale office precinct development project in Amsterdam, the South-Axis, where many international corporations maintain their European head offices. "[They] ask for sustainable buildings," he continued; "they need this to meet their [corporate social responsibility] targets, to put it in their reports" (int. 64). In the mid-2000s the council was launched by representatives of the construction and property sectors aiming to serve this market for sustainable buildings. The first question it sought to address was whether it would develop a certification and classification program itself, or adopt an existing one. It realized that if it took too long with implementing a program it might lose out to rival green building councils. A serious contestant was the German Green Building Council, which by then was actively involved in "European roadshows seeking to obtain contracts for the implementation of [its certification and classification program] in other countries" — an insight shared by a senior manager from the German Green Building Council (int. 2). BREEAM provided the Dutch council with the best opportunity to brand the program as a Dutch product for the Dutch property and construction market and was selected accordingly. This process is reflected by the development of LEED in the United States and its adaptation. LEED was implemented in 2000 by the United States Green Building Council. With LEED the council sought to respond to commercial opportunities for sustainable buildings, and to market their performance (USGBC, 2013d). Initially LEED applied to offices in the United States only, but in a similar way to BREEAM it was quickly expanded to include a wide range of building types and city developments. The council also understood the international and commercial potential of LEED as a brand and has actively exported it: LEED is applied in more than 125 countries and territories around the world (USGBC, 2013c). Chapter 8 further discusses the adaptation of LEED in India, and the motivations — many financial — that the United States Green Building Council had to export its program there.

In short, not only is there a market for buildings with higher levels of sustainability performance than that required by mandated building codes, planning legislation, or conventional practice; there also is a competitive market for voluntary certification and classification programs for sustainable buildings.

Program Performance: Three Case Studies

Assessment of the performance of certification and classification programs for sustainable buildings is anything but easy. The number of buildings constructed under a program and the class of certificates issued offer an indication of the popularity of a program, interviewees argued, but not about how well a program contributes to decarbonizing the built environment. For example, at the outset BREEAM-NL exhibited promising performance. Since the program was launched in 2009, 45 percent of all future commercial construction work in the Netherlands has been registered for future certification or has been certified.[2] Nonetheless, registrations make up two-thirds of this number, and many registered buildings might not advance to the development phase. Of the certified projects 80 percent have gained certification in the three highest classes of certification, which indicates considerable compliance beyond the requirements of Dutch building regulation. However, whether that performance will be achieved by constructed buildings remains to be seen. About 40 percent of all certificates are issued for building designs, and another 30 percent for constructed buildings. For these two categories the ultimate performance depends on how closely contractors follow certified designs and how well BREEAM-NL inspectors assess their work to make sure that buildings delivered meet the certified criteria (cf. Scofield, 2013; Shrestha & Kulkarni, 2013; N. Taylor, Jones, Searcy, & Miller, 2014).

Time and again interviewees emphasized that certifications may too easily give the illusion of energy efficient and low-carbon buildings without those buildings achieving promised performance — simply because changes are made to the certified design or because contractors make errors that are unnoticed by program administrators (cf. Belzer, Mosey, Plympton, & Dagher, 2007; Scofield, 2013). They argued that only by assessing and certifying the performance of buildings during use would meaningful improvement of building assessment and performance be achieved. Keeping this in mind, the performance of BREEAM-NL might be considered in a different light: of all registered and certified buildings only 6 percent have been certified in the three highest classes their performance while in operation; and even for those buildings it might be questioned how much they outperform noncertified buildings in terms of energy efficiency and carbon emissions. Interviewees stressed the risk of labeling programs that award the class of certification exclusively on the basis of accumulated credits. "It is an exercise in collecting credits," a sustainability consultant at one of the Netherlands' leading consultancy firms explained. She illustrated this with a striking example: "We worked on a project within the Rotterdam Docklands and we had to make sure to achieve a certain number of credits [to achieve a specific class of certification]. The design team added a public transport terminal, which adds a credit or two, but there are no buses going that way" (int. 68).

While interviewees were generally positive about certification and classification programs for having raised awareness about building sustainability in the property and construction sectors, these constraints were mentioned over and over again. Another recurring observation by the interviews is that this category of voluntary programs is most promising in the high end of the market for new commercial property — mostly offices — and government-owned or leased buildings. Buildings in the high end of the commercial property market are often owned or leased by major corporations that seek sustainable office space as part of their social corporate responsibility policies, and governments often strive to lead by example in commissioning or leasing sustainable buildings, explained interviewees. They further explained that this category of voluntary programs has not yet made considerable inroads in the market for existing property. "One would expect people to choose in-operation certification, but that's not what is happening. It has to do with return rates," the senior manager at the Dutch Green Building Council clarified. "With new development the costs of sustainability are marginal compared to the development as a whole. Yet, with existing property things are different. Returns have been promised to investors, long-term contracts are signed. Investing in sustainability then suddenly looks significant as compared to rental rates" (int. 64). Likewise, this category struggles in the market for residential property. Interviewees explained that for homeowners it is often location and short-term costs that matter, rather than sustainability credentials that might mean long-term gains. A closer look at three of the programs studied reveals a number of additional issues related to their performance.

LEED, United States: Delving into the Statistics

Like BREEAM, LEED is a certification and classification program that builds on labeling. It was launched in 2000 by the United States Green Building Council and, again like BREEAM, has at first glance achieved impressive results. By 2015 more than forty-five thousand projects had been certified in more than 150 countries and territories around the world, although 90 percent of certified buildings are located in the United States. In sheer size LEED dwarfs the performance of BREEAM: about 400 million square meters of building space is LEED certified, while roughly 50 million square meters is BREEAM-certified.[3] In 2014 it was awarded a United Nations top environmental prize, the Champions of the Earth Award, for its transformative impact on the property and construction sectors. Because of its relative age; its wide application, particularly in the United States; its rich longitudinal database; and an ongoing scholarly interest in the program, LEED provides an ideal initial in-depth case study with which to explore the performance of this category of voluntary programs.

Initially LEED maintained a strong focus on new commercial property development, but over the years it has branched out to include more building types, both new and existing; interiors; and even neighborhood development projects. Of certificates issued in the United States, 60 percent relate to commercial property and 40 percent to residential property; and 92 percent relate to new development projects, while 8 percent relate to existing buildings. LEED allows for certification of building designs ("as designed"), completed buildings ("as built"), and buildings in use ("in operation") — the latter category makes up about 7 percent of all certificates issued in the United States. Certificates are issued in four classes based on a summarized weighted outcome of all credits awarded to a building: Platinum, issued to 11 percent of certified buildings (indicating that at least 75 percent of the maximum number of credits possible was awarded); Gold, issued to 30 percent (at least 55 percent of credits); Silver, issued to 35 percent (at least 45 percent of credits); and Certified, issued to 25 percent (at least 35 percent of credits).

Comparable to the other certification and classification programs studied, LEED seeks beyond-compliance behavior from certified buildings and building projects (rule-takers). In terms of energy efficiency, for example, an "as designed" or "as built" building is required to show at least a 14 percent energy efficiency improvement against a baseline building; or to meet the energy efficiency requirements stipulated in the American Society of Heating, Refrigerating, and Air-Conditioning Engineers (ASHREA) Standard 90.1 (Roderick, McEwan, Wheatley, & Alonso, 2009). The baseline is based on conventional construction practice in the United States, and the ASHREA standard is widely applied throughout the United States to govern building energy efficiency — sometimes as a voluntary standard, sometimes included in mandatory state and local building regulation (see also Appendix A). Buildings seeking "in operation" classification are required to show at least a 20 percent energy efficiency improvement against a baseline building (USGBC, 2010).

These requirements are, generally, not considered to be very challenging (cf. Roderick et al., 2009; Yudelson & Meyer, 2013) — for example, meeting the ASHREA standard does not require beyond-compliance performance in the states that have included this standard in their mandatory building codes. Still, buildings certified "as designed" or "as built" are repeatedly found not to meet their certified expected performance — this may be a result of changes in design after certification, construction flaws unnoticed by LEED inspectors, or occupants who do not use the building as expected (District of Columbia Department of the Environment, 2012; Gifford, 2009; Newsham et al., 2009; Todd, Pyke, & Tufts, 2013). Studies have even indicated that LEED-certified buildings do not outperform conventional buildings in terms of energy efficiency or carbon emissions (Scofield, 2009) and in certain examples they perform worse than conventional buildings (Scofield, 2013).

Also problematic is that LEED allows consumers and developers to play the system. The ability to mix and match credits under LEED and other programs studied was critiqued by interviewees for undermining the potential for achieving substantial decarbonization of the built environment (also, Hoffman & Henn, 2009). While the ability to mix and match credits allows property developers and owners to assemble sustainability solutions that best suit their buildings, the risk is that they choose low-cost solutions that have high credits over high-cost solutions with low credits — irrespective of whether the solution chosen contributes to improved energy efficiency or reduced carbon intensity. As the introduction to an article on a LEED-sustainable building website explains, "The road to green certification is paved with low-hanging fruit. ... This cheat sheet with 22 shortcuts will get you to LEED certification without a lot of trouble" (Seville, 2011). While the article's foray into certification schemes is tongue in cheek, the shortcuts constitute credible advice: "If [the] house [you seek to obtain certification for] is big, make sure you have lots of rooms that can be classified as bedrooms to offset the point penalty for larger homes" and "Install one efficient showerhead (just one!) per stall, high efficiency toilets and lavatories (all of them) and get 6 [credits]." All together these shortcuts add up to 70 LEED credits, which would place most projects close to — if not above — the 85-credit threshold required to achieve Platinum certification. Equally problematic, argue some interviewees, is that programs such as LEED allow for the certification of buildings that are entirely unsustainable or only contribute to unsustainable urban behavior: Can casinos in the Nevada desert that use many gallons of water merely for aesthetics and parking garages in city centers that only promote fossil-fuel based private transport truly be considered sustainable buildings (see also Alter, 2008; USA Today, 2013)?

This is, then, the broader context in which the performance of programs like LEED needs to be considered. When getting behind the statistics it becomes clear that a building-by-building performance assessment of actual energy consumption is needed for buildings with "as designed" and "as built" certification if one is to understand their carbon intensities. This is what "in operation" certification is intended to achieve: it certifies buildings on the basis of actual performance data, rather than on expected performance data, and periodically reassesses this performance. However, "in operation" certification is rarely adopted. But even without a building-by-building performance assessment a general apprehension of the performance of LEED can be obtained: more than 800,000 commercial buildings have been constructed in the United States since LEED was launched: of these some 25,000 have been LEED certified — 3 percent. For residential buildings the numbers are even less promising: some 21 million homes and housing units have been developed in this period in the United States, of which less than 0.5 percent have been LEED certified.[4]

Green Star, Australia: A Carefully Groomed Narrative of Success

Green Star is another instance of a certification and classification program based on labeling. Comparable to BREEAM and LEED, it certifies buildings in terms of the total number of credits collected in a range of categories — including project management, indoor environment quality, energy efficiency, and carbon emissions. When the Green Building Council of Australia introduced it in 2003 it marketed Green Star as seeking to influence and reward the absolute leaders of the Australian commercial property market — and presented it as more ambitious than programs such as BREEAM and LEED (GBCA, 2012). "We faced this question with Green Star: do you aim for the top five per cent of the market and neglect the other 95 percent?" a senior board member of the Green Building Council explained. "Aiming too high means that you lose engagement with the field; aiming too low and you're not interesting for leaders. The top 25 percent appeared a way to address the leaders in the market, without losing engagement. If you address the leaders, you will push the followers" (int. 22). To indicate its emphasis on rewarding only the top quartile and to portray itself as more ambitious than other programs, Green Star awards three certification classes, the minimum of which is a "4 Star" rating (referred to as "Best Practice"), followed by 5 Star ("Australian Excellence"), and 6 Star ("World Leadership").

When compared to other arrangements these indicators appear to oversell themselves: "World Leadership" Green Star buildings are found considerably less energy efficient than buildings certified under European systems (Yudelson & Meyer, 2013), and because of differences in energy assessment methods and performance criteria Green Star tends to award relatively higher certification classes than do BREEAM and LEED for buildings with similar levels of energy performance (Roderick et al., 2009). In terms of carbon emissions and energy efficiency — pivotal in decarbonizing the built environment — the lowest certification class, 4 stars, requires developers and property owners to show at least 10 percent better performance than requirements set by the National Construction Code of Australia (GBCA, 2014). This is a lenient rule: in light of the relatively low performance requirements in this code much higher building energy efficiency and carbon emissions are possible, even at net-cost benefit, as discussed in Chapter 2 (also IEA, 2013). Carefully chosen terminology — "Best Practice" and "World Leadership" — seeks only to create an illusion of high-performing buildings in Australia, some critical interviewees argued.

Adding to this illusion of leadership is the presentation of performance data by the Green Building Council of Australia. In brochures celebrating a decade of Green Star it reports that by 2013 18 percent of Australia's office space in central business districts in major cities was Green Star—Certified (GBCA, 2012, 2013a, 2013b) — while Green Star also allows for certification of other buildings types and city development projects, the number of these buildings certified in these areas is marginal (GBCA, 2015). The 18 percent office market coverage appears impressive, and the council uses it to demonstrate its influence in changing the Australian construction and property sectors. Governmental organizations and others also use the successes claimed by the council to highlight an assumed change in these sectors toward higher levels of sustainable building and city development (GBCA, 2013a). At the same time the data presented omit mention that only 10 percent of certificates are issued in the 6 star class, equating to only 1.8 percent of Australia's office space displaying ambitious Green Star performance (GBCA, 2013b). Such brochure material also does not mention that only since 2012 have "in operation" certificates been issued: the 18 percent predominantly reflects "as designed" or "as built" certificates — certificates that have many complications as to whether certified urban sustainability credentials have been met: "There has always been the tension with Green Star that your design can reflect those credentials," a senior manager at one of Australia's major property development firms observed, "but when your building is constructed and goes into operation and the contractor is not held accountable to adhere to certain conditions, he might get a little sloppy. And from there on it's just a downhill slide" (int. 44).

Other data presented by the council indicate similar ambiguity: in the same series of brochures it reports that Green Star—certified buildings on average produce 62 percent fewer greenhouse gas emissions and consume 66 percent less electricity and 51 percent less potable water than comparable Australian buildings (GBCA, 2013c). Yet it brushes aside an essential contributing factor: the introduction of mandatory building energy efficiency requirements in Australia in the mid-1990s (see Appendix A). These have logically resulted in higher energy efficiency and reduced carbon emissions of all relatively new buildings (most Green Star certificates are issued to new development). As with the example of LEED, earlier, the data presented can be questioned, again, for relying heavily on expected performance from "as designed" and "as built" certification and not on measured performance of buildings in use. The popular Australian media are surprisingly uncritical in their use of data provided by the

Green Building Council and report that "builders embrace [the] Green Star message," that because of Green Star "sustainable building gathers pace," and that for more than a decade Green Star has been "crucial to lifting sustainability standards" in Australia (Chandler, 2012; Hastings, 2013; Hurley, 2010).

Interviewees were wary that the certification industry's hyperbolic emphasis on leadership and the media attention generated by programs such as Green Star might provide perverse incentives. As with the other programs, problems of rule-takers' cynically taking advantage of the way credits are awarded were mentioned. "The credits system may be a trigger for people to install features that they are not going to use," a building energy consultant in Sydney explained. "There are examples where a builder knew appliances would not be used or would not function. That is a waste of resources, and misuse or even abuse of the framework. It is a cheap way of buying some credits" (int. 46). More problematic, some interviewees argued, is that certification of a building becomes an end in itself for the construction and property sectors and not a means toward a more sustainable built environment. "It might be OK to knock down a ten-storey building and replace it with an eleven-storey Green Star building, just because it is five-star Green Star," an administrator in an Australian state capital city observed. "On face value that's fantastic, but where's the life-cycle analysis? Where was the rigor when looking at minimizing resource consumption, minimizing waste to landfills, minimizing carbon emissions, maximizing the capacity of the city?" he continued, maintaining that the positive performance of the new Green Star building might well be undone by the lost embedded energy in the demolished one (int. 50).

NABERS, Australia: Combining Mandatory Participation with Voluntary Performance

The pattern of marginal uptake of voluntary certification and classification programs by rule-takers and a marginal improvement of building energy efficiency and carbon intensity beyond mandatory requirements or conventional practice was echoed in all examples studied, with the exception of NABERS in Australia. NABERS is applied in 77 percent of the office market in Australia. Certificates are only issued for "in operation" performance (based on information supplied by the utilities), and 50 percent of all certified buildings are in classes that indicate energy efficiency improvements of at least 20 percent compared to conventional practice — 4.5–6 stars.[5] What explains this performance?

NABERS builds on rating: it rates the energy and water efficiency of existing buildings on a 6-star scale, with 2.5–3 stars representing average market performance (NSW Government, 2011a). This "average market performance" is not the same as compliance with requirements set by the National Construction Code of Australia. NABERS ratings apply to existing buildings and the Code does not set requirements for existing buildings — as is the case in many other countries (see also Chapter 2). Compliance with the code corresponds with a NABERS rating of around 4 stars (Steinfeld, Bruce, & Watt, 2011). NABERS was implemented, as mentioned before, by the state of New South Wales in 1998 to gain insight into the resource consumption of the existing building stock and to influence the office market. It was expected that insight into building energy and water performance would drive demand for energy- and water-efficient office space, resulting in an upgrading of offices. Office upgrades in their turn were expected to contribute to ambitious carbon emission reduction targets set by state and local governments, a senior administrator of NABERS explained (int. 40). The program was quickly adopted by other state governments, and in 2005 the Australian Commonwealth government adopted NABERS as a nationwide voluntary arrangement.

The high uptake of NABERS in the office market is explained by the introduction of the Building Energy Efficiency Disclosure Act of 2010, which applies to office buildings with a net lettable area greater than two thousand square meters and requires its owner or tenant to disclose the energy efficiency rating when it goes on the market for sale or lease, or when an existing lease is renewed. The act requires that a NABERS energy certificate is made available, but it does not stipulate that a specific class of certification for a building has to be met. Nonetheless, half of the certificates issued are for buildings that indicate energy efficiency performance of at least 20 percent beyond average market performance. Interviewees explained that NABERS provides an important signaling function: "We have received pressure from tenants that when we disclosed [the rating] to them they said: This is ridiculous. You guys have to increase this. Why am I paying so much for your inefficient building?" a senior manager at one of Australia's major property owners observed (int. 44). The program provides an easy-to-understand metric for office users, interviewees explained further, and because of the mandatory disclosure requirements all large offices can now be compared by office users. "It is clearly linked to cost. Energy is a large part of the cost of buildings. So this is a very clear and tangible way of assessing costs," the senior administrator of NABERS observed. "[With NABERS] you can relate the cost-savings to the star rating. And the other way around, if you want to improve your building you can assess if it is cost-effective to make the improvement. We experience that as one of the biggest drivers" (int. 40).

Most promising about the Act is that it has particularly stimulated certification of relatively small offices, rented by small and medium-sized firms that often have short-term leases (int. 40; Bannister, 2012). For this group of firms and buildings, programs such as BREEAM, LEED, and Green Star were considered unattractive: "We are talking about the top end of town [that seeks BREEAM, LEED, or Green Star certification]. Think government, blue-chip companies, financial institutions, lawyers and accounting firms. But there is another level where the consumer does not currently see the benefit of sustainable buildings," a senior manager at a major Australian development firm explained. "And even if they do see the benefit, they probably are not willing to pay a premium for it. This is the next major challenge. We need to get the B and C-Grade buildings performing sustainably," he continued (int. 47). Since the introduction of the act in 2010, the market coverage of NABERS has grown from 50 to 77 percent, but the number of yearly issued certificates has grown much faster from some five hundred to fifteen hundred — indicating that particularly smaller-sized offices are now being certified. The impact of the act becomes apparent also when looking beyond office buildings and energy efficiency. NABERS allows for certification of other building types as well — including retail and residential buildings — but the act does not apply to these. The uptake of NABERS for other building types is minimal, however (Iyer-Raniga, Moore, & Wasiluk, 2014). Similarly, NABERS certification for water efficiency is not mandatory under the act and the uptake of this certification is considerably lower than the uptake of NABERS certification for building energy efficiency — it is applied in 46 percent of the office market in Australia.

However, the introduction of the act should not be given too much credit. NABERS certification is sought for existing office space, including office space that is on the market for the first time. The Australian office market experienced a period of rapid growth between 2010 and 2014, which partly explains the growth in the uptake of NABERS certification (Property Council of Australia, 2014). Also, in 2010 mandatory energy efficiency requirements in the National Construction Code of Australia were increased in stringency and all new office space now has to meet requirements equivalent to those for NABERS 4-star ratings. This partly explains the relatively high percentage of buildings with beyond-average market performance ratings — 4–6 stars. Finally, other voluntary programs in Australia have begun to use NABERS as a benchmark or rule to accommodate. Green Star requires, for example, at least a 4-star NABERS classification for buildings that seek Green Star certification — including existing buildings. Similarly, CitySwitch Green Office (discussed in Chapter 5) incentivizes its rule-takers to achieve a 4-star NABERS classification. Growth of rule-takers under such programs logically results in a growth of buildings certified under NABERS.

Key Findings

The analysis of a set of voluntary certification and classification programs for sustainable buildings has provided insight into why and how governments and nongovernments are involved in these programs and factors influencing their performance. In broad terms, the narrative of certification and classification programs presented in this chapter confirms the theoretical account presented in Chapter 3. At the same time the broad narrative and the case studies highlight a number of novel considerations regarding these voluntary programs. The concluding section of this chapter teases out these significant findings.

Certification and Classification: A Murky Business

Different approaches to classification (benchmarking, rating, labeling) and different forms of certification (as designed, as built, in operation) make this category of programs different from those applied in areas such as forest products, food, or environmental management (Auld, 2014; Bartley, 2003; Zobel, 2013). Labeling in particular allows for flexibility and enables participants to determine how they should comply with the rules and criteria underlying a program. Often such "performance-based" regulation is considered to stimulate innovation and help firms in overcoming the regulatory straitjacket said to burden the construction and property sectors (K. M. Fowler & Rauch, 2006a). For the labeling arrangements studied it has become clear, however, that the freedom property developers and owners have to mix and match criteria often results in cheating: situations in which they seek to secure high certification classes with minimal outlay and without concern for whether the combination of criteria met results in meaningful levels of built environment sustainability.

Another issue that stands out in the design of these arrangements are the three different forms of certification. Specific problems were found with "as designed" and "as built" certifications: they often do not live up to their certified performance. This problem is well known to the rule-makers of these arrangements, a problem that saw some resolution in the introduction of "in operation" certification from the late 2000s onward, certifying the actual performance of a building in terms of its energy consumption and carbon emissions when in operation. The failing of this "in operation" certification, however, is its marginal application. And whereas issued "as designed" and "as built" certificates do not expire — in all likelihood maintaining specious claims for a growing number of buildings that do not live up to their certified performance, and which property owners nevertheless continue to use to market these buildings' sustainability credentials — "in operation" certification inconveniently requires updating.

Introduction and rapid uptake of "in operation" certification are unlikely: for rule-takers it is more difficult to achieve this form of certification, and for rule-makers it requires increased enforcement effort — entailing monetary costs that ultimately have to be borne by rule-takers. A broader move to "in operation" assessment would be expected to result in a loss of participants or at the very least a decrease in the issue of high-class certificates. The large participant base — the total amount of certified space or the total number of buildings certified — and the high-class certificates issued are effectively used by rule-makers to cultivate and market a narrative of leading practice. This narrative is needed to justify their function in the industry, to attract future rule-takers and thus income, and if possible to make their programs appealing to organizations in other locations in need of voluntary regulation. Interviewees repeatedly expressed concerns about this market for voluntary programs and the profit made by rule-makers. For rule-makers sustainability certification of buildings is big business — financially and politically.

Lenient Rules, Lenient Enforcement, High Rewards

In general, the programs studied were found to have set lenient rules, confronted enforcement complications comparable to mandatory building codes, and offered relatively high rewards. Certification is sometimes awarded for behavior that is commensurate with or only marginally beyond compliance with mandatory regulation or conventional industry practice — LEED, for example, awards considerable credits for compliance with the ASHREA standard, which is a conventional code for building energy efficiency in the United States. Some programs set more challenging rules or set varying levels of rules for different classes of certification, but interviewees did not consider that any of the programs made plausible attempts to improve sustainability. "BREEAM is not for innovators, not for those leading in the industry. It's a checklist. It works for people who want to do something with sustainability, but do not exactly know what," the sustainability consultant from the Netherlands contended, "but it does not push the envelope of what can be done" (int. 68). In addition, the ability to take advantage of these programs seems to be counterproductive, particularly in the higher classes of certification. Most arrangements have in place conditional rules for basic sustainability indicators that each certified building is required to meet — often relating to building energy efficiency and carbon emissions. This implies that even buildings in low-certification classes meet these requirements, but the example of the cheat sheet for LEED highlights how relatively high points awarded for cheap and easy solutions can make all the difference between a low, medium, or high certification class — even when those solutions do not further improve the energy efficiency or reduce the carbon intensity of the certified building (for another example, see M. Brown, 2010).

The poor performance of "as built" and "as designed" certificates documented in the literature reflects poor enforcement practice. While most programs rely on their third-party assessors to evaluate building designs and construction work, these third-party assessors are themselves often trained and accredited by program administrators. They can perhaps be better understood as at arms' length from the administrators rather than as entirely independent third parties. Interviewees repeatedly referred to the certification process as a "tick the box" exercise designed to conjure authority for claims about poorly performing buildings — this issue mirrors the literature discussed in Chapter 3, but it also returns to the complications of enforcing mandatory building codes discussed in Chapter 2. Moving to "in operation" certification could help to overcome this enforcement problem because it builds on actual performance data and not expected performance. However, for reasons of market-driven conservatism in voluntary programs, and unwillingness on the part of governments to enact and enforce strict mandatory requirements, it is highly unlikely that this solution will be widely adopted in the near future.

This combination of lenient rules, complications with enforcement, and the almost certain high rewards for participants — higher rental or sales revenue of certified buildings ranging from 5 to 10 percent compared to that of noncertified buildings (Bloom, Nobe, & Nobe, 2011; BREEAM, 2014; Deng et al., 2012; Eichholtz et al., 2010; Newell, MacFarlane, & Kok, 2011) — is a risk-enhancing mix of design conditions. Interviewees often painted a picture of profit-seeking property developers and owners abusing these programs in order to obtain the highest level of certification at the lowest cost. While roughly accurate, and supported by the literature on this category of voluntary programs for sustainable buildings, this picture should not overshadow another perspective: these programs have resulted in a range of innovative and ambitious buildings and city development projects with demonstrated high levels of built environment performance. At least in the high end of the commercial property market these programs have helped to place decarbonization of the built environment on the agenda of property developers and owners, and have provided them a means to bridge supply and demand in the market for these buildings (see also Yudelson & Meyer, 2013).

Risks of Mandating Voluntary Programs

That being said in praise of these programs, the bottom line is that they have not yet achieved sweeping results. LEED, the largest program studied, has certified 3 percent of all new commercial property and less than 0.5 percent of all residential property built in the United States since the program was introduced in 2000. Energy Star Buildings has certified 3 percent of all new commercial property also, and Energy Star for Homes 7 percent of all new residential property since the programs were introduced in the United States in 1999.[6] EnviroDevelopment has certified 6 percent of all residential property since it was introduced in Australia in 2006.[7] More promising in terms of uptake are Green Star, which has certified 18 percent of all new offices built in Australia since the program was introduced in 2003, and BREEAM-NL, which has certified some 45 percent of all new commercial property — predominantly offices — since the program was introduced in the Netherlands in 2009. However, most of these programs rely heavily on "as designed" and "as built" certification and issue a large part of certificates in the lower classes. This raises numerous questions around the performance of the buildings they certify, as highlighted throughout this chapter.

A more effective means of addressing these problems might instead be to mandate these voluntary programs. While the notion of a mandatory voluntary program appears to be an oxymoron, a number of governments in Australia do stipulate compliance with Green Star requirements, and a not-insignificant minority of governments in the United States oblige compliance with LEED specifications. The City of New York passed Local Law 86 in 2005, requiring that development projects receiving particular government funding have to meet the midclass LEED Silver certification (City of New York, 2005). Some counties and cities in North Carolina award density bonuses for builders who conform to LEED criteria (North Carolina General Assembly, 2008), and the state of Maryland has a tax credit program for construction work that received LEED Gold certification (Maryland Energy Administration, 2012) — in some other regions of the United States, however, anti-LEED policies exist (see, e.g., Kansas Committee on Energy and Environment, 2013). As highlighted earlier, LEED is also heavily incorporated in governments' sustainable procurement criteria, requiring that government-occupied buildings need to conform to certain LEED classifications (USGBC, 2013b).

Adopting or referring to standards developed by nongovernmental organiations is an easy and cost-effective way for governments to introduce sustainable development requirements. Yet the uptake and mandating of LEED and Green Star—like programs by governments are not without risk: criteria and regulation in these programs emerge under different accountability and legitimacy rules than public regulation. Although the United States Green Building Council represents a wide range of stakeholders, governments included, it does not have the democratic legitimacy that governments normally wield. Mandating these programs carries the risk that the process of public scrutiny for decisions on sustainable buildings and decarbonizing the built environment are bypassed (Corbett & Muthulingam, 2007; Schindler, 2010; Schmidt & Fischlein, 2010). This pertains all the more because many credits in these programs are awarded for applying materials or services certified under other voluntary programs developed by other nongovernment actors.[8]

Are Hybrid Programs the Way Forward?

The exception to the rule in terms of performance is NABERS, which has achieved coverage of 77 percent in the Australian office market since it was introduced as a nationwide program in 2005. And not only is the uptake of NABERS considerable; the program has awarded about 50 percent of its certificates for classes that indicate at least 20 percent energy efficiency improvements compared to conventional practice — and because NABERS only issues "in operation" certification there is a high level of confidence that buildings indeed perform as certified. The combination of mandatory certification with voluntary classification in this program seems to have contributed to this success. Because all owners and users of office space of two thousand square meters and up are exposed to the energy performance of these buildings, a level of equality in access to sustainable office space has emerged. In the other programs property owners and users can decide to enter the market for such buildings or not. In particular, owners of existing buildings, small and medium-sized firms as users of buildings, and homeowners were considered not attracted to this market for sustainable buildings, interviewees stressed, whether this is because they do not have social corporate responsibility policies in place or simply do not value the long-term financial and other advantages of sustainable buildings over short-term costs.

While inspirational, NABERS' performance should nonetheless be understood in its specific context. The hybrid approach of combining mandatory and voluntary aspects within a program is no guarantee for success, as a comparable set of programs in Europe indicates. Under EU legislation, the energy performance of all residential property that goes on the market for sale should be disclosed through an energy efficiency certificate, but the level of energy performance — and thus the level of certification — is voluntary. While mandatory since 2010, programs in the various European member states that built on this hybrid design have not created a demand for improved energy efficiency in the residential property market (Brounen & Kok, 2011; Dixon, Keeping, & Roberts, 2008).[9] In Australia the office market is relatively compact — estimated to be forty-five hundred buildings only[10] — and highly concentrated in the central business districts of a relatively small number of cities. Building owners compete visibly with each other, a circumstance that might have accelerated competition. Finally, it is laudable that about 50 percent of Australian buildings perform beyond conventional practice, but this is in part because the conventional practice of Australian office buildings was poor when the benchmark for NABERS was set. Building energy efficiency requirements were only introduced in the 1990s, suggesting that most buildings included in this conventional practice had meager energy efficiency at the outset (see further Appendix A).

5   Urban Governance Networks
Generating and Sharing Knowledge

"Even without financial incentives [as provided by certification and classification programs] you can achieve a lot simply by connecting people and organizations, and by disseminating knowledge" — so a program administrator from the Netherlands stated about the value of the second category of voluntary programs discussed in this book (int. 75). These programs seek to generate and share knowledge on how to construct and retrofit sustainable buildings, and how building user behavior can be changed to reduce resource consumption — in other words, knowledge generation occurring concurrently with construction and use. Chapter 3 distinguished two subsets of programs within this category: those that focus on individual rule-takers, in which the flow of knowledge is generally from rule-maker to rule-taker; and those that focus on a collective of rule-takers and rule-makers. In the latter, knowledge flows among rule-takers, and rule-makers act as intermediaries for knowledge dissemination.

The programs studied in this chapter align with a larger trend of governance experimentation: the process of testing and refining governance instruments through their implementation (Ansell & Bartenberger, 2016; De Burca, 2010; Evans, Karvonen & Raven, 2016; Sabel & Zeitlin, 2011; Sanderson, 2002). Those studied in this chapter were selected, however, because they aim for more than purely experimenting and drawing lessons. They have all set ambitious targets in terms of the number of rule-takers they seek to attract, the extent to which they wish to change their behavior, or both. In addition to the two main questions raised in Chapter 1, this chapter seeks to understand whether this combination of governance experimentation and achievement of such ambitious results is realistic. Table 5.1 gives a brief overview of the programs that were researched for this chapter (Appendix B provides a more extensive description of each program).

Table 5.1 indicates that the programs in this chapter have a broader range of designs than the certification and classification programs addressed in Chapter 4. Governments play a strong role as rule-makers in all programs studied. "Government continues to be an important

Table 5.1 *Overview of Knowledge Generation and Sharing Programs Studied*

Name	Brief Description	Form Ind.	Coll.
Better Building Partnership (Australia, 2011)	Program for reduced commercial property related carbon emissions. Joins the City of Sydney government and the city's major property owners; strong focus on existing commercial property. It aims for a 70 percent reduction of 2006 emissions by 2030		X
Better Buildings Challenge (United States, 2011)	Program for reduced commercial property related carbon emissions. Joins the United States federal government and commercial property owners; sole focus on existing commercial property. It aims for a 20 percent reduction of 2010 emissions by 2020	X	
Chicago Green Office Challenge (United States, 2008)	Program for reduced resource consumption by offices. Challenges office users in Chicago to reduce their resource consumption more than other office users in the program. It has not set a specific target, but aligns with the city's ambition to reduce building-related energy consumption by 15 percent. To be achieved by 2020	X	
CitySwitch Green Office (Australia, 2010)	Program for reduced resource consumption of offices. Challenges office users in Australia to reduce their resource consumption and achieve a specified classification (4 stars) under NABERS*	X	
Energiesprong (Netherlands 2010)	Series of programs for reduced resource consumption at building level. Strong focus on existing residential property. Different targets are set for different programs. The most ambitious aim for carbon-neutral property development		X
Green Deals (Netherlands, 2011)	Series of programs for reduced resource consumption at building level. Focus on new and existing property and commercial and residential property. Different targets are set for different programs. The most ambitious aim for carbon-neutral property development		X
Retrofit Chicago (United States, 2012)	Program for reduced commercial property related carbon emissions. Joins the City of Chicago government and the city's major property owners; strong focus on existing commercial property. Spin-off of the Better Buildings Challenge. It aims for a 20 percent reduction of 2010 energy consumption by 2017	X	
Zonnig Huren (Netherlands, 2012)	Program for reduced residential property related energy consumption. It seeks an uptake of renewable energy technology in (social) housing corporation-owned property. It has not set a specific target		X

Note: Ind. = focus on individual rule-takers; Coll. = focus on collective of rule-takers
* For discussion of NABERS see Chapter 3

actor in the transition toward a low-carbon built environment," another program administrator in the Netherlands observed. "Market conditions are often absent, mainly because of a lack of knowledge about what can be done at firm level, a lack of demand from consumers, and a lack of supply from producers. This requires long-term thinking, and governments provide that" (int. 79). Governments' motivations for being involved as rule-makers echo the motivations discussed in Chapter 3: these programs often align with larger policy programs for carbon emission reductions at national, regional, or local level and seek reductions in areas where governments cannot easily implement mandatory requirements. Through these knowledge generation and sharing programs governments reach out to firms in the construction and property sectors and seek to support them in reducing their building-related resource consumption and carbon emissions. Their primary role in these programs is that of knowledge broker, but this role is taken up slightly differently in the two subsets of programs discussed here. This difference is addressed first in the section that follows. Then the chapter discusses four programs in depth in order to develop our understanding of this category of voluntary programs. The chapter concludes with reflections concerning critical findings.

Government as Knowledge Broker

In all knowledge-generation and sharing programs studied, governments and their representatives act as knowledge brokers (cf., Cillo, 2005; Meyer, 2010): they document experiences by rule-takers and convert these into transferable knowledge; they make this knowledge available to rule-takers participating in the programs and often to non-participants as well; and they often market this knowledge through popular media outlets. An illustrative example from the set of programs studied is the Green Office Challenge in Chicago, US. The program challenges office tenants to reduce their energy and water consumption. The program was introduced in 2008 and contributes to the city's ambition of a 15 percent reduction of 1990 levels of building-related energy consumption by 2020 (City of Chicago, 2011). Under the program, rule-takers are actively competing against each other to become the most energy and water efficient and least carbon emitting tenant in the Chicago central business district – they do not, however, commit to a personal target. The program is administered by a non-profit organisation on behalf of the city and supports rule-takers with tailored information on how they can improve their energy and water efficiency. It further transforms the experiences of these rule-takers in case-studies and best-practice reports, and this documented knowledge is available to rule-takers on the program's website. "We invite them to provide us with best practices and that works really well," a program administrator observed. "We then put those online, which is a unique branding opportunity for them. We give them space, and it is very low-impact for them" (int. 186). The website also facilitates the competition by making available all rule-takers' energy and water consumption data as provided by the utilities. To induce rule-takers go the extra mile a yearly awards ceremony occurs to highlight leading practice. In all four programs that conform to the first sub-type of programs (those that focus on individual rule-makers in which the information flow generally is from rule-taker to rule-maker), governments are purported to act merely in this way: they introduce incentives for prospective rule-takers, transmute experiences into documented knowledge, and make this knowledge available to all rule-takers and often also to non-participants – the Green Office Challenge is the only example where knowledge is made available exclusively to rule-takers.

In the four programs that fit the second sub-type of programs (those that focus on a collective of rule-takers and rule-makers), governments are more actively involved in the generation of knowledge. In addition to translating experience into knowledge, they participate in the process of knowledge generation. Illustrative is Energiesprong ("Energy Leap") in the Netherlands. The program was implemented 2010 and seeks to generate knowledge of how to reduce the energy consumption of the built environment throughout the Netherlands. It is administered by a quasi-autonomous government agency and invites governments, firms, citizens, and civil society organisations to propose ideas on how to achieve significant building energy efficiency improvements. The agency supports the most promising ideas with administrative and financial support, information, leadership recognition, and opportunities to build close links with policymakers. More importantly, it is actively involved in transferring ideas for energy efficiency improvements to pilot projects to test those ideas. By 2015, it was actively involved in 28 projects, varying from small-scale pilot programs that seek to understand how small retail units can be retrofitted to become energy neutral, to large-scale projects that incentivise four main social housing corporations to retrofit 111,000 houses to become energy neutral (Platform 31, 2014). Knowledge generated is documented in case studies and best-practice reports, and also made available online.

Program Performance: Four Case Studies

Not for the first time interviewees observed that assessing the performance of this category of voluntary programs is not easy. Some stated that the combined goals of developing knowledge of how to achieve sustainable buildings and actually achieving them may result in conflicting situations. Consider a program that translates experience of the complications of achieving sustainable buildings into knowledge documents, but falls short in actually achieving such buildings (see also discussion on direct and indirect outcomes in Chapter 3). Zonnig Huren ("Sunny Leasing"), a program in the Netherlands, provides an illustrative example. Zonnig Huren joins some thirty Dutch social housing corporations. It is administered by a consultancy firm and supported by the corporations' national advocacy group and the Dutch Ministry of Finance. Together these corporations own some 25 percent of all 2.4 million corporation-owned rental units in the Netherlands. The group consists of some forty rule-takers, mainly large corporations — roughly four hundred large and small corporations are active in the Netherlands (int. 93). Under the program corporations aim to retrofit a part of their property, typically by installing photovoltaic solar panels. It was expected that they would find it easier to upgrade their property when experiences from other corporations could be used as a point of departure — by participating in the program rule-takers commit themselves to making their experiences available. Rule-takers accept the overall program goal of retrofitting a substantial part of Dutch rental property rather than individual targets (Atrivé, 2012).

By 2015 the upgrading of the anticipated number of housing units lagged behind ambitions: only some 30 percent of the anticipated forty thousand housing units had been retrofitted. Although failing to achieve its instrumental goals, the program has ironically been successful in terms of processual experimentation. In seeking to retrofit property, housing corporations confronted more regulatory, political, and financial barriers than initially anticipated. They experienced difficulties of including the costs of upgrades in social housing rental rates. They became aware of fluctuations in energy costs, subsidies, and political preferences for or against renewable energy — making it difficult for them to develop long-term business plans. They realized that renewable energy retrofits demand knowledge and experience that many corporation staff lack, and that it is often difficult to communicate the advantages of renewable energy to tenants (Agentschap NL, 2013). "By and large retrofitting is not financially viable for the corporation," a representative of one of the participating housing corporations explained. "We won't see our investment returned within the remaining exploitation period. It is luxury. And in the current [financially difficult] market it is a choice between surviving as an organization and not caring about the environment, or perishing by being sustainable" (int. 65). Interviewees explained further that by setting high expectations this program has made itself vulnerable to easy critique for not achieving desired outcomes, even while it has generated important knowledge regarding why these outcomes have not yet been achieved. This schism was also identified in some of the other programs discussed in this chapter: opponents of the program (and voluntary programs more generally) point to the failure in meeting goals set; those in support of it, however, can easily brush aside the underperformance and point to its value in creating critical knowledge.

Zonnig Huren is illustrative of another risk also. "Returns for tenants, landlords and the environment," its homepage claims[1] — a typical example of the ecological modernization narrative that underlies many of the programs studied. Rule-takers under the program realized, however, that achieving these financial returns was not easy for them or for their tenants. The strong focus on financial returns might have made rule-takers particularly disillusioned about the program because they were difficult to achieve. More problematically, some interviewees maintained, experiences like these might make rule-takers more skeptical of sustainable building practice than they were before participating. A voluntary program in such circumstances may cause more harm than good. Closer examination of the following four programs reveals a number of additional issues related to the performance of this category of voluntary programs.

Cityswitch, Australia: Preaching to the Converted

CitySwitch underlines the trend uncovered by certification and classification programs discussed in Chapter 4: while some individual participants indicated considerable improvements of building-related resource consumption and carbon emissions, the performance of their program as a whole appeared insignificant when contrasted with the sustainable building challenge faced. It is further illustrative of two specific risks related to the full set of voluntary programs studied: their administrators might have incentives to portray program performance in a more positive light than it deserves, and programs might attract those who are already leaders in the construction and property sectors, rather than those who lag behind.

CitySwitch was launched in 2010 by the Sydney City Council as part of the city's ambition to reduce its carbon emissions by 70 percent of 2006 emissions by 2030 (City of Sydney, 2008, 2011). An administrator explained that when CitySwitch was introduced it had become clear that building certification and classification (discussed in Chapter 4) could not be solely relied on for achieving desired citywide reductions of consumption and carbon emissions (int. 41). The involvement of building users — particularly office tenants — was seen as a promising avenue. After its introduction in Sydney it quickly attracted attention in other cities in Australia, and it was made a nationwide program in 2011. It is administered by local governments with support from a national body. It requires office tenants who commit to the program to achieve at least a 4-star rating under the NABERS certification and classification program — a class that indicates beyond-average market performance in terms of building energy consumption (see Chapter 4). In return they are supported by local governments with local platforms for obtaining and sharing knowledge — often in the form of workshops and seminars — and administrative and sometimes financial support. "[The] key of the program is learning," a local program administrator explained, "and we can best be understood as a facilitator in this learning process through the meetings and lectures we organize" (int. 35). The national CitySwitch administration provides rule-takers with a broader knowledge platform: a website with toolkits, workbooks, case studies, links to other programs, information about financing energy efficiency upgrades, and legislative requirements. Another significant activity of the national administration is celebrating and rewarding leadership: it hosts an annual awards ceremony to celebrate the best-performing rule-takers, and it promotes rule-takers' performance through ongoing media campaigns. The national administrator claimed of the performance of CitySwitch in 2015 that "[in 2014, CitySwitch rule-takers] achieved reductions of over 85,000 tonnes of carbon emissions and 75 GWh energy, delivering savings of over [AUD] $14 million to [participants] and energy savings equivalent to the energy use of 12,712 average homes."[2]

But what does this reported performance signify? The 75 GWh savings by 650 participants in 2014 corresponds with a 13–16 percent reduction of their energy consumption in 2011 — when CitySwitch was launched nationally.[3] At first glance this constitutes a moderate improvement of building energy efficiency, but it is not overly impressive when keeping in mind that Australian office tenants are reported to waste 50 percent of their energy in ways that can be easily addressed (Greensense, 2013; see further Chapter 2). When contrasted with the full Australian office market's energy consumption of 2011 the program's performance is even less impressive: its 2014 energy consumption reductions correspond to 0.8 percent of 2011 consumption. This has a considerably less successful ring to it than "energy savings equivalent to the energy use of 12,712 average homes."[4] The national administrator, however, has a strong incentive to frame this performance as a considerable success. To understand why, some further exploration of the program is required.

Not all rule-takers comply with the requirement to achieve a 4-star NABERS rating or higher (CitySwitch, 2015). This noncompliance, however, is not penalized, so explained a national administrator, and noncompliant rule-takers are not excluded from the network (int. 41). Rule-takers further tend to fail to comply with the requirement of providing NABERS ratings (obtaining ratings is expensive and may cost up to AU$5,000, sometimes more than the cost for installing energy efficient measures), but are not disciplined for this either: "This [non-reporting] distorts the data we have. Based on the current data only very flawed predictions of reductions can be made," the administrator observed (int. 41). The reported performance data are likely to constitute a theoretical best-case scenario, with real performance being substantially lower than recorded numbers. Regardless, predictions are required and numbers have to be reported, the administrator continued, because the local councils that support the program (administratively, financially, or both) require quantitative results to account for the program at local level. This gives administrators a strong incentive to present performance data in the best light possible — funding depends on it. Lenient enforcement has also resulted in an unwanted side effect. Because rule-takers are often not penalized for violating program rules, they have a strong incentive to report NABERS ratings only after carrying out retrofits: a high jump in NABERS ratings makes them likely candidates to win an award and receive industry attention at the yearly awards ceremony. Alternatively, they join the program only after making improvements, or provide flawed performance data when they join that they can improve upon easily. Thus the story behind "those improvements remains outside our focus," the administrator concluded, suggesting that the information provided on the website may also be flawed (int. 41).

The strong emphasis of CitySwitch on awarding leading practice might unintentionally work against the program. Besides awarding achievement of a 4-star or higher NABERS rating, it does not provide many other incentives to prospective rule-takers. Knowledge and case studies on how to reduce energy consumption are freely available through the program website; members do not receive significant financial support; and the recognition received from administrators does not have the marketing value of certification and classification programs (see Chapter 4). The program appears attractive only to those most likely to achieve leading performance. This was confirmed by the national administrator. "It is about leadership; it is about being seen to participate. The program helps leaders to feel good about what it is they are doing, and have a place to speak about it," she explained. "The awarding scheme helps in this and we very much aim to market [their performance] to the best of our ability. But do they win business with it? Probably not" (int. 41). A local administrator considered this prevailing attention to leadership the major shortcoming of the program. "What we found is that the first things people in [City X] ask are, 'Well, what's in it for me?' And, [after we explain to them the advantages of improved energy efficiency], 'Well, I can do that anyway. What is it that council is going to pay for?'" he explained (int. 50). He suspects that CitySwitch is not attractive to less-ambitious tenants, a suspicion that is confirmed by data on rule-takers. For a prolonged period new rule-takers have on average had higher NABERS ratings than nonparticipating office tenants, which indicates that CitySwitch attracts the already leading tenants in the office market and not laggards (CitySwitch, 2013, 2014b, 2015).

Strikingly, an almost identical narrative unfolds from the Chicago Green Office Challenge — a voluntary program with an almost identical design. As explained earlier, this program seeks to incentivize office tenants in Chicago's central business district to reduce energy consumption and supports them with knowledge on how to achieve this, and a yearly awards ceremony celebrates leading practice. In 2015, some 170 office tenants were participating in the program (representing a handful of tenants in Chicago's central business district) and collectively achieved energy reductions "equivalent to taking 43 homes off the grid for one year," the program administrator reports on its website[5] — this corresponds with less than 0.01 percent of all commercial building—related energy consumption in Chicago (see also City of Chicago, 2014). When asked to explain the major complication faced in achieving desired outcomes, one of the Green Office Challenge administrators observed: "[After some years] we realized that we were hitting a wall. [We attract] the early adapters, anyone who is already a leader in this field. And we have difficulties getting those on board who have heard of the program but do not see a need to participate" (int. 186).

Better Buildings Challenge, United States: The Program That Claims to Have It All

The Better Buildings Challenge conforms to the pattern uncovered thus far: some individual participants demonstrate considerable beyond-compliance performance, but the overall outcomes of the program are marginal, at best, when compared to the sustainable building challenge faced. It also indicates a pattern among a number of the voluntary programs studied: relatively marginal performance in terms of rule-takers attracted, relatively marginal overall performance of the program, but nevertheless is the program's an overall contribution to improved built environment sustainability presented by its administrators as a major success.

The Better Buildings Challenge is part of the larger United States Department of Energy's Better Buildings Initiative (White House, 2011a), a component of the Obama administration's Climate Action Plan (White House, 2013). Through this initiative the Obama administration sought to reduce the U.S. commercial property sector's 2010 energy consumption by 20 percent by 2020, a goal the challenge is unlikely to achieve. The program was launched by President Obama in 2011 and presented as "the fastest, easiest, and cheapest ways to save money, cut down on harmful pollution, and create good jobs" (White House, 2011b). Rule-takers in the challenge commit to reducing their energy consumption by 20 percent or more over the period of ten years compared to a base year. They may set this base year up to three years before joining the challenge and agree to conduct an energy efficiency assessment of their building portfolio in order to determine their personal benchmark. They agree further to develop and implement an energy plan to achieve their stated ambitions, and to report results: data that show their energy performance, but also how they have achieved improvements. In return the department supports them with technical and administrative assistance, connects them with firms that can help them in saving energy, and publicly recognises their participation and performance. The department further transforms rule-takers' experiences to knowledge documents and makes this knowledge available through a program website. Unique to the challenge is that it supports participants in sourcing funds for their energy upgrades. The program acknowledges that property owners often experience difficulties in obtaining funds for retrofits (see also Chapter 2 and Chapter 6) and seeks to tackle this problem by making funds available for retrofits. By 2015 a total of U.S.$5.5 billion was committed to the program — about half by private investors and the other half by the Obama administration.

Most buildings the challenge seeks to upgrade were built under lenient mandatory building energy requirements, and rule-takers should find it easy to harvest the "low-hanging fruit" in terms of energy upgrades (IEA, 2013). Some indeed do: the department highlights that the best performers have already achieved energy consumption reductions of up to 40 percent — and they have achieved this through conventional and low-tech building envelope upgrades and retrofitted duct systems (U.S. Department of Energy, 2014a, 2015). In sheer numbers the program's performance appears impressive also. By 2015, 3.5 billion square feet (325 million square meters) of commercial space was committed to the challenge, representing thirty-two thousand properties, and in 2014 a total of 58 trillion Btu energy savings was achieved (US Department of Energy, 2015). On average, participants had reduced their energy intensity

by 2 percent compared to their base year, about 14 percent of participants had already achieved 20 percent or more reductions, and another
25 percent had achieved at least 10 percent reductions (U.S. Department
of Energy, 2014b). What do these numbers mean in relative terms? The
answer, as with the Green Office Challenge and CitySwitch is, not a lot.
By 2015 the United States held 90 billion square feet of commercial
property (8 billion square meters), representing some 5.6 million buildings. The challenge covers about 4 percent of this space, and 0.6 percent
of the number of buildings — indicating that it is predominantly large
property owners that participate. The relative energy savings achieved
represent less than 0.3 percent of the 20 quadrillion Btu commercial
building—related energy consumption in the United States in 2014.[6]
While the relative performance of the program is limited, it is nevertheless presented as a considerable achievement by the Department of
Energy: "The federal government has shown success in its commitment
to identify new opportunities to save taxpayer dollars, reduce energy
and water costs, and cut harmful pollution. To date, the federal government has contracted for nearly $2 billion in energy efficiency perform-
ance contracting projects, and is working toward a total of $4 billion by
2016. These investments have created over 15,000 jobs and reduced over
680,000 tons of GHG emissions," the program's 2015 annual report
stresses (U.S. Department of Energy, 2015).

What accounts for a program that on paper has it all — generating and
sharing knowledge, supporting property owners in acquiring funds for
their retrofits, and having the full support of the federal government —
while achieving such marginal results? Comparable to CitySwitch, it
appears that the program's dominant focus on rewarding leadership is
only of interest to a small group of property owners. The program
director explained the underlying strategy: "We want to make the case
that not everyone has to start at square one. We want other organisations
to follow what the leaders have done" (quoted in Zimmerman, 2012).
The first group of rule-takers were hand-picked by the department
because of their past performance as leaders in the area of environmental
sustainability — including organizations such as 3M and Lend Lease,
which in 2015 were among the absolute top performers in the program.
"The hope is that the success that they've had becomes solutions
that other organisations can use so that leaders in the Better Buildings
Challenge are serving as mentors for other organisations," the program
director clarified (quoted in Lack, 2012). This is why the department
actively develops written case studies and best practice documents based
on the data provided by participating rule-takers in knowledge documents
that can be used by others. However, these others might very well face

different problems than the leaders. The leaders, major corporations with large property portfolios, have a corporate image to maintain, have dedicated property staff, and can replicate experiences throughout their property portfolios, so explained interviewees. The large majority of commercial property owners, the "others," possess only a single or a few buildings, do not employ dedicated property staff, and are required by the process of upgrading the energy efficiency of their businesses to interrupt their daily business — or that of their tenants. As with a number of the other voluntary programs studied, the lessons drawn from the Better Building Challenge might very well fail to resonate with a large majority of property owners.

Green Deal, Netherlands: Generating Knowledge throughout a Country

Green Deal is illustrative of another recurring pattern in the voluntary programs studied. Comparable to a range of other programs, it builds on a win–win narrative of cost savings for rule-takers through more efficient building construction and use practices to reduce the negative impact of the built environment — often termed ecoefficiency. However, this process can readily produce two specific undesired outcomes. The first occurs when the starting point of cost savings pushes rule-takers to opt for marginal sustainable building improvements with high cost savings over proposals with substantive improvement but low or no cost savings. The second pertains in the absence of short-term and substantial cost savings, whereupon rule-takers turn away from these programs disillusioned, strengthened in their belief that sustainable buildings are costly and difficult to achieve.

Launched in 2011, Green Deal is a policy program that allows the national government of the Netherlands to enter into voluntary programs with other governments, firms, citizens, and civil society organizations. When introducing Green Deal the government explained: "The Netherlands opts for green growth. Economic growth that takes into account the environment and sustainable development."[7] Through Green Deal the government invites others to propose ideas for voluntary programs that aim to generate knowledge on how barriers to decarbonizing the Dutch economy can be overcome. It has a strong focus on decarbonizing the built environment, with approximately 40 percent of 160 voluntary programs addressing sustainable buildings and sustainable building use. The most promising ideas for voluntary programs receive financial, administrative, or other support. Outlines specify what makes for a promising idea, which includes the potential for upscaling the program and achieving measurable results, for example, buildings constructed, or energy consumption reduced. Approximately one-quarter of proposed ideas are supported (Kwink Groep, 2013). Once a program is selected for support, the Netherlands Enterprise Agency — at arm's length from the Ministry of Finance — enters a voluntary program with those who proposed it. The agency assists participants in surmounting regulatory barriers where possible, acts as a neutral intermediary in drawing various parties together, or supports them in finding financial or administrative support for the realization of their idea — it does not provide funds directly, however (Agentschap NL, 2012). A program runs for a period of two to three years and is monitored and evaluated by the Green Deal Board — representing various industry sectors — to ensure public accountability (Green Deal Board, 2012). Knowledge generated is made available through a website with case studies and best practices, and a series of reports.[8]

Voluntary programs developed under Green Deal include certification and classification programs, programs to incentivize the use of renewable energy at precinct level, and a program that incentivizes the cement industry to reduce its overall carbon emissions. Administrators and rule-takers involved were generally positive about these voluntary programs. A representative of the Ministry of the Interior, which is responsible for the essential mandatory governance instruments that regulate the built environment, explained that "it took a long time to give the idea of sustainability and sustainable buildings a specific place within the Dutch building codes. And these are only mandatory for new commercial and residential development" (int. 59). He was particularly appreciative of the various voluntary programs under Green Deal because these were developed more quickly than mandatory requirements could have been established, focused on new and existing buildings as well as building use, and set generally more ambitious requirements than mandatory building codes. He expected that the programs developed under Green Deal would help to promote broader norms on sustainable buildings in the Dutch construction and property sectors, making it easier, ultimately, for the national government to introduce more ambitious mandatory requirements.

Rule-takers explained that they value the voluntary programs because they provide an efficient means for addressing the complicated and often interacting barriers they face in constructing or retrofitting sustainable buildings, or for changing the way buildings are used. One of them illustrated this with a simple example: overcoming the financial barriers that hamper retrofits is not just an issue of obtaining the support of banks and financial institutions — it often also involves changing statutory regulation (int. 213). Tenants might not want to carry out energy retrofits because they run the risk of losing their investment were their landlord to go out of business: Dutch bankruptcy law considers all items installed in or attached to a building — including installations owned by tenants — as part of that building, and in a bankruptcy case sells a building with all items fixed to it. Or, a landlord might not be willing to carry out energy retrofits because Dutch rental law restricts landlords in increasing rent, even when the benefits of such upgrades go directly to tenants in the form of reduced energy bills. This rule-taker specifically valued the voluntary program he was involved in because it eased the upgrading process by assisting with involvement of relevant parties — government agencies responsible for financial regulation, bankruptcy law, and rental law; financial institutions and banks; landlords and tenants — and collaboratively worked toward a solution documented and made available to others who face similar issues.

That being said, the various voluntary programs and the Green Deal program as a whole were criticized as well — by interviewees and in external evaluations (cf. Kwink Groep, 2013; Rotmans, 2011). The national government is critiqued for spreading its resources too thin by supporting a large number of voluntary programs, for selecting ideas for voluntary programs that have a moderate level of ambition, and for backing ideas that would have been implemented without government support — the program addressing the cement industry mentioned earlier, for example, is merely a continuation of a program that was already in existence. Interviewees were critical of the small scale of many voluntary programs developed (some focus on a single or only a handful of buildings) and of the scalability of knowledge generated. "A number of programs seem to stimulate conventional practice or practice that would not have much of an impact even if it were taken up on a large scale," the same rule-taker stated. "More ambitious selection criteria would be desirable, although that might result in situations in which a program is only of interest for a small group of elite players" (int. 213). The win–win narrative underlying the larger program was critiqued also. Interviewees argued that the strong focus on cost savings through resource efficiency might incentivize rule-takers to propose ideas for marginal sustainable building improvements with high cost savings rather than submit proposals with substantive improvement but low or no cost savings. Similarly, the national government might be biased in selecting ideas on the basis of their potential for economic growth as opposed to selecting them on the basis of their potential for decarbonizing the built environment. In addition, they explained, because of the strong focus on cost savings, rule-takers might easily become disillusioned when expected cost savings do not materialize — an issue that resonated with experiences shared by the rule-takers in Zonnig Huren ("Sunny Leasing," discussed earlier). Interviewees explained further that there is a risk that voluntary programs are merely established in order to demonstrate that action has been taken. "We seem to stop experimenting after a program-and-a-half to focus again on the next one," a representative of a construction sector peak body noted (int. 69). Others added that this specific type of program might even result in participation fatigue because there are too many voluntary programs in which firms can be involved. "The trouble with these programs is that firms often commit to ambitious outcomes even when they know upfront that they won't be able to achieve these," a policy maker from the city of Rotterdam observed. "We are running the risk that firms no longer want to participate because of bad experiences in earlier programs, or simply because so many programs seek to achieve almost similar goals" (int. 73). They warned, finally, that the voluntary programs, however well designed, do not represent real-world settings: comparable to the circumstances of CitySwitch, knowledge generated could be flawed. As a result, programs might conclude with overly high expectations of the ability to scale up the knowledge generated in a pilot program (and are reported doing so: Kwink Groep, 2013). "What happens now is that we draw lessons from results, but not from the process toward those results," the representative of a construction sector peak body indicated (int. 69). Rule-takers in the voluntary programs are, he argued, likely to be more ambitious and willing to go the extra mile to make a program work than they normally would be — a problem often pointed out in the literature on experimental governance (e.g., Vreugdenhil, Slinger, Thissen, & Ker Rault, 2010). They might have an ulterior interest for adopting a program — for instance, being ahead of competition were the program to be scaled up — an interest that nonparticipants lack, which might result in resistance from nonparticipants when they are asked to take similar voluntary action in expanded versions of the program.

Better Buildings Partnership, Sydney, Australia: A Successful Outlier

Within the full set of voluntary programs studied the Better Buildings Partnership is an outlier: it is among the most ambitious in terms of goals set in building-related carbon emission reductions, and it is among the most successful in terms of achieving its goal. The partnership highlights the possibilities of retrofitting office buildings in a best-case scenario characterized by a highly ambitious rule-maker, highly ambitious and well-funded rule-takers, and a relatively small geographical area of application.

The partnership joins the Sydney City Council with the city's fourteen major property owners, who collectively own more than 50 percent of the city's commercial property. Because considerable reductions of energy use and carbon emissions are possible at building level, Sydney City Council staff realized that if only these fourteen major property owners would retrofit their predominantly existing property, the city would take a huge step toward achieving its ambition of cutting its greenhouse gas emissions by 70 percent of 2006 emissions by 2030 (City of Sydney, 2011). When the partnership was implemented in 2011, it had also become clear that these property owners were unlikely to retrofit their buildings rapidly through certification and classification programs, as experienced under CitySwitch, and the City Council sought alternative governance instruments. Inspired by similar voluntary programs for commercial property owners in London and Toronto, the partnership was introduced: in it property owners make a commitment to the mayor of Sydney to reduce their existing property's carbon emissions by the stipulated amount, and in return the city supports them in achieving this goal. Unique to the partnership is that it involves its rule-takers in city development policy processes so that they can plan their future investments accordingly. "It provides them the opportunity to actually influence and to be inside the tent with the city, and with the city's ambitious agenda," a Sydney City Council policy maker explained. "And from a city point of view we need them as well. While we think we can get the best experts, we need their expertise and experiences as well to show us and challenge us to get the best solutions" (int. 42).

Through the partnership the property owners share their experiences with retrofitting buildings and the council provides a platform for sharing these experiences to the larger construction and property community: it transforms experiences to documented knowledge and administers a website with case studies and best practices on office building retrofits.[9] The partnership assists the council in understanding how it can make changes to the city's infrastructure in such a way that it helps property owners to achieve their goals. For example, one of the pivotal energy supply infrastructure changes envisaged by the council is the development of a decentralized energy network for Sydney that relies on trigeneration — the "tri-" stands for the three outputs of (natural or renewable) gas-fired engines. These engines produce low-carbon-intensive electricity, hot water for heating buildings, and cold water for cooling buildings.[10] Trigeneration engines fit in the basements of office buildings but require infrastructure upgrading to connect nearby buildings. Installing a trigeneration engine significantly improves a building's energy efficiency and a trigeneration network would significantly reduce Sydney's carbon emissions. It is particularly because of the close collaboration and alignment of individual and collective goals that the program is expected to achieve promising results for individual rule-takers and for the city as a whole. "There is only so much they can do with their own portfolio and their own buildings. They know that the next step, the next reach of reductions, they cannot just do that alone," the policy maker continued. "They would rather do it in collaboration with the building owner next door, or the city and thereby networking with all the building owners in the city. The next jump [can only be achieved] by actually working together" (int. 42).

In 2015 it reported being halfway to meeting its emissions reduction target (Better Buildings Partnership, 2015). This is outstanding performance that is not replicated by any other program studied for this book – although a number of the improvements had been made (or were planned) by the participating property owners in the five years before the program was implemented. In other words, the 2006 benchmark skews the reported performance of the program (Better Buildings Partnership, 2015). A number of characteristics are important in explaining this performance. The partnership is an exclusive, elite group of property sector leaders, within which highly professional senior managers represent their respective organizations in the partnership. The rule-takers are strongly committed to the partnership: they have the financial means for undertaking retrofits (their combined building stock is valued at AU $105 billion), and they have a high level of certainty that they will see their investments returned, as Sydney's central business district will likely remain one of Australia's prime office markets. Finally, the council is strongly committed to the partnership. The Partnership is one of its flagship voluntary programs that contribute to the city's ambition that it "will be seen as a global leader for best practice in sustainability in buildings, precincts and urban development" (Better Buildings Partnership, 2015, 8). The program, participating property owners, and their performance are actively marketed by the council in national and international forums.

That the partnership would achieve such results so quickly was not expected by administrators or participants. When interviewed in 2011 and asked what they thought of the partnership a senior manager representing one of the participants stated: "We are waiting for the city to roll out their plans. To push it a bit more. Maybe the Better Building Partnership has got in too early. The value for us is in being at the table with our competitors and peers. I'm not sure what other value actually comes from the initiative than just being a part of what everybody is a part of at the moment" (int. 44). Administrators interviewed in 2011 expected that demands for better-performing office space by office tenants would be a particularly significant incentive for the fourteen property owners to commit to the partnership (int. 41 and int. 42). In 2010, mandatory energy efficiency disclosure of office space through a NABERS certificate and CitySwitch was introduced (NABERS: see Chapter 3; CitySwitch: see previous discussion). Both inform office tenants about the building energy performance of the offices they rent. This expected increase in demand for better-performing office space is, however, not as strong as expected, a program administrator explained in a follow-up interview in 2014 (int. 42). The partnership is now actively involved in informing and educating tenants about the advantages of leasing low-energy, non-carbon-intensive office space (Blundell, 2014). It does so, among others, through active engagement with CitySwitch and has begun to experiment with green leases, which set out obligations of landlords and tenants of office buildings with high levels of urban sustainability.

Besides praise of the partnership, it should be kept in mind that it covers a relatively small area: the Sydney City Council governs the Sydney central business district and some surrounding inner city suburbs — 25 square kilometers; in contrast, the greater metropolitan area of Sydney measures 12,300 square kilometers — and the partnership applies to some one hundred buildings only. Property owners and government staff in other major cities in Australia such as Melbourne and Brisbane explained that they cannot duplicate the Better Buildings Partnership. This is predominantly because their cities do not have the advantage of having a relatively small group of owners who control a large share of commercial property, which would allow them to set up a comparable network. An administrator in another Australian state capital city explained further that Sydney provides property owners who commit to the partnership a reputational advantage that smaller cities — such as his — cannot offer:

We host the back offices of the big companies. It is in the interest of these big companies to have the city where they have their headquarters, the city that they want to be the springboard to the world from, to have these cities hum and look fantastic. It is not necessarily of interest to them to have their back offices be a high-cost work environment, with [higher levels of built environment] sustainability, higher rental costs and all that. Urban reality is that the shake-out of resources and the big thinking of plans, the attracting of [government] money, happens in big cities [such as Sydney]. (int. 50)

Comparable experiences to those of the partnership were also reported in another elite network: Retrofit Chicago. This program seeks to reduce energy consumption of office buildings in Chicago by at least 20 percent over a period of five years. The program was launched by the City of Chicago in 2012 and resembles a number of design conditions of the partnership: it builds on close collaboration between the city council and participating commercial property owners; it seeks to generate and share knowledge on office retrofits; and it rewards rule-takers with media exposure in local, national, and international forums. In addition, Retrofit Chicago supports its rule-takers in securing funds for their retrofits — it is a spin-off program of the nationwide Better Buildings Challenge. By 2015, some forty-five property owners — represented by a small number of professional property managers — had committed fifty buildings to the program, and in its first three years of implementation participants had reduced their building-related energy consumption by 7 percent of the 2010 baseline.[11]

Significant Findings

The narrative that has unfolded through the set of knowledge generation and sharing programs again largely confirms the theoretical account presented in Chapter 3. It further supports and gives weight to the range of findings from the certification and classification programs studied in Chapter 4, while also adducing several novel conceptions. The following concluding section addresses the crucial findings from this part of the study.

Conflicting Ambitions?

The voluntary programs studied in this chapter have bold ambitions. They seek to generate knowledge on state-of-the-art approaches for reduced building-related resource consumption and carbon emissions. They also seek to encourage leadership in these mattersand to achieve considerable numbers of sustainable buildings. And they attempt to do all this under the rubric of ecological modernization — the assumption that economic gains are attainable through increased environmentally sustainable behavior. But is this combined set of ambitions realistic? Leading performance at the forefront of what is possible in terms of sustainable buildings combined with large-scale, financially driven uptake appears contradictory. If a program indeed meets its ambitions in terms of comprehensive adoption of leading sustainable building practice, the inevitable question is, Why have its rule-takers not achieved this without the program?

    The mix of ambitions provides opponents and supporters of these voluntary programs ammunition with which to criticize or support the outcomes achieved. Opponents may disparage outcomes as not truly groundbreaking. Was it that challenging for the 14 percent of rule-takers in the Better Buildings Challenge to improve their building energy efficiency by 20 percent in four years? Documented case studies indicate that these results have been achieved through conventional practice — building upgrades such as wall and roof insulation and more energy efficient heating and ventilation systems. If their performance is considered outstanding, then what explains the average performance of rule-takers of a little more than 2 percent efficiency improvements? Do relative energy savings of the program — 0.3 percent in 2014 — justify these efforts? Supporters of this category of voluntary programs might brush this censure aside, pointing to the valuable knowledge gained, and to the marginal performance as an optimistic indication that change is possible. "Even when you do not achieve a specific number of buildings, still much may be achieved," a program administrator in Boston argued. "It's a ripple effect. It's about collateral benefit. Some lessons and effects simply are not quantifiable" (int. 192).

More problematic than this conflict between gaining knowledge and achieving sweeping change is the strangely resolute contradiction between inciting innovation and achieving economic gain (cf. Hayden, 2014; Helm, 2012; Matthews, 2015). Innovative practice inevitably requires economic risk. The concept of ecological modernization and the related win–win narrative that rule-makers often use to attract rule-takers can be counterproductive when anticipated financial gains do not materialize. It may also result in situations, as indicated by Green Deals in the Netherlands, for instance, in which conventional but guaranteed profitability is preferred to an innovative but financially underperforming (but still cost-neutral) environmental alternative.

Leadership Fixation

A related risk in this category of voluntary programs is the pervading emphasis on rewarding leadership. While encouraging leadership has normative appeal, it entails practical complications. As interviewees explained, not all prospective rule-takers can or want to be leaders in their sector — the extremes of success would amount to an industry composed exclusively of leaders — and not all knowledge created by leading rule-takers will resonate with other firms and individuals that a program targets. They further explained that prospective rule-takers might consider the marketing of leading performance within a program — through annual awards ceremonies and by promoting program leaders in the popular media — as too small an incentive to join a program. Also, does not winning an award imply that a participating rule-taker is a loser? A solution to this winner—loser dichotomy is to introduce "a wide range of awards to ensure that every participant has an opportunity to win," an administrator of the Chicago Green Office Challenge explained. "Participants are very concerned about their public standing," and winning an award helps them to improve their image of corporate responsibility, she continued (int. 186). Yet, this strategy of award inflation is analogous to an industry of leaders: the award currency is devalued and the function of peer distinction is lost.

Leadership overemphasis also places pressure on rule-takers to excel, which might prompt them to stretch or even violate program rules to achieve this status. Seeking to win an award or media attention from program administrators, rule-takers might join a program by providing skewed data on their preparticipation performance, refrain from reporting performance data during participation, or only join a program after they have taken action that might favor their recognition as a leader. Situations of playing the system were found in the Australian program CitySwitch, but are likely to be present in other programs also. The Better Building Challenge in the United States, for example, allows prospective rule-takers to set the benchmark against which their performance is measured up to three years before participating; it makes logical sense for a rule-taker to choose a year and benchmark that allow for most improvement when joining the program. While participants who cheat with program rules might establish the most impressive best practices results for program administrators to report on, the knowledge generated from their experiences would not contribute to means of decarbonizing the built environment.

This leadership fixation might also result in a related risk: because administrators of these programs are very enthusiastic in marketing the leading performance of rule-takers in the popular media, they create the illusion that the construction and property sectors are proactive and successful in voluntarily decarbonizing the built environment. The Better Buildings Challenge keeps track of articles "in national, regional, business, and trade media [that highlight rule-takers] for their leadership in improving the energy efficiency of commercial and public buildings, multifamily housing, and industrial plants" and provides links to more than 150 of such articles published in 2014 alone.[12] In light of the relative performance of the program in 2014 — a 0.3 percent reduction of commercial building-related energy consumption — this is extraordinary media coverage. Likewise, administrators of less successful programs might decide not to share information, only adding to the illusion that these voluntary programs are generally successful. "We keep our data to ourselves now," an administrator of a voluntary program in the United States shared. "We are being compared to other programs. Other programs that do much better, but that run much longer also. We will show our data when there are clear successes to show" (int. 187).

Performance in Perspective

Comparable to the certification and classification programs studied in Chapter 4, the knowledge generation and sharing programs studied here have not yet achieved extensive results in terms of uptake or reduced building-related resource consumption and carbon emissions. While program administrators tend to depict program performance in the best possible light — program funding or other support often depends on outcomes achieved — the bottom line is that program performance is feeble when compared to the sustainable building challenge faced. This raises an important question: is there truly any low-hanging fruit in the process of decarbonizing the built environment? It is often argued that the possibility of achieving swift returns from improving resource efficiency or reducing carbon intensity is the prevailing promise of the construction and property sectors in addressing climate change (Georgiadou, Hacking, & Guthrie, 2012; Hoppe, Bressers, & Lulofs, 2011; WGBC, 2013). But even when supported and celebrated, firms and individuals in the construction and property sectors do not rush to join these programs.

Another concern about the performance of the programs discussed is that they result in tinkering at the edges of the sustainable building challenge rather than in solutions that address the fundamental problems. Programs such as CitySwitch in Australia, Zonnig Huren ("Sunny Leasing") in the Netherlands, and the Better Buildings Challenge in the United States predominantly exist to make rule-takers aware of by-now rather conventional possibilities to reduce building-related energy efficiency. They do not challenge rule-takers to move much beyond well-trialed practice: attaining a NABERS 4-Star rating under CitySwitch requires only improving a building to just above the average of the Australian market performance of new commercial buildings; achieving a 20 percent energy efficiency reduction under the Better Buildings Challenge over a period of ten years is modest in light of, for example, the 10 percent energy efficiency improvements of a considerable number of United Kingdom government buildings over the course of one year (see Chapter 2; Cabinet Office, 2011). That being said, the programs that do challenge rule-takers to generate knowledge on nonconventional solutions for decarbonizing the built environment — Energiesprong

("Energy Leap") and Green Deals in the Netherlands — are hamstrung by their ambition to find solutions that result in economic growth as well as improved built environment sustainability. By escaping the paradigm of ecological modernization, rule-makers might allocate a part of their means to support rule-makers seeking to establish sustainable buildings that generate no financial gain or even a small financial loss. The city of Amsterdam's revolving loan fund, discussed in Chapter 6, is an illustrative example of this idea.

The exception to this rule of relatively poor performance is the Better Buildings Partnership in Sydney. It has attracted all the rule-makers it targets — Sydney's major commercial property owners; in 2014 it even branched out to allow smaller commercial property owners to join the program — and is well under way in achieving its ambitious target. But this performance should again be understood in its specific context: the program relies on a small network of ambitious property owners in control of a large proportion of the city's commercial property, and an ambitious city government. As interviewees explained, this program design might achieve less promising results in contexts that deal with larger numbers of less affluent property owners — making the design unattractive for small and medium-sized firms and homeowners.

6   Innovative Climate Financing
Providing Funds

Chapters 4 and 5 highlighted that the high expectations of voluntary programs for sustainable buildings and cities often do not materialize in real-world settings. The majority of the programs studied indicate marginal performance in terms of attracting rule-takers and of making an overall contribution to improved built environment sustainability. The programs studied thus far generally attract some leaders within the construction and property sectors and incentivize them to make modest reductions to their building-related resource consumption or carbon emissions. Interviewees were aware of these performance patterns. They pointed to two related reasons for this marginal performance: the dominant motivator for prospective rule-takers to commit to a program is financial gain, they argued; and, programs are of interest to leaders in the construction and property sectors, but not to those who make up the majority of the market, that is, the early and late majority and laggards.

"What I've learned is that the voluntary needs to come with a tangible benefit," an Australian program manager explained. "If you step away a bit you find that [rule-makers of voluntary programs] need to find out what their value proposition is. Without finance the value is often limited to promotion, networks, and knowledge" (int. 26). She maintained, as did other interviewees, that the bottom line for many property developers and owners is a financial one. Individuals and firms may have good intentions before joining a program, but these dampen when they realize the initial costs of sustainable buildings. "What you often see is that the sustainable building ambition of governments and local firms is very high, but as soon as people begin thinking about the financial side those ambitions decline. Money makes things more real it seems," a senior sustainable building consultant in the Netherlands added (int. 70). Interviewees explained that financial considerations are particularly relevant for homeowners and small and medium-sized firms. "Of course, at the top-end of any market it is important to demonstrate leadership. That is why they are the top end," the CEO of an Australian construction and property sector peak body explained. "One of the ways to show leadership these days is to be environmentally sensible and understand those issues. So that's a criteria that more and more leaders meet. But there is a very large component of businesses and offices and residential buildings that are not at that top end, and do not feel leadership pressure" (int. 43). While organizations and individuals in other market segments might show environmental awareness also, this CEO questioned whether it was for similar reasons. "They say: 'Look: there is a market out there, but people are earning only so much salary. If we stick to all these sustainability requirements we've got to sell them 200,000 dollar apartments, but people can only pay 100,000 dollars. So we have a problem.' And it is the same in commercial buildings as well. It's about the economics" (int. 43).

The financial hesitation of property developers and owners is amplified by another issue. As explained in Chapter 3, banks and other finance providers are hesitant in providing funds for sustainable building development and use — and that holds also for the provision of funds for building retrofits. They fear that the sustainability credentials of buildings are not reflected in their market value, thereby creating risk if their owners cannot repay the loans of mortgages provided should they have to sell their property (Bals et al., 2006; World Bank, 2011a). The final category of voluntary programs studied in this book seeks to overcome the financial hesitation of property developers and owners; they seek to remove the risks experienced by banks and other finance providers, or to provide funding directly to sustainable building development and retrofit projects with potential for considerable resource or carbon reductions that are unable to find conventional funding. Rule-makers of these programs argue that by improving the resource efficiency of buildings their owners save money — they face lower electricity and water bills than in owning or leasing conventional buildings. These cost savings can offset investment funds. In other words, comparable to many of the programs in Chapters 4 and 5, those discussed here also support an ecological modernization narrative: that economic progress and environmental sustainability can go hand in hand. Table 6.1 gives a brief overview of the programs discussed in this chapter (see also Appendix B).

Table 6.1 indicates that the programs studied for this chapter have a broad range of designs — comparable to the range of information generation and sharing programs studied in Chapter 5. Yet again, they can be clustered in two broad subsets: programs that bridge governments, third-party fund providers such as banks and financial institutions, and property owners; and programs that directly fund sustainable building development and use, and set specific requirements to funds provided. In what follows each subset is initially introduced. The chapter then

Table 6.1 *Overview of Funds-Provision Programs Studied*

Name	Brief Description	Risks	Dir.
		Form	
1200 Buildings (Australia, 2010)	Program that bridges the City of Melbourne government, finance providers, and commercial property owners; it aims for a 38 percent reduction of rule-takers' building-related energy consumption	X	
Additional Credit for Energy Efficient Homes (Netherlands, 2012)	Voluntary mortgages for potential homeowners to make energy efficiency improvements to new or existing residential property	X	
Amsterdam Investment Fund (Netherlands, 2011)	Revolving loan fund that financially supports projects that add to the city of Amsterdam's environmental sustainability goals.		X
Billion Dollar Green Challenge (United States, 2011)	Program that challenges colleges and universities to set up self-managed revolving loan funds for building retrofits; sole focus on existing commercial property		X
Building Innovation Fund (Australia, 2008)	Program that funded only the most promising building retrofit proposals from a pool of proposed retrofits in the state of South Australia, which had a sole focus on existing commercial property.		X
E$^+$ Green Building (United States, 2011)	Program that seeks to stimulate the construction of "energy plus" residential property in Boston (property that generates more energy than it consumes)		X
Energy Efficient Mortgage (United States, 1995)	Voluntary mortgages for (future) homeowners to make energy efficiency improvements to new or existing residential property	X	
Environmental Upgrade Agreements (Australia, 2011)	Program that bridges the City of Sydney government, finance providers, and commercial property owners	X	
PACE (United States, 2008)	Program that allows municipalities to issue bonds for commercial building retrofits; applied in thirty states in the United States	X	
Small Business Improvement Fund (United States, 2000)	Program that builds on tax increment financing to offer financial support to building upgrades and retrofits of small firms based in Chicago		X
Sustainable Development Grant (Australia, 2007)	Program that funded only the most promising building retrofit proposals from a pool of proposed retrofits in Brisbane, it had a sole focus on existing commercial property		X

Note: Risks = programs that focus on removing risks experienced by third-party fund providers; Dir. = programs that provide funds directly to rule-takers that commit to program rules; PACE = Property Assessed Clean Energy discusses three examples in depth to gain a better understanding of the opportunities and constraints of this category of voluntary programs for decarbonizing the built environment and concludes with a reflection on critical findings.

Removing Risks Experienced by Third-Party Fund Providers

The first subset of programs join governments, banks and other fund providers, on the one hand, and property owners, on the other. Most distinctive about this subset of programs is that they seek to obviate the risks experienced by banks and finance providers, or offer them other rewards that make them willing to provide funds for sustainable building development and retrofits. At the same time these programs have been introduced with the expectation that once potential property developments have access to funds for sustainable buildings or retrofits, they will be more willing to acquire buildings with higher-than-conventional levels of sustainability, or will be more willing to retrofit their existing buildings. Two specific designs for such programs were uncovered in this study: environmental upgrade financing and energy efficiency mortgages.

Environmental Upgrade Financing

In environmental upgrade financing programs governments act as intermediaries to obviate risks experienced by banks and other finance providers in supplying funds for sustainable building retrofits. In the programs studied governments obtain funds — from banks or other providers — and supply these to rule-takers. Rule-takers commit to using these funds for retrofitting existing buildings in line with program rules. This design was introduced in the United States as a nationwide program in 2008: Property Assessed Clean Energy (PACE).

PACE helps commercial property owners to access long-term loans for energy retrofits and upgrades.[1] Loans are sought from local governments, and PACE provides a framework and guidelines for government and property owners to reach agreements on how loans are being used. PACE allows rule-makers (local governments) and rule-takers (property owners) to enter into tailored agreements that account for the specific circumstances of rule-takers and their property. Once they have entered into an agreement, the local government issues a bond on behalf of the property owners that can be purchased by a third-party finance provider. After obtaining funds, the local government supplies these to the property owner, who uses it for energy efficiency retrofits and upgrades according to the agreement. The local government recoups these funds — with interest — through an additional property tax on the property of the rule-taker and repays the funds and interest to the third-party finance provider. In order to be allowed to impose this additional property tax, PACE requires that state and local government enact legislation that allows for PACE financing. By 2015, thirty states had enacted such legislation, and thirteen states were actively using it (PACE Now, 2015).

Administrators of local PACE programs in San Francisco and Sacramento (int. 179; int. 184) considered one of the main strengths of the program its tying funds provided to the building and not the building owner: because the funds provided are recouped through the additional property tax, the duty to repay the funds moves to the new property owner if the building changes ownership. Another main strength, they explained, is the involvement of local government as risk-taker. "The repayment obligation is secured through the property taxes and that allows us to advertise [the bonds] over a 20-year repayment period at competitive rates. It is a secure new class of asset investment that provides longer-term repayment periods. It creates positive cash flows," a program administrator in San Francisco stated. "What's more, the bond can even be passed over to the tenants. That makes it a uniquely powerful program," he concluded (int. 179). This latter aspect of the program helps to overcome the split-incentive problem, discussed in Chapter 2, in which the building owner pays for energy retrofits while the tenant obtains the financial advantages.

Local governments in Australia have implemented voluntary programs that build on a comparable design, albeit with some differences: 1200 Buildings in Melbourne, implemented in 2010; and Environmental Upgrade Agreements in Sydney, implemented in 2011. These programs differ from PACE in how governments seek to obtain funds. Instead of issuing bonds on behalf of property owners, as under the PACE program, the governments of Melbourne and Sydney have entered into agreements with finance providers and borrow funds directly to supply these to property owners. Funds are repaid by property owners through a newly introduced property tax, which required legislative changes in both cities. In both Melbourne and Sydney the environmental upgrade financing programs set strict criteria for rule-takers: the Melbourne program, for example, requires that property owners commit to improving the energy efficiency of their buildings by 38 percent by 2020 (da Silva, 2011).These commitments relate to the cities' larger ambitions of reducing resource consumption and carbon emissions — this again differs from PACE, which allows for greater specificity of agreements between local governments and property owners. When interviewed in 2011, just after 1200 Buildings in Melbourne was launched, one of its administrators was convinced that the program would quickly attract a substantial number of rule-takers. "The finance incentive [provided by the program] has created a strong value proposition and that is something that building owners are interested in" (int. 26). Later in the research project it became clear, however, that the program struggles considerably with attracting rule-takers — as do the other programs: in the period 2008–2015, some 350 commercial buildings were retrofitted under PACE; since 2010 fewer than 50 buildings have been participating in the 1200 Buildings program in Melbourne; and since 2011 fewer than five agreements had been signed under the Environmental Upgrade Agreements in Sydney. The performance case study of 1200 Buildings, which follows, explores why commercial property owners evince so little interest in environmental upgrade financing.

Energy Efficiency Mortgages

Energy efficiency mortgages also seek to remove risks experienced by finance providers while providing funds to prospective homeowners to support the costs of energy efficiency measures for their new or existing homes. These mortgages have a long history in the United States: the U.S. Federal Housing Administration implemented the Energy Efficient Mortgage Program in 1995. It recognizes that homeowners can reduce their utility expenses through energy retrofits or upgrades of their houses — increasing their capacity to repay mortgages — and allows those who seek to do so to top up their approved mortgage. It considers energy savings as additional disposable income that improves borrowers' ability to pay and thus reduces the risk for finance providers (U.S. Department of Housing and Urban Development, 1995). Homeowners are allowed additional mortgages that are less than the expected savings from energy upgrades of new or existing homes — estimated energy savings must be determined through an acknowledged system or by an acknowledged energy consultant. Maximum mortgage limits are set to 5 percent of the property. Mortgages issued under the Energy Efficient Mortgage Program are insured by the Federal Housing Administration, which secures finance providers against loan default. The program has resulted in a number of spin-off programs. The states of Colorado, Maine, and New York trialed Energy Star Mortgages: by injecting capital into energy efficiency mortgages they aimed to lower the interest rates for borrowers, making it more attractive to them to undertake home energy upgrades. Typically these mortgages are marketed as a win–win opportunity: homeowners can save costs by reducing their energy consumption, which at the same time reduces the carbon emissions of their homes (Kats et al., 2012).

A different take on energy efficiency mortgages is the Tijdelijke Regeling Hypothecair Krediet ("Additional Credit for Energy Efficient Homes") program, implemented by the Netherlands Ministry of Finance in 2012. It is a temporary lifting of restrictive home mortgage regulation for the period 2012–2018 allowing mortgage suppliers to issue higher mortgages to lenders who seek to improve the energy efficiency of their future house. In 2012 they were allowed to lend up to 6 percent more than the value of the house at the time of transaction (with a maximum of eight thousand euros), decreasing by one percentage point per year until the temporary program is phased out in 2019. A specific temporary rule allows mortgage suppliers to lend up to twenty-five thousand euros more than the value of the house at the time of transaction to lenders who seek to make their prospective house energy neutral (Dutch Ministry of Finance, 2012). This program sits within a larger policy of providing government-backed mortgages to enable financing for sustainable construction.

Reviews of these energy efficiency mortgages in the United States and the Netherlands indicate that their impact is insufficient to address the problem (ACEEE, 2013; Dwars, 2013; Kats et al., 2012). The largest and oldest of these, the United States Federal Housing Administration's Energy Efficient Mortgage Program, issued fewer than six thousand mortgages in the period 2006–2014 (Federal Housing Administration, 2011, 2012, 2013, 2014). To put these numbers in perspective: in its best year thus far, 2011, of close to 15 million mortgages issued throughout the United States, a mere 1,065 were issued under the program — representing less than 0.1 percent of mortgages that year — less than one in ten thousand. These reviews highlight a number of problems that explain the low uptake of the programs. On the demand side there is limited interest in energy efficiency retrofit; homeowners simply do not demand these mortgages because they are generally not interested in retrofitting their homes. Those who are interested in doing so often have funds for retrofits or consider the paperwork and other related administrative efforts too much trouble for the relatively small additional mortgage provided through these programs (Kolstad, 2014). On the supply side finance providers are hesitant to participate. One of their recurring arguments is that technical energy retrofits and upgrades do not guarantee energy savings by consumers because consumer behavior plays an important role as well. Consumers might feel justified in using more energy since they occupy an energy efficient house — the rebound effect discussed in Chapter 2 — with the result that cost savings decrease, making them less capable of paying back the additional mortgage (Allen, Barth, & Yago, 2012; BuildingBusiness, 2015).

Earmarked Funding

The second subset of programs is not concerned with the risks experienced by banks and other third-party finance providers, but seeks to alleviate the financial concerns of rule-takers by providing funds for low-carbon building development or retrofits directly. Funds provided are often earmarked to achieve specific outcomes — for instance, a specified reduction of energy consumption — but the programs leave it to rule-takers as to how they achieve these outcomes. These programs are built on the assumption that if rule-takers are allowed to find their own solutions to achieve an outcome, they will come up with innovative solutions. "For me it really shows what the market is capable of. You often see ambition [in government] to lift the minimal standards, but then the interest groups squeal and say 'that cannot be done,'" a senior policy officer in the government of South Australia observed. "But with a [funding program that challenges them] you see that it can be done" (int. 51). This characteristic distinguishes these programs from more traditional subsidies, which often specify the solution to achieve the outcome (for instance, subsidies that support homeowners in the cost of installing solar panels), as opposed to challenging them to identify and install innovative solutions themselves (Irvine et al., 2012; Stewart, 2006). Two specific designs for such programs were uncovered in this study: competitive funding and revolving and self-provided funds.

Competitive Funding

Competitive funding typically challenges citizens, governments, firms, civil society groups, and other organizations to propose ideas for the development or retrofitting of sustainable buildings with high levels of performance that move well beyond mandatory requirements or conventional practice. These programs strongly discriminate among prospective rule-takers who apply for funds and provide funds only to the most promising proposals in terms of built environment sustainability (cf. Matthews, 2015; Mazzucato, 2015; Simpson & Clifton, 2014). This strong discrimination as to who is funded and who is not sets these programs even further apart from conventional subsidies — conventional subsidies built on the idea of equal accessibility.

Competitive funding programs with these characteristics were identified in the United States and Australia.

The Australian programs — the Sustainable Development Grant, in the city of Brisbane (2007–2010), and the Building Innovation Fund, in the state of South Australia (2008–2012) — have a straightforward design: a government agency earmarks a fixed amount of funds for property development and retrofitting that demonstrate high levels of built environment sustainability performance; property developers and property owners seeking funds can submit proposals, and those likely to achieve best performance are awarded funds. To ensure the most promising proposals were selected, the Brisbane program used a system comparable to the certification and classification programs discussed in Chapter 4: a proposal was awarded credits in different categories, and a threshold credit score had to be met to be eligible for funding. The higher the total score the larger the grant provided. The threshold score was comparable with achieving at least a 4-Star classification under the certification and classification program Green Star (see Chapter 4). The South Australian program worked with a jury — consisting of government representatives, the property sector, and academia — that assessed proposals and awarded funds. Here proposals were required to move well beyond mandatory requirements. In both programs funding covered a proportion of the costs, and only for an energy efficiency improvement or other intervention that could not otherwise obtain funding, but did not cover a development or retrofitting project in its entirety. "The funds provided are relatively small," an administrator in Brisbane said, "and the question is whether it actually influences whether a project would go ahead or not." In a typical project supported under the Brisbane program the funding was less than 1 percent of a total of AU$19.5 million in construction costs.[2] "They do, however, push developers and planners to think to go further, to push the boundaries of [sustainable building practice]," he continued; "that is the strength of it" (int. 27).

Administrators of the E$^+$Green Building program in Boston shared similar experiences. The program challenges designers and property developers to propose and construct new multiunit residential housing in Boston that achieves at least LEED Platinum certification (the highest tier under the certification and classification program; see Chapter 4) and have to be energy positive ("E$^+$") once built. That is, buildings should generate more energy than they consume. A significant aspect of the program involves design competitions. In 2011, for example, a design competition was held for housing development on three inner Boston development sites. These sites were government property and highly sought-after by developers. Instead of selling the sites to the highest bidder the city government decided to make the sites the incentive of a design competition: they would be awarded to those teams of designers and property developers who proposed the most promising ideas for energy positive housing development. In addition, a monetary reward was included. A total of fourteen teams participated in the 2011 competition. Program administrators explained that these teams had increased prospective targets for sustainable housing development in the United States — one of the designs accrued fifty-six more credits than the ninety necessary to achieve LEED Platinum certification[3] — but with available and fairly conventional technological solutions and without significant additional costs compared to those of conventional housing development. The winning designs now act as showcases for City of Boston staff: "I take my colleagues [to these projects] and show them around," one of the program administrators observed, "and when they sit with their next development project they ask [the applicant of a building permit or the developer], 'Why are you not doing this?'" (int. 193). Moreover, explained his colleague, "it has changed the mind-set of the nonwinners as well. They realized that they can develop high-performing buildings in a cost-effective way, and some will now realize their designs on other sites" (int. 192).

Such potential spillover effects of showcase projects was mentioned by other program administrators as well. Australian program administrators had also experienced that "nonwinners" would go ahead with their projects simply because they had developed a firm understanding of the investment costs and operational cost savings of energy efficiency upgrades, which provided them with a business case in favor of development. That being said in favor of these programs, interviewees explained that the overall impact of such programs is marginal. Funds allocated for these programs are relatively small — fewer than twenty buildings supported by the Sustainable Development Grant and the Building Innovation Fund combined. Also, the programs do not attract very large numbers of prospective rule-takers. In 2011 Boston was, for example, home to twenty-three hundred registered architects and some 850 architecture and building design firms.[4] One would expect that a design competition with such high stakes would be of interest to more of them than those participating in the fourteen teams — all the more so during a period when the construction and property sectors were affected by the aftermath of the global financial crisis.

Revolving Loan Funds and Self-Provided Funds

What would be more ideal than having a fund for sustainable building development and retrofit that replenishes itself? That ideal is, in a nutshell, the premise of revolving loan funds and self-provided funds. Revolving loan funds are gaining popularity as a means with which to support sustainable development. Funds are "revolving" because once they are paid back to the central fund, it can issue new loans to other projects (Boyd, 2013; Chou et al., 2014; Indvik, Foley, & Orlowski, 2013). Such funds have been established in the United States and the Netherlands.[5]

The Amsterdam Energy Fund is a typical example of a revolving loan fund. It was established by the Amsterdam City Council in 2011 to fund projects that contribute to the built environment sustainability goals of the city, which include a 40 percent reduction of 1990 carbon emissions by 2025 and a 70 percent reduction by 2040 (City of Amsterdam, 2011). Within the fund €70 million is earmarked to provide financial support to building and city development projects that seek energy reductions or local energy generation. It funds two types of projects: safe investment projects with a high likelihood of repaying loans supplied and less reliable projects that might not be able to return the loaned funds. The first category comprises 80 percent of loans issued, and it funds fairly conventional and low-risk energy upgrades such as the instalment of more than ten thousand solar panels on the city's flagship soccer stadium. The other 20 percent of loans are issued to highly innovative projects, for instance, citizen-run energy utilities. Losses that might occur from this second category of loans are covered by profit made in the first category. By 2015 the fund had invested some €14 million in twenty-nine projects, predominantly in the safe investment category.[6] Because of its slow uptake and strong focus on safe investments in now-conventional sustainable building solutions, the fund faces considerable criticism at the local level. It is hailed, however, by the C40 Cities Climate Leadership Group, an international network of the world's largest cities, for being among the world's most promising voluntary programs for accelerating the transition to a low-carbon built environment.[7] The performance case study, which follows, explores the fund further, seeking to understand its conflicting reception.

A unique take on revolving loan funds is the Billion Dollar Green Challenge in the United States. The program was implemented in 2011 by the Sustainable Endowments Institute, a project within the Rockefeller Foundation, and challenges prospective rule-takers to invest a total of U.S.$1 billion in self-managed revolving loan funds to finance energy efficiency improvements of educational facilities. Rule-takers in this instance are educational institutions — universities and colleges — and environmental nonprofit organizations. The challenge does not provide funds itself, but proselytizes the concept and advantages of revolving loan funds throughout the United States' education sector. It supports rule-takers with guidelines on how to establish a self-managed revolving loan fund, with computer software to track their own performance and to compare it with that of other rule-takers, and with case studies from other rule-takers on how to improve the energy efficiency of educational buildings (Bornstein, 2015). The challenge does not require its participants to achieve a specified increase in energy efficiency.[8] By 2015, some fifty universities and colleges had participated in the challenge, with U.S.$110 million committed to self-managed revolving loan funds.

Another example of a self-provided fund is the Small Business Innovation Fund in Chicago. It was introduced in 2000 by the city of Chicago to generate local funds for local building upgrades. Although implemented well before the city launched its agenda on improved urban sustainability (see Chapter 5), the program has gradually moved closer to contributing to this agenda (SomerCor, 2014). The fund is not revolving in the sense that it issues loans that can be reissued once paid back, but it is revolving in the sense that it generates funds from local districts and invests these in the districts where they are generated. It is funded through tax increment financing, a method that uses future tax gains to subsidise current improvements. Property owners can apply for funding if their property is situated in a tax increment financing area. Administrators of the fund award financial support to the most promising proposals, and since 2000 some eight hundred grants have been issued. Tax increment financing is a common governance instrument in the United States, but it is not well known in other countries. The fund is therefore considered in more depth in the following performance case studies.

Program Performance: Three Case Studies

By now it comes as no surprise that the performance of the voluntary programs studied is limited in comparison to the sustainability challenge faced. Interview accounts and additional data highlight that this category for voluntary programs particularly struggles with attracting rule-takers. For example, by 2015, seven years after its launch, PACE in the United States had been applied to 350 commercial projects and had generated U.S.$130 million in private funds.[9] While the energy efficiency improvements of these projects are impressive — 62 percent on average compared to the pre retrofitting condition — the total number of projects PACE has been applied to is insignificant when compared to the volume of U.S. commercial building stock. Keeping in mind that this building stock represents some 5.6 million buildings (see Chapter 5), commercial buildings retrofitted through PACE are about as uncommon as energy efficiency mortgages issued for residential buildings in the United States.

Still, PACE administrators use the jargon of "leaders" and "success stories" in marketing the program[10] and the popular media channel this narrative: "Tax Programs to Finance Clean Energy Catch On" is the headline of a 2013 *New York Times* article that in highly positive terms discusses the vast potential and popularity of PACE (Cardwell, 2013). In line with the previous chapters, the following three case studies seek to delve into the details of these programs in order to gain an understanding of the performance prospects of this category.

1200 Buildings, Melbourne, Australia: Funds Are Not Attractive to Everyone

1200 Buildings aims to fund retrofits of two-thirds of buildings in Melbourne's central business district by 2020 — some twelve hundred buildings — and supports building owners in acquiring low-cost finance to do so. The program was developed by the City of Melbourne and implemented in 2010; it contributes to the city's larger ambition of becoming a world leader in urban sustainability. The program considers that existing buildings can easily reduce 38 percent of their energy consumption, giving the program a potential of reducing the city's emissions by 25 percent. When launched it was also expected to create eight hundred jobs and generate AU$1.3 billion in economic activity (Energy Efficiency Council, 2010).

The program resembles PACE in the United States, but was an Australian first: it provides the framework for a three-way agreement among a building owner, the City of Melbourne, and a finance provider. Under these agreements the property owner obtains funds from a finance provider and at the same time the city places a charge on the property this owner seeks to retrofit — comparable to a council rate or property tax. The rate is equal to the repayment associated with the funds provided. It is collected by the city and transferred to the finance provider. Because the charge rests on the land — and not the property owner — the loan is tied to the property. When the property goes on the market for sale, the current owner can pay out the loan in full or transfer it to the new owner (da Silva, 2011). Legislative change at state level was required to allow for this new charge: "Basically we eliminate the risks for banks so that they can lend money at lower rates," a City of Melbourne policy maker explained, "but it was very difficult to get the legislation changed" (int. 8). This process took more than two years and made officials in other cities initially look on the program as too complicated for implementation in their jurisdiction. In 2012 a senior policy maker in Brisbane explained, "We are interested in the program in Melbourne, but the

major challenge is the legislative change needed to establish the relationship and relations between the council, the bank, and the building
owner" (int. 27). By 2015, however, three other Australian states had
also passed legislation allowing for this type of environmental upgrade
financing for commercial building retrofits — New South Wales, South
Australia, and Western Australia.

Under 1200 Buildings building owners commit to using funds for
building retrofits that result in at least a 38 percent reduction of energy
consumption within five years of obtaining the funds. They are allowed
to share the costs of the loan with their tenants, but only if the latter
voluntarily agree to do so. This opens the way for building tenants to
discuss building upgrades with their landlords. In addition to these
funds, participants are provided with information on how to undertake
retrofits and are allowed to use the program's logo for marketing activities to indicate their leading performance in the Melbourne commercial
property market. At time of introduction the program was hailed as the
"holy grail to funding green retrofits" by an Australian property sector
website (Perinotto, 2010), and it won a prestigious C40 Cities Climate
Change Leadership Award in 2013 for being a world-leading governance
innovation for improved urban sustainability.[11] Yet, by 2015, halfway
through its lifetime, the program indicated difficulty in achieving its
expected outcomes; by then twenty-five property owners had committed
to retrofit a total of forty-two buildings under the program — or a mere
3.5 percent of the 1200 buildings it targets.[12] What can explain this low
participation in a program that provides many attractive incentives:
financial support, reputational benefits, and information on how to conduct retrofits?

The pivotal complication appears to be the participant base targeted:
approximately half of commercial property in Melbourne's central business district belongs to private owners — small and medium-sized firms
and individuals — and not large professional corporations (City of
Melbourne, 2013). "Private owners often do not have the corporate
structures and resources to research, facilitate and track building performance," the team leader of the program observed (quoted in: Aliento,
2014). They are often not aware of the energy performance of the
building or buildings they own and take a passive stance on building
energy performance. More than large firms, they consider building
energy retrofits as a sunk cost rather than an investment that might
generate a cash flow in the form of energy cost savings (Perinotto,
2014a). Also, the properties owned by these small and medium-sized
firms do not change ownership or tenancies frequently and therefore
remain unnoticed according to Australia's Building Energy Efficiency

Disclosure Act, which requires property owners to carry out building energy assessments when office space goes on the market for sale or lease (discussed in Chapter 4). An additional complication is that they predominantly own midtier buildings (referred to as B-grade in Australia: buildings smaller than ten thousand square meters). This type of buildings is not sought after by premium tenants, such as governmental agencies and corporate tenants, who normally require their landlords to provide them with high-performing office space — including high levels of built environment sustainability (City of Melbourne, 2013). As a result, their owners are not pressured by the tenant market to retrofit their buildings — and to participate in a program such as 1200 Buildings. In this regard their characteristics more closely resemble those of homeowners in how they address the sustainability performance of their property, rather than those of large firms.

Furthermore, the reputational benefits of the program are of little interest to small and medium-sized firms and individual commercial property owners. The vast majority of participants in the program are large corporate property owners and, comparable to the participants in Sydney's Better Building Partnership (see Chapter 5), they may feel peer pressure to retrofit their buildings. They all seek to attract premium tenants and, more importantly, they report to a larger stakeholder base. Participating in a program such as 1200 Buildings bolsters their image of social corporate responsibility. The program markets the significant benefits for participants exactly in these terms: "Improving corporate image," "Lower environmental footprint and greenhouse gas emissions," and "Making the building more attractive to investors."[13] The program does little, however, in marketing itself as an attractive opportunity for small and medium-sized firms and individual commercial property owners. A final and related complication is that the program administrators and private owners perceive the problem in radically divergent ways: where the program considers a retrofit a full-scale energy upgrade of a building that results in long-term gains, small firms and individual owners think of retrofitting as maintenance and repairing broken assets that are short-term costs (City of Melbourne, 2013). They see little justification for long-term investments in their property: "It's a long lag time," a program administrator stated; "it's about changing building owners' thinking in short-term benefits to thinking in long-term benefits" (int. 26). Strikingly, an administrator of a PACE program in San Francisco spoke of comparable experiences: "There is a demand problem. Although it is a very secure program, property owners do not prioritize [building retrofits] very much," he noted. "Initially the question was, Can we really get private financing for retrofitting buildings?

And the answer is yes. Now the question is: Can we get building owners to participate? We do not know. You can create a great program, but without customers it is not doing much. We need to find out the mindset of building owners" (int. 179).

Amsterdam Investment Fund: A Questionable Awardee

Of voluntary programs considered, the Amsterdam Investment Fund provides perhaps the most intriguing example of inappropriate overemphasis on leadership — and the risks that can accompany it. The fund was proposed in 2009 as a vehicle for investing income generated from selling bonds the city owned in a privatized electricity utility, worth €750 million. "The underlying idea of the fund was property for property," a fund administrator explained; "the money from the bonds has to be invested in local sustainability projects, in city development, and in projects that contribute to the local economy and Amsterdam's innovativeness" (int. 67). The Amsterdam City Council took up this idea and agreed on installing a €200 million revolving loan fund that would issue loans of at least €2.5 million to support building and city development projects that improve Amsterdam's economic competitiveness, urban sustainability, and social aspects (Teulings, 2013).

The fund differs from conventional revolving loan funds. Rather than functioning as self-managed funds, such as the fund established under the Billion Dollar Green Challenge, it operates as a market fund and seeks to make profit. The fund seeks to spur innovation, particularly in the area of urban sustainability. However, supporting innovative ideas requires risk, and not all funded projects might be able to pay back loans. To conserve the extent of this fund and thereby safeguard its continuance, it provides financial support both to low-risk, secure enterprises (80 percent) and in a smaller proportion (20 percent) to highly innovative projects with a lower likelihood of being able to repay loans. A criterion for funding (in both categories) is an expected return of at least 4.5 percent per year — this generates income to cover possible losses made in the second category. The same administrator explained: "The Fund Functions like any market fund. We are not supplying cheap loans or subsidies. Our idea is that projects need durable capital, not a cheap financial impulse" (int. 67).

The Fund has received international acclaim. In 2014 it received a prestigious C40 Cities Climate Leadership Award — a similar award was given to 1200 Buildings in 2013 (discussed previosuly). These awards seek, as explained on the C40 website, to "[reward] important, innovative policies and programmes that reduce emissions and improve sustainability" and to "recognize those successes, catalyze ambition, and share lessons with cities around the world."[14] The C40 Cities Climate Leadership Group was particularly positive about the fund because "in 2010, the Fund's investments helped Amsterdam achieve a 20% emission reduction as compared to 1990 levels," and "The response has been strong so far, and is expected to remain so in the future. A key outcome of the Fund is that both citizens and organisations are able to increase the energy efficiency of their homes/offices, and thereby gain protection against increasing energy bills."[15] This praise — and the media attention that accompanies it — is used by the City of Amsterdam to underline their leading position in the transition to low-carbon cities.[16] Strikingly, at the local level the fund has become a topic of much debate and criticism for not achieving expected results (Boonstra, 2013). How can a single program generate such opposing reactions?

A closer look at the program reveals that the C40 Group award was partly for anticipated outcomes rather than for results. A 2013 evaluation of the fund reveals considerable problems (Teulings, 2013): the City Council had extracted €90 million for investments in projects it considered societally relevant but that would not result in financial returns; it had allocated €45 million to launch another revolving loan fund, and had only invested some €19 million within the goals of the fund — less than 10 percent of the original funds allocated. The 2013 review also observed that the specific selection criteria for projects led to conflict in practice: by requiring a market return of at least 4.5 percent on investments, the fund placed innovative projects in a difficult position. The nature of an innovative solution is that it cannot normally guarantee a positive return. The fund has also been criticized because of the relatively large minimum size of the loans it has provided: a loan of €2.5 million or more is not suitable for small projects, which excludes firms and individuals who seek support for small projects from the fund. This issue was also mentioned as a limitation of the PACE program in San Francisco. While it is possible to issue small bonds for small retrofitting projects under PACE, these are not sought after by investors. Small bonds generate relatively high administration costs and minimal investor interest. "Investors only want to buy the 500,000 dollar bonds," a PACE administrator explained, "but there are many 100,000 dollar or smaller solar projects that need funding too" (int. 179).

Before the 2013 evaluation the fund was already subject to intense political debate in the Amsterdam City Council, with the opposition claiming that it was an unnecessarily convoluted instrument used to bankroll existing construction investments; that it was used to finance €1.2 million in administration costs for four years of nonproductivity;

and that the council ought instead to have invested in important social areas such as unemployment (van Zoelen, 2014). It used the fund and its lack of measurable outcomes as a means with which to attack the City Council and publicly question its capacity to govern (Boonstra, 2013). In response, the City Council continued its practice of using the fund for ulterior purposes, this time in the role of scapegoat: it announced that the model was flawed and determined to redesign it on the basis of the recent invaluable experience it provided (Amsterdam City Council, 2013). The redesign of the fund resulted in rebranding: since 2013 it has been the Amsterdam Energy Fund. It still consists of two parts, with 20 percent of the funds invested to yield "societal return." This component is administered by the City of Amsterdam and issues a wide range of loans for energy efficiency upgrades and local energy production as low as €5,000. The second 80 percent component (€45 million) is available for financially viable projects; it is referred to as the Amsterdam Climate and Energy Fund and is managed by private sector fund providers. It issues loans from €0.5 million to €5 million and requires a minimum return on investments of 7 percent. Management of the fund is outsourced for a number of reasons: "You need a specific type of person to work on this," an administrator of the fund explained; "it's no longer just opening the subsidy-tap, letting the money flow, and things will be OK. You need people who think commercially and it is hard to find those in a public organization" (int. 67). But this was not the only reason to involve private sector fund managers, he continued. By doing so the fund is placed at a distance from policy makers and politicians: "Initially, we faced a lot of politics. 'What is it you will do with the money? Is it your role as government to play bank? Are not you interfering with the market?' politicians asked. But the biggest challenge was to cut the fund loose from policy making," he concluded. "You do not want them to pick and choose projects. They live by the day" (int. 67).

With all this in mind it is striking that the C40 Climate Leadership Group awarded the fund a prestigious prize in 2014. When looking closely at the C40 Group's description of the fund it becomes clear, however, that they present a highly idealized appreciation of its performance. It refers to "a powerful financing instrument ... which has €75 million net worth," determining that "all businesses, residents, housing associations and community organisations are contributing toward reaching Amsterdam's 2040 energy goals," and that the fund had helped Amsterdam in achieving 20 percent reduction of 1990 emission levels by 2010. These claims are closer to wishful thinking than facts: in 2010 the fund was not yet operating, and by the time the C40 Group honored the fund with an award in 2014 it had already changed name, size, and focus;

had been the topic of fierce and ongoing political debate; and had only awarded 10 percent of initially reserved funds, making for a far less inspirational exemplar of "city leadership" than the version the fund presented on the C40 Group's website.

Small Business Improvement Fund, Chicago, United States: Borrowing from the Future

The Small Business Improvement Fund was implemented by the City of Chicago in 2000 — it stands out from the other programs studied in that, comparable to the certification and classification program NABERS (see Chapter 4), it combines aspects of mandatory and voluntary requirements. The program builds on tax increment financing, a public financing method applied throughout the United States (Baker, Cook, McCann, Temenos, & Ward, 2016; Squires & Lord, 2012; Weber, 2013). Tax increment financing uses future tax incomes to fund current improvements that are expected to result in yearly tax income increases. In a nutshell, a city government establishes a tax increment financing district by drawing a line around part of a city — for instance, around specific postal code zones. Property taxes for this area are frozen at a certain level that is capable of providing revenue for basic services, such as primary education or police services. Any tax revenue above this level is used to fund upgrades of the built environment within that tax increment financing zone — for instance, energy retrofits of buildings. A common assumption underlying tax increment financing is that these upgrades will result in higher tax revenues in the future because property in a well-maintained neighborhood might increase in value — property tax is often linked to property value. Tax increment financing allows city governments in the United States to issue bonds or borrow money to fund built environment upgrades, assuming that this future additional income in tax revenues is sufficient to repay the bonds or money borrowed. Typically, funds obtained are provided to property owners as a grant to finance their building upgrades.

In Chicago, the Small Business Improvement Fund is one of the vehicles used to use tax funds for supporting building retrofits and upgrades. Under the program rule-takers have to pay the initial costs of a retrofit, and if they meet program criteria they are reimbursed — but they can only apply for reimbursement of 25–75 percent of these costs. The choice not to fund projects fully was deliberately made: "People have to be able to pay for it in the first place themselves," a Small Business Improvement Fund administrator observed; "that makes them more conscious of how money is spent" (int. 185). Of course, the downside of this structure is that only those who are able to pay initial costs can use it — a conventional critique of traditional subsidies discussed in Chapter 2. To overcome this specific issue the fund supports prospective rule-takers in finding lenders to provide the initial costs. "The main program objective is keeping businesses in Chicago," the administrator explained. "The easy choice for them is moving out to the suburbs and gobbling up green fields — the harder choice is to stay and retrofit their buildings" (int. 185). It finances a wide range of building retrofits: from restoration of historic building facades to upgrading of building heating, ventilation, air-conditioning, and cooling systems. These are not required to meet a specific sustainable building performance goal, but over the years administrators have moved toward advising applicants to seek reductions of building-related resource consumption. The fund operates in partnership with a local electricity utility that operates a lighting retrofit program and a local gas utility that runs a heating system retrofitting program; it is also influenced by the larger built environment sustainability goals of the City of Chicago (see Chapter 5).

Tax increment financing is not without criticism. It may cause gentrification of city districts when property prices rise so much that existing businesses and residents can no longer pay the housing costs. It may indirectly drain tax revenues from schools and other public services by attracting new residents and businesses that increase demands for these public services. And it may politicize and skew the allocation of funds in favor of larger firms, particularly because aldermen normally retain a large say in who is awarded the funding. They are likely to favor larger firms as they provide jobs and add to the economic viability of a district — of course, there also is a likelihood that large firms are more capable of influencing council representatives than are small firms and residents (Lefcoe, 2011; Pacewicz, 2013). The Small Business Improvement Fund was implemented specifically to overcome large-firm favoritism (NCBG, 2003). When tax increment financing was introduced in Chicago funds tended to flow to the larger firms: "They had all kinds of lawyers that specialized in getting these funds," explained the administrator, "and small firms got upset. They felt they were paying into a pool of money, but that they did not get anything from it" (int. 185). Here smaller firms were considered those with less than 100 full-time staff and a maximum of U.S.$5 million in gross sales (special rules apply to new firms, and landlords and tenants). To ensure the apolitical allocation of funds, administration was outsourced to a nonprofit development firm.

To obtain funding, prospective rule-takers lodge a retrofitting or upgrade proposal with the fund administrator. They are strongly advised to consult administrators, who strongly encourage ambitious sustainable building improvements, about proposals. Upon submission administrators assess applications against the fund's eligibility criteria. If eligible, they are placed on a waiting list and awarded financial support when it becomes available. If there is more demand than supply in a district, then a lottery is held to determine resource allocation. Those not awarded through lottery are placed on a waiting list for the next round of funding. By 2015, the fund had issued some sixteen hundred grants with an average value of U.S.$42,000, and data indicate that over the years funds are increasingly issued for building energy upgrades. The fund differs from most other programs, not only in that it combines aspects of mandatory and voluntary requirements — paying property tax is mandatory; applying for funds is voluntary — it also differs from these in that it does not seek to reward leadership. The sustainable building retrofits and upgrades proposed and supported generally focus on well-trialed technologies such as energy efficient lighting or solar panels. The overall impact of the program is limited in terms of reducing Chicago's building-related carbon emissions: it covers 104 tax increment financing districts, indicating that the sixteen hundred grants are thinly spread. Even in a large district such as Hollywood/Sheridan, which encompasses forty-four city blocks of residential and commercial buildings, at best four relatively minor building upgrades are funded annually.[17]

Significant Findings

This third empirical chapter largely confirms the findings of the previous two: voluntary programs for sustainable buildings generally attract little interest from the pool of prospective rule-takers they target and do not incentivize them to make substantial improvements to buildings or the ways they are used. In what follows the significant findings from this part of the study are considered.

Limited Interest from Prospective Rule-Takers

The funding programs studied are sobering: they indicate that even when property developers or owners are given relatively easy access to financing for sustainable building development or retrofitting, they do not line up in great numbers. Environmental upgrade financing programs, such as PACE in the United States and 1200 Buildings in Melbourne, have only attracted a marginal number of the pool of prospective rule-takers they target. Energy efficiency mortgages are rarely sought by (prospective)

homeowners in the United States and the Netherlands. Only a small
number of local architects and property developers participated in competitions for funding, such as E$^+$ Green Building in Boston, the Sustainable Development Grant in the city of Brisbane, and the Building
Innovation Fund in the state of South Australia. Similarly, the fifty
universities and colleges that participate in the Billion Dollar Green
Challenge represent a mere 1 percent of the five thousand universities
and colleges in the United States.[18]

What explains this lack of interest? In part this might again be
explained by the enduring fixation on fostering industry leadership. With
the exception of the Small Business Improvement Fund and energy
efficiency mortgages, all programs studied build on a narrative of leadership. However, as explained in the conclusion to Chapter 5, the leadership narrative may not resonate with all prospective rule-takers. This
issue is best illustrated by 1200 Buildings in Melbourne, where program
administrators have come to realize that the opportunity to engage
directly with the city government and be recognized for leadership is
attractive to major property owners, but not to small and medium-sized
firms and individual property owners. They do not maintain an image of
corporate responsibility, and they are not required to account for their
environmental sustainability performance to stakeholders and investors.
For small business and individual owners the competitive advantage of
retrofitting their buildings might be of less value than for large property
owners. Small firms and owners often occupy their own buildings or
enter into long-term leases with their tenants. They are simply not in the
market for premium tenants such as governmental agencies and large
corporations, which typically seek sustainable office space.

A further related explanation for this lack of interest is that the programs studied fail to address the problems of hyperbolic discounting
and split incentives. As explained earlier (see Chapter 2), hyperbolic
discounting refers to the tendency of individuals and organizations to
discount the long-term financial gains deriving from investment in building upgrades; the split incentive problem describes the situation in which
the current building owner or landlord who bears the cost of a building
upgrade does not receive the financial benefits of it, which instead accrue
to a future building owner or a tenant. Again, both problems are illustrated by 1200 Buildings in Melbourne. Seeking to overcome these
problems, its administrators have gradually redesigned the program. In
particular, the program's website now resembles that of the Better
Buildings Partnership in Sydney (see Chapter 5): it now provides information about how to obtain funding for retrofits and includes case
studies, best practice, and lessons learned by current rule-takers that

inform prospective rule-takers about the broader advantages of the program. In addition, so explained an administrator, the program seeks to build bridges with other programs to help overcome the split incentive problem: "We are now more and more interacting with CitySwitch [an information generation and sharing program for office tenants in Australia; see Chapter 5]. If we have one or more CitySwitch signatories in a [potential 1200 Buildings] building then we try to establish that link. We try to connect the two [landlord and tenant], so that they can inform each other on how to move further" (int. 26).

Public Funds, Politics, and Equality

"Money makes things more real" (int. 70), a senior sustainable building consultant in the Netherlands explained regarding the loss of interest in voluntary programs when confronted by the cost of sustainability solutions. Money makes matters more political also, as this research has illustrated. The Amsterdam Energy Fund attracted considerable censure from policy makers and politicians who maintained the funds could be better used for alternative policy goals. As the administrator of the fund explained, one of the major complications in its establishment was the realized need to distance it from policy makers and politicians. This choice has, however, not only given some politicians ammunition with which to disparage the fund and those who introduced it, but also provided those in power the means with which to capitalize on the rhetoric of environmental sustainability — however briefly — while pursuing a conventional planning agenda. Further to this, it appears that the adoption of financial risk by governments for voluntary programs returns these programs to the realm of traditional governance that subjects funding and accountability to interminable political debate and public furor — problems that voluntary programs are frequently expected to overcome (see Chapter 3). Programs such as 1200 Buildings in Melbourne and PACE in the United States, for example, require legislative changes that allow local governments to take the risk of borrowing money or issuing bonds to support rule-takers in retrofitting their buildings. These are slow and lengthy processes, considered by some policy makers interviewed as too much trouble to implement in their own jurisdiction.

Another complication of voluntary programs that rely on public funds in this category is the tension between the strong discrimination of awarding prospective rule-takers with funds and the source of that funding. The Small Business Improvement Fund in Chicago illustrates this complication: it was established to overcome inequalities in the allocation of tax increment financing, which prior to introduction of this

Amsterdam Energy fund was largely awarded to major firms because they could afford submission specialists and they could more easily influence council representatives. Interviewees did not point out similar processes in the other programs studied, but one can imagine that the owner of the City of Amsterdam's flagship soccer stadium — the Amsterdam ArenA, which was supported with a €1.6 million loan by the Amsterdam Energy fund[19] — has more access to professional support in applying for funding than has the amateur soccer team just down the street from it. If not designed or managed well, programs like these can use public funds to increase inequality.

Borrowing from the Future

A final complication of these programs worth highlighting is the risk inherent in their underlying strategy — borrowing from the future. Most programs discussed in this chapter expect that projects that are awarded funds will produce means of repaying those funds in the future because their energy or other resource reductions save them costs. This expectation is, however, made under the assumption that the costs of energy or other resource consumption will not alter significantly and, more problematically, that once a building upgrade is carried out a rule-taker will not increase initial energy use. There is considerable evidence of rebound effects among building users after upgrades or retrofits have been carried out (see Chapter 2). Most of the studied programs assume, further, that building upgrades or retrofits are carried out as proposed in the funding process. A design for a sustainable building or even a constructed or retrofitted sustainable building might not achieve its expected energy reductions simply because contractors can make mistakes or institute cheaper shortcuts in carrying out the work that are unnoticed (see Chapter 4). In sum, these programs build their expectations of future financial returns on three assumptions concerning the future: stable energy prices, stable relative energy use, and proper construction work. Fluctuation in any of these factors will negatively affect the ability of rule-takers to repay funds provided — which is indeed one of the motivations for banks to be hesitant in supporting energy efficiency mortgages. A related risk of these programs is that they may add to the already considerable financial debts of cities and nations if rule-takers are not capable of repaying loans.

7 Separating the Wheat from the Chaff

A Crisp-Set Qualitative Comparative Analysis (csQCA)

"Are these [voluntary programs] the silver bullet?" a policy maker in Sydney questioned when I interviewed him in 2012. He answered his own question immediately: "Probably not. But it is just another angle I think we have to try out and we will see the results over the next few years" (int. 42). The previous three empirical chapters largely confirm his expectation that voluntary programs for sustainable buildings are not the silver bullet when it comes to accelerating decarbonization of the built environment. To recap these chapters, Table 7.1 offers an overview of the performance of the programs studied — where possible it provides quantitative data; where not, it provides qualitative descriptors.

The picture presented in Table 7.1 is consistent, but not encouraging. The twenty-six programs studied highlight that rule-takers have little interest in these programs, and that the programs' contribution to reducing building-related resource consumption (predominantly energy consumption during operation) or carbon emissions is minimal. The programs experience most interest in the area of new office buildings in the central business districts of major cities. These buildings are normally occupied (owned or rented) by major firms and government agencies that require sustainable building space. Smaller firms and occupants of residential property are less interested in sustainable buildings, interviewees explained time and again. "Look, the commercial market has been hit and it has taken less than ten years," a building sustainability expert at a major Australian consultancy firm explained. "But this does not relate to the residential market or the small firms. In the commercial market sustainable building is seen as creating value, and as necessary to compete on a level where other people do this too. The residential buildings and mixed-used buildings are different. People do not want to pay for it there" (int. 23). They further highlighted that voluntary programs have not yet been able to generate much interest among owners and occupants of existing buildings. "What you see now is a flight from existing buildings to new sustainable buildings," a manager at a major Australian property investment firm observed. "But what do you do with the

Table 7.1 *Summary of Voluntary Programs Studied in This Book*

Name (Year of Introduction)	Participating Rule-Takers Relative to Pool of Prospective Rule-Takers	Average Reductions by Rule-Takers	Reductions in Perspective
1200 Buildings (2010)	4 percent	Unknown (too few buildings retrofitted yet)	Insignificant*† compared to Melbourne's commercial building energy consumption
Additional credit for energy efficient homes (2012)	Less than 1 percent	Unknown (too few houses constructed or retrofitted)	Insignificant compared to the Netherlands' residential building energy consumption
Amsterdam Investment Fund (2011)	Less than 5 percent (handful of projects funded)	Unknown (too few buildings retrofitted yet)	Marginal contribution to the city of Amsterdam's ambition of 20 percent carbon reductions by 2020
Better Buildings Challenge (2011)	Less than 1 percent (representing 4 percent of commercial building space)	2 percent (with a quarter of participants having achieved at least 10 percent)	Less than 0.5 percent of commercial building energy consumption in the United States
Better Buildings Partnership (2011)	100 percent (all fourteen initially targeted rule-takers)	35 percent (on track to reach 70 percent by 2020)	Applies to Sydney's central business district only; larger Sydney metropolitan area 500 times larger
Billion Dollar Green Challenge (2011)	1 percent	More than 20 percent	Insignificant compared to energy consumption of U.S. educational facilities
BREEAM-NL (2009)	45 percent (of future commercial buildings)	More than 20 percent (but paper performance)**	Possible meaningful contribution, but risk that buildings do not perform as certified once built
Building Innovation Fund (2008)	Less than 2 percent †	More than 20 percent	Insignificant compared to Adelaide's commercial building energy consumption

Table 7.1 (*cont.*)

Name (Year of Introduction)	Participating Rule-Takers Relative to Pool of Prospective Rule-Takers	Average Reductions by Rule-Takers	Reductions in Perspective
Chicago Green Office Challenge (2008)	Less than 1 percent	Less than 10 percent	Insignificant compared to Chicago's commercial building energy consumption
CitySwitch Green Office (2010)	6 percent	13–16 percent	Less than 1 percent of office building energy consumption in Australia in 2011
E⁺ Green Building (2011)	Less than 2 percent[†]	More than 20 percent	Insignificant compared to Boston's residential building energy consumption
Energy Efficient Mortgage (1995)	Less than 1 percent	Unknown (no data available)	Insignificant compared to U.S. residential building energy consumption
Energiesprong (2010)	Unknown (no data available)	Unknown (no data available)	Unknown
Energy Star Building (1999)	3 percent	More than 20 percent (but paper performance)**	Less than 1 percent of U.S. residential building energy consumption
Energy Star for Homes (1999)	7 percent	More than 20 percent (but paper performance)**	Approximately 1.5 percent of U.S. commercial building energy consumption
EnviroDevelopment (2006)	6 percent (of new residential buildings)	More than 20 percent	Approximately 1 percent of Australian residential building energy consumption
Environmental Upgrade Agreements (2011)	Less than 1 percent	Unknown (too few buildings retrofitted yet)	Insignificant compared to state of New South Wales commercial building energy consumption
Green Deals (2011)	Unknown (no data available)	Unknown (no data available)	Unknown
Green Star (2003)	18 percent (of new office buildings)	More than 20 percent (but paper performance)**	Approximately 4 percent of Australian office building energy consumption

Table 7.1 (*cont.*)

Name (Year of Introduction)	Participating Rule-Takers Relative to Pool of Prospective Rule-Takers	Average Reductions by Rule-Takers	Reductions in Perspective
LEED (2000)	3 percent (of new office buildings)	More than 20 percent (but paper performance)**	Approximately 0.5 percent of U.S. commercial building energy consumption
NABERS (1998)	77 percent	More than 20 percent	Approximately 15 percent of Australian office building energy consumption
PACE (2008)	Less than 1 percent (of commercial property)	62 percent	Insignificant compared to U.S. commercial building energy consumption
Retrofit Chicago (2012)	More than 5 percent (of major office buildings)	7 percent	Approximately 1.5 percent of Chicago's office building energy consumption
Small Business Improvement Fund (2000)	Less than 5 percent	Less than 20 percent	Insignificant compared to Chicago's commercial building energy consumption
Sustainable Development Grant (2007)	Less than 2 percent†	More than 20 percent	Insignificant compared to Brisbane's commercial building energy consumption
Zonnig Huren (2012)	Less than 2 percent	More than 20 percent	Insignificant compared to Netherlands residential building energy consumption

Notes: * The qualitative descriptor "insignificant" indicates a maximum of 0.5 percent.
** The term "paper performance" indicates that these are expected reductions, not observed reductions; for example, most certification and classification programs studied have issued certificates for the design of a building and not the performance of a building in operation (see Chapter 4).
† The number of rule-takers as part of possible participants applying for funds or participating in the competition.
Abbreviations: BREEAM-NL = Dutch application of BRE Environmental Assessment Method; LEED = Leadership in Energy and Environmental Design; NABERS = National Australian Built Environment Rating System; PACE = Property Assessed Clean Energy.

existing buildings? That's a question the industry is struggling with. Retrofitting is a tough job" (int. 53).

Although the results in Table 7.1 are almost identically feeble, the previous chapters do not immediately indicate a single condition or obvious set of conditions that explains why these programs perform so poorly as an approach to decarbonizing the built environment. This chapter collects the empirical findings and contrasts them with the theoretical template outlined in Chapter 3. It moves beyond the individual cases and categories discussed in the earlier chapters, seeking to draw lessons from cross-case comparisons of the full set of cases studied. Such broader insight is necessary if we are to understand the value and potential of voluntary programs for sustainable building and city development — the goal is that this synthesis will not merely complement existing understanding, but rather resituate and reform our approaches to achieving desirable, sustainable societal outcomes.

Bringing It All Together

Of the programs discussed, what common factor performs well in attracting rule-takers? What unites the programs under which rule-takers have made meaningful reductions in their building-related resource consumption or carbon emissions? Similarly, what is common to those that do not achieve these desired outcomes? To answer these questions a benchmark needs to be set to distinguish the more promising programs from the less promising ones. Throughout the book it has been emphasized that existing buildings hold huge potential for improved resource efficiency and reduced carbon emissions, and that technology and insights on behavioral change are available to construct new buildings or retrofit existing ones — at net cost benefit — that are 30–80 percent less resource and carbon intensive than conventional ones. But what can reasonably be expected from voluntary programs in attracting rule-takers and improving their behavior?

The literature on voluntary programs is well aware that they can amount to window dressing or greenwash if they do not require meaningful improvements, or they may be used to create the illusion of addressing societal or environmental problems (Giddens, 2009; Wood, 2003). Such insights, combined with the potential of buildings for improvement, make it tempting to set an ambitious benchmark for separating the wheat from the chaff in the voluntary programs studied. Nonetheless, another perspective present in the literature argues we should not be too harsh in evaluating voluntary programs, their rule-makers, and their rule-takers: voluntary programs function as modest additions to mandatory governance instruments, not as replacements of these (Berliner & Prakash, 2014; Coglianese & Nash, 2014). To distinguish the more promising programs from the less promising ones studied in this book, I therefore use benchmarks that seek a happy medium between often-low mandatory requirements for sustainable buildings and the high potential that today's buildings and those of the future hold for decarbonizing the built environment, combined with empirical data from the full set of programs studied.[1]

With this in mind, in what follows I consider a program that is promising in attracting rule-takers within the full set studied if at least 15 percent of the full pool of prospective rule-takers have joined the program after a period of ten years — or are on track to achieving it.[2] This number broadly corresponds with the coverage of an innovation that is assumed necessary for it to have the potential to become considered mainstream — it corresponds with the leaders and early adopters in a market (Moore, 2002; E. M. Rogers, 1995). In interviews rule-makers concurred that they target specifically these two groups. "When we developed the instrument we became aware there were two groups interested in it," an administrator of one of the Australian certification and classification programs observed. "Those that were already doing leading stuff in terms of sustainable buildings but had no means to market it, and those who thought sustainable buildings are a good idea but had no clue of how to go about it. And so the program was developed" (int. 30). Similarly, a policy maker in New York explained: "We try to capture the early adopters in the sector. Timewise it is not effective to do otherwise. They motivate the others. If we can engage with them we can understand our audience and then move further. It is much easier if you first have ten large firms and then go to the next and say: 'Look, we have these ten; why are you not doing anything?'"(int. 195).

Within the full set of programs studied, I then consider a program that is promising in improving its rule-takers' behavior if these reduce their building-related resource consumption or carbon emissions by 20 percent over a period of ten years. While this number is relatively low in comparison to possible reductions in the construction and property sectors (see Chapter 2), it corresponds with a yearly reduction of 2 percent, reflecting the median yearly reduction of the programs studied. It corresponds further with built environment—related energy consumption and carbon emission reduction ambitions for 2020 and beyond, as expressed by national governments in the Netherlands and United States during the period of study (see Appendix A). In other words, within the full set of programs studied, the 20 percent benchmark makes for a meaningful crossover point with which to distinguish the programs with performance potential from those with little or none (Ragin, 2008; Rihoux & Ragin, 2009; Schneider & Wagemann, 2012). A 20 percent reduction of building-related resource consumption or carbon emissions over a ten-year period is not sufficient to address the sustainable building challenge faced, however (as discussed in Chapter 2). Throughout this study I have provided examples of successful attainment of worthwhile targets within short time frames and with the use of prevailing conventional solutions.

In what follows, crisp set qualitative comparative analysis (csQCA) is carried out to cluster the programs in terms of more and less promising performance, based on these two benchmarks. The process of this analysis was explained in Chapter 1, but some further explanation is required here for those unfamiliar with the method (see also Appendix C). As its starting point QCA expects that conditions (rules, enforcement, rewards of voluntary programs, the involvement of local governments, and the type of diffusion networks) interact in causing outcomes (the number of rule-takers in a program and their performance). It further assumes that different types of combinations of interacting conditions may result in similar outcomes. The first assumption is referred to as conjunctural causation, the second as equifinality. Within QCA, types of interacting conditions are referred to as "paths," and a full typology is referred to as a "solution." A "consistency score" indicates how well a path and the full solution reflect the data; a "coverage score" indicates how many of the data are explained by the paths and solution uncovered. In QCA, associations between conditions and outcomes are expressed in terms of necessity and sufficiency. Necessity refers to a situation in which the outcome (the number of rule-takers in a program and their performance) cannot be produced without the condition (such as the rules, enforcement, and rewards of voluntary programs; the involvement of local governments; and the type of diffusion networks): if the outcome is present, the condition is present. Sufficiency refers to a situation in which a condition itself can produce the outcome without the help of other conditions — humans need oxygen to sustain life (oxygen is a necessary condition for human life), but oxygen by itself is not sufficient to sustain life (food and water, for instance, are other necessary conditions).

Analyzing the Programs Further

An essential step in QCA is data calibration. Data are calibrated to correspond with Boolean algebra and logic simplification. Table 7.2 presents the programs studied as calibrated data sets. Note that the numerical information provided throughout this chapter is a description

Table 1.2 *Observed Conditions and Outcomes (Raw Data Matrix)*

Program Name	Conditions							Outcomes	
	Rules	Enforcement	Financial Rewards	Non-Financial Rewards	Leadership Rewards	Local Government as Rule-Maker	Diffusion Network	Attracting Rule-Takers (15 percent)	Improved Rule-Taker Behaviour (20 percent)
1200 Buildings	1	1	1	0	1	1	0	0	?
Additional credit for energy efficient homes	1	0	1	0	0	0	0	0	?
Amsterdam Investment Fund	0	1	1	0	1	1	0	0	?
Better Buildings Challenge	1	1	1	1	1	0	0	0	0
Better Buildings Partnership	1	1	1	1	1	1	1	1	1
Billion Dollar Green Challenge	0	0	1	1	1	0	0	0	1
BREEAM-NL (commercial)	0	1	1	0	0	0	1	1	1
Building Innovation Fund	0	0	1	0	1	1	0	0	1
Chicago Green Office Challenge	1	1	0	1	1	1	0	0	0
CitySwitch Green Office	1	0	0	1	1	1	0	0	1
E+ Green Building	1	1	0	0	1	1	0	0	1
Energy Efficient Mortgage	0	1	1	0	0	0	0	0	?
Energiesprong	1	0	0	1	0	0	0	?	?
Energy Star Building	1	1	1	0	0	0	0	0	1

143

Table 7.2 (*cont.*)

Program Name	Conditions							Outcomes	
	Rules	Enforcement	Financial Rewards	Non-Financial Rewards	Leadership Rewards	Local Government as Rule-Maker	Diffusion Network	Attracting Rule-Takers (15 percent)	Improved Rule-Taker Behaviour (20 percent)
Energy Star for Homes	1	1	1	0	0	0	0	0	1
EnviroDevelopment	1	1	1	0	0	0	0	0	1
Environmental Upgrade Agreements	1	0	1	0	0	1	0	0	?
Green Deals	1	0	1	0	1	0	0	?	?
Green Star (offices)	0	1	1	0	1	0	1	1	1
LEED (commercial)	0	1	1	0	1	0	0	0	1
NABERS (offices)	0	1	1	0	0	0	1	1	1
PACE	1	1	1	0	1	1	0	0	1
Retrofit Chicago (major office buildings)	1	1	0	0	1	1	1	0	1
Small Business Improvement Fund	1	0	1	0	0	1	0	0	0
Sustainable Development Grant	1	1	1	0	0	1	0	0	1
Zonnig Huren	1	1	1	1	0	0	1	0	1

Notes: Codes: 0 and 1 are explained in what follows; ? = no reliable data, or no data

Source: Appendix B (Voluntary Program Snapshots).

144

of data patterns that underlie the data set, not simplistic reductions of the qualitative data obtained and discussed in the previous chapters — QCA uses numerical symbols, but it is a qualitative method. The conditions in Table 7.2 relate directly to the theoretical template presented in Chapter 3 — they are expected to affect the performance of the programs studied. To recapitulate, the model of analysis for this research has inherited three main conditions from the club theory perspective: "rules," "enforcement," and "rewards." From the previous three empirical chapters it has become clear that rewards exist in various forms, and for the analyses I distinguish "financial rewards," "nonfinancial rewards," and "leadership rewards." From the urban transformation literature the "involvement of local government" as rule-maker was adopted as a relevant condition, and the diffusion of innovations literature contributed the "diffusion network" as a condition capable of explaining the performance of voluntary programs. The outcomes of interest are the two performance indicators discussed previously.

In terms of calibration of conditions, for rules, a score of 1 indicates that a program requires its rule-takers to achieve at least a 20 percent reduction of their building-related resources or carbon emissions over a ten-year period. A score of 0 indicates that such a requirement is not stated. NABERS, for example, does not require this performance, but on average its rule-takers do achieve it. The Better Buildings Challenge is an example of the opposite. For enforcement, a score of 1 indicates stringent enforcement of these rules, considered as third-party enforcement or enforcement based on the performance data of a building obtained when in use. This accords with the literature on voluntary programs, discussed in Chapter 3, as well as with the empirical observations in the earlier chapters. A score of 0 indicates more lenient forms of enforcement, such as self-reporting or administrator assessment. CitySwitch Green Office is illustrative of the risk of administrator assessment, which has been expressed in the broader literature: administrators often have incentives to ignore noncompliance. Further, Chapter 4 discussed the relevance of using ex-post rather than ex-ante performance data: even under a condition of third-party enforcement such as in LEED, certified building designs that comply with program rules may not perform as such once built and in operation. As was illustrated in Chapter 2, it is particularly difficult to evaluate whether or not a building will meet requirements — mandatory or voluntary — once completed. Certification and classification programs that mainly rely on third-party enforcement as opposed to enforcement based on ex-post data are therefore excluded from the assessment of common factors for the programs by which rule-takers have made meaningful reductions in resource consumption or carbon emissions.

Calibration of the other conditions is straightforward: for financial rewards, a score of 1 indicates that rule-takers are assured of gaining financial rewards from committing to a program, whether through reduced operation costs or higher sales or rental prices of their property; a score of 0 indicates no assurance of financial reward. For nonfinancial rewards, a score of 1 indicates that rule-takers are assured of receiving other rewards by committing to a program, such as information on sustainable building development or use; a score of 0 indicates no such rewards. For leadership, a score of 1 indicates commitment to a program is considered a means to showcase leadership in the construction or property sector; a score of 0 indicates that committing to a program is not considered to allow for showcasing such leadership. For local government, a score of 1 indicates that local government is involved in the program as rule-maker, and a score of 0 indicates it is not. For the diffusion network, finally, a score of 1 indicates a network that makes it likely that a prospective rule-taker is frequently exposed to a voluntary program (e.g., a relatively small group of frequently interacting prospective rule-takers, or an authoritative industry body supporting the program; see Chapter 3); a score of 0 indicates a network that makes it less likely that a prospective rule-taker is frequently exposed to the program. All causal assumptions and causal directions are based on the literature discussed in Chapter 3.

The two performance indicators relate to the earlier discussion: A score of 1 indicates that a program has attracted 15 percent of the full pool of prospective rule-takers it targets over a ten-year period; a score of 0 indicates it has not. Likewise, a score of 1 indicates that rule-takers have reduced their building-related resource consumption by 20 percent over a ten-year period, while a score of 0 indicates they have not. Programs younger than ten years were treated as indicated before. Finally, a question mark indicates that no reliable data are available for the programs studied that allow for inclusion of that program in the following analyses.

What Attracts Rule-Takers?

To understand what attracts rule-takers to the programs studied, the data are first analyzed for necessary conditions before they are exposed to more complex analysis to identify configurations of sufficient conditions. A test for necessity seeks to understand whether the outcome of interest can only be produced if a specific condition or combination of conditions is present. Table 7.3 displays the results of the analysis for necessity.

Conditions should only be considered necessary if their consistency scores are very high (consistency indicates how strongly the condition

Table 7.3 *Necessary Conditions for Attracting Rule-Takers*

Conditions	Consistency Score	Coverage Score
Stringent rules	0.25	0.06
Stringent enforcement	1.00	0.24
Assured financial rewards	1.00	0.20
Nonfinancial rewards	0.25	0.17
Leadership rewards	0.50	0.15
Local government involvement	0.25	0.08
Positive impact of diffusion network	1.00	0.67

relates to the performance outcome); a cutoff point of 0.90 is advised (Rihoux & Ragin, 2009, 45). Table 7.3 points to three such conditions: "stringent enforcement," "assured financial rewards," and "positive impact of diffusion network." The low coverage scores for "stringent enforcement" and "assured financial rewards" indicate that these are likely to be trivial necessary conditions (Schneider & Wagemann, 2012). The high coverage score of "positive impact of diffusion network" indicates that it plays a relevant role in explaining why prospective rule-takers join a voluntary program. To understand whether and how conditions interact (conjunctural causation) and whether there are one or more types of interacting conditions related to this specific performance outcome (equifinality), an analysis for sufficient conditions is conducted next.

To gain insight into the issues of equifinality and conjunctural causation, the data are analyzed logically to reduce the empirically observed configurations (Rihoux & Ragin, 2009, chapter 5, box 8.1; Schneider & Wagemann, 2012, chapter 11). A first step in this analysis is to create a truth table; the truth table for this part of the study is represented in Table 7.4.

The truth table depicts all configurations of conditions that are logically possible. With the seven conditions included in this study, the number of logically possible combinations is 128 (2^7). All 24 empirical observations with an observed outcome on the performance indicator (attracting rule-takers) are included in this table (rows 1–19) — each observation is unpacked as a configuration of conditions. For example, the first row represents voluntary programs with lenient rules (a score of 0), stringent enforcement (1), assured financial rewards for rule-takers (1), no nonfinancial rewards for rule-takers (0), no leadership rewards for rule-takers (0), no local government involvement (0), a diffusion network that likely exposes prospective rule-takers to the program frequently (1),

Table 7.4 *Truth Table for Attracting Rule-Takers*

	Conditions							Outcomes	
Row	Rules	Enforcement	Financial Rewards	Nonfinancial Rewards	Leadership Rewards	Local Government as Rule-Maker	Diffusion Network	Frequency	Attracting Rule-Takers
1	0	1	1	0	0	0	1	2	1
2	0	1	1	0	1	0	1	1	1
3	1	1	1	1	1	1	1	1	1
4	1	1	1	0	0	0	0	3	0
5	1	0	1	0	1	1	0	2	0
6	1	1	1	0	1	1	0	2	0
7	0	0	1	1	1	1	0	1	0
8	0	1	1	0	1	0	0	1	0
9	0	0	1	0	0	0	0	1	0
10	0	1	1	0	1	0	0	1	0
11	0	1	1	1	1	1	1	1	0
12	1	0	0	0	1	1	0	1	0
13	1	0	1	0	1	1	1	1	0
14	1	0	0	1	1	0	0	1	0
15	1	1	1	0	0	0	0	1	0
16	1	1	1	1	1	1	0	1	0
17	1	1	1	1	1	1	0	1	0
18	1	1	1	1	0	1	1	1	0
19	1	1	1	1	1	0	0	1	0

Rows 20–128: Logical remainders

148

Table 7.5 *Intermediate Solution for Attracting Rule-Takers*

		Coverage			
Solution	Formula	Raw	Unique	Consistency	Programs
Path RT.1	rule*ENF*FIN*NETW	0.75	0.75	1.00	BREEAM-NL, Green Star, NABERS
Path RT.2	ENF*FIN* NON- FIN*LEAD*LG*NETW	0.25	0.25	1.00	Better Buildings Partnership
Solution coverage: 1.00					
Solution consistency: 1.00					

Note: Uppercase indicates the condition is present; lowercase indicates the condition is absent Abbreviations: Rule = rules (sustainable building requirements); Enf = enforcement of rules; Fin = assured financial rewards for rule-takers; Non-fin = nonfinancial rewards for rule-takers (e.g., information); Lead = possibility to showcase leadership in the construction or property sector for rule-takers; LG = local government as rule-maker; Netw = positive impact of diffusion network; * = logical AND

and a program that has attracted at least 15 percent of the full pool of targeted rule-takers (1). The frequency score indicates that two programs meet these conditions: BREEAM in the Netherlands and NABERS in Australia. The truth table also includes possible configurations, but without empirical observations — the logical remainders in rows 20 to 128.

The truth table is used to enable logical minimization of the data. Following Ragin (2008), all empirical observations are considered in the analysis (also, Schneider & Wagemann, 2012). From here on, standard analysis is carried out in FS/QCA 2.5 (version 2.5; www.compasss.org; Ragin & Davey, 2014). Table 7.5 represents the intermediate solution resulting from this analysis. An intermediate solution includes counterfactuals in the minimization process. I use counterfactuals for all conditions, following the method discussed in Chapter 3: if a condition is present, a positive relation with the performance is expected. However, counterfactuals are not included for "rules" and "enforcement" as the literature was found to conflict on these two conditions — for these I rely on empirical observation only.

Table 7.5 adopts a straightforward notation and presentation of causal configurations ("paths") that are sufficient to cause the outcome of interest (attracting rule-takers) — uppercase script indicates the condition is present and lowercase script indicates the condition is absent in a causal configuration. It designates two configurations as related to attracting at least 15 percent of the pool of prospective rule-takers (path RT.1 and path RT.2). The solution coverage (1.00) is high (Ragin, 2008), indicating that the solution strongly relates to the outcome observed (see further Schneider & Wagemann, 2012, section 5.3). The solution consistency (1.00) is high as well, indicating that the solution is of high empirical importance in reaching the outcome. The paths can be considered as two causal recipes that are individually sufficient to cause the outcome. Because some conditions recur in the various paths, the full solution can be formulated as:

$$
\text{Attracting rule-takers} \rightarrow ENF*NETW*FIN
\begin{cases}
\text{rule} \\
+ \\
NON\text{-}FIN*LEAD*LG
\end{cases}
\tag{7.1}
$$

In this equation, the multiplication symbol (*) represents the logical AND, and the sum symbol (+) represents the logical OR; again, upper-case script indicates the condition is present and lowercase script indicates the condition is absent in a causal configuration. The preceding equation (1) can be read as: voluntary programs that have attracted 15 percent or more of the full pool of rule-takers they target over a ten-year period, or are on track to doing so, are characterized by:

- Stringent enforcement, a diffusion network that likely exposes prospective rule-takers frequently to the program, assured financial rewards for rule-takers, and lenient rules (path RT.1); or,
- Stringent enforcement, a diffusion network that likely exposes prospective rule-takers frequently to the program, assured financial rewards for rule-takers, nonfinancial rewards for rule-takers, leadership rewards for rule-takers, and local government involvement (path RT.2).

Some Observations

The preceding equation (1) indicates both conjunctural causation (different conditions interact in causing the performance outcome) and equifinality (different configurations of conditions result in the same performance outcome).[3] Perhaps more striking is that in all three programs that indicate promising performance, stringent enforcement is a necessary condition, but it nonetheless plays a small part in explaining the outcome (it is an INUS condition — an insufficient but necessary part of an unnecessary but sufficient condition) resulting from the analysis of necessary conditions (Table 7.3). Clearly, these stringent requirements did not deter rule-takers from joining the programs.

In all paths the assurance of financial reward was, however, found to be a necessary condition for prospective participants to commit to a program. Yet, comparable to stringent enforcement, it is an INUS condition and plays a small part in explaining the outcome. Other rewards appear relevant as well. Indeed, while many interviewees observed that financial rewards are attractive for prospective rule-takers, they also indicated that they may not be attractive enough. "Keep in mind that here in the U.S. the cost of energy is about five dollars per square foot, whereas the cost of staff is about a hundred or two hundred dollars per square foot. ... Building managers are more worried about their staff than their energy," a senior economist at an environmental nongovernmental organiation explained regarding why financial incentives may not be as significant to attracting rule-takers as is sometimes thought: "So what would happen if we could demonstrate and market that people are more productive in sustainable buildings? That would change the story" (int. 181).

What Discourages Prospective Rule-Takers?

An obvious question to pose at this point is whether the inverse of the conditions and clusters of conditions in the programs studied result in the opposite performance outcome. In other words, if a condition is observed as necessary or sufficient in a path related to "attracting rule-takers" will it always be absent in paths related to "not attracting rule-takers." For example, all programs that evince promising outcomes in terms of attracting rule-takers were characterized by financial rewards, but is this condition always absent in programs that are less promising in attracting participants? The literature on voluntary programs often assumes this symmetry between causal conditions and program performance, but the question is not often studied empirically. To determine whether or not this symmetry is present, the data are again subjected to analysis of necessity, in Table 7.6.

Table 7.6 points to one necessary condition that meets the consistency score cutoff of 0.9: the absence of a diffusion network that frequently exposes prospective rule-takers to the program. The relatively high coverage score of this condition further indicates that it plays a relevant role in discouraging prospective rule-takers from joining the programs studied.

Table 7.7 presents the outcome of this analysis for sufficient conditions. The same procedure is followed as for the earlier analysis for sufficient conditions, and because the same data set is used, the truth table represented in Table 7.3 also holds for this analysis, except with inverse scores for the performance outcome "attracting rule-takers."

Table 7.6 *Necessary Conditions for Discouraging Prospective Rule-Takers*

Conditions	Consistency Score	Coverage Score
Lenient rules	0.25	0.63
Lenient enforcement	0.35	1.00
No assured financial rewards	0.20	1.00
No nonfinancial rewards	0.75	0.83
No leadership rewards	0.45	0.82
No local government involvement	0.45	0.75
No positive impact of diffusion network	0.90	1.00

Table 7.7 indicates eight causal recipes that are individually sufficient to discourage prospective rule-takers from participating in the programs studied. The solution coverage and solution consistency are again high (both 1.00), indicating that the solution strongly relates to the outcome observed and that it is of high empirical importance in reaching the outcome. As with the earlier analysis of sufficient conditions, a number of conditions recur in the distinct paths and the full solution can be formulated as:

$$
\text{Discouraging prospective rule-takers} \rightarrow
\begin{cases}
\text{netw}* \begin{cases}
\text{non-fin}* \begin{cases} \text{ENF} \\ + \\ \text{lead} \\ + \\ \text{rule} \end{cases} \\
+ \\
\text{RULE}* \begin{cases} \text{ENF}*\text{lg} \\ + \\ \text{fin} \end{cases} \\
+ \\
\text{rule}*\text{enf}*\text{NON-FIN}*\text{lg}
\end{cases} \\
+ \\
\text{RULE}* \begin{cases} \text{ENF}*\text{lead}*\text{lg} \\ + \\ \text{enf}*\text{fin}*\text{non-fin} \end{cases}
\end{cases}
\tag{7.2}
$$

The preceding equation (2) can be read as: voluntary programs that have not attracted 15 percent of the full pool of rule-takers they target over a ten-year period, or are not on track to doing so, are characterized by:

Table 7.7 Intermediate Solution for Discouraging Prospective Rule-Takers

Solution	Formula	Coverage		Consistency	Programs
		Raw	Unique		
Path NRT.1	ENF*non-fin*netw	0.50	0.10	1.00	1200 Buildings, Amsterdam Investment Fund, E$^+$ Green Building, Energy Efficiency Mortgage, Energy Star Building, Energy Star for Homes, EnviroDevelopment, LEED, PACE, Sustainable Development Grant
Path NRT.2	non-fin*lead*netw	0.40	0.15	1.00	Additional Credit for Energy Efficient Homes, Energy Star Building, Energy Star for Homes, EnviroDevelopment, Environmental Upgrade Agreements, Small Business Improvement Fund, Sustainable Development Grant
Path NRT.3	rule *non-fin*netw	0.20	0.05	1.00	Amsterdam Investment Fund, Building Innovation Fund, Energy Efficiency Mortgage, LEED
Path NRT.4	RULE*ENF*lead*lg	0.20	0.05	1.00	Energy Star Building, Energy Star for Homes, EnviroDevelopment, Zonnig Huren
Path NRT.5	RULE*ENF*lg*netw	0.20	0.05	1.00	Better Buildings Challenge, Energy Star Building, Energy Star for Homes, EnviroDevelopment
Path NRT.6	RULE*fin*netw	0.15	0.11	1.00	Chicago Green Office Challenge, CitySwitch, E$^+$ Green Buildings
Path NRT.7	rule*enf*NON-FIN*lg*netw	0.05	0.05	1.00	Billion Dollar Green Challenge
Path NRT.8	RULE*enf*fin*non-fin	0.05	0.05	1.00	Retrofit Chicago

Solution coverage: 1.00
Solution consistency: 1.00

Notes: Uppercase indicates the condition is present; lowercase indicates the condition is absent

Abbreviations: Rule = rules (sustainable building requirements); Enf = enforcement of rules; Fin = assured financial rewards for rule-takers; Nonfin = nonfinancial rewards for rule-takers (e.g., information); Lead = possibility to showcase leadership in the construction or property sectors for rule-takers; LG = local government as rule-maker; Netw = positive impact of diffusion network; * = logical AND

153

- The absence of a diffusion network that exposes prospective rule-takers frequently to the program, and the absence of nonfinancial gains for rule-takers, and stringent enforcement (path NRT.1); or,
- The absence of a diffusion network that exposes prospective rule-takers frequently to the program, and the absence of nonfinancial gains for rule-takers, and the absence of leadership rewards for rule-takers (path NRT.2); or,
- The absence of a diffusion network that exposes prospective rule-takers frequently to the program, and the absence of nonfinancial gains for rule-takers, and lenient rules (path NRT.3); or,
- The absence of a diffusion network that exposes prospective rule-takers frequently to the program, and stringent rules, and stringent enforcement, and the absence of local government involvement (path NRT.5), or,
- The absence of a diffusion network that exposes prospective rule-takers frequently to the program, and stringent rules, and the absence of financial rewards for rule-takers (path NRT.6), or,
- The absence of a diffusion network that exposes prospective rule-takers frequently to the program, and lenient rules, and lenient enforcement, and nonfinancial rewards for rule-takers, and the absence of local government involvement (path NRT.7); or,
- Stringent rules, and stringent enforcement, and the absence of leadership rewards for rule-takers, and the absence of local government involvement (path NRT.4); or,
- Stringent rules, and lenient enforcement, and the absence of financial rewards for rule-takers, and the absence of nonfinancial rewards for rule-takers (path NRT.8).

Some Observations

Particularly remarkable is the nonsymmetrical relationship between what attracts rule-takers to and what discourages them from participating in the voluntary programs for sustainable buildings studied. Where the presence of a diffusion network that exposes prospective rule-takers frequently to the program was a necessary condition in all of the paths that show promising performance in terms of attracting rule-takers, the absence of this network is not a necessary condition in all of the paths that depict less promising performance. As one of the program administrators explained: "You just cannot push businesses into it. We learned that however much work we put into outreach you still only reach those who already slightly get it. You do not get the ones who do not have some basic understanding or are already a bit concerned about sustainability.

That is a hard lesson we have learned. We thought: 'We can go out there and convince people about sustainability.' But that is not how it works. It is much more effective to work through the people who already participate. It is about concentric circles. To show what is possible through the current participants and then hope you create a ripple effect" (int. 194).

Also notable is the role that the conditions "rules" and "enforcement" play. In two of the configurations (path NRT.3 and path NRT.7) the voluntary programs are characterized by lenient rules, and in two configurations (paths NRT.7 and NRT.8) the voluntary programs are characterized by lenient enforcement. This goes against the causal direction that these two conditions have in the other configurations. This provides empirical evidence for the literature discussed earlier regarding voluntary programs, which suggests that stringent and lenient rules, as well as stringent and lenient enforcement, may attract or discourage commitment to a voluntary program by prospective and existing rule-takers (Potoski & Prakash, 2009). As this study indicates, their impact on program performance depends on how they combine with other conditions.

The various paths further illustrate that in interaction with other conditions the causal direction of the rewards to rule-takers may play out differently than anticipated: path NRT.7 indicates nonfinancial rewards for rule-takers as an INUS condition — this goes against the expectation that (high) rewards attract prospective rule-takers. It is also striking that only in a few configurations is the absence of financial rewards for rule-takers an INUS condition. This further emphasizes that financial rewards play a less strong role in attracting rule-takers than is often assumed.

Finally, both analyses for sufficient conditions (Table 7.5 and 7.7) indicate no clustering of country contexts under specific paths. This supports my choice of these countries as discussed in Chapter 1 for the purpose of this study the potential differences in the contextual conditions of this set of countries appear not to have a definitive influence on the performance of the programs studied. That is not to say that these countries' contexts do not affect this poor performance at all. The absence of strong mandatory requirements for low-carbon building development and an experienced financial risk of low-carbon building development (strengthened by the global financial crisis of 2008–2011) were mentioned by interviewees, time and again, as reasons why individuals and organizations are not attracted to these programs.

What Makes Rule-Takers Improve Their Behavior?

It is now of interest to understand what is common to the programs studied in which rule-takers have achieved building-related resource

Table 7.8 *Necessary Conditions for Improved Rule-Taker Behavior*

Conditions	Consistency Score	Coverage Score
Stringent rules	0.73	0.73
Stringent enforcement	0.73	0.80
Assured financial rewards	0.73	0.80
Nonfinancial rewards	0.36	0.67
Leadership rewards	0.72	0.80
Local government involvement	0.64	0.78
Positive impact of diffusion network	0.37	1.00

consumption or carbon emission reductions of 20 percent over a ten-year period, or are on track to do so — I have discussed the motivation for this crossover point for promising and less promising performance previously. In what follows, analyses for necessity and sufficiency are carried out. These analyses consider the performance of rule-takers within the programs, and not the performance of a program as a whole. In other words, where Table 7.1 evaluates most of the programs as having an insignificant or marginal contribution to reducing resource consumption or carbon emissions of the full pool of prospective rule-takers or buildings they target, the following analyses are only concerned with whether a program meets the crossover point and, if so, why. Bearing in mind that the performance data of reductions achieved by Green Star in Australia, BREEAM in the Netherlands, and Energy Star Buildings, Energy Star for Homes, and LEED in the United States are largely based on ex-ante prediction and not ex-post performance data, these programs are excluded from the analysis. That being said, this implies that de facto, only the configuration of conditions that make up LEED is excluded from the analysis of sufficient conditions, since BREEAM and Green Star have configurations similar to that of NABERS, and Energy Star Building and Energy Star for Homes have configurations similar to that of EnviroDevelopment — both NABERS and EnviroDevelopment are included in the analysis.

To understand whether any of the conditions are necessary for this performance outcome the data are, again, subjected to analysis of necessity; Table 7.8 presents the results.

Table 7.8 shows that no condition meets the consistency score cutoff point of 0.9 to consider it a necessary condition for improved rule-taker behavior — building-related resource consumption or carbon emission reductions of 20 percent or more. At question then, is: what combination or combinations of conditions is or are sufficient for improving rule-taker behavior? An analysis for sufficient conditions will assist here, but first a truth table is necessary, as represented in Table 7.9.

Table 7.9 can be read in a similar manner to Table 7.4. It presents the configurations of conditions constituting the fourteen voluntary programs where the performance outcome (reductions by rule-takers) was empirically observed — excluding five certification and classification programs for reasons discussed earlier. As before, an analysis for sufficient conditions is conducted for logical minimization of the data. For this analysis counterfactuals for all conditions are again applied following the direction discussed in Chapter 3: that is, if a condition is present, a positive relation with the performance is expected; this includes the conditions "rules" and "enforcement."[4] Table 7.10 presents the outcome of this analysis for sufficient conditions.

Table 7.10 presents seven causal recipes that are individually sufficient to incentivize rule-takers in the programs studied to reduce their building-related resource consumption or carbon emissions by 20 percent. The high solution coverage and solution consistency (both 1.00) indicate that the solution strongly relates to the outcome observed and that it is of high empirical importance in reaching the outcome. Following the earlier analyses the full solution can be formulated as:

$$
\text{Improved rule-taker behaviour} \rightarrow
\left\{
\begin{array}{l}
\text{FIN} * \left\{
\begin{array}{l}
\text{RULE*ENF*} \left\{
\begin{array}{l}
\text{non-fin} \\
+ \\
\text{NETW}
\end{array}
\right. \\
+ \\
\text{rule*enf*LEAD*} \left\{
\begin{array}{l}
\text{LG} \\
+ \\
\text{NON-FIN}
\end{array}
\right. \\
+ \\
\text{LEAD*} \left\{
\begin{array}{l}
\text{ENF*NETW} \\
+ \\
\text{RULE*NON-FIN*LG}
\end{array}
\right.
\end{array}
\right. \\
+ \\
\text{RULE*ENF*non-fin*LEAD*LG}
\end{array}
\right.
\qquad (7.3)
$$

The preceding equation (3) can be read as: voluntary programs that have incentivized their rule-takers to reduce building-related resource

Table 7.9 *Truth Table for Improved Rule-Taker Behavior*

	Conditions							Outcome	
Row	Rules	Enforcement	Financial Rewards	Nonfinancial Rewards	Leadership Rewards	Local Government as Rule-Maker	Diffusion Network	Frequency	Improved Rule-Taker Behavior
1	0	0	1	0	1	1	0		1
2	0	0	1	1	1	0	0		1
3	0	1	1	0	1	0	1		1
4	1	0	0	1	1	1	0		1
5	1	1	0	0	1	1	0		1
6	1	1	0	0	1	0	1		1
7	1	1	1	0	0	1	0		1
8	1	1	1	0	0	1	0		1
9	1	1	1	0	1	1	1		1
10	1	1	1	1	0	0	0		1
11	1	1	1	1	1	1	1		1
12	1	0	1	0	0	1	1		0
13	1	1	0	1	1	1	0		0
14	1	1	1	1	1	0	0		0
Rows 15–128: Logical remainders									

Table 7.10 *Intermediate Solution for Improved Rule-Taker Behavior*

Solution	Formula	Coverage Raw	Unique	Consistency	Programs
Path Red.1	RULE*ENF*FIN*non-fin	0.27	0.19	1.00	EnviroDevelopment, PACE, Sustainable Development Grant
Path Red.2	RULES*ENF*non-fin*LEAD*LG	0.27	0.19	1.00	E$^+$ Green Building, PACE, Retrofit Chicago
Path Red.3	ENF*FIN*LEAD*NETW	0.18	0.09	1.00	Better Buildings Partnership, NABERS
Path Red.4	RULE*ENF*FIN*NETW	0.18	0.09	1.00	Better Buildings Partnership, Zonnig Huren
Path Red.5	rule*enf*FIN*LEAD*LG	0.09	0.09	1.00	Building Innovation Fund
Path Red.6	rule*enf*FIN* NON-FIN*LEAD	0.09	0.09	1.00	Billion Dollar Green Challenge
Path Red.7	RULE*enf*NON-FIN*LEAD*LG	0.09	0.09	1.00	CitySwitch Green Office

Solution coverage: 1.00
Solution consistency: 1.00

Notes: Uppercase indicates the condition is present; lowercase indicates the condition is absent

Abbreviations: Rule = rules (sustainable building requirements); Enf = enforcement of rules; Fin = assured financial rewards for rule-takers; Non-fin = nonfinancial rewards for rule-takers (e.g., information); Lead = possibility to showcase leadership in the construction or property sector for rule-takers; LG = local government as rule-maker; Netw = positive impact of diffusion network; * = logical AND.

consumption or carbon emissions by 20 percent over a ten-year period, or are on track to do so, are characterized by:

- Assured financial rewards for rule-takers, and stringent rules, and stringent enforcement, and nonfinancial rewards for rule-takers (path Red.1); or,
- Assured financial rewards for rule-takers, and stringent rules, and stringent enforcement, and a diffusion network that frequently exposes rule-takers to the program (path Red.4); or,
- Assured financial rewards for rule-takers, and lenient rules, and lenient enforcement, and local government involvement (path Red.5); or,
- Assured financial rewards for rule-takers, and lenient rules, and lenient enforcement, and nonfinancial rewards for participants (path Red.6); or,
- Assured financial rewards for rule-takers, and leadership rewards for rule-takers, and stringent enforcement, and a diffusion network that frequently exposes rule-takers to the program (path Red.3); or,
- Assured financial rewards for rule-takers, and leadership rewards for rule-takers, and stringent rules, and nonfinancial rewards for rule-takers, and local government involvement (path Red.6); or,
- Stringent rules, and stringent rewards, and the absence of nonfinancial rewards for rule-takers, and leadership rewards for rule-takers, and local government involvement (path Red.2).

Some Observations

Noteworthy here is the role the condition "financial rewards" plays in the performance outcomes, which differs from its earlier function. It recurred as a trivial necessary condition in the analyses for necessary conditions for the performance outcome "attracting rule-takers," but was not found a necessary condition for the outcome "improved rule-taker behavior." The knowledge shared by interviewees throughout the book highlights the complex nature of this condition in its interaction with other conditions. Nonetheless, this specific finding sheds some new light on this interaction: financial gains appear to be relevant to some prospective rule-takers as a motivator to commit to a program, and become less important for rule-takers once they have decided to participate in a voluntary program.

Another observation worth highlighting is the absence of nonfinancial rewards as an INUS condition in two of the paths identified (path Red.1 and path Red.2). The absence of this condition goes, again, against its expected causal direction (see Chapter 3). A likely explanation is that the presence of other rewards is more important to rule-takers than the absence of nonfinancial rewards.

What Explains Shirking Behavior by Rule-Takers?

Again the opposite question can be posed: what explains that in some programs studied rule-takers have not achieved building-related resource consumption or carbon emissions of 20 percent over a ten-year period, or are not on track to do so? Answering this question helps us to understand whether causal conditions and observed outcomes have a symmetrical relationship or not. More interestingly perhaps, since all programs that have not been able to incentivize rule-takers to improve their behavior along these lines nonetheless require them to meet this goal (see Table 7.2), the data also allow us to explore why rule-takers in these programs exhibit shirking behavior. This question is repeatedly posed in the literature, but rarely is it scrutinized empirically (Darnall & Sides, 2008; Lubell, 2004; Lyon & Maxwell, 2007; Potoski & Prakash, 2009).

Following on from the earlier analyses, Table 7.11 presents the results of the analysis for necessary conditions. Note that for this analysis the influence of rules on achieving the outcome is not included — after all, shirking behavior implies that rule-takers do not live up to the rules of a program. For this reason those programs that do not set stringent rules have been excluded from the analysis.[5]

Only one condition is identified as necessary for shirking behavior, the absence of a diffusion network that exposes rule-takers frequently to the program; but because the coverage score for this condition is relatively low, it is likely to play a trivial role in causing the outcome. Table 7.11 points again to a nonsymmetrical relationship between the conditions and how they affect rule-taker behavior: the presence of a diffusion network that exposes rule-takers to a program was not found to be a

Table 7.11 *Necessary Conditions for Shirking Behavior*

Conditions	Consistency Score	Coverage Score
Lenient enforcement	0.33	0.25
No assured financial rewards	0.33	0.50
No nonfinancial rewards	0.33	0.17
No leadership rewards	0.33	0.25
No local government involvement	0.33	0.33
No positive impact of diffusion network	1.00	0.38

Table 7.12 *Intermediate Solution for Shirking Behavior*

		Coverage			
Solution	Formula	Raw	Unique	Consistency	Programs
Path Shirk.1	ENF*fin*NON-FIN*netw	0.33	0.33	1.00	Chicago Green Office Challenge
Path Shirk.2	ENF*NON-FIN*lg*netw	0.33	0.33	1.00	Better Buildings Challenge
Path Shirk.3	enf*FIN* non-fin*lead*netw	0.33	0.33	1.00	Small Business Improvement Fund

Solution coverage: 1.00
Solution consistency: 1.00

Notes: Uppercase indicates the condition is present; lowercase indicates the condition is absent
Abbreviations: Enf = enforcement of rules; Fin = assured financial rewards for rule-takers; Non-fin = nonfinancial rewards for rule-takers (e.g., information); Lead = possibility to showcase leadership in the construction or property sector for rule-takers; LG = local government as rule-maker; Netw = positive impact of diffusion network; * = logical AND

trivial necessary condition in programs that were promising in improving rule-taker behavior. To improve understanding of this nonsymmetry an analysis for sufficient conditions is needed. The truth tables — Table 7.9 and Table 7.12 — present the results of this analysis.

Table 7.12 illustrates that three causal recipes explain shirking behavior in the set of voluntary programs studied. They can be simplified further in the following equation:

$$\text{Shirking behaviour} \to \text{netw} * \left\{ \begin{array}{l} \text{ENF*NON-FIN*} \left\{ \begin{array}{l} \text{fin} \\ + \\ \text{lg} \end{array} \right. \\ + \\ \text{enf*FIN*non-fin*lead} \end{array} \right. \tag{7.4}$$

The preceding equation (4) can be read as: programs subject to shirking behavior, as well as programs that show marginal performance of rule-takers in terms of reducing their building-related resource consumption or carbon emissions, are characterized by:

- The absence of a diffusion network that exposes rule-takers frequently to the program, and stringent enforcement, and nonfinancial rewards for rule-takers, and the absence of assured financial rewards for rule-takers (path Shirk.1); or,
- The absence of a diffusion network that exposes rule-takers frequently to the program, and stringent enforcement, and nonfinancial rewards for rule-takers, and the absence of local government involvement (path Shirk.2); or,
- The absence of a diffusion network that exposes rule-takers frequently to the program, and lenient enforcement, and assured financial rewards for rule-takers, and the absence of nonfinancial rewards for rule-takers, and the absence of leadership rewards for rule-takers (path Shirk.3).

Some Observations

Here a caveat is required: this part of the analysis draws on only three empirical observations of shirking behavior. The internal validity of the findings is strong — as indicated by the high solution coverage and consistency scores — but the external validity of this finding is marginal because of the very small number of empirical observations. That being said, this part of the analysis draws an important empirical insight: again the observed nonsymmetrical relationship between causal conditions and program performance outcomes is prominent. This observation stresses that it cannot be assumed that if a promising performance outcome is observed when a specific condition is present, a nonpromising (or otherwise different) performance outcome will occur when that condition is not present — this study illustrates that this insight holds for individual conditions as well as for clusters of interacting conditions.

Significant Findings

This chapter has further analyzed the twenty-six voluntary programs studied in the earlier empirical chapters, as well as more closely scrutinized their performance. It has illustrated that when considered from a distance these programs have an insignificant impact on reducing the building-related resource consumption or carbon emissions of the full pool of individuals, firms, or buildings they target. This is, unfortunately, the bottom-line insight from this study: voluntary programs for sustainable building and city development and transformation do not appear to be a promising answer to speeding and scaling up the decarbonization of the built environment. This empirical observation does by no means downplay all the effort by rule-makers and rule-takers, or the vast amount of highly sustainable buildings developed, and the changed building use that they have realized. Yet, the sustainable building challenge is too complicated and too pressing for voluntary programs, which are not able to effect meaningful impact within the time frame required — an issue I return to in Chapter 9. That being said, some significant findings stand out from comparative analysis of the full set of programs studied— insight that may help to design more promising governance interventions for the decarbonization of the built environment, and that complement the broader understanding of the capacity of voluntary programs to address societal problems: these are briefly summarized in this final section.

Conjunctural Causation and Equifinality: Good News, Actually

The four sets of analyses for necessary and sufficient conditions all point out that the various conditions under analysis combine in causing their effects: none of the paths identified as related to any of the outcomes studied is characterized by a single condition. The analyses also show that various combinations of conditions can be related to similar outcomes: all solutions uncovered were characterized by at least two and a maximum of eight paths. In other words, this chapter has provided empirical evidence for conjunctural causation and equifinality. Although the analyses have considerably simplified the data collected, the various paths and solutions uncovered may at first glance not look simple. After all, they indicate that promising and less promising performance of the voluntary programs studied are characterized by a complex interaction of different conditions. From the study no ideal-type designs or contexts for voluntary programs can be abstracted that can be expected to "work" or "fail."

That being said, the identification of conjunctural causation and equifinality can also be interpreted in a more positive light — it suggests that different designs of voluntary programs for sustainable buildings may yield similar results. For example, if a rule-maker seeks to implement a program that is promising in terms of improving rule-takers' behavior, but that is not capable of reaching out to them through a diffusion network or rewarding their leading performance in the construction and property sectors (thus excluding programs fitting paths Red.2 and Red.3), the rule-maker might still be able to develop a program that provides enough incentives otherwise (e.g., those fitting paths Red.1 and Red.4). In similar vein, rule-makers who struggle to attract rule-takers may have to make only small adjustments to their programs to turn the tide, rather than overhaul the program.

Role of Rules and Enforcement: Fuzzy, as Expected

Besides providing empirical support for the assumption that conjunctural causation and equifinality are at play in how the conditions of interest affect the performance of the programs, the study has also provided empirical support for the individual conditions. For the majority of conditions included in the analyses the causal direction was generally as expected: if a condition is present it relates to promising performance outcomes; if it is absent it relates to less promising performance outcomes. Even the expected "fuzzy" relationship between stringent and lenient rules and stringent and lenient enforcement and the performance of the programs was empirically observed. This strengthens earlier work on voluntary programs that indeed assumes that program rules and enforcement have a complex impact on their performance (Potoski & Prakash, 2009).

These empirical observations stress the explanatory value of the theoretical template presented in Chapter 3. There are two exceptions, however. The presence of financial rewards was identified as an INUS condition in path Shirk.3; and similarly, the presence of nonfinancial rewards was identified as an INUS condition in path NRT.7, path Shirk.1, and path Shirk.2, whereas its absence was identified as an INUS condition in path Red.1 and path Red.2. These observations are contrary to the expected causal direction of these two reward conditions (see Chapter 3). Different explanations stand out. First, the positive influence of the presence of other rewards may cancel out the negative influence of the absence of these, or vice versa. Second, nonfinancial rewards such as information supply may be interpreted differently by various rule-takers. To some it might be an attractive incentive; to others the processing of such information might be an additional burden of participating in a program. A third explanation may be that my operationalization of, particularly, nonfinancial gains is too broad, and future studies may wish to use more fine-grained operationaliations — for instance, by distinguishing nonfinancial rewards in access to information, access to policy makers, access to a peer network, and so on (see also Chapter 3).

Role of Financial Rewards: Less Evident than Expected

Intriguing is the empirical observation that the presence or absence of assured financial rewards is less present in the various solutions than is often expected in the literature on voluntary programs — and less evident than was argued by many interviewees. In some programs that are considered promising in terms of attracting participants or improving their performance, assured financial rewards are present, but this condition combines with other conditions in how it relates to program performance, and assured financial rewards are not observed as a necessary condition. Perhaps more striking is the empirical observation that the absence of assured financial rewards is not a necessary condition in any of the programs studied that showcase less promising outcomes, and only a sufficient condition in a few of the paths that relate to less promising outcomes. For the set of programs studied these rewards are a motivator for prospective rule-takers to participate and improve their behavior, but their absence is not a motivator to decline to participate or to refrain from improving behavior. Rule-makers may have to change their dominant sales pitch that these programs are in the financial interest of rule-takers, and that it is predominantly financial gain that makes these programs attractive to them.

That is not to say that rule-makers should cease marketing the financial gains for prospective rule-takers — these rewards appear to be a strong motivator for those who do commit to these programs — but rule-makers may need to broaden their marketing strategy by, for example, stressing the ease of participation or, as one of the interviewees explained, by marketing the additional benefits of sustainable buildings, such as improved staff performance. Alternatively, most of the programs studied are administered by governmental agencies, and their staff may not be the most suited to selling these programs to prospective rule-takers (a comparable observation is made by Moore, 2002). "What is important is the sales pitch. It takes people a long time to cross the line and join the program. But council people do not join council because they like to sell. They are not sales people," a program administrator in Australia explained: "The challenge for government is to find the right people to sell the program to participants. But if you do not pay the wages that come with those skills it is going to be hard to find the people that can actually perform in the program" (int. 41). This insight was replicated almost verbatim by a program administrator in the Netherlands, who stated: "You need a specific type of person to work within the program. It is a staffing issue. It is about facilitation. It requires a different mind-set. For government it is hard to find the right people who can do this" (int. 67).

Role of Leadership Rewards: Overly Propagated by Rule-Makers?

A similar observation is made for the leadership rewards to rule-takers when committing to a program. Although rule-makers expect much of industry recognition — and many of the programs are firmly built on a leadership narrative, as has become clear from the empirical chapters — leadership rewards were not found to be a necessary condition for attracting rule-takers. Comparable to the assured financial rewards, the absence of leadership rewards appears not, as a rule, to discourage participants from committing to the programs studied or refraining from improving their behavior once they join.

This empirical observation questions the strong focus on leadership and the leadership narrative that is communicated by the administrators of many of the voluntary programs studied. As with marketing of assured financial rewards, the leadership narrative may not resonate with all types of prospective rule-takers for these programs, and a different narrative may be needed — an issue I will return to in Chapter 9.

Role of Local Governments: Overly Propagated by Academics and NGOs?

All of the observed solutions support the assumption that local government involvement is positively related to desired outcomes of voluntary programs for sustainable buildings. The broader study points out, however, that the involvement of local government in a voluntary program is by no means a guarantee that it will outperform those without local government involvement. Comparable to the role of national governments and nongovernments, the role of local governments interacts with the rewards that accrue to rule-takers, the stringency of program rules and their enforcement, and the type of diffusion network through which program administrators reach out to prospective rule-takers. In addition, local government involvement or its absence was not an INUS condition in many of the individual paths observed.

These empirical observations question the foundation of arguments for city council—based localization of environmental governance because they are the level closest to citizens (Aust, 2015; UNCED, 1992). When it comes to sustainable building and city development and use, smaller local governments in particular may not have the capacity to keep up to date with sustainability developments, or may lack the capacity to ensure that rule-takers act in accordance with their commitments in voluntary programs (cf. Cheshire et al., 2014). Likewise, large firms with property in different locations may prefer to commit to a regional, national, or even international voluntary program over a local one as it saves multiple interactions with different program administrators and need to invest in understanding regionally divergent program rules and compliance mechanisms. Voluntary programs administered by local governments may further lack the "brand value" that larger programs provide to participants.

The Role of Diffusion Networks: Underappreciated by Rule-Makers?

Where rule-makers appear to have too much focus on marketing and providing assured financial and leadership awards, they also underappreciate the role of the diffusion network in disseminating knowledge of voluntary programs to prospective rule-takers. Looking back once more at Table 7.1 and the observations made in this book it becomes clear that attracting rule-takers requires the capacity to identify and persuade them: the Dutch Green Building Council that administers BREEAM-NL was launched by the relatively small group of dominant property developers in the Netherlands, a geographically small, densely populated country; the Green Building Council in Australia that administers Green Star only needs to cater to a handful of major cities;[6] NABERS in Australia is known to all prospective rule-takers simply because they are legally required to supply a NABERS certificate when they put their property on the market for sale or lease; and the City of Sydney had to reach out to only fourteen property owners when it launched the Better Building Partnership.

Now compare this with the diffusion network faced by the United States Green Building Council, which administers LEED, or that faced by the United States Department of Energy, which administers the Better Buildings Challenge, or even the network faced by the City of Melbourne in seeking to reach out to more than five hundred property owners under the 1200 Buildings program. Not only do they face a much larger pool of prospective rule-takers; these prospective rule-takers are likely to be less well connected than their counterparts in BREEAM-NL, Green Star, and the Better Building Partnership and are also less likely to be exposed to buildings constructed or retrofitted under these programs — the value of seeing and experiencing sustainable buildings resulting from these programs should not be underestimated, as various interviewees stressed (see also E. M. Rogers, 1995).

Nonsymmetry between Conditions and Performance: Not Such Good News, Unfortunately

Finally, while I started this concluding section with a positive note on conjunctural causation and equifinality because they indicate that marginal changes to a program may yield considerably different outcomes and that different program designs may yield a similar, desired outcome, I consider the nonsymmetry observed between conditions and program performance to be less hopeful. This nonsymmetry indicates that voluntary programs for sustainability, at least the set of twenty-six programs studied in this book, are a highly complex category of governance interventions.

Despite all their flaws (see Chapter 2), the effects of mandatory building codes are relatively straightforward and predictable: increase their stringency and ensure enforcement and the quality of the built environment will improve; reduce their stringency or go soft on enforcement and the quality of the built environment deteriorates. Although voluntary programs allow for nuanced structures — for instance, a model that compensates for stringent rules by introducing greater financial and leadership rewards — the outcome of a change in design or context of a voluntary program is very difficult to predict, even in broad terms. The nonsymmetry between conditions and performance indicates that it is relevant to understand in detail why particular voluntary programs appear to be effective: we can thereby understand and replicate them. It is also important to determine in detail why other programs fail in order to recognize the combinations of circumstances and program structures that result in failure; for instance, the lack of a diffusion network that frequently exposes prospective rule-takers to a program, coupled with insufficient information gain can lead to insufficient program uptake. When designing and implementing a voluntary program, merely seeking to build on positive characteristics — or seeking to avoid the negative ones, for that matter — is not sufficient to ensure promising outcomes. The findings from the analyses presented in this chapter underline that the transferability of voluntary programs is complicated (cf. Bai, Roberts, & Chen, 2010). "Look, there is much interest in our program from other organizations, and they seek to replicate it," a program administrator in Australia explained, "but what happens is that they cherry-pick things and then it all falls down. For some reason they do not understand the big picture, how it all fits together. So inevitably they make an error. They do not copy correctly. They go partway. But by going partway you miss out on it all" (int. 52).

8   Voluntary Programs for Sustainable Cities Elsewhere
Certification and Classification in India, Malaysia, and Singapore

Voluntary programs for sustainable building are also looked on favorably in contexts other than relatively rich and developed countries in the Global North. They are considered to be a promising means of accelerating the transition to more sustainable cities in countries in the Global South and other non-OECD countries (see Chapter 1). In this chapter I focus on voluntary programs in a number of these countries in seeking to understand whether they present similar or different opportunities and constraints to those uncovered in Australia, the Netherlands, and the United States. In this chapter I invert the research design followed thus far. Whereas the previous chapters considered differently designed voluntary programs within broadly similar contexts, this chapter is interested in similarly designed programs in different contexts. The focus is on nine certification and classification programs (see Chapter 4) in India, Malaysia, and Singapore. Table 8.1 provides a summary of the programs studied here (see also Appendix B).

Table 8.1 identifies a similar pattern to that identified for the certification and classification programs in Australia, the Netherlands, and the United States: they have different foci and different approaches to classification (rating, benchmarking, and labeling – see Chapter 4 for terminology) and award certificates to building designs, completed buildings, and buildings in use. This indicates, again, that from the outset it is often not immediately clear what a certificate and a specific class of certification mean. This is one of many similarities among these programs in all countries studied, but there are considerable differences also. In what follows, the move to voluntary programs in India, Malaysia, and Singapore is further explored. As in the earlier chapters, four programs are singled out for in-depth discussing to improve our understanding of the impact of these differences in separate national contexts.

Table 8.1 *Overview of Certification and Classification Programs Studied*

Name	Brief Description	Classification	Indicators	ad	ab	io
				Form		
Eco-Housing (Pune, India, 2004)	Comprehensive sustainable building program for housing development in Pune	Labeling	Stars (1–5)	X*		
Eco-Office (Singapore, 2002)	Program for reduced energy, water, and paper consumption by office users	Rating	Logo			X
Green Building Index (Malaysia, 2009)	Comprehensive sustainable building program; dominant application in new commercial property market	Labeling	Certified, Silver, Gold, Platinum	X*		
Green Label (Singapore, 1992)	Program for resource-efficient building materials, consumer products, and services	Benchmarking	Logo	X		
Green Mark (Singapore, 2005)	Comprehensive sustainable building program; partly mandatory for new development and major retrofits	Labeling	Certified, Gold, Gold Plus, Platinum	X*		
Green Township (Malaysia, 2009)	Comprehensive sustainable building program for city development	Benchmarking	Logo	X		
GRIHA (India, 2007)	Comprehensive sustainable building program; dominant application in new commercial property market	Labeling	Stars (1–5)	X*		
LEED-India (India, 2001)	Comprehensive sustainable building program; dominant application in new commercial property market	Labeling	Certified, Silver, Gold, Platinum	X	X	
LCCFA (Malaysia, 2011)	Comprehensive sustainable building program for city development	Labeling	Stars (1–6)	X	X	

Notes: ad = as designed certification; ab = as built certification; io = in operation certification (see further Chapter 4)

Program abbreviations: GRIHA = Green Rating for Integrated Habitat Assessment; LEED = Leadership in Energy and Environmental Design; LCCFA = Low-Carbon Cities Framework and Assessment System

* Issued certificates are subject to periodic renewal (de facto "in operation" certification)

Why the Turn to Voluntary Programs in India, Malaysia, and Singapore?

Interviewees in India, Malaysia, and Singapore repeatedly mentioned international pressure as a motivator for their governments to implement voluntary or quasi-voluntary programs for sustainable building and city development and transformation. In particular, the international Climate Change Conference in Copenhagen (COP 15) in December 2009 was considered a turning point for climate change and environmental policies. "Many things have changed since Copenhagen. Peer pressure has increased, and with the numbers on the table [emission and development targets] it will be more and more difficult to give a credible account of not being involved," a senior policy maker in Singapore explained, "Also, donor countries will likely base their aid on green policies in recipient countries. This will make it more and more important to have green policies in place for countries in the region," he continued, stressing further the role of international pressure as a motivator (int. 131). In his experience this was among the critical reasons for Singapore to introduce the certification and classification program Green Mark. Similar impetus was reported for the implementation of Green Rating for Integrated Habitat Assessment (GRIHA) and Eco-Housing in India, and the Low-Carbon Cities Framework and Assessment System (LCCFA) and Green Townships in Malaysia. These voluntary programs all sit within larger policy programs that mark turning points in these countries' responses to climate change: the Eleventh and Twelfth Five Year Plans in India (covering the period 2007–2017), the 2009 National Green Technology Policy in Malaysia, and the various Sustainable Singapore Blueprints in Singapore (the most recent launched in 2014). These policy programs were influenced by the outcomes of COP 15, which activated rapidly developing countries in the Asian region to indicate moves toward more environmentally sustainable development (Riazi, Skitmore, & Cheung, 2011; Appendix A).

Interviewees in India and Malaysia explained further that voluntary programs have the advantage that they can be developed and implemented relatively easily and quickly. The complex division of powers to regulate buildings and cities among local, regional, and national governments in these countries normally impedes the introduction of mandatory regulations (Darko et al., 2013; KeTTHA, 2011). Such requirements are virtually nonexistent in India and Malaysia (see also Chapter 2; Appendix A). For example, GRIHA in India could be adapted from existing certification and classification arrangements such as BREEAM and LEED (see Chapter 4) and was in operation two years after initial steps were taken to develop it; and LEED-India is a direct adaptation of LEED. The Green Building Index in Malaysia also closely models these internationally applied certification and classification programs, which at the time the Green Building Index was developed exhibited promising results.[1] Interviewees further referred to motivation inducements used in such programs in Australia, the Netherlands, and the United States: these programs are of interest to private sector organizations in the construction and property industries as there is some market demand for property with higher sustainability credentials than required by legislation. In India and Malaysia these organizations have collaborated in Green Building Council—like organizations and have developed and implemented certification and classification programs.

An additional impetus was mentioned by interviewees in Singapore: through Green Mark the national government aimed to expand its regional political influence. A representative of the ASEAN[2] financial sector explained that Singapore aspires to regional leadership in terms of energy efficiency. To achieve this, he continued, it needs to entice international investors and businesses that would probably "feel uncomfortable with a too-strong command-and-control approach to policy making" (int. 118). The voluntary nature of Green Mark as one of Singapore's flagship sustainability programs indicates the national government's willingness to allow some flexibility in sustainable building and city development while retaining a dominant governance role. By running its own certification program the Singapore Building and Construction Authority further had the opportunity to expand its influence rapidly in the ASEAN region, representatives of the authority explained. It has been very active in exporting Green Mark and markets it intensely as an Asian product suited to the tropics. Green Mark is now adopted by more than ten countries, including China, Malaysia, Vietnam, Thailand, and Indonesia. In the process of expanding its sustainable building influence, Singapore actively exports its experience and knowledge of sustainable building and city development throughout the region.

Program Performance: Case Studies

Comparable to the programs studied in Australia, the Netherlands, and the United States, those studied in India and Malaysia indicate poor performance: fewer than 100 GRIHA-certified projects have been built since the program was introduced in 2007; some 200 completed projects have been certified under LEED-India since 2001; fewer than 10 projects under Eco Housing since 2004; and some 280 under the Malaysian Green Building Index since 2005. Again this indicates an uptake of these programs of far less than 15 percent of the targeted market. Also comparable to the Global North programs discussed, their uptake is largely in high-end commercial office projects and government commissioned work. The two dedicated city development programs in Malaysia, Green Townships and LCCFA, have remained dormant over the course of the research project. While implemented in 2009 and 2011, respectively, neither of the programs had certified any city development project by 2015. The exception to this rule of low uptake is Green Mark in Singapore. The program was introduced in 2005, and by 2015 24 percent of Singapore's built environment was Green Mark certified, with 35 percent of certificates issued in the highest performance class, Platinum — indicating that these buildings are at least 20 percent more energy efficient than mandatorily required (BCA, 2010, 2014a, 2014c).

A closer look at GRIHA, LEED-India, the Green Building Index, and Green Mark reveals that all programs exhibit similar constraints to those in Australia, the Netherlands, and the United States. It further becomes clear that the specific contexts of India and Malaysia present additional challenges to the performance of these programs, and that the hybrid mandatory—voluntary approach to Green Mark has resulted in similar performance outcomes to those of the hybrid mandatory—voluntary program NABERS in Australia discussed earlier (see Chapter 4).

Certification and Classification in India: Voluntary Programs and a Culture of Corruption

Various voluntary certification and classification programs have been implemented in India. The government-supported Energy and Resources Institute (TERI) introduced the Green Rating for Integrated Habitat Assessment certification scheme (GRIHA) in 2007 (Ministry of New and Renewable Energy, 2012). In 2004 the Pune Municipal Corporation (the building authority in the city of Pune) introduced Eco-Housing, a certification scheme for environmentally sustainable housing development. This instrument was developed in collaboration with the United States Agency for International Development (USAID), the University of Pune, the University of Ahmedabad, the International Institute for Energy Conservation (IIEC), and TERI (IIEC, 2009). Finally, the Indian Green Building Council, a construction and property sector peak body, adopted LEED in 2001, with adaptations for the Indian context (IGBC, 2013).

According to their administrators these programs show promising performance. The Indian Green Building Council reports that LEED-India is applied to close to three thousand building projects with a total built-up space of more than 2.5 billion square feet (235 million square meters) throughout India (IGBC, 2015), and administrators of Eco-Housing report that some 16 million square feet (1.5 million square meters) is committed to the program.[3] But what do these numbers actually mean? Scratching at this impressive veneer, it is again apparent that the answer is, Not much. The figures presented by program administrators are wishful thinking at best, so explained interviewees, and typically illustrate design aspirations. To begin with, in their reporting, program administrators combine certified with precertified projects. Project developers can seek precertification — often based on a brief assessment of building plans — as this may help them to market their future buildings. It remains to be seen, however, whether these prospective buildings will actually be constructed. Eco-Housing is illustrative here: less than 3 percent of certified buildings (including precertified) has been completed. Interviewees mentioned similar numbers for LEED-India. "These programs show intention," the principal of an architectural firm mentioned, "but not actual performance. Probably less than 1 percent of new buildings in India are certified" (int. 154). This low number is confirmed by other sources — at one of the sustainable building conferences I visited, for example, a leading figure in the Indian Green Building Council mentioned: "We now have 1.4 or 1.5 million square feet of LEED-India certified buildings. Yet, the existing building stock of India is about 35 to 40 billion square feet" (int. 176).[4]

Interviewees and additional data pointed out that particularly in a context where corruption is the rule rather than the exception, such as the property and construction industries in India (CAP, 2012; Vittal, 2012), voluntary certification and classification programs risk being violated. For the administrators of GRIHA this was the reason to certify buildings only after completion, when their performance could be measured. "It is all about mind-set. People here are used to getting away with violations," a GRIHA administrator observed; "this is why GRIHA measures performance in-operation and not expected performance as designed; this is especially important in a culture where lenient compliance is often the norm" (int. 199). The prospect of submitting developed buildings to direct measurement, however, appears to be less appreciated by property developers and owners: since 2007 fewer than 100 GRIHA-certified projects have been realized throughout India.[5] Another problem interviewees and additional data raised is that these programs are only applied in the absolute top end of the property sector — new flagship office buildings and government commissioned work in major cities — and not in the majority of buildings. This is where property developers see a market in which prospective property owners and occupants are willing to pay a premium for sustainable buildings. But in other areas they do not envisage a profitable market. Also, as interviewees explained, the structure of these programs may discourage specific groups of rule-takers. "In being holistic [these programs] may be less appealing to medium and small-size enterprises," the principal of an architectural firm observed. "For them energy use and cost savings are important, but not far-reaching concepts of sustainable buildings [promoted by these programs]" (int. 154). Another reason mentioned is the lack of mandatory requirements for sustainable building and city development. "It needs mandatory backing. Currently LEED-India and GRIHA are not mandatory. There is no incentive for people to participate," an architect mentioned. "It needs to be tied with [mandatory] regulations to work" (int. 165). Besides limited uptake of this type of program, it may result in a situation in which environmentally sustainable buildings and city districts are only achievable for a very small portion of the Indian population: housing units developed under the Eco-Housing program in Pune sell at 10 million Indian rupees (U.S.$150,000), a sum well beyond the reach of most of Pune's citizens.[6]

Finally, countries in the Global South, such as India, are looked on favorably by voluntary program administrators in the Global North as markets for expansion. The implementation and adaptation of LEED in India are illustrative here. The United States Green Building Council was actively involved in establishing the Indian Green Building Council. This is a nonprofit organization under the aegis of the Confederation of Indian Industry — itself an association of Indian businesses. The United States Green Building Council had an active role and interest in launching the Indian council: "The initiation of the Indian Green Building Council was supported by the U.S. Green Building Council and the U.S. government, with USAID funds," a senior member of the United States Green Building Council explained. There is a history of American building associations — the plumbers' association, the glazing association — supporting the founding of similar associations in India, he went on to explain, but "there was also an interest to sell the U.S. LEED [program] in India" (int. 173). A salient detail is that the Indian Green Building Council is phasing out LEED-India certification by 2018. It initially licensed LEED only for the certification of commercial buildings — predominantly offices. Since then it has redesigned the LEED framework for a series of certification and classification programs under its own brand name and as of 2015 used these for certification of sustainable buildings in India (IGBC, 2013). To maintain its influence in India, the United States Green Building Council formed a strategic partnership in 2014 with the Energy Resources Institute — the organization that administers GRIHA (USGBC, 2014).

Certification and Classification in Malaysia: Voluntary Programs without a Mandatory Benchmark

Interview accounts and data from the Malaysian voluntary programs studied accord with India's program history. Common barriers to large-scale uptake and desired performance of voluntary programs are persistent corruption in the construction sectors; the initial costs of sustainable building development, and the limited ability of small and medium firms and households to bear these; and the absence of benchmarks for mandatory building codes and planning legislation. Interviewees were particularly vocal about this last barrier: "One of the major issues is that there is no [environmental or sustainable building] act to enforce all these [voluntary programs]," a policy maker at the Malaysian Ministry of Energy, Green Technology and Water categorically stated (int. 142). He explained that without a mandatory benchmark for sustainable building and city development these programs have little to offer to prospective rule-takers. On the one hand, they may feel that any requirement for sustainable building and city development is too much, simply because they are not forced to take any action by the government. On the other hand, they may feel that in the absence of mandatory requirements, voluntary programs do not provide enough marketing value — "beyond compliance" performance is meaningless when there is no mandatory benchmark to which the market can refer.

That being said, various organizations have sought to fill this gap in mandatory regulation. One of these is the Green Building Index, a comprehensive certification and classification program that relies on labeling. The program was developed and implemented in 2009 by the Malaysia Green Building Confederation, a group of industry associations and nongovernment organizations promoting sustainable building practice. Although international certification programs such as LEED were making inroads in Malaysia at that time,[7] the Malaysian Green Building Confederation has developed the Green Building Index specifically because its members considered international programs unsuitable for the Malaysian context. "The problem with [LEED] is that it is too much focused on an international setting, and that it doesn't keep a focus on local Malaysian circumstances," a representative of the confederation observed. "To give an example: the Green Building Index has a strong focus on transport because there is such a big transport problem in Malaysia. [LEED,] however, has a low focus on transport. I mean, [LEED] makes sense in [other countries], but less so in Malaysia" (int. 138). This opinion is at odds with the more than 125 countries and territories that have found LEED suitable for local application (USGBC, 2013c).

In light of this view it is also surprising that the Green Building Index strongly resembles the design of LEED (see also Appendix B), so much so that administrators of a competitive certification and classification program in Malaysia, the program Green Real Estate, argued that "the Green Building Index uses LEED as a point of departure. But LEED-like thinking doesn't make sense for us" (int. 135). This competing program was developed by a number of private sector organizations, predominantly major property developers and owners. They considered that "the Green Building Index has a monopoly [in Malaysia]," particularly because councils force developers to use the index for government-commissioned buildings (int. 135). To cater to an alternative segment of the market they initiated Green Real Estate, which is "pretty much based on Green Mark [from Singapore; see later discussion]" (int. 135). The Malaysia Green Building Confederation is, in its turn, critical of the Green Building Index and its reliance on Green Mark: "By copying Green Mark, Green Real Estate may miss the fit with local context," the representative of the confederation stated. Adding to this competition between certification and classification tools in Malaysia, the national government of Malaysia has entered into an agreement with the United Kingdom—based BREEAM program (see Chapter 4) to develop sustainable building development programs for the Malaysian construction sector.[8] Reflecting on such developments, the representative of the confederation concluded: "There is a danger that different programs polarize the markets instead of driving the market toward more sustainable practice" (int. 138).

Interviewees appreciated the development and implementation of various voluntary certification and classification programs that seek to fill in the gap in mandatory regulation and legislation in Malaysia. They were concerned, however, that lacking a mandatory benchmark, it can be too easy for nongovernmental organizations to develop and market voluntary programs. Competition among various certification and classification programs, combined with the absence of mandatory benchmarks, may create a race to the bottom in program rules (see Braithwaite & Drahos, 2000; Potoski & Prakash, 2013a). They argued that voluntary programs should provide an alternative for, or complement to, mandatory requirements, but should not be the only form of requirement for sustainable building and city development. "Are [these programs] sufficient?" a representative of the Malaysian Institute of Architects asked rhetorically. "Probably not," he continued; "there need to be more incentives from government or mandatory requirements. If you make [sustainable building] mandatory then everyone has to follow it; through [these programs] you only reach those who are savvy enough" (int. 137).

But lacking societal pressure for low-carbon development, lacking polit-ical will, and lacking industry support, change in the mandatory sphere was not expected. "There is some awareness [of sustainable buildings and cities], but it is not much. Not among policy makers, not among the general public, not in industry," the policy maker at the Malaysian Ministry of Energy, Green Technology and Water observed; "there is not much engagement with industry: we lack [mandatory requirements] to back all these initiatives; developers often tell their clients that sustainable technology is expensive, and environmental policy in Malaysia is more about supporting the economy than about sustainability" (int. 142). This condition made him concerned about the lost opportunities of these voluntary programs to accelerate the transition to low-carbon building in Malaysia.

Certification and Classification in Singapore: When Government Requires Participation

Singapore has made sustainable development one of its major policy goals (see Appendix A). The certification and classification program Green Mark is one of the flagship programs introduced by the Singapore government to achieve this goal. The program is a typical example of labeling: it allows for the certification of buildings, building blocks, and city districts based on their overall performance in terms of water and energy consumption, impact on the natural environment, indoor environ-mental quality, and "innovations and other green features" (BCA, 2012). Detailed requirements are set for these indicators, and credits are awarded for meeting individual targets. The total sum of credits defines the class awarded: "Certified" (50–74 credits), "Gold" (75–84 credits), "Gold Plus" (85–89 credits), and "Platinum" (90 credits and up). The Platinum class does not reflect maximum performance per se. Nonresi-dential buildings, for example, can achieve a total of credits that is higher than double the number required for Platinum certification (190 credits in total; BCA, 2013a). Minimum requirements relate to energy efficiency (at least 30 of 116 possible credits) and the other indicators combined (at least 20 of 74 possible credits) to ensure balance in the uptake of the various performance requirements.

Certification classes were voluntary when Green Mark was introduced in 2005, but this is no longer the case. As of 2008 the Singapore Government had required Gold certification for new construction work larger than two thousand square meters.[9] In 2013 mandatory regulation was further tightened. Gold certification is required for commercial property larger than fifteen thousand meters if property owners or users decide to renovate it. This has made Green Mark a vital part of mandatory urban sustainability requirements in Singapore (Deng et al., 2012). A senior bureaucrat involved in the development and implementation of Green Mark explained that exposing property developers and owners to relatively low mandatory classes might make them aware that it is not complicated or costly to achieve the voluntary higher classes and then seek to attain these (int. 110).

The increased mandatory requirements contribute to meeting the Singapore government's ambition to have 80 percent of its built environment certified by 2030. The requirements are complemented with various financial incentives that support property owners in achieving high Green Mark classes, as well as a yearly awards ceremony recognizing outstanding Green Mark performance (BCA, 2012). The Singapore government ensures this ceremony receives media attention, placing the work and the names of the winners and nominees in the spotlight. Representatives of the construction and property sectors regularly referred to the ceremony and its awards as "the Oscars in the industry" (int. 129), explaining that being awarded an "Oscar" will likely generate future work. "In effect, what we did, we had the carrot and the stick," another senior bureaucrat explained. "The legislation, the stick, sets a minimum mark [Gold class certification]. And then, for the rest, we used the incentive scheme to go Gold Plus and Platinum. And that has been quite effective" (int. 109). This insight accords with Green Mark performance data. When legislation and financial incentives were introduced in 2008, some 5 percent of Singapore's built environment was certified; by 2014 this was 24 percent, indicating that Green Mark is on track to meet the government's goal (BCA, 2010, 2014a, 2014c). Performance data further indicate positive uptake of "beyond compliance" certification: 21 percent of certificates issued in 2014 were Gold Plus, and 35 percent were Platinum — similar performance is reported for earlier years (BCA, 2013b). When compared to another certification and classification program in Singapore, Eco Office, this bureaucrat's assessment appears to be accurate. Eco Office is a voluntary program that certifies office tenants on the basis of their energy, water, and paper consumption. The program was introduced in 2002 by the Singapore Environment Council — a nongovernment organization that receives funding from the Singapore government — and one of Singapore's major development firms. The program begun as a means to reduce resource consumption in Singapore, and in 2014 it was exported to Malaysia and Indonesia. But this is where the comparison with Green Mark ends. Contrary to Green Mark, participation in Eco Office is not mandated by the Singapore government. This may in part explain its marginal uptake: by 2014, the program had attracted eighty participants, more than half of these government agencies.[10] This represents a very small proportion of Singapore's office tenants.[11]

Care needs to be taken, however, in concluding that the combination of sticks and carrots in Green Mark has been "quite effective," as claimed. Looking behind the scenes of the performance data a more complex story unfolds. Singapore experienced a construction boom in the early 2010s, which ended by the mid-2010s (Stevenson, 2015). With certification compulsory in this period it logically follows that the overall certified built environment has grown. The poor uptake of Green Mark for existing buildings — as anywhere, the majority of built-up space — may foreshadow the future performance of Green Mark now that the construction boom has ended. In 2014, for example, only 18 percent of certificates issued were awarded to existing buildings — in the history of Green Mark this is the best year in terms of certificates awarded to existing buildings (BCA, 2014b). Interviewees explained that most existing buildings in Singapore are residential units, and these often change ownership quickly. Their owners are not likely to retrofit their unit because "they will not see the return of their investment," an academic at the Energy Studies Institute explained (int. 122), or because they do not desire to enter a tedious process of retrofitting their unit (see also BCA, 2011).

Representatives of the Singapore property and construction sectors added a further explanation: the high uptake of "beyond compliance" certification results from developers expecting more profitable rental rates or sales prices from buildings in high classes compared to lower classes — research confirms these higher returns (Deng et al., 2012). This, they argued, also introduces the possibility that developers seek high certification classes driven by financial interest only. "Basically [property developers] see a market. And developers often hope to find a shortcut to meet the Platinum requirements," an academic at the Energy Research Institute shared. And, mimicking a developer, he continued, "Tell me how this can easily achieve Platinum. Tell me — what is the cheapest option?" (int. 120). This observation was corroborated by other interviewees. "The main problem is that Green Mark is very feature-based. If I add this, if I add that, I get the credits of it. But no one looks whether that feature is good for a project," an academic at the Department of Building noted. "Very often you see cases where they have installed green features, but it doesn't work out well because they did not look at the whole [building or city development project]" (int. 97). The problems voiced in these comments underlie some of the typical complications of labeling discussed in Chapter 4: compared to rating it does not offer detailed information as to the specific urban sustainability performance of a certified building or development project. Under Green Mark, for example, mandatory Gold class certification is possible without meeting any requirements for water efficiency (BCA, 2013a). In addition, the classification terminology used suggests that the higher classes considerably outperform the lower ones. However, the extent of improvements between each step in the higher classes diminishes: it takes twenty-five credits to move from Certified to Gold, ten credits from Gold to Gold Plus, and only five credits from Gold Plus to Platinum — and this highest class of certification can be achieved by meeting less than half of all possible Green Mark criteria.

Significant Findings

Insight derived from the certification and classification programs in India, Malaysia, and Singapore largely confirms the narrative presented in Chapter 4, which considered similarly designed programs in Australia, the Netherlands, and the United States. The programs studied in the current chapter have also revealed a number of additional perspectives regarding the impact of the local context on program performance (particularly in India and Malaysia), and the potential of combining mandatory and voluntary aspects in the governance of low-carbon buildings and cities (in Singapore). These significant findings are addressed in detail in what follows.

Overall Poor Performance of Certification and Classification Programs

The overall performance of the programs studied — in terms of attracting rule-takers — largely confirms the pattern uncovered in the earlier empirical chapters. Certification and classification programs only appeal to the expensive end of the construction and property sectors, where there is demand for sustainable buildings and clients have the means to pay additional costs charged by providers. "Why don't people do this? You have to ask the question, 'Why not?'" the CEO of one of Malaysia's major development firms said. "It's about misconceptions. People think it is expensive and difficult. Doing things a different way is risky, and many organizations don't want to take risks" (int. 141). This assessment rings true, even for Singapore, where adoption numbers by rule-takers in the quasi-voluntary program Green Mark have been relatively significant. A developer in Singapore explained: "Cost is always an issue. There still is a lack of awareness at the homeowner level: they are less willing to pay for [sustainable buildings]" (int. 104). A senior bureaucrat at the Singapore Housing Development Authority suggested that rule-makers "need to focus more on educating homeowners" to increase their awareness and raise their demand for low-carbon houses (int. 125).

Nevertheless, the relatively promising performance of Green Mark in terms of achieving considerable "beyond compliance" behavior is an exception requiring scrutiny. This "beyond compliance" behavior for Green Mark is considerably higher than for LEED in the United States or Green Star in Australia, and is closer to that of NABERS in Australia. In comparison: 35 percent of all certificates under Green Mark are issued in the highest class (Platinum) and 42 percent in the highest classes of NABERS (5-Star and 6-Star).[12] At the same time, only 11 percent of LEED certificates are issued in the highest class (Platinum), and 9 percent in the highest class of Green Star (6 Stars). The important similarity between Green Mark and NABERS is that they built on mandatory participation and voluntary compliance levels, whereas LEED and Green Star both rely on voluntary participation. I will return to this difference in the conclusion of the book — Chapter 9.

Unfavorable Economic Circumstances, Lack of Mandatory Requirements, and Corruption

Even more than those in Australia, the Netherlands, and the United States, interviewees in India and Malaysia referred to unfavorable economic conditions as one of the reasons why voluntary certification programs are unable to attract large numbers of rule-takers. They were particularly conscious that many voluntary certification and classification programs rely heavily on the application of novel, energy efficient building materials and products. "Why is all this technology not being used?", an architect in India countered in response to my interview question on this topic. "Well, only the top 5 percent of the Indian population can afford the current green technologies; if you only have ten rupees in your hand, you're not going to buy a 5-Star energy efficient air conditioner" (int. 202). This made some of them wonder whether voluntary programs that have been developed in the Global North can or should be transferred to the Global South — an issue I return to in the next section. Another contextual condition referred to by interviewees as explaining the poor performance of the certification and classification programs in India and Malaysia is the lack of mandatory requirements for low-carbon building and city development. They held the opinion that in the absence of such conditions voluntary programs may either ask too much of prospective rule-takers or provide too little incentive. Both of these perceptions concerning the more extreme contextual conditions in India and Malaysia substantiate the theoretical account given in Chapter 3 — these inferences need to be drawn with some caution, however, as they all build on anecdotal data.

An additional contextual condition referred to by interviewees — and confirmed by other data sources as explanatory for the poor performance of certification and classification programs in India and Malaysia — is a persistent culture of corruption (Ismael, 2009; Vittal, 2012). Interviewees in these countries argued that specifically for sectors such as construction and property, which are characterized by large sums of money changing hands, voluntary programs may too easily lead to corruption. In addition, so explained interviewees, the lack of institutional capital in India and Malaysia may further hamper the development and implementation of voluntary programs for sustainable building and city development. Lacking qualified staff, governments are unable to develop and implement voluntary programs themselves, or to assess the reliability of those developed and implemented by others. As an architect in India observed, "[Our policy makers] take what has been developed [in the Global North], but forget that it was not developed for the same level of development or under the same levels of corruption or inequity as we face here" (int. 197).

Transferability of Programs from the Global North to the Global South

Interviewees were particularly critical of the transfer of Global North voluntary programs to the Global South. Not only might the institutional context hamper the copying-and-pasting of voluntary programs, but the programs' content and focus may also be incompatible with Global South understanding of sustainable building, or unsuited to building development methods. As illustrated in the empirical chapters, the programs studied in Australia, the Netherlands, and the United States focus on reduced resource consumption or carbon emissions through technological solutions. But is this technology necessary, affordable, or consistent with desired outcomes in rapidly developing economies? Some interviewees wondered: "Especially in the West there is much stress on efficiency and substitution in sustainability debates. It is all about getting more bang for the buck, and then making the buck more sustainable," an architect in India said. "But why consume so much at all? The sufficiency issue is not addressed in Western sustainability thinking, and voluntary programs such as LEED legitimize this consumption" (int. 197).

It perhaps goes too far to consider this transfer of voluntary programs from the Global North to the Global South as a process of neocolonialism, but the model of neocolonial relations is nevertheless broadly applicable: rule-makers in the Global North actively pioneering a new market by establishing domestic monopolies in developing nations. This chapter explained how the United States Green Building Council was actively involved in the implementation of LEED in India — partly because it sees a growing market for LEED application. Now that the Green Building Council of India has decided to discontinue LEED-India, the USGBC has formed a strategic partnership with the Energy Resources Institute — the organization that administers GRIHA — to maintain its influence in the sustainable building market in India (USGBC, 2014). Likewise, the administrators of BREEAM have entered into an agreement with the national government of Malaysia to develop a certification and classification program for the Malaysian market. And finally, the Singapore government aimed to expand its political influence in the region by actively exporting Green Star to countries such as China, Malaysia, and Vietnam — in doing so it is also capitalizing on the market for sustainable building certification in these countries. While some countries in the Global South adapt programs from the Global North, others consider the hegemony of programs such as LEED and BREEAM a primary motivator to develop local certification and classification programs themselves — for instance, in Singapore and Malaysia (Green Mark and the Green Building Index). "LEED does not make sense for us. You cannot apply certain things here in the tropics," a managing director of one of Malaysia's largest property developers observed (int. 135). Strikingly, however, both Green Mark and the Green Building Index use Global North templates, and the organization that administers these programs actively seeks to export them to the region.

In addition, so explained interviewees, the construction sector in countries such as India and Malaysia is often low-tech when compared to that of countries in the Global North: labor is cheap, making it financially profitable for developers and contractors to have work carried out on construction sites, as opposed to using more expensive premanufactured building parts, as is normal practice in developed economies (Kamal, Haron, Ulang, & Baharum, 2012). In situ construction often results in more environmental problems than the use of premanufactured building parts — it requires greater use of packaging material, transport, and on-site activities that may result in local air or water pollution (Kamar, Hamid, Ghani, Egbu, & Arif, 2010; Shamsuddin, Zakaria, Mohamed, & Mustaffar, 2012). Voluntary programs from the Global North, however, often do not accommodate such low-tech development processes.

9   Beyond the Leadership Delusion
What Role for Voluntary Programs in Decarbonizing Buildings and Cities?

In the previous chapters I have stayed close to the data collected on the thirty-five voluntary programs for low-carbon, resource efficient, and environmentally sustainable buildings and cities, and stayed close to the theoretical template developed in Chapter 3. In this concluding chapter I allow myself a little more freedom. I do so in two ways. First, I am more normative than in earlier chapters and open up my focus not only to the environmental consequences of voluntary programs for sustainable buildings and cities (their opportunities and constraints in decarbonizing the built environment), but also to some of their other societal consequences — particularly in terms of equity. Second, I am more forward looking about how to improve the performance of voluntary programs. These projections move well beyond the thirty-five programs studied, and are of interest to those concerned with climate change mitigation, with sustainable buildings and cities, and with the efficacy of voluntary programs and other innovative and experimental forms of governance as a policy tool in modifying the behavior of all kinds of individuals and organizations — and not merely those in the construction and property sectors.

This final chapter more closely considers a number of these issues. First, it begins with reflections on the theoretical template presented in Chapter 3, and the hypotheses stated in that chapter. It then reflects on the value of voluntary programs for decarbonizing the built environment in developed economies (predominantly OECD countries) and in rapidly developing economies and other non-OECD countries. I then raise one of my core criticisms of the voluntary programs studied: they run the risk of creating — and in part have created — a leadership delusion about sustainable buildings and the transition to low-carbon built environments. In addition, I consider how, in my opinion, the lessons from these programs can be used to move beyond this leadership delusion to govern a large-scale, and, I hope, speedy, transition to sustainable building and city development and use. In the final section of this chapter I give thought to the broader topics related to voluntary programs for sustainable buildings and cities as stated in Chapter 1: what are the risks of the narrow understanding of environmental sustainability on which most voluntary programs are founded? To what extent is the paradigm of ecological modernization — which underlies most of the programs studied — promising in decarbonizing the built environment in the Global North and South? Why, in the face of a major environmental crisis, do the majority of sustainability solutions, such as the voluntary programs studied here, address symptoms rather than fundamental issues?

The Value of the Theoretical Template: Improving Understanding of Voluntary Programs

In Chapter 1 I explained that the theoretical template used in this book is the result of an iterative process of moving backward and forward between data and theory. The empirical synthesis chapter, Chapter 7, highlighted that the theoretical template I applied explains all variance in the conditions of voluntary programs for which performance outcomes were empirically observed (twenty-four programs for the performance outcome "attracting rule-takers" and fourteen for the performance outcome "affecting rule-taker behavior").

Reflections on the Hypotheses Regarding Voluntary Program Performance

In Chapter 3, three sets of hypotheses were made concerning the performance of the voluntary programs studied. These hypotheses were based on one of the most dominant perspectives for studying voluntary program performance, the club theory perspective (Potoski & Prakash, 2009), using realist evaluation practice (Pawson, 2013; Pawson & Tilley, 1997). They help to assess the explanatory reach of the club theory perspective for the studied voluntary programs.

The first set of hypotheses is not confirmed by the programs studied. To begin, the contention *voluntary programs for sustainable buildings that combine relatively lenient rules with relatively high rewards attract a relatively large number of rule-takers* (H1.1), is observed in three certification and classification programs — BREEAM-NL, Green Star, and NABERS. At the same time, however, a range of programs contradicts this: these programs have lenient rules and high rewards, but do not attract a relatively large number of rule-takers (set at 15 percent of the full pool of prospective rule-takers) — these include Energy Efficiency Mortgages and LEED; and, some programs have stringent rules and either high or low rewards, but do attract a relatively large number of rule-takers — these include Retrofit Chicago and CitySwitch Green Office. Then, the additional component *these programs substantially fail to improve the behavior of these rule-takers in terms of reducing their building-related resource consumption or carbon emissions* (H1.2) is disconfirmed by the same three certification and classification programs: their rule-takers do, on average, achieve substantial resource consumption or carbon emission reductions (set at a 20 percent improvement of mandatory requirements, or conventional practice performance for these programs). It may be argued that this performance is questionable for BREEAM-NL and Green Star because they have, thus far, predominantly certified expected performance instead of actual performance of buildings in use. Nonetheless, NABERS relies solely on actual performance data, which are considered to offer trustworthy insight into program performance. Finally, the part *in this specific design stringent monitoring and enforcement is a nonnecessary condition for improving rule-taker performance* (H1.3) is again disconfirmed by these three certification and classification programs, as they all build on third-party monitoring and enforcement, or data concerning resource consumption from buildings that are in use. This specific part of this set of hypotheses is further controverted by the analysis for sufficient conditions for the outcome "improved rule-taker behavior" (see Table 7.10): stringent enforcement is part of four of the eight paths that explain this performance outcome.

Likewise, the second set of hypotheses is not confirmed by the programs studied. To begin, the part *voluntary programs for sustainable buildings that combine relatively stringent rules with relatively high rewards attract small groups of dedicated rule-takers* (H2.1) is observed in a number of programs — including the Better Buildings Partnership and Retrofit Chicago. However, another program following this design, CitySwitch Green Office, disconfirms this because it has attracted a relatively high number of rule-takers. The next section, *these programs succeed in improving substantially the behavior of these rule-takers in terms of reducing their building-related resource consumption or carbon emissions* (H2.2), is observed in, for example, the Better Buildings Partnership, but not in others, for instance, CitySwitch Green Office. The final part, *in this specific design stringent monitoring and enforcement are necessary conditions for improving rule-taker behavior* (H2.3), is also observed in the Better Buildings Partnership, but not in CitySwitch Green Office.

The third hypothesis is again not confirmed by the full set of programs studied: *voluntary programs that provide direct monetary gains outperform those providing other rewards, in terms of attracting rule-takers and improving their behavior* (H3). While the presence of financial reward is observed in all voluntary programs that have achieved promising results in terms of attracting participants, this condition combines with other rewards in some of these programs. For the programs that have not achieved promising results, and for those more specifically that have failed or succeeded in terms of improving rule-taker behavior, the presence or absence of financial rewards is not observed in the pattern predicted by this hypothesis.

In sum, none of the sets of hypotheses and all their distinct parts are confirmed by the set of twenty-six voluntary programs studied. This stresses further the limited explanatory power of the existing literature and theorizing on voluntary programs that these hypotheses relied on — predominantly literature on the design conditions of such programs (e.g., Borck & Coglianese, 2009; DeLeon & Rivera, 2010; Potoski & Prakash, 2009) — and accentuates the importance of exposing this theorizing to other conditions when studying real-world examples of voluntary programs.

Reflections on the Causal Conditions Applied

The book has provided empirical evidence for the assumed causal direction of only two of the conditions included in the theoretical template. In short, for the conditions "local government involvement" and "type of diffusion network" the assumed positive causal direction was indeed identified: if any of these conditions were present at normal or high levels, they were found to have a positive impact on program performance. The book has uniquely provided empirical evidence for the assumed complex relationships between the conditions "rules" and "monitoring and enforcement" and program performance: stringent rules or monitoring and enforcement may relate to both promising and less promising program performance, as do lenient rules or monitoring and enforcement. This complex relationship is often assumed in the literature (Potoski & Prakash, 2009), but thus far has not been substantiated within a single study for both stringent and lenient rules, and stringent and lenient monitoring and enforcement. More precisely, this book has provided unique empirical insight into how stringent and lenient rules, or stringent and lenient monitoring and enforcement, combine with other conditions in affecting program performance outcomes.

The book has also provided unique empirical insight into the set of reward conditions included in the theoretical framework — assured financial rewards, nonfinancial rewards, and leadership rewards. It has illustrated how sometimes low levels or even total absence of one type of reward appears to be compensated for by the slight or substantial presence of another type of reward, and vice versa. For example, in one of the paths related to improved rule-takers' behavior the absence of nonfinancial rewards is compensated for by the presence of leadership rewards (path Red.2), and in another path its absence is compensated by the presence of assured financial rewards (path Red.1). That being said, because the study builds on QCA logic and tools (set theory and Boolean algebra), it needs to be borne in mind that the combination of all interacting conditions in the paths explains the performance outcome — in this case the two paths differ, since in one path assured financial rewards are present (path Red.1), and in the other the combination of leadership rewards and local government involvement is present (path Red.2; see Chapter 7 for these paths).

Reflections on the Observed Conjunctural Causation, Equifinality, and Nonsymmetry

Considering the same examples, I have already expressed some hope of positively affecting the performance of voluntary programs because of empirically observing conjunctural causation and equifinality — in other words, various conditions combine in affecting program performance, and different combinations of conditions may cause the same outcome (as in the example of path Red.1 and path Red.2). This indicates that differently designed voluntary programs may lead to similar outcomes. For example, a local government that seeks to develop a voluntary program but lacks means to reward prospective participants financially (and thus rules out the program design represented by path Red.1) may still yield desired performance results by providing leadership rewards, for example, by actively marketing program performance in the popular media, or by an annual awards ceremony (which follows the program design depicted by path Red.2). It also indicates that marginal adjustments to less promising programs may produce considerable outcomes.

However, I have expressed concerns about the empirically observed nonsymmetry in the relationship between conditions and program performance. While this observation is unique in itself, and its identification is valuable from a scholarly perspective — to the best of my knowledge it has not yet been identified in earlier empirical studies of voluntary programs — this nonsymmetry is accompanied by considerable practical complications. Simply put, it implies that it cannot be assumed that what affects voluntary program performance positively when present (e.g., assured high financial reward) also affects this performance negatively when absent (e.g., low or no assured financial reward). To those involved in the development and administration of voluntary programs it is therefore important not only to understand what aspects of voluntary programs work in their specific context, but also what aspects do not work in their context. Cherry-picking the positive aspects of other voluntary programs cannot be expected to yield desired outcomes; nor can simply inversing an incentive when it is found to yield undesired results in its current state (for instance, changing low to high financial rewards). Unfortunately, we humans appear to be biased toward thinking in symmetrical cause-and-effect relations and find it difficult to deal with nonsymmetrical possibilities (Kahneman, 2011).[1]

Finally, the inclusion of both "successful" and less successful programs in the study has resulted in the methodological observation that the less successful programs provide a much richer understanding of voluntary program performance than the successful ones. For example, the voluntary programs with promising results in terms of attracting rule-takers and improving their behavior largely confirm the assumed relation between financial rewards and these outcomes. On the contrary, the programs that do not show promising results for these outcomes demonstrate a much more complex relation with financial rewards. Some of the less promising programs confirm the assumed relation, while others contradict it. This indicates that in studying innovative and experimental governance interventions such as voluntary programs it is relevant to include both successful and unsuccessful cases.

The Role of the Diffusion Network

Perhaps the most valuable addition to the literature and theorizing on voluntary programs is the inclusion of the diffusion network in the theoretical framework. As an individual condition it does not explain any of the variance in the programs studied, but in combination with the other conditions it became the missing piece in this study's empirical puzzle. This calls on future researchers of, and those more practically involved in, voluntary programs (and other innovative governance instruments) to think more carefully about the role of the diffusion network when seeking to understand voluntary program performance. Throughout the book I have quoted a range of program administrators and rule-takers who, in one way or the other, stress the importance of the diffusion network. Often they explained the importance of peer-to-peer communication in reaching out to prospective rule-takers, as was the case for the Better Building Partnership and the Chicago Green Office Challenge. Another example of using the diffusion network is including construction and property sector peak bodies, and a number of their representatives have spoken in the empirical chapters. Yet another way is to activate "change agents" related to prospective rule-takers. "We run a program and only building owners are eligible to apply. But in practice often the biggest advocates for this are engineering consultants. They may have a solution, but need a client to implement it and a building to apply it [to]," a senior policy maker in the state of South Australia observed. In his experience these consultants are essential in contacting the property owners the program targets (int. 51). A more drastic way of using a diffusion network is by mandatorily requiring exposure to a voluntary program, as illustrated by NABERS in Australia and Green Mark in Singapore, or by having authority figures involved to advocate for the program. This all strongly reflects insight from the diffusion of innovations literature and calls for the introduction of a "diffusion network perspective" to existing theorizing on voluntary programs.

A Word of Caution

As with any research project, the findings presented here should be considered in light of the methods applied. The caveats of applying QCA methodology constitute standard reading in a series of textbooks (Goertz & Mahony, 2012; Ragin, 2008; Rihoux & Ragin, 2009; Schneider & Wagemann, 2012), and Appendix C explains how I have dealt with these in this study. Still, it should be kept in mind that this study builds on a sample of thirty-five real-world voluntary programs. They were selected for their capacity to maximize the utility of information available in explaining their performance (Flyvbjerg, 2015). The thirty-five cases are but a fraction of all the possible voluntary programs for sustainable building and urban transformation that have been implemented worldwide (van der Heijden, 2014a). I nevertheless expect that these thirty-five programs provide a knowledge base and a perspective of their opportunities and constraints that are broad enough to improve our understanding of the performance of voluntary programs more generally. The extent to which the breadth of knowledge and perspective are limited is balanced by the depth and rigor of the systematic analysis outlined in the empirical chapters. In addition, I would suggest that those studying other sets of voluntary programs for sustainable building and urban transformation, or voluntary programs in other sectors, or in countries other than those considered here are likely to find similar performance patterns and interactions between outcomes and conditions to those revealed in this book. However, it is unlikely they will find identical patterns and interactions: this study allows for "moderatum generalization" (Payne & Williams, 2005). In particular, I expect that differences in contextual conditions (different sectors, countries, types of actor, and diffusion networks) and their interaction with voluntary program design conditions (rules, enforcement, rewards) will result in empirical observations that diverge from this study and others.

What Exactly Explains the Overall Poor Performance of the Voluntary Programs Studied?

That all being said in favor of the scholarly contribution of this study, its primary finding is that voluntary programs for low-carbon building and city development are not a promising means of hastening and scaling up the decarbonization of the built environment in highly developed, rich economies such as Australia, the Netherlands, and the United States — nor in other countries with different contextual conditions, including India, Malaysia, and Singapore. How can it be that this approach to governance yields such poor results? When looking back over the full study several reasons that may explain the overall poor performance of voluntary programs for sustainable development arise.

A Very, Very Long Tail without a Head — Power Laws Do Not Hold Here

The first is a symptomatic problem related to the built environment in highly developed, rich economies (predominantly OECD countries): Most building-related resource consumption and carbon emissions can be attributed to the operational phase of existing buildings (80 percent, see Chapter 2) and this is roughly halved between the residential and commercial sectors. In other words, because these buildings already exist, the crucial issue is to retrofit or upgrade them, to achieve a drastic change in building use or, preferably, a combination of both. Contrary to that in many other markets for consumable goods, rapid and large-scale decarbonization of the built environment in these developed economies is not expected to result from changing supply — unless, of course, building energy supply would switch from nonrenewable to renewable resources — but from changing consumption.

The critical problem of the consumption side of the built environment is that it has a very long tail: many small voluntary improvements are possible in hundreds of millions of individual buildings owned by hundreds of millions of individual property owners (cf. UNEP, 2009). This means that power laws do not hold here. Power laws, more popularly known as the 80/20 rule, build on the idea of scale variance and argue that by capturing the small group of, for example, top carbon emitters ("20 percent" — the relatively small number of major consumers or producers: the "head"), the vast majority of carbon emissions is addressed ("80 percent") and that the remaining small percentage of carbon emissions is produced by a very large group (the "tail," see further Kane, 2014). Unlike many other sectors, there is no "head" in the construction and property sectors that is responsible for the vast majority of consumption or emissions.[2,3] The built environment is not characterized by "winner takes all" markets and processes, which appear to be a necessary condition in order for voluntary programs that follow an exclusive club model to achieve promising outcomes.

In sum, administrators of voluntary programs for low-carbon building and city development thus need to convince many individual prospective rule-takers of the advantages of joining their program for it to have any noticeable effect — this holds even for specialist and targeted voluntary programs, such as 1200 Buildings in Melbourne. To complicate matters further, the very long tail of prospective rule-takers is highly fragmented, implying that different groups of prospective rule-takers ask for different types of voluntary programs and different communication channels and narratives to reach them. This pertains all the more because voluntary programs do not constitute a continuous innovation but often a discontinuous one, requiring prospective rule-takers to gain knowledge, invest money and time, and change the way they have been doing business or using their buildings for a long time (cf. MacVaugh & Schiavone, 2010; E. M. Rogers, 1995). As has become clear throughout the book, program administrators struggle with reaching out to prospective rule-takers and convincing them to participate for exactly these reasons.

The Marginal and Perhaps Negative Impact of Context

Related to the problem of the very long tail without a head is the marginal, perhaps even negative impact of the context of the voluntary programs studied. Policy makers in all countries explained that mandatory building codes for sustainable building development and use are modest compared to technological possibilities and are sometimes even absent (cf. IEA, 2008, 2013). Thus, even when a voluntary program requires its prospective rule-takers to make "significant" improvements, it often only tinkers at the margins of the sustainable building challenge. The only voluntary program studied that has set very stringent requirements for its rule-takers is the Better Buildings Partnership in Sydney, which aims for a 70 percent reduction of building energy consumption over a ten-year period — but, as explained in Chapter 5, because of its relatively small scale (one hundred buildings) its relative impact is limited.

Another problem related to the context of the programs studied is that there is very little societal pressure to decarbonize the built environment. Households and small and medium-sized firms generally do not ask for buildings with sustainability credentials, as was stressed time and again by interviewees. But large-scale, more general societal pressure is also absent. Typical environmental NGOs that are normally very capable of increasing social pressure on various issues, such as Greenpeace or the World Wildlife Fund, have thus far overlooked the area of sustainable construction. The issue of sustainable building lacks the sentimental popular appeal of a polar bear on a sheet of ice, and possibly also lacks the "feel-good reinforcement factor" of purchasing sustainably produced Fair Trade coffee (cf. Hoffman, 2015; Hughes & Macbeth, 2005). This was best illustrated by a senior manager at a Dutch housing corporation interest group who said: "Home owners think of solar panels as sympathetic — much more so than, say, the insulation of the facade of their house. The latter is not sexy, but perhaps more effective" (int. 93).

Finally, the problem of hyperbolic discounting (whereby future, long-term gains are dismissed in light of the short-term costs required to achieve them) is particularly strong in the construction and property sectors, and its effects were only strengthened by the global financial crisis of 2008–2011. Interviewees in all countries often highlighted that the "current financial climate" did not permit sufficient financial space to develop sustainable buildings or retrofit existing ones. There is even a risk that the problem of hyperbolic discounting as practiced by prospective and existing rule-takers spills over to rule-makers: "We shouldn't forget our position in the market," a policy maker in the city of Rotterdam in the Netherlands reminded me. "It's a fine balance between economy and ecology, which is especially true in a time like this [referring to the global financial crisis]. If we ask to much of firms they will base themselves in another city" (int. 73).

Voluntary Programs Unfit to Fill Regulatory Voids — Perhaps Because There Is No Low-Hanging Fruit?

In sum, neither the targeted market (the construction and property sectors) nor its context (existing building codes and planning legislation, economic circumstances, and societal pressure)is favorable for voluntary programs for sustainable building and city development to be successful in attracting large numbers of rule-takers and significantly improving their behavior and their buildings. Many of the challenges faced by mandatory sustainable building regulation are also confronted by voluntary programs. This insight supports earlier studies that determine that reliance on voluntary programs to fill regulatory voids is doomed to failure (cf. Short, 2013). While the knowledge generated through these voluntary programs is very valuable and their uptake even holds potential to trigger a shift in norms in the construction and property sectors (spillover effects, cf. Cole & Valdebenito, 2013; Lim & Prakash, 2014; Yudelson & Meyer, 2013), they are unsuitable to address effectively the specific characteristics of — and deeply embedded problems in — the construction and property sectors and the sustainable building challenge more generally.

Besides, being unable to address these symptomatic and structural problems, the voluntary programs studied also take a major risk by marketing an enduring narrative of ecological modernization, ecoefficiency, and green growth — reliant on the assumption that the economy and the natural environment gain from these programs, particularly because rule-takers save costs by reducing their resource consumption or carbon emissions (cf., Dryzek, 2005; Hayden, 2014; Matthews, 2015). Policy makers, private sector representatives, and academics alike often claim that there is much low-hanging fruit in the construction and property sectors — referring to assumed low-cost but significant reduction potential of building-related resource consumption and carbon emissions — and the voluntary programs studied accept this claim (Hoppe et al., 2011; Vandenbergh, Barkenbus, & Gilligan, 2008). As rule-takers interviewed repeatedly argued, however, these promised cost savings do not materialize within the expected time frame — which in the case of Zonnig Huren ("Sunny Leasing") in the Netherlands, for example, left rule-takers disillusioned. It appears to be time for rule-makers and other advocates of voluntary programs for sustainable buildings to step away from the low-hanging fruit narrative: making the required changes to the built environment within the required time frame is not going to be easy and is not going to be profitable, at least not in the short term. Not acting is, however, going to be more costly in the long run, and voluntary programs may be designed and implemented in such a way as to make the transition to a low-carbon built environment as easy and cost-efficient as possible. How? That is the topic of a following section.

Voluntary Programs in Rapidly Developing Economies: A Much More Complicated and Risky Context

A word of caution seems necessary for voluntary sustainable building programs in rapidly developing countries. The performance outcomes of the programs studied in India and Malaysia were as unpromising as of those studied in Australia, the Netherlands, and the United States. However, as Chapter 8 highlighted, in contexts characterized by low institutional capital and contexts that have a culture of corruption, voluntary programs may face even more complications than a lack of interest among rule-takers. Low institutional capital typically entails lack of oversight by authorities, which leads to the greater likelihood that such programs are prone to corruption. Involved parties have considerable interest in meeting program requirements, or in attracting large numbers of participants to their program. This problem was identified in the programs studied in Australia, the Netherlands, and the United States and is likely to be strengthened in countries with a known culture of corruption such as India and Malaysia.[4]

Equally problematic is the active exportation of Global North voluntary programs to the Global South. Dissimilar building and construction practices, different understandings of and approaches to ownership of property, differences in institutional capital, incomparable cultures of compliance and corruption mean that programs developed in and for the Global North should not be expected to fit the contexts of countries in the Global South. While it is laudable that green building councils in the Global North want to support their developing counterparts, such support should involve more than self-interested expansion of the Global North's market for voluntary programs — particularly certification and classification programs. Financial and administrative support in the development of local programs that suit the local context may ultimately yield better outcomes.

The Leadership Delusion and Beyond: "We've Got to Toughen Up Here"

What strikes me most when I look back at the set of voluntary programs studied is the dominance of a leadership narrative in the way programs are marketed by administrators, in the way rule-makers and rule-takers talked about these programs, and in the way they are depicted in the popular media. A board member of the Australian Green Building Council, the organisation that administers Green Star, sought to motivate members of the program by stating: "If you address the leaders, you will push the followers" (int. 22). "Government said they would only lease certified buildings and that has really kick-started the sustainability move here. It's showing leadership," the managing director of a large property investment firm in Australia told me when discussing Green Star (int. 53). "For participants it is important that they are recognized in taking leadership," an administrator of CitySwitch Green Office in Australia stated (int. 36); and an administrator of 1200 Buildings in Melbourne concluded: "You will never get anywhere without leadership.

You need leadership. And our program provides a platform [for property owners] to show leadership" (int. 26). An administrator of Energie-sprong ("Energy Leap") in the Netherlands argued that the program is a success because "we have found the leaders in the industry. We are known as a brand. You are here because you have heard about us" (int. 79). "Most of the progressive companies in India now seem to [have their buildings certified under LEED-India]. It's about their corporate image. They want to be seen as leaders," the principal of an Indian sustainability consultancy firm explained (int. 154). And, finally, an administrator of Retrofit Chicago stated: "In the newspaper we praise [participating] buildings for being good for the community. Other building owners see that and they say 'we want to be leaders too. We want to participate in this program too'" (int. 188).

Throughout the empirical chapters I discussed how most programs studied actively market a narrative of leadership (in the sense of pioneers or "front-runners," see Teisman, van Buuren, & Gerrits, 2009) as one of the means of attracting rule-takers, and the ways in which they market the performance of rule-takers as showcasing leadership in the area of sustainable building practice. I have also provided examples of the popular media echoing this narrative of leadership. For example, the United States Green Building Council actively promotes the uptake of LEED in the United States and in doing so generates much positive attention: the *New York Times* dedicated more than 125 articles to the program over the last decade. In contrast, the voluntary Energy Star Home certification and classification program administered by the United States Environmental Protection Agency was mentioned in fewer than 10 articles during the same period.[5] Compared to the United States Green Building Council, the agency is less active in promoting the performance of the program. Even more, LEED was awarded the United Nations' top environmental prize, the Champions of the Earth Awards, and 1200 Buildings and the Amsterdam Investment Fund have both received a Climate Leadership Award from the C40 Cities group for their "leading position" in and "transformative impact" on the construction and property sectors.

All this talk of facilitating leadership, showcasing leading practice and behavior, and rewarding leaders has, I argue, resulted in a "leadership delusion." A narrative is presented that reads as if the construction and property sectors have embraced sustainable building practice and are actively working to decarbonize the built environment. But no such thing is the case when the "leading performance" of the programs, their rule-makers, and their rule-takers in all but one of the programs studied is feeble at best. This leadership delusion is understandable — it is in the interest of rule-makers and rule-takers to recite this narrative to one another and the world at large — but it is also hazardous because it can remove political and societal attention from the sustainability challenge that needs to be addressed, and it can also create a false sense of security. Does this suggest that we should cease using voluntary programs in this area? I hesitate to counsel abandonment of voluntarism and self-regulation in the absence of an implemented alternative framework. Nevertheless, as rethinking the purpose and continued use of these programs is an urgent necessity, I favor a future for voluntary programs within larger regulatory frameworks for decarbonizing the built environment. A sustainable building consultant summed up his experience with voluntary programs in Australia: "You have the leaders in these programs that keep going further, and then regulation should come in and pick up the laggards" (int. 29). This sentiment was shared by more interviewees when challenged to share their personal opinions about the value of voluntary programs: "Mandatory is the way to go. And that probably is a funny answer from somebody who runs a voluntary program," an administrator in Australia conceded. "Well, there probably is room for both. But if we make the changes in the time line we need to make them, then we've got to toughen up here" (int. 41). Of course, voluntary programs are often implemented as moderate complements to mandatory requirements, and as such expectations of their performance may need to remain low (Berliner & Prakash, 2014; Coglianese & Nash, 2014). Regardless of this, the research does indicate directions that might aid in achieving more desirable voluntary program outcomes than those reported throughout this book.[6]

Beyond Leadership: Toward a Focus on Early Adopters and Early Majorities

The voluntary programs studied face the exact problems explored in the literature on the diffusion of innovations. Many of them have not made the transition from a very small group of absolute leaders in the industry to a larger group of early adopters that is essential to mainstream them. More problematically, hardly any program has made the transition from the early market (comprising leaders and early adopters — here defined as 15 percent of the full pool of potential rule-takers a program targets) to the mainstream market (made up of the early and late majority). "We are constantly engaging with the same people," a program administrator in the United States observed: "We are always questioning how we can get the people that are now out of our network into the program" (int. 194). The first impediment to diffusion from leaders to early adopters results when early adopters are unable to discover the advantages of a voluntary program or when its risks are not commensurate with the rewards (cf. Moore, 2002). This is most visible in the low uptake of the highest classes of voluntary certification and classification programs. "It simply is not viable to develop a Green Star 6-Star rated multiunit residential project. Unless, of course, you want it to be a flagship development of your portfolio and you know you're going to make a loss on it," a sustainability manager at a major property developer in Australia explained (int. 44). This observed obstacle to diffusion questions the efficacy of highly popular awards ceremonies, as well as the strong focus of Green Star— and LEED-like programs on marketing the highly innovative 6-Star and Platinum-classed buildings, as opposed to slightly more conventional 5-Star and Gold-classed ones — the latter may be more inspirational to early adopters than the former.

More problematic is the "gap" in diffusion between early adopters and the early majority. Here the leadership narrative advocated by rule-makers might be wholly inapplicable to its audience: prospective rule-takers with the characteristics of the early or late majority are unlikely to be inspired by language about leadership, innovation, or being ahead of the pack (cf. E. M. Rogers, 1995). They are typically seeking low-risk changes to their conventional practice. The actively marketed success stories of leading rule-takers likely do not resonate with this group of prospective rule-takers (cf. G. Marshall, 2014). Small firms in the United States are so dissimilar to multinationals such as 3M or Lend Lease that the lessons learned from the leading performance of these organizations in a program like the Better Buildings Challenge simply have no value to them. Rule-makers and program administrators need to become more aware of the vast heterogeneity present in the "long tail" of the construction and property sectors and plan their diffusion strategies accordingly. It is necessary to include a diffusion network perspective in the development, implementation, and evaluation of voluntary programs.

Beyond Voluntary and Mandatory: Toward Hybrids

One way of bridging these impediments and gaps in diffusion networks is to move beyond the dichotomy of mandatory and voluntary programs. NABERS in Australia, the Small Business Improvement Fund in Chicago, and Green Mark in Singapore are examples of hybrid governance instruments that combine aspects of mandatory requirements and voluntary programs. All prospective rule-takers are exposed to NABERS and Green Mark simply because participation is mandatory, but the level of compliance with the programs is voluntary. Administrators of these programs argued that by exposing rule-takers to the programs they might understand the ease or viability of achieving higher-than-mandatory levels of classification. Because certification and classification programs replicate the design of mandatory building codes in many countries it may be expected that a change to hybrid certification and classification schemes can be implemented with relative ease — it makes for the least discontinuous innovation of the various program designs studied.

The Small Business Improvement Fund, which builds on tax increment financing, is another inspiring design in that it provides an answer to the pervasive problem of hyperbolic discounting and loss aversion of property owners. Simply taxing property owners in the present and offering them the opportunity to retrofit or upgrade their prospective building with finance provided by the taxes raised, might induce them to become more active in seeking to benefit directly from those tax monies already paid. The concept of tax increment financing is not without criticism (Lefcoe, 2011; Pacewicz, 2013). However, the notion of changing the default for prospective rule-takers — from choosing to put aside funds for a retrofit, to being required by mandate to do so — provides a promising avenue down which to prod people into making choices that will result in societally desirable outcomes and has yielded encouraging results in the area of building-related energy consumption reductions (Cabinet Office, 2011; Kosters & van der Heijden, 2015; Thaler & Sunstein, 2009). An alternative to this design would be to change from voluntary opting-in to allowing for voluntary opting-out of programs — for example, providing energy efficiency mortgages for future homeowners as the default option, but permitting them to decline the arrangement.

Yet another alternative is to design for synergies between mandatory requirements and voluntary programs. The promising performance of NABERS in Australia — and arguably also Green Star — is partly the result of mandatory energy efficiency disclosure regulation; and the promising performance of BREEAM-NL is to some degree the consequence of sustainable procurement requirements for governments in the Netherlands, which stipulate that new governmental office space, whether owned or leased, has to meet a specific or comparable level of BREEAM-NL performance criteria. Piggybacking voluntary programs on mandatory regimes may be considered by the construction and property sectors as less intrusive government intervention than the ratcheting up of mandatory building codes. These few examples are drawn from what might be a substantial pool of hybrid designs: future scholarship will need to improve our understanding of their potential for accelerating the transition toward a low-carbon built environment.

Beyond Short-Term or No-Term: Toward Rolling Rule Regimes

Another novel way of thinking about voluntary programs and mandatory requirements is to join the two in a "rolling rule regime" (Sabel, Fung, Karkkainen, Cohen, & Rogers, 2000; Silver, Scott, & Kazepov, 2010). "Voluntary programs are almost the R&D [research and development] section of mandatory schemes. It is where innovative behavior does happen. And it does test out a lot of people's systems and processes, and they show that robust programs are possible and they can deliver advantages," the CEO of a major environmental consultancy firm in Australia explained. "And when mandatory schemes come along, they then already are significantly in the process. It is not starting from scratch. They do not have to reinvent the wheel, and all the learning already has happened" (int. 32). Interviewees further argued that voluntary programs allow rule-takers to conceive novel building designs, or to use the most innovative technological solutions that are not currently accepted under mandatory requirements.

Another prominent shortcoming of the voluntary programs studied is that they either focus on the very short term or do not have a time horizon in which they want to achieve a certain goal. Short-term programs are not given time to achieve transformative change. In existing circumstances it is likely that only large leading firms in the construction and property sectors are willing to take the risk in joining such programs — the Better Buildings Challenge is an example — and the lessons learned from these programs are unlikely to inspire others to follow their lead. Programs without a time frame run the risk that anything goes: LEED has been in operation for more than fifteen years and its relative transformative impact in terms of buildings constructed or retrofitted is marginal. During that same time, LEED has provided numerous examples — in all classes of certification and for a wide range of property types — that could function as influential templates for the industry: inspiration to construct buildings that consume considerably lower volume of resources and produce a much lower volume of carbon emissions than conventional buildings. But how can it be that a building that was a pioneering LEED exemplar some fifteen years ago is still not conventional practice? A rolling rule regime may solve this issue by mandating that today's leading practice in a voluntary program will be the bottom line in mandatory building codes within, say, ten years. This still incentivizes and rewards leaders and early adopters in the early market, as they have the opportunity to set the future bottom line and possess the experience necessary to achieve it, but it would also actively push the mainstream market (the early and late majority) to follow suit within the time frame set. A rolling rule regime would also help to overcome the noticeable risk that voluntary programs without a time horizon become sluggish over time: "They may limit innovation in the industry when parties start to consider these [programs'] standards as the lowest common denominator," an administrator of one of the Australian certification and classification programs warned (int. 30).

Last, but Not Least: Fundamental Questions

And with that I have come to the final section of this book. In summing up I reflect on the fundamental questions posed in the first pages.

What Role for Voluntary Programs in Decarbonizing the Built Environment?

The two questions underlying this book are: *To what extent and how do voluntary programs contribute to the construction, maintenance, and use of resource-efficient and low-carbon buildings and cities? What future application of these voluntary programs may help to accelerate decarbonization of the built environment?* The thirty-five programs studied throughout the book do not present a hopeful picture of the extent of which voluntary programs help to accelerate and scale up decarbonization of the built environment. While they have generated a wealth of valuable lessons, best practices, and exemplars of resource efficient and low-carbon development, relative to the sustainability challenge faced their overall impact is lower than negligible. The programs studied have further made clear that answering the "how" question is anything but easy. Various design, context, actor, and diffusion network conditions interact in affecting voluntary program performance. There does not appear to be a blueprint for a program that is guaranteed to yield desired outcomes. While at first glance this is a decidedly negative finding, the positive news is that in combination with the actors involved, its contexts, and the type of diffusion network used, various program designs may yield desired outcomes. In other words, we do not have to write off voluntary programs for sustainable buildings as a category of governance instruments that is doomed to fail.

What the research discussed here does suggest, however, is the likelihood that the role of voluntary programs for sustainable buildings and cities should only continue as a component of larger regulatory frameworks for decarbonizing the built environment: this answers the second question. I have already argued that rule-makers and program administrators need to think beyond the early market — the leaders and early adopters — and question how they can harness the majority market if they wish their voluntary programs to have significant impact. I have also argued that moving beyond the dichotomy of mandatory and voluntary programs toward hybrid governance instruments and the inclusion of voluntary programs in rolling-rule regimes may be a more hopeful application of voluntary programs than strictly consigning them to roles that complement mandatory building codes and planning legislation.

Beyond Ecological Modernization and Sustainable Building Inequalities

In this book I have used the term "sustainable buildings and cities" as a shorthand for the development, retrofitting, and use of buildings and cities in ways that require less resource volume and result in reduced carbon emissions than are stipulated by mandatory regulation or conventional market practice. I am aware that this narrow focus on ecoefficiency does not address fundamental questions of ongoing development in a finite world, or fundamental questions about inequalities among different groups of people who may or may not be able to afford sustainable buildings, whether this is within a city or between populations in the Global North and Global South. The focus on ecoefficiency, and on ecological modernization more broadly (the paradigm that addressing climate change risks results in economic growth) is an empirical reality of the programs studied. Throughout the book it has become clear that this focus on ecoefficiency yields marginal results, and that the focus on ecological modernization may be counterproductive when rule-takers do not see promises of financial returns fulfilled — or it may simply appear to be too hazardous to the large group of potential rule-takers in the majority market.

The problem of inequalities resulting from "sustainable building practice" is beginning to enter academic and policy debates (Bulkeley, Castan Broto, & Edwards, 2015; Eames et al., 2013; Robinson & Cole, 2015) — and relates to earlier debates on environmental, health, and other social —economic inequalities resulting from environmental policy choices (Downey & Hawkins, 2008; Lopez, 2002). This book adds to those debates: most of the programs studied yield desirable outcomes in the high end of the commercial construction and property sectors (new office buildings for major corporations in the central business districts of large cities), but not in other areas. Interviewees stressed that small and medium-sized firms and homeowners consider sustainable building practice as too expensive or too complicated. Program administrators (rule-makers) tend to gravitate to program designs that serve large firms because the sustainable building practice of such firms reflects well on the program. For program administrators these large firms are the "low-hanging fruit," but one may question whether these firms require all of the support they receive through these programs. This reservation holds all the more when considering that many of the voluntary programs studied are administered by government agencies, and that means that taxpayers are funding prosperous, capable major corporations. Another risk is that sustainable buildings developed under these programs become a status symbol that is not equally accessible for all. As highlighted in Chapter 8, the sustainable housing units developed under the voluntary Eco-Housing program in Pune, India, sell at 10 million Indian rupees (U.S.$150,000), a sum that is well out of reach for most of Pune's citizens.

Beyond Technosustainability and Voluntary Programs as Industry Captured Regulatory Capitalism

Related to the preceding the voluntary programs studied in this book predominantly address technological solutions to decarbonizing the built environment and have a limited focus on behavioral change. This reflects another empirical reality that resonates with other voluntary programs and governance innovations for sustainable building around the globe (see also, van der Heijden, 2014a). Interviewees considered this a shortcoming of many of the programs studied. "Look, you can build a ten-star building, but if you put a one-star family in it it's not going to work," an administrator of an Australian certification and classification program observed (int. 30). Interviewees in India were particularly critical of the dominant focus of programs on achieving ecoefficiency through technosustainability: "There is a tension between efficiency and sufficiency that is not addressed," an architect argued (int. 205). They argued for programs that concentrate more on behavioral change to reduce building-related resource consumption and carbon emissions than on technological solutions. Keeping in mind the risks of rebound effects — the possibility that occupants use more energy in a sustainable building than in a conventional one as they feel justified in having already contributed to sustainability — there is much to say for increasing our attention to behavioral change. But the energy required to produce sustainable technology and the carbon emissions resulting from it (embodied energy and carbon emissions) also supports a transfer of focus to programs that address the behavior of building users. In light of the rapidly growing built environment around the globe due to ongoing urbanization, the Jevons paradox looms: reductions achieved through technosustainability are outpaced by rapid growth in resource consumption and carbon emissions (cf. Alcott, 2005).

That most voluntary programs studied focus on technological rather than behavioral solutions is not surprising. Certification and classification programs especially are influenced by manufacturers of building materials, which maintain shortsighted self-interest in ensuring that the construction and property sectors consume ever-increasing volumes of their products. "You've got to bear in mind that in terms of sustainable technology there are a lot of vested interests," the CEO of an international building design firm explained (int. 160), citing examples of concerted lobbying by manufacturers for their products to be accepted by certification programs as compliant with set standards (see also, Gonzalez, 2009; Papadopoulos, 2015). "The whole thing [certification and classification programs] is hijacked by people who drive personal interests and do not seek sustainability per se," stated an individual who maintained LEED and Green Star accreditations, allowing assessment of building compliance in both programs (int. 210). The voluntary programs studied are exemplary of what has become known as regulatory capitalism — the regulation and governance of the global political economy through governance instruments by actors outside the traditional legislature (Braithwaite & Drahos, 2000; Levi-Faur, 2006). These programs are subject to considerable risk of capture by powerful industry and lobby groups willing to co-opt regulatory regimes for their own agenda.

Beyond Correcting and toward Directing

In conclusion, then, this book should be seen as a plea to policy makers, governments, industry representatives, and researchers to cease tinkering at the edges of what is possible with voluntary programs and instead to implement regulatory frameworks that swiftly decarbonize the built environment and create sustainable buildings and cities.[7] Voluntary programs hold potential to scale up and accelerate this transition, but the way they are used now is doing more harm than good. The leadership delusion distracts from the full scale of the sustainable building challenge faced, conceals the overall poor performance of the construction and property sectors, and can provide a questionable rationale for dubious "sustainable" building practice.[8] The relatively low and unambitious requirements set for prospective and existing rule-takers may lock their buildings into suboptimal performance while allowing owners to feel they have done enough for many years in the future (see also, UNEP, 2009). Finally, the focus on ecological modernization and technoefficiency can be counterproductive when promised financial rewards do not materialize or when the growth of building-related resource consumption and carbon emissions outpaces the reductions achieved — through rebound effects, the Jevons paradox, or both.

Two fitting observations by interviewees will complete this discussion. One of the primary challenges that need to be overcome is the fragmentation of the construction and property sectors in general, and the fragmentation of the sustainable building movement in particular. "My overall insight, after having been in the industry for decades now, is that the sustainable building movement is very fragmented," a senior director at one of the world's largest insurance companies stated. "Everyone moves in the same direction, but hardly anyone is working together; some do, but most are in their own little tower" (int. 183). Much more than traditional governance instruments for sustainable buildings, voluntary programs provide a means of establishing synergies within and acceleration of the sustainability movement. They may even provide a means with which to overcome the piecemeal fashion of addressing the sustainable building challenge that is inherent in mandatory building codes and planning legislation (cf. Eames et al., 2013). They allow for local, regional, national, and international knowledge generation and sharing, and thus can provide bridges between siloed industries and trades, and give governments, firms, citizens, and civil society organizations a platform for collaboration on what needs to be a mutual goal of decarbonizing the built environment.

Most importantly, however, is the need to overcome the mediocre ambitions of voluntary programs for sustainable buildings. "So far we have been interested in buildings that are less bad," a board member of the Green Building Council of Australia told me. "Buildings that use less energy, use less water, use less [volume of] materials. This is what we have been capable of doing. But it is time to stop looking at buildings that do less bad; we should start looking at buildings that do good" (int. 22). Voluntary programs are ideally suited to challenge the leaders and early adopters in the construction and property sectors to develop innovative buildings and cities that "do good" and to develop innovative ways of using buildings and cities that do good — thereby setting the direction for the future of sustainable building and city development and use. But these innovations require vast increases in scale, which necessitate a different way of conceiving of where voluntary programs should sit in the larger regulatory framework for decarbonizing the built environment — a different way of thinking about how to affect — to *redirect* — the majority market. This book has provided a number of alternatives for doing so.

Where Next? Forward, Sideway

That leaves us asking where this research might lead. As would any author, I hope that this book will inspire others to conduct research along similar lines — or alternatively to motivate others not to carry out such research: as I have mentioned, undertaking and reporting on a medium-n study have many challenges. The ultimate proof of the impact of the normative and projective thinking presented in this concluding chapter will be realized in ongoing analysis, so it is for this reason that I invite others to put this thinking to the test in future research. In terms of a research agenda for the future, several issues have moved to the fore in this book that require further analysis. Some of these issues necessitate innovation that develops and expands the field, while others call for comparison and disciplinary assessment in order to secure the fundamentals of environmental sustainability in building and city development and transformation. In other words, I foresee the need for ongoing research that is both progressive and foundational: both forward and sideway.

An initial body of future scholarship might explore the explanatory capacity of the theoretical template introduced in this book. In particular, the diffusion network perspective developed and addressed in the various chapters would constitute a point of departure in future studies: to what extent might it help to elucidate other policy areas or programs in other countries? What is its explanatory capability in situations of more or less fragmented diffusion networks than those in the construction and property sectors? A second body of future scholarship might explore where and how hybrid governance interventions that combine aspects of mandatory and voluntary programs are applied throughout the world, and in what sectors. It may question whether these hybrids are capable of overcoming the shortfalls of mandatory and voluntary programs and combine their strengths. This scholarship could focus particularly on the transferability and scalability of effective models and good practices resulting from hybrids. To what extent are hybrid governance interventions promising for scaling up and for transfer? A third body of future scholarship might move away from sustainable building and city regulation through mandatory and voluntary programs altogether to ask broader questions: What alternative governance interventions could help to overcome the problem of existing property rights in the transition to a more sustainable built environment? What governance interventions are available to local governments to bypass slow-moving and often lenient mandatory requirements? And last, but not least, what governance interventions will help city users — mayors and commercial property owners included — understand that it is their behavior and changing it for the better that matter more than erecting yet another low-carbon building or city precinct?

Appendix A Country Snapshots

Focusing on the development of governance for low-carbon and sustainable buildings and cities, this appendix presents snapshots — concise outlines of the current and future direction of nations studied in this book: Australia, India, Malaysia, the Netherlands, Singapore, and the United States. For each country the sustainable building challenge faced is explored, as are the dominant governance instruments in this area, their development since the 1970s (the era when countries began to introduce building energy efficiency requirements), and the complications faced by these instruments in realizing sustainable buildings and cities. For each country the move to innovative governance instruments that build on voluntary commitment is explored, with specific attention to the dominant actors involved in these instruments and their motivations for implementing them. Where possible, cross-references are included to prevent repetition. The extensive references and footnotes provide interested readers resources for pursuing a particular topic.

Australia

Eighty-nine percent of Australians live in cities (Standing Committee on Environment and Heritage, 2005).[1] The country's urbanization level is projected to grow to 91 percent by 2030 — combined with population growth this constitutes an additional urban population of 5 million people by 2030: an annual growth rate of approximately 1.4 percent (Australian Government, 2010). Australia's sustainable building challenge predominantly comprises improving its existing cities and buildings: its cities create more urban sprawl than almost anywhere in the world; the vast majority of its building stock predates the mandatory energy efficiency regulations of the mid-1990s; and its cities transform at the rate of 2 percent per year—including growth and replacement of existing buildings (ASBEC, 2008; City Mayors, 2007; Haughton & Hunter, 1994; Johanson, 2011). The construction, maintenance, and use of buildings account for approximately 25 percent of Australia's annual carbon emissions,[2] approximately four metric tons per capita annually — placing Australians on par with citizens in the Netherlands (CIE, 2007; Greenhouse Office, 1999a, 1999b; Saul, Sherwood, McAdam, Stephens, & Slezak, 2012).[3]

Dominant Governance Instruments for Sustainable Buildings

The power to regulate land use resides with state and territory governments, which largely delegate this to local councils. Funds for realizing land-use policy goals are allocated by the Australian Commonwealth Government.[4] This gives it considerable power in governing urban affairs, the development and use of buildings included. It takes further responsibility for sustainable building and city development through the National Urban Policy and the Building Code of Australia (McLoughlin & Huxley, 1986; McManus, 2005; Sandercock, 1990; Thompson & Maginn, 2012). The National Urban Policy (of 2011) requires that all states, territories, and local councils have planning systems that seek improved city layouts, development of increasingly environmentally sensitive buildings, and preparations for climate change and natural disasters (Albanese, 2013). The Building Code of Australia pursues improved sustainability in buildings primarily through building energy efficiency codes. These were introduced in 1997 and have since been increased in stringency. This advisory code is adopted by all states and territories (ABCB, 2010).

Two other relevant instruments are the National Australian Built Environment Rating Scheme, or NABERS (NSW Government, 2011b), and the Nationwide House Energy Rating Scheme, or NaTHERS (Department of Industry, 2014). Both were introduced as voluntary instruments for disclosure of building energy performance. Since 2010, NABERS has been mandatory for existing and new office spaces larger than two thousand square meters; since 2006 NaTHERS has been mandatory for the construction of new homes. NABERS provides an example of an innovative hybrid governance instrument that combines aspects of voluntary and more traditional mandatory instruments — it is further addressed in Chapter 4.

The commonwealth government has implemented various subsidies and economic instruments designed to stimulate the uptake of photovoltaic solar power at building level. The most recent was the Solar Credit Programme (2009–2012), which sought to make solar power attractive to households and small businesses — subsidizing about 50 percent of their costs (Australian Government, 2012; Martin, 2012). To improve its attractiveness it was combined with favorable feed-in tariffs (the price paid for energy fed back into the grid) offered by state and territory governments (Energy Matters, 2013). However, the program was terminated as a result of a considerable number of fraud cases, changes of governments and resistance to the program by new governments, and a reduction of feed-in tariffs owing to the financial risks the originally high tariffs were to governments (ACCC, 2011; Lloyd, 2013).

Complications and Critique

Australia's three-tier system of urban governance has been criticized, particularly for the hindrance it causes to urban development when higher- and lower-level authorities have to agree on proposals, resulting in a patchwork of plans and ambitions at the local level (Bond, 2011; COAG, 2012b). Dominant governance instruments are censured for falling short in reducing resource consumption and carbon emissions of buildings and cities. The Building Code of Australia applies only to the development of new buildings and major retrofits of existing ones. Owners and users of the vast stock of existing buildings are not expected to make financial investments for sustainable building improvements without incentive (AGO, 2006; Deloitte, 2013; Whelan, 2012). This is particularly problematic because mandatory building energy efficiency requirements were introduced relatively late in Australia and are lenient when compared to those in the United States and Europe (IEA, 2013). For these reasons, even younger building stock has poor sustainable building performance (AGO, 2006; ASBEC, 2008; Bond, 2011; Johanson, 2011; Maller & Horne, 2011).

Australia's other principal instruments are also criticized for poor performance. The National Urban Policy is too abstract to achieve its goals, lacking in clear targets and indicators to measure the performance of Australian cities (Gleeson, Darbas, & Lawson, 2004; Kelly, 2013; Ludlam, 2013). NABERS is flawed in not requiring physical alterations to buildings with low energy performance (see Chapter 4); NaTHERS applies only to newly constructed houses (Bond, 2011); and the Solar Credit Programme and other similar subsidies have been highly inequitable in disadvantaging low-income households (McIntosh & Wilkinson, 2010). Added to this, the effectiveness of enforcement of these instruments has been brought into question in view of high levels of noncompliance with mandatory building energy efficiency requirements that are reported (Healthy Environs, 2015; Pitt & Sherry, 2014).

Complicating this governance further, the Australian construction and property sectors are extraordinarily conservative, opposing cultural and technological change that allows for resource efficient, low-carbon buildings. This is expected to complicate the implementation of future mandatory governance instruments such as increased building energy efficiency requirements or more stringent planning legislation (Kajewski, 2001; Loosemore, 2013, 2014).

Turning to Voluntary Programs

Acknowledging the shortfalls of these instruments, governments of major Australian cities are active in trialing innovative voluntary alternatives in Brisbane, Melbourne, and Sydney — with Adelaide and Perth following suit. They have various reasons for doing so. State and territory governments require cities to draw up plans that contribute to achieving the commonwealth government's ambitions of a 20 percent reduction of 2000 levels of greenhouse emissions by 2050 — this relates to the National Urban Policy (Australian Parliament, 2011; COAG, 2011). Between 2005 and 2010, the development of these plans resulted in healthy competition among Australia's three largest cities over carbon emission reductions (City of Brisbane, 2009; City of Melbourne, 2008; City of Sydney, 2008; see also Chapter 1). They set reduction targets reaching significantly beyond those of the commonwealth government. Lacking well-performing governance instruments to achieve these goals, however, and lacking the power to mandate better performance of existing or future buildings, they turned to trialing innovative governance instruments that build on voluntary commitments (Beatley, 2009; Government Property Group, 2010).

In addition, some actors in the construction and property sectors recognize the market potential of developments with sustainable building performance beyond mandatory requirements or the conventional market standard. Inspired by an international trend of certification and classification instruments, they have developed a number of these for the Australian market: Green Star and EnviroDevelopment are the primary instances (see Chapter 4). These help in making sustainable building credentials visible, showcasing industry expertise, and tapping a market of consumers willing to finance high levels of sustainable building performance (EnviroDevelopment, 2014; GBCA, 2012).

India

India's population of 1.28 billion people (in 2015) is largely rural: 32 percent of Indians live in cities.[5] Rapid change is expected, however. The urban population is projected to rise to 41 percent by 2030 — combined with population growth this corresponds with an additional urban population of 215 million people by 2030 (as of 2015); an annual compound growth rate of approximately 3 percent (UN, 2014).[6] However, building and city related resource consumption and carbon emissions are projected to grow faster than India's urban population: the urbanizsation trend combines with rapid economic development, the rise of India's middle class, and suburbanization — trends that in themselves result in increased resource consumption and carbon emissions (Global Commission on the Economy and Climate, 2014; Government of India, 2013; Heymann, 2011).[7] Cities in India are projected to transform by 5–10 percent per year over the next decades — a projection that includes ambitions of the Government of India to achieve a slum-free India by 2022 (Government of India, 2013; IIHS, 2011; McKinsey, 2010). Governing this transition is central to India's sustainable building challenge. Yet it also relates to its current buildings and cities: existing urban planning and land use policies have resulted in overexpansive suburban and periurban development; many of its large cities face pressing housing shortages, lack of basic amenities, and poor infrastructure; while mandatory governance instruments and processes for sustainable buildings are virtually absent (Aijaz, 2012; Global Commission on the Economy and Climate, 2014; Kumar & Managi, 2012; Roy, 2009).[8]

Dominant Governance Instruments for Sustainable Buildings

Urban governance in India, including governance for sustainable buildings, is the result of a complex allocation of powers and responsibilities among governments at national, regional, and local levels, as well as interactions with other policy areas (see Aijaz, 2012; Markandey & Reddy Anant, 2011; Pinto, 2008; Sen, 2013). That said, the national government of India plays a large role in the administration of urban development and has introduced a range of governance instruments that seek to address sustainable buildings, mainly through urban planning, building energy efficiency policies, and building codes.

Urban planning requirements, including sustainable buildings, are addressed through the National Housing and Habitat Policy (of 1998) (Government of India, 2001). Related to this policy, the Jawaharlal Nehru National Urban Renewal Mission (of 2005) supports sixty-seven major cities in urban development projects and local governance reforms (Jain, 2010); and the National Mission on Sustainable Habitat (of 2008) promotes sustainable buildings through improvements of building energy efficiency, urban planning, and reduced carbon emissions (Government of India, 2008). Through the Rajiv Awas Yojana (of 2013), a policy that envisions a slum-free India by 2022, the national government seeks to provide affordable housing, basic infrastructure, and social amenities (Government of India, 2013). This allows it to influence directly the resource efficiency and carbon intensity of future building stock.

Building energy efficiency is targeted through the Energy Conservation Building Code (of 2007), which sets minimum energy efficiency requirements for building exteriors, electric systems, water heating and pumping systems, and lighting, heating, ventilation, and cooling systems (M. Evans, Shui, & Somasundaram, 2009; Kumar & Managi, 2012). The code is voluntary and state governments are advised to adopt it — by 2014 only two states had (Vedela, Bilolokar, Jaiswal, Connolly, & Deol, 2014).

Complications, Criticisms

Ample criticism has been made of India's complex institutional setting for governing sustainable buildings: overlapping responsibilities among the three levels of government create coordination problems; governance variance among states hampers national goals; and governments responsible for urban matters are often weak and poorly organized (Aijaz, 2012; Kunmar, 2013; Shah & Joshi, 2010). Related criticism condemns the haphazard, often poor administration of urban planning at the local level, which is often wholly absent in smaller cities; government corruption undermines urban policy implementation and is reportedly becoming worse;[9] and mandatory requirements and policies are erratically and often improperly enforced (CAP, 2012; Mahadevia, Joshi, & Sharma, 2009; McKinsey, 2010). Such criticism of the current state of affairs raises concern in light of the rapid urban development projected for India (TERI, 2009; UN-HABITAT, 2013).

The dominant governance instruments introduced since the late 1990s are also decried for not applying to the existing building stock; the Energy Conservation Building Code is condemned for being voluntary rather than mandatory; and the Government of India is criticized for setting lenient requirements in the code and for implementing it relatively late (GBPN, 2013; Vedela et al., 2014). Comparable to Australia, even the newer parts of India's built environment exhibit mediocre sustainable building performance (IEA, 2013; Sen, 2013; TERI, 2009).

Governance for sustainable buildings in India is complicated further by a conservative and low-tech construction sector, which along with the property sector is resistant to technological and organizational change, while corruption is common to both sectors. This is expected to hamper the future implementation of mandatory governance instruments for sustainable construction (Bergoeing, Loayza, & Piquillem, 2010; KPMG, 2011).

Turning to Voluntary Programs

Facing these complications, governments at different levels and throughout India have begun trialing innovative governance instruments. This development is primarily due to the shortcomings experienced with planning legislation and building codes, and readily available information about experiences with innovative governance instruments as a possible solution to these.[10] Replicating international examples, the Government of India has implemented a number of certification and classification programs such as labeling programs for household and office electric appliances, and certification programs for buildings and cities (Kumar & Managi, 2012; Ministry of New and Renewable Energy, 2012). But other motivations exist.

Governments in India face international pressure for reduced resource consumption and carbon emissions and are at the same time supported by international governments and other organizsations in achieving such reductions (Gallucci, 2015; Michaelowa & Michaelowa, 2012; Rong, 2010). Support organizations supply not only financial backing, but also experience with internationally derived innovative governance instruments to trial in the Indian context (CDP, 2014; Cities Alliance, 2008; UNDP, 2013a; World Bank, 2011b). For example, India's first city-to-city network that supports cities in achieving the goals of the Jawaharlal Nehru National Urban Renewal Mission, the Peer Experience and Reflective Learning Network — or PEARL — received financial and administrative support and considerable media coverage from the World Bank and Cities Alliance (Cities Alliance, 2008; World Bank, 2011b). Another example is the Energy Conservation and Commercialization Bilateral Project Agreement between the Government of India and the United States (in force from 2000 to 2011), which sought improved energy efficiency of buildings and cities by considering, among other issues, how the Energy Conservation Building Code could be implemented best (USAID ECO-III Project, 2010).

Finally, again comparable to Australia, some actors in the property and construction industries in India acknowledge the market potential of buildings and city districts with sustainable building performance beyond mandatory requirements or conventional performance. Following international examples, they have developed a number of innovative governance instruments for the Indian market (with LEED-India being the dominant voluntary program for sustainable buildings at the time of writing this book; see Chapter 8). These allow industry members to showcase their leading practice or to access a specific consumer market (IGBC, 2013; Mumbai First, 2014).

Malaysia

Malaysia has urbanized rapidly over the last four decades: 73 percent of its 2015 population of 31 million people live in cities — an increase of 30 percent since the 1970s.[11] The urban population is projected to grow slowly to 75 percent by 2030 — combined with population growth this corresponds with an additional urban population of 6 million people by 2030 (as of 2015): an annual compound growth rate of approximately 1.7 percent.[12] The fast pace of urbanization in the past has resulted in quickly built and overall low-quality building stock, and problems with these structures are expected to increase. Current cities are sprawling;[13] they face the challenge of needing to improve slum areas; and economic growth is projected to increase household energy consumption — often kerosene — and building-related carbon emissions rapidly (Bari, Begum, Jaafar, Abidin, & Pereira, 2010; LESTARI, 1998; Zaid, Myeda, Mahyudding, & Sulaiman, 2014).[14] As in India, this economic growth is likely to result in increased building and city related resource consumption and carbon emissions. Improvements are sought in replacement of buildings rather than in retrofits, as well as in city development projects. Malaysia's sustainable building challenge will thus concentrate on governing such development. However, it is questionable whether existing governance instruments possess the capacity to ensure high levels of environmental sustainability performance in such development (Fong, 2013; Zaid et al., 2014).

Dominant Governance Instruments for Sustainable Buildings

Sustainable building development and use in Malaysia are governed through planning legislation and building codes.[15] Three levels of government are involved in urban planning: the Government of Malaysia, predominantly through its Five-Year Plans and National Physical Plan; regional and state governments, through State Structure Plans and State Economic Plans; and local councils and municipal governments, through Local Plans and Metropolitan Plans. Building codes, standards, and design guidelines are developed by the Department of Standards Malaysia (national level), but are advisory only.[16] Local councils and cities are not mandated to adopt the codes developed by this department and may develop and enforce their own standards, and they do, producing much diversity at local level (APEC/USAID, 2013; Ponrahono, no date).

Two other relevant instruments are in place to govern sustainable buildings: the National Green Technology Policy (of 2009) and the

Construction Industry Masters Plan (of 2006). The former codifies a number of ambitions concerning the construction, maintenance, and use of buildings and sets requirements for the adoption of green technology in these processes (Idris & Ismail, 2011; Yeow, 2010). The latter was developed by the Malaysian Construction Industry Development Board, a corporate body, and seeks to improve the productivity, efficiency, and cost-effectiveness of the Malaysian construction sector. It expresses ambitions in terms of improved resource efficiency of the sector and improved environmental practice on the part of relevant individuals and organizations (Kamar et al., 2010; Sundaraj, 2007). Both, however, are reliant upon voluntary implementation and do not set mandatory requirements for property developers, owners, or users.

Complications and Critique

As in India, considerable criticism has been generated by Malaysia's complex institutional setting for governing sustainable buildings: overlapping responsibilities of governments result in coordination problems — at local and regional levels a cacophony of governance instruments hampers attainment of national goals; and agencies responsible for urban affairs are typically poorly organized (APEC/USAID, 2013; Jawan, 2009; Riazi et al., 2011). Further criticism disparages the voluntariness of building codes and instruments, such as the Construction Industry Master Plan; their late introduction and lenient requirements; poor enforcement of these instruments; and corruption and abuse of power by governmental actors (Abidin, 2010; APEC/USAID, 2013; Hezri & Hasan, 2006; Ismael, 2009). The various urban policies are also regarded unfavorably for their concentration on new development as a solution to problems with existing buildings and cities; for hypocritically adopting the rhetoric of resource efficiency and reduced carbon emissions while maintaining economic growth and prosperity as their main goal (Hezri & Hasan, 2006; Ismael, 2009; Shaffi, Ali, & Othman, 2006).

Also comparable to India and many other developing economies is Malaysia's low-tech construction sector, which complicates governance for sustainable buildings: inexpensive labor costs make it profitable for developers and contractors to construct buildings on-site as opposed to using more expensive premanufactured building components (Kamal et al., 2012). On-site construction often results in more environmental problems than the use of premanufactured building parts — it requires greater use of packaging material, transport, and on-site activities that result in local air or water pollution (Kamar et al., 2010; Shamsuddin et al., 2012).[17] The Malaysian construction industry is further criticized for its conservatism, with developers and contractors preferring conventional construction processes over sustainable ones, in part because they feel that construction projects with improved levels of building sustainability are more expensive than conventional forms (Abidin, 2010; Idris & Ismail, 2011; Makri, 2014).

Turning to Voluntary Programs

Governments and related organiations in Malaysia have begun trialing novel governance instruments in an attempt to overcome complications experienced with building codes, planning legislation, and other traditional governance instruments. Building on international experience, for example, the Government of Malaysia has supported the development of certification and classification programs. The Green Building Index is one of these — see Chapter 8 — and relates directly to goals expressed in the 2009 National Green Technology Policy and the Construction Industry Master Plan 2006–2015 (Hashim, Darus, Salleh, Haw, & Rashid, 2008; Riazi et al., 2011). Comparable to India, Malaysia is also confronted by international pressure for reduced resource consumption and carbon emissions, and international support for developing and implementing alternative governance instruments (Fong, 2013; Hezri & Hasan, 2006). Finally, with occasional government collaboration, some actors in the construction and property sectors have developed innovative governance instruments for the Malaysian market that allow them to showcase leading practice or access a specific consumer market (Rosly, 2011).

The Netherlands

Like Australia, the Netherlands is highly urbanized: 89 percent of its populace of 17 million (in 2015) is urban.[18] Its population is expected to remain stable until 2030, and no change in urbanization is projected (CBS, 2010). The Netherlands appears to have the potential to be a leading country in terms of resource efficiency and low-carbon buildings and cities: it has high-density cities, low per capita road supply, and houses that are considerably smaller than those in Australia or the United States (E. Fowler, 1995; G. James, 2009; Newman, 2014). However, building-related carbon emissions are approximately four metric tons per capita annually — roughly the same as that of Australia[19] (Ministry of Infrastructure and the Environment, 2013; Tigchelaar, 2012). The sustainable buildings challenge of the Netherlands relates to its existing building stock: a large measure of this predates the early 1980s when energy efficiency requirements were introduced, and it transforms slowly by some 2 percent per year (Beerepoot & Beerepoot, 2007; Hoppe, 2009; Soeter, 2010; Sunikka & Boon, 2003).

Dominant Governance Instruments for Sustainable Buildings

Governance for sustainable buildings is the responsibility of the Government of the Netherlands and local councils — provinces (regional level) have some minor responsibilities (ensuring regional coherence among local councils, among others). Dominant governance instruments for sustainable buildings in the Netherlands are national planning legislation (Wet Ruimtelijke Ordening) and the Dutch Building Codes (Bouwbesluit), both implemented by the national government and administered by local councils (Van Bueren & Priemus, 2002; van der Heijden, Visscher, & Meijer, 2007). National planning legislation requires local councils to draft local urban development plans, and provinces to produce regional plans that set limits on the urban growth of Dutch cities. The Dutch Building Codes seek improved sustainability in buildings, predominantly through building energy efficiency codes — in the mid-1960s insulation requirements were introduced for new buildings, and in the 1980s energy efficiency requirements for heating installation. These requirements have been increased in stringency since and are among the most stringent in the world (IEA, 2008; van Straalen, de Winter, Coppens, & Vermande, 2007).

Two other relevant instruments affect these codes: the European Energy Performance of Buildings Directive (EPBD) and the Ecodesign Directive (EC, 2009, 2010). The EPBD (introduced in 2001 and amended in 2010) requires that European member states set minimum energy efficiency requirements for residential and commercial buildings and provide fiscal and financial incentives to encourage sustainable construction with higher energy efficiency levels than required by legislation, and that building owners publicly display energy performance certificates. The European Ecodesign Directive (of 2009) requires member states, among others, to set mandatory ecological requirements for energy using and energy related products, including construction-related products such as windows, heating systems, and insulation.

The national government has set in place a number of subsidy programs and other financial instruments to support households and firms in improving the energy performance of their buildings. Energy Investment Deductions existed from 2009 to 2010 for upgrades of commercial buildings. In the same period a subsided household energy advice program was implemented to promote improvements to dwellings. From 2012 to 2013 a subsidy program supported homeowners in the installation of small-scale solar photovoltaic systems (Ministry of Infrastructure and the Environment, 2013).

Complications and Criticisms

The Dutch Building Codes, the EPDB, and the Ecodesign Directive are criticized in particular for their focus on new construction and major retrofits, while ignoring existing building stock. As in Australia, it is not expected that households and firms will make voluntary changes to their existing buildings without incentive (Meijer, Itart, & Sunikka-Blank, 2009; Ministry of Infrastructure and the Environment, 2013). Another notable comparison with Australia is that the mandatory building energy efficiency requirements are leniently enforced, raising significant questions about the energy performance of buildings that have been constructed since these requirements were introduced (van der Heijden & Van Bueren, 2013; Vringer, van Middelkoop, & Hoogervorst, 2014).

Other instruments also receive criticism. The EPDB's mandatory energy performance certificate system performs poorly: certificates have to be available at the sale or rental of a property, unless future building owners or tenants sign a waiver. The waiver option is the norm, particularly in the residential sector, resulting in very low uptake of these certificates — this indicates that energy efficiency is of only limited market impact when buying or renting a house (Brounen & Kok, 2011; Tweede Kamer der Staten Generaal, 2012). The various short-term subsidies that have been used also face censure: for attracting free riders who would have carried out energy efficiency improvements without the subsidies; for being unfair to low-income households; and for their creating a high administrative burden (Murphy, 2012, 2014; van Rooijen & van Wees, 2006).

Finally, as in the other countries studied, the Dutch construction and property industries are highly fragmented, conservative, and resistant to cultural and technological change (Klein Woolthuis, 2010; Rotmans, 2010; Van Bueren & Priemus, 2002). Such resistance impedes the implementation of future mandatory governance instruments for sustainable buildings. Industry and political representatives frequently invoke the global financial crisis (2008) and its aftermath as a means of avoiding transition to improved sustainable buildings (BouwendNederland, 2012; Gemeente Oldenzaal, 2014).

Turning to Voluntary Programs

Responding to these shortcomings, the national government has taken a keen interest in innovative governance instruments — as to a lesser extent have Dutch local councils, citizens, and firms. A main driver for the national government is the European Committee's binding legislation requiring member states to attain 20 percent reduction of 1990 levels of energy consumption and carbon emissions by 2020(EC, 2009). Innovative governance instruments developed by the national government build on a history and tradition of covenants and negotiated agreements in the Netherlands (Jordan, Wurzel, & Zito, 2005). The national government has drafted covenants with building contractors, energy suppliers, social housing organizations, and local councils, among others (Ministry of Economic Affairs, 2013b; Ministry of Infrastructure and the Environment, 2013). Local councils have entered into similar agreements with local representatives of the construction and property sectors, as well as with households (Municipality of Amsterdam, 2003; Municipality of De Bilt, 2010).

Also, as in the other countries studied, some players in the Dutch construction and property sectors acknowledge the market potential of products and services with higher levels of sustainability credentials than are required by Dutch or European legislation. This has resulted in a number of governance instruments that allow them to showcase their expertise in this area and to access the market for buildings with high levels of sustainable building performance (DGBC, 2014a). The dominant voluntary program is BREEAM-NL, discussed in Chapter 4.

Singapore

Singapore is home to 5.4 million people.[20] The city-state population is projected to grow by an additional 1.1 million people (above the 2015 level) by 2030, an annual compound growth rate of approximately 1.2 percent (Government of Singapore, 2013). As a small island city-state, Singapore is enormously restricted in its development space: its sustainable building challenge relates primarily to facilitating its anticipated population growth within this physical limitation (Dale, 1999; T.-C. Wong, Yuen, & Goldblum, 2008). But some challenges also derive from its existing building stock: the country depends on the import of resources critical to the operation of the city, including electricity and water (Ministry of the Environment and Water Resources, 2014). The construction, maintenance, and use of buildings account for 50 percent of Singapore's energy consumption.[21] Building related carbon emissions, however, are low in Singapore: about one metric ton per capita annually (National Climate Change Secretariat, 2012).[22]

Dominant Governance Instruments for Sustainable Buildings

Land scarcity in Singapore has necessitated planning ahead and making optimal use of space (Yue, 2001). Singapore has a vulnerable economy that depends on services and exports, and it has to import almost all of its resources. This is reflected in Singapore's energy policies, which are firmly directed towards energy efficiency and reduced energy consumption, particularly at building level (Lin-Heng & Youngho, 2004). As a city, Singapore is also distinctive in that it is administered by a national government — pledges made in international forums are directly translated into city policies (T.-C. Wong et al., 2008).

Three governance instruments are dominant in Singapore's transition to higher levels of sustainable building: Master Plans, Green Building Masterplans, and the Green Mark building codes (BCA, 2012, 2014a; URA, 2014). Master Plans are developed every five years — the most recent was introduced in 2014 — and seek to optimize the use of Singapore's limited space by setting economic, social, and environmental objectives. Three Green Building Masterplans have been introduced since 2006, the most recent in 2014, targeting the development and adoption of buildings with high levels of sustainability performance, as well as large-scale retrofits of the existing building stock of Singapore.[23] Green Mark is a building certification and classification program that makes visible specific aspects of a building, such as its energy and water consumption, its impact on the natural environment, and its indoor environmental quality (see Chapter 8). It is the equivalent of mandatory building codes in other countries.

Through the development and management of public housing the government can directly influence the sustainable building performance of future construction: more than 80 percent of Singaporeans live in public housing, and 95 percent of it is owner-occupied.[24] It is also active in the retrofitting and upgrading of city precincts in a number of programs that are highly government subsidized (Fernandez, 2011; J. Wong, Teh, Wang, & Chia, 2013). Other subsidies, retrofitting programs, and incentives are in place, and many of these correspond with the Green Mark program and seek a further increase in its uptake (BCA, 2014a; Hamilton-Hart, 2006).

Complications and Criticisms

Singapore is frequently referred to as a successful example of direct government intervention — by Singaporeans and non-Singaporeans alike (Dale, 1999; T.-C. Wong et al., 2008; Yue, 2001).[25] Its approach to governing and realizing sustainable building is a model for low-carbon city development projects in China and India (Cram, 2015; Pheng, Liu, & Wu, 2009; T.-C. Wong, 2011). That is not to say there is no criticism: sustainable building development has only recently been made an aspect of mandatory building codes, and studies point out that individuals and organizations in the construction and property sectors have little experience with developing, maintaining, and managing sustainable buildings. These studies suggest that educating and informing individuals and firms in these sectors are necessary parts of the transition to higher levels of sustainable building performance (Chan, Qian, & Lam, 2009; Deng et al., 2012; Hwang & Tan, 2012). Another recurring point of criticism is the government's dominant involvement in sustainable building development and use, which has resulted in the adoption of a passive stance by the construction and property sectors (Chan et al., 2009; Kein, Ofori, & Briffett, 1999).

Turning to Voluntary Programs

Although not experiencing the large shortfalls in building code and planning legislation targets common to other countries, the Singapore Government has nevertheless begun trialing advanced governance instruments. Green Mark is one of these. It is a building certification and classification program (see Chapter 8) that provides the base for other governance instruments, such as incentive programs for building retrofits and awareness-raising programs (BCA, 2013c; Kishnani, 2013). In addition, the Singapore government and the Singapore Environment Council, a government-supported NGO, have introduced instruments that incentivize occupants and tenants of houses and offices to reduce their consumption of energy and water (Singapore Environment Council, 2013a). Furthermore, the Singapore Green Building Council, a construction and property sector peak body, is actively involved in promoting Green Mark in Singapore and seeking acknowledgment for leading practice by individuals and firms in the construction and property sectors (BCA, 2013c).

United States

The United States' population of 320 million people is largely urban: 82 percent live in cities.[26] An urbanization rate of 87 percent is projected for 2030 — combined with population growth, this corresponds with an additional urban population of 53 million people by 2030: an annual compound growth rate of approximately 1.2 percent. Comparable to

Australia, the sustainable building challenge of the United States is concerned with improving its existing cities and buildings: its metropolitan regions are typified by extensive suburban sprawl; a large proportion of its building stock predates the 1970s, when building energy efficiency requirements were introduced (although not implemented in all states); and they transform by approximately 2 percent per year (Barras, 2009; Beatley, 2009; City Mayors, 2007; Garvin, 2014; Newman & Kenworthy, 1999). The construction, maintenance, and use of buildings account for approximately 40 percent of the United States' annual carbon emissions. Building related carbon emissions correspond to approximately seven metric tons per capita annually — considerably more than that of citizens in the other countries considered in this book (Cluett & Amann, 2014; Kwatra & Essig, 2014; McKinsey, 2009b).[27]

Dominant Governance Instruments for Sustainable Buildings

The power to regulate land use resides with state and local governments.[28] Their powers and responsibilities for planning legislation are laid down in the Standard Zoning Enabling Act 1924 and the Standard City Planning Enabling Act 1928. However, the federal government maintains significant impact on the development of cities in the United States through federal funding. It also has a strong impact on sustainable buildings, particularly through the National Environmental Policy Act 1969, which requires, among other things, an environmental impact statement for all development activities "significantly affecting the quality of the human environment" (NEPA, section 102(2)(c), as cited in: Garvin, 2014, 519). Related statutes at state level set similar requirements.

While the country does not have a set of mandatory building codes, recognized organizations develop codes and standards, often in collaboration with local, state, and federal governments, for adoption by state or local governments. Owing to this haphazard response, considerable disparity exists in states and local uptake of these codes (EPA, 2013).[29] The most widely adopted instruments for governing sustainable buildings are the International Energy Conservation Code (of 2000), the International Green Construction Code (of 2012), and the American Society of Heating, Refrigerating, and Air-Conditioning Engineers (ASHREA) Standard 90.1 (1975). These codes have increased in stringency since their introduction. Where implemented, they apply to new construction work, and occasionally to major renovations (Bartlett, Halverson, & Shankle, 2003; Halverson, Shui, & Evans, 2009).

Complications and Criticisms

As with the other countries, critique of the three-tier system of urban governance is common, particularly in regard to the complex system of local and state planning and zoning legislation, and the multilevel system of the National Environmental Policy Act and related legislation (Garvin, 2014; Papadopoulos, 2015). The reach of dominant governance instruments receives criticism also: they prevailingly apply to new construction work, avoiding existing building stock and city planning (CEC, 2008; IEA, 2007). It is not expected that owners and users of existing buildings make financial investments to improve sustainable building performance without incentive (Halverson et al., 2009; McGraw Hill, 2013). Another prominent similarity with the other countries is a reported culture of lenient enforcement of building energy efficiency codes due to lack of agency funding, underqualified staff, and readiness to use the prioritization of structural, health, and fire safety codes as justification for marginalizing or ignoring energy efficiency concerns (Meres, Sigmon, DeWein, Garett, & Brown, 2012; Stellberg, 2013).

Again comparable to the other countries studied, the construction and property industries are typified as conservative and reactive, highly fragmented, with substantial investment in existing industry infrastructure that will likely hamper the introduction of future regulation for sustainable building development (Choucri, 1991; Hardie & Manley, 2008; Katshiwagi, 2010; Lepatner, 2008). For example, in New York, a city considered to be among the world's leaders in innovative governance approaches for sustainable buildings (C40 Cities, 2014), Mayor Bloomberg faced enormous resistance from the local construction and property sectors when he proposed to introduce mandatory energy retrofits for existing buildings. In a time of global economic stress, they argued, his proposals involved untenable financial risk (Cheatham, 2009). Ardent cultural resistance to governmental involvement in property in the United States also impedes the introduction of additional mandatory requirements (Diamond & Noonan, 1996).

Turning to Innovative Governance Instruments

Understanding the limitations of these dominant governance instruments, governments at various levels have begun trialing innovative instruments. The Environmental Protection Agency and the Department of Energy are active in this area at the national level, but also on state and even local council levels various innovative regimes have been introduced. For state governments and local councils similar reasons to those present in Australian cities appear to apply: by promoting and improving the environmental performance of the built environment a state or city or policy maker can distinguish itself from others, potentially attracting investors or voters (cf. Cheshire et al., 2014). EPA and Department of Energy involvement assists in establishing control over urban development and sustainable buildings, and their involvement in innovative governance instruments provides a means with which to bypass their formal constitutional powers (Borzel, 2001; Genschel, 1997; U.S. Department of Energy, 2014c).

In addition, citizens and firms have developed a number of governance instruments, including voluntary programs, to help to promote their leadership or the specific performance of their products or services (Green Globes, 2014; RESNET, 2014; USGBC, 2013d).

Appendix B Voluntary Program Snapshots

This appendix presents a snapshot of each voluntary program studied in this book, including crucial information on its design, development, and implementation. It seeks to provide a concise account of a number of defining factors: how long the program has been in force, its aims whether and how its rules relate to mandatory requirements for sustainable building and city development and use, and whether those rules stipulate specific "beyond compliance" behavior, who monitors and enforces compliance, and the rewards for rule-takers participating successfully in the program.

This appendix seeks to help the reader to understand the data presented in Chapter 4 (certification and classification programs), Chapter 5 (information generation and sharing programs), Chapter 6 (funds-provision programs), and Chapter 8 (programs in India, Malaysia, and Singapore), as well as the comparative qualitative analyses presented in Chapter 7. The references provided in the snapshots suggest further readings that explore the programs studied. In addition, for the snapshot of each program at least one relevant website is included, and where available reference to performance data.[1]

Certification and Classification Programs (Chapter 4)

BREEAM-NL (The Netherlands, 2009)

This certification and classification program was implemented in 2009 by the Dutch Green Building Council, a nonprofit organisation with strong ties to the property and construction industries. It is the Dutch adaptation of the internationally used Building Research Establishment Environmental Assessment Method (BREEAM), initially developed and implemented in 1990 in the United Kingdom (Cole & Valdebenito, 2013). BREEAM-NL acknowledges sustainability credentials of buildings (residential and commercial property), city district developments, and demolition projects that move beyond the Dutch Building Decree and other mandated requirements. The Dutch Green Building Council aims to harmonize BREEAM-NL with Dutch building codes and planning legislation. The program is mainly applied to newly developed commercial property — offices and industrial buildings (DGBC, 2015).

In line with other labeling-based programs, BREEAM-NL builds on a set of criteria a building or development project has to meet in order to be certified in a range of categories: management, health, energy, transport, water, construction material, waste, and land use. Where possible these are directly correlated with the mandatory Dutch building codes (DGBC, 2014b). Credits are awarded for each criterion met, and the higher the total number of credits the higher the class of certification — a maximum of 100 credits is awarded. It is left to the applicants to mix and match categories and criteria they wish to meet, and a number of criteria are compulsory. Certification can be obtained in the categories "as built" (when a building design and the constructed building meet BREEAM-NL requirements) and "performance" (when a building in operation meets BREEAM-NL requirements). The latter category of certification is subject to periodic renewal. The program awards five classes of certification. Assessments are carried out by third parties; however, these parties are trained and recognized by the Dutch Green Building Council.

To explain the ratings of this system, a 4-Star classed building is required to be 24 percent greater than standard compliance with energy efficiency requirements in Dutch building codes; while a 5-Star classed building requires 51 percent. No requirements are set for lower classes of certification. The ease of acquiring points varies considerably: a 20 percent improvement of energy efficiency results in three points; bicycle racks and shower facilities for cyclists yield two points (DGBC, 2014b). Once a building or city development project is certified, property developers or owners may use the BREEAM-NL logo and the star classification for promotional activities.

> website (in Dutch only): www.breeam.nl
> Performance data: www.breeam.nl/projecten/statistieken
> website BREEAM (international): www.breeam.org

Energy Star Homes and Energy Star Buildings (United States, 1995)

These certification and classification programs were developed and implemented in 1995 by the United States Environmental Protection Agency; they followed on from the Green Lights program (US EPA, 1993; Videras & Alberini, 2000; see further Chapter 3). Both programs are ratings based: Energy Star Homes for new residential development,

Energy Star Buildings for new commercial development. The focus of both programs is on energy performance only. Homes and buildings can be certified in five star classes, with a 5-Star classification indicating the highest energy efficiency performance (EPA, 1997).

Energy Star requirements for homes and other buildings relate to wall and window insulation, equipment for heating and cooling, and lighting and other fixed appliances. A maximum of 100 credits can be awarded to a home or building. Certificates are issued "as built" and for some building types are subject to periodic renewal. Assessment of construction work is carried out by acknowledged third party inspectors, and certificates are issued by the Environmental Protection Agency. A building certified in the lowest class is at least 15 percent more energy efficient than a building that complies with conventional energy efficiency requirements in the United States; a building in the highest class is 30 percent more energy efficient (EPA, 1997) — but note that no national mandatory energy efficiency requirements apply in the United States (see also Appendix A). Once a building is certified, property developers or owners may use the Energy Star logo and the star classification for promotional activities.

> website: www.energystar.gov
> Performance data Energy Star Homes: www.energystar.gov/index.cfm?fuseaction=new_homes_partners.locator&s=mega
> Performance data Energy Star buildings: www.energystar.gov/index.cfm?fuseaction=labeled_buildings.locator

EnviroDevelopment (Australia, 2006)

Certification and classification program developed and implemented in 2006 by the Urban Development Institute of Australia, a peak industry body with strong support from the Queensland government. It acknowledges sustainability credentials of buildings and city development projects that exceed compliance with the Building Code of Australia. The program is benchmark based and tailored to different development types: master-planned communities (projects larger than fifteen hundred dwellings), residential subdivision (projects up to fifteen hundred dwellings), senior or retirement living, multiunit residential projects, and industrial, retail, education, and health care buildings. It can be applied to individual buildings, but in practice it is used for large-scale development projects (EnviroDevelopment, 2014).

In line with other certification and classification programs it builds on a set of criteria a building or development project has to meet in order to be certified. Among other conditions, it requires a reduction of 20 percent of greenhouse gas emissions and 20 percent of water consumption compared to specifications of the Building Code of Australia (EnviroDevelopment, no date). Assessment of development projects against the EnviroDevelopment criteria is carried out by third party assessors. Certification is subject to yearly renewal. It differs from other certification and classification programs, however, in that it does not accumulate criteria in its final level of certification, as the popular labeling-based programs do. Instead, it awards certification in different categories of performance: ecosystems, waste, energy, materials, water, and community. Once a development project is certified, property developers and owners can use the EnviroDevelopment logo, a series of colored leaves on a branch representing the categories of certification (EnviroDevelopment, 2010). Each leaf indicates that the development project performs better than the benchmark set for that category but does not indicate how the project's performance compares with that of other certified projects in that category.

> website: www.envirodevelopment.com.au
> Overview of projects: www.envirodevelopment.com.au/01_cms/
> details.asp?ID=57

Green Star (Australia, 2003)

This is a certification and classification program developed and implemented in 2003 by the Green Building Council of Australia, a nonprofit organization with close relations to the property and construction industries. Initially it was targeted at the top 25 percent of the commercial property market (GBCA, 2012). It acknowledges urban sustainability credentials of buildings and city development projects that supersede compliance with the Building Code of Australia. It is an example of labeling-based certification, tailored to different development types: offices, office interiors, educational buildings, industrial buildings, multi-unit residential buildings, retail centers, health care buildings, public buildings, and precinct development projects. The program is mainly applied to commercial property (GBCA, 2015).

In line with other labeling-based programs, Green Star builds on a set of criteria a building or development project has to meet in order to be certified. Its standards do not directly relate to the Building Code of Australia, or other mandatory requirements in Australia (GBCA, no date). The more criteria met, the higher the class of certification. Assessment of projects is conducted by a third party assessor. Certification can be obtained in the categories "as designed" (when a building design meets Green Star requirements), "as built" (when the constructed building meets Green Star requirements), and "performance" (when a building in operation meets Green Star requirements). The latter category of certification is subject to periodic renewal. Green Star awards three classes of certification: 4 Star (lowest tier), 5 Star (midtier), and 6 Star (highest tier). When introduced, it was decided not to issue certificates for relatively low "beyond compliance" behavior (GBCA, 2012). Certification in the 4-Star class, however, requires a building only to perform slightly better in terms of energy efficiency than compliance with the Building Code of Australia (see also Chapter 4; Appendix A). Once a project is certified under Green Star, property developers and owners may use the Green Star logo and star classification for promotional activities.

website: www.gbca.org.au/green-star
Performance data: www.gbca.org.au/project-directory.asp

LEED (Leadership in Energy and Environmental Design; United States, 2000)

This is a certification and classification program developed and implemented in 2000 by the United States Green Building Council, a tax-exempt membership-based nongovernmental organization closely associated with the construction and property industries. It acknowledges sustainability credentials of buildings and city development projects. LEED is one of the oldest and most widely applied labeling-based programs, and many of the certification and classification programs discussed in this book build on LEED. LEED is tailored to different development types: homes, commercial buildings, interiors, and neighborhood development projects. The program is primarily applied to new commercial property (USGBC, 2013a).

Comparable to the other labeling-based programs, LEED builds on a set of criteria a building or development project has to meet in order to be certified. Its requirements for energy efficiency relate directly to common mandatory requirements in the United States. The more criteria met, the higher the class of certification. LEED certification is granted by the Green Building Certification Institute, the organization that also carries out assessments. While the institute seeks to portray the assessment as a third party process, it is more fitting to consider it an administrator-led process: the Green Building Certification Institute is a United States Green Building Council affiliate organization

(Keller, 2012). Certification is issued in the categories "as designed," "as built," and "in operation" — only the latter category is subject to periodic renewal. LEED awards five classes of certification. Once a project is certified under LEED, property developers and owners may use the LEED logo and the classification issued for promotional activities.

> website: www.usgbc.org/leed
> Performance data: www.usgbc.org/projects
> Additional performance data: www.gbig.org/collections/14544

NABERS (National Building Energy Rating System, Australia: Regional 1998; National 2005)

NABERS is a certification and classification program developed and implemented in 1998 by the New South Wales Government Sustainable Energy Development Authority — a state level agency; now the Office of Environment and Heritage — and adopted by the Australian Commonwealth Government in 2005. It is a ratings-based program for existing and new buildings, focusing on energy and water consumption. Buildings can be certified in six star classes, including half stars, with a 6-Star NABERS classification indicating the highest level of energy or water efficiency (NABERS, 2013). The program was initially developed to certify energy consumption of office buildings only. While it has expanded its reach to include other building types, it is still mostly applied to office buildings. It has also been included in the Australian Building Energy Efficiency Discloser Act of 2010 (see Chapter 4; Appendix A).

NABERS certifies the actual energy and water consumption of buildings in use. To generate the rating, the actual performance data are adjusted for a building's size and occupancy, the climate conditions in which it operates, the hours of its use, the level of services it provides, and the energy sources it uses. A building with a 2.5–3-Star rating indicates average performance as compared to other buildings in its class. A building with a 4-Star rating performs at the same level as a newly developed building under the Building Code of Australia (Steinfeld et al., 2011). Assessment is undertaken by a third party assessor and certificates are issued by the New South Wales Government Office of Environment and Heritage. Because no mandatory energy efficiency requirements apply to existing buildings, NABERS de facto certifies beyond compliance performance. Certification is subject to renewal: with office buildings, for instance, a certificate has to be renewed when a building of two thousand square meters or larger goes on the market for sale or lease. Building owners and tenants may use the NABERS logo and star classification for promotional activities. NABERS is incorporated into a range of other Australian innovative governance programs studied, including Green Star and CitySwitch Green Office (see Chapters 4 and 5).

> website: www.nabers.gov.au
> Performance data: www.nabers.gov.au/AnnualReport/life-of-program-statistics.html

Information Generation and Sharing Programs (Chapter 5)

Better Building Partnership (City of Sydney, Australia, 2011)

This is a voluntary program launched by the by the Sydney City Council in 2011, joining the council and the city of Sydney's fourteen major property owners. It aims to reduce the carbon emissions, waste, energy, and water consumption in buildings belonging to these major property owners. Together, these property owners account for more than 50 percent of all commercial property in Sydney's central business district. The program requires its rule-takers to reduce their existing buildings' carbon emissions in 2030 by 70 percent compared to 2006 emissions (Better Buildings Partnership, 2013).

Participating property owners in the partnership sign a letter to the mayor of Sydney pledging that they will make improvements to their buildings to achieve this goal. In return the city of Sydney keeps these property owners involved in prospective policy deliberations so that they can plan their property portfolios accordingly. It further seeks to reduce regulatory barriers these property owners face in retrofitting their property, as well as financial barriers to doing so. In addition, the city of Sydney promotes the "beyond compliance" performance and leadership of the rule-takers in the program in various media outlets, including a website that is dedicated to the program. The program builds on self-reporting of performance data by its rule-takers and makes these data publicly available through the program's website and annual reports (e.g., Better Buildings Partnership, 2013). Compliance data are relatively easy to verify as they predominantly relate to energy consumption information provided by utilities and energy suppliers. More recently the program has begun to focus on barriers faced by office tenants in improving their urban sustainability behavior. By linking and seeking to overcome barriers faced by office tenants *and* the property owners of their buildings, the program hopes to create synergies that accelerate the improvement of urban sustainability in Sydney's central business district (Blundell, 2014).

Webite: www.sydneybetterbuilding.com.au
Performance data: www.sydneybetterbuildings.com.au/projects/ benchmarking-and-reporting

Better Buildings Challenge (United States, 2011)

This is a voluntary program launched by the federal government in 2011 that joins the federal government, state and local governments, educational organizations, housing providers, and firms — mostly large corporations, including manufacturing, retailers, and fast-food companies. Rule-takers commit to at least 20 percent energy consumption improvement over the course of ten years. For doing so they receive rewards such as federal government recognition, media attention, financial and technical assistance from the U.S. federal government, and best practice sharing through a peer network. It is part of the larger Better Buildings Initiative that seeks to catalyze private sector investment in commercial building upgrades.

As no mandatory building energy efficiency requirements apply in the United States, the minimum 20 percent increase target asks for beyond compliance performance. Because the baseline against which this performance is to be achieved is set at rule-taker level — their energy consumption in one of the three years before they entered the collaboration — the performance of the full pool of rule-takers cannot be compared; the program rewards initially poor performing firms that find it easy to make improvements over initially well-performing firms; the latter find it much more complicated to make improvements. The program builds on self-assessment, verified by the program administrator, in practice the United States Department of Energy. Rule-takers are strongly advised to use the Energy Star Portfolio Manager — a reporting tool within the Energy Star program discussed earlier — or other reporting tools approved by the program administrator.

website: www.energy.gov/eere/better-buildings
Performance data: www4.eere.energy.gov/challenge/home

Chicago Green Office Challenge (Chicago, United States, 2008)

This is a voluntary program launched by the City of Chicago Council in 2008 in collaboration with the international cities network International

Council for Local Environmental Initiatives (ICLEI). It challenges office users to reduce energy and water consumption, to produce less waste, to implement sustainable procurement practice, and to commute by public transport, bicycle, or foot. To ensure that rule-takers engage in the program the collaboration organizes competitive office-to-office challenges: rule-takers use software to keep track of their own performance and the data they supply are compared by the collaboration's administrators — and made visible to other rule-takers — to ascertain who is performing best (ICLEI, 2009). It is one of the first examples in which "gamification" is used to improve office tenants' behavior. The program is sponsored by a major supplier of office products, Office Depot, and administered by the Delta Institute, a Chicago-based nonprofit.

The program does not set minimum requirements for rule-takers, but because no mandatory requirements are established in the United States in terms of the energy performance of existing buildings and their users, the collaboration requires beyond compliance performance. Rule-takers achieve energy reductions of about 10 percent (int. 186). The program builds on self-assessment by rule-takers, but data provided by rule-takers are relatively easy to fact check as they predominantly relate to energy and water consumption data supplied by utilities.

website: www.greenpsf.com/go/community/index/chicago

Cityswitch Green Office (Australia, 2010 Sydney, 2011 National)

This is a voluntary program launched by the Sydney City Council in 2010 to join the council and office tenants, which became a nationwide program in 2011 (CitySwitch, 2014a). It is administered by local councils and state governments and serves as a platform for office tenants to learn about energy efficiency, share information, network, and showcase good practices. A yearly awards ceremony recognizes leading practice in different categories.

By participating in the network, office tenants make agreements with councils about their future environmental performance. Commitment to the program involves rule-takers' voluntarily undertaking a set of energy actions and providing an annual report on their achievements. Specifically, tenants agree to meet a specific rating within the voluntary NABERS program (discussed under certification and classification programs). The required rating for CitySwitch rule-takers (4 stars under NABERS) approximates modest beyond compliance performance with mandatory requirements for new office development in Australia (Steinfeld et al., 2011). Compliance with NABERS requirements is evaluated by third party assessors. However, interviews with CitySwitch administrators indicated that not meeting the agreed NABERS rating is not penalized under the program (see Chapter 5). In return for participation in the program, councils provide tenants with support to meet these goals. Certain councils provide financial support to office tenants, while others facilitate meetings and ensure an ongoing supply and distribution of information. The national CitySwitch organization maintains a website that provides information to rule-takers and non-rule-takers alike, including case studies, best practices, and information about other programs for improved urban sustainability in Australia. More recently the program has begun to focus on the interaction between tenants and landlords, and the barriers they face when seeking improved urban sustainability of existing office buildings. CitySwitch rule-takers are permitted to use the promotional CitySwitch logo to promote their leading practice.

> website: www.cityswitch.net.au
> Performance data: from yearly progress reports.

Energiesprong ("Energy Leap"; Netherlands, 2010–2015)

This is a cluster of voluntary programs led by Platform 31, a quasi-autonomous agency partly funded by the government of the Netherlands. Launched in 2010, it is a fusion of a number of knowledge institutes in the Netherlands,[2] joining the Ministry of Housing, Planning and Urban Development; the Ministry of Finance; and the social housing, private housing, and commercial property sectors. Energiesprong has a variety of incentives for realizing pilot sustainable building projects, for creating knowledge on improved urban sustainability in the Netherlands, and for experimenting with various innovative governance programs: monetary rewards, administrative support, information, leadership recognition, and the ability to build close relations with policy makers. By the end of 2014 it had established twenty-eight voluntary governance programs: these varied from small-scale pilot projects that seek to understand how small retail units can be retrofitted to become energy neutral, to large-scale projects that incentivize four main social housing corporations to retrofit 111,000 houses to become energy neutral. Significant for Platform 31 is that initiatives result in scalable programs that have developed knowledge of how the energy and carbon intensity of the Dutch built environment can be reduced (Platform 31, 2014).

Platform 31 and rule-takers develop targets — for instance, retrofitting a given number of offices to ensure energy neutrality, retrofitting privately owned houses to reduce 80 percent of energy consumption, or developing city district designs with high levels of urban sustainability — to which rule-takers commit, and that Platform 31 supports them in meeting. These targets generally require considerable beyond compliance behavior of rule-takers. Platform 31 has a number of preselection criteria for prospective rule-takers to meet. For some of the voluntary programs third party assessment is used; others rely on self-assessment, administrator assessment, or government assessment.

> website (in Dutch only): www.energiesprong.nl
> Performance data (in Dutch only): www.energiesprong.nl/nederlandenergieneutraal

Green Deals (Netherlands, 2011)

Launched in 2011, Green Deals comprises a series of voluntary programs that join the government of the Netherlands (the Ministry of Finance) and other parties. Through these programs the national government supports urban sustainability projects — often financially but also by reducing regulatory barriers — and in doing so it aims to achieve targets set by the European Union for a 20 percent reduction of energy consumption and carbon emissions by 2020 (Ministry of Economic Affairs, 2013b). Since 2011 more than two hundred agreements have been entered into; close to sixty have a specific focus on increased sustainable building development and use, ranging from local renewable energy projects to the development of certification and classification programs for urban sustainability (Ministry of Economic Affairs, 2013a). Rule-takers propose a Green Deal to the Ministry of Finance, which then assesses its viability and expected beyond compliance urban sustainability performance — only projects that hold promise of considerable beyond compliance performance are included. The Green Deal Board — representing business, civil society organizations, and government (but not academia) — monitors and assesses the performance of the Green Deals (Green Deal Board, 2012).

For this book specific Green Deals were studied in detail: a series of negotiated agreements in the city of Amsterdam that are pilot projects for improved urban sustainability of new and existing buildings and other developments; a series of interacting innovative local governance programs implemented in the city of Haarlem that seek to reduce residential building resource energy consumption by at least 20 percent compared to that of conventional standards; and a pilot study that seeks to determine whether and how the notion of circular economy — high-quality use and reuse of resources — can be applied to existing and new buildings. These deals aimed to result in scalable models that improved building energy efficiency throughout the Netherlands (van der Heijden, 2014c).

> website (in Dutch only): www.rvo.nl/onderwerpen/duurzaam-
> ondernemen/groene-economie/green-deal/green-deal-afspra
> ken-en-partijen
> Performance data (in Dutch only): www.ondernemendgroen.nl/
> greendeals/pages/default.aspx

Retrofit Chicago Commercial Buildings Initiative (Chicago, United States, 2012)

This is a voluntary program launched by the city of Chicago government in 2012. It joins the city government, commercial property owners, and private sector fund providers. Through the program the city government seeks to reduce the energy use of Chicago's office space, which complements the city's overall ambition to reduce resource consumption and carbon emissions (NRDC, 2014). The program is Chicago's commitment to the Better Buildings Challenge (discussed previously).

By participating in the network, commercial property owners enter into an agreement with the city of Chicago to reduce the energy consumption of their property by at least 20 percent over a five-year period. In its first two years the Initiative attracted forty-eight mostly iconic office buildings in the central business district, and rule-takers had on average reduced their energy use by 7 percent — with some rule-takers already meeting the 20 percent reduction goal (NRDC, 2014). Energy improvements were achieved particularly through low-tech and low intrusive interventions ("low hanging fruit") such as changing to energy efficiency LED lighting; installing motion sensors on heating, cooling, and lighting systems; upgrading heating and cooling systems; and improving the use of office equipment such as computer monitors (Retrofit Chicago, 2015). In return for participating the city of Chicago facilitates network and marketing opportunities for property owners, helps to locate funding sources for retrofits, and creates case studies and models from the knowledge generated for other property owners to follow.

> website: www.retrofitchicagocbi.org

Zonnig Huren; ("Sunny Leasing," The Netherlands, 2012)

This is a voluntary program launched by a Dutch consultancy firm and some thirty Dutch social housing corporations in 2012, with support from their advocacy group Aedes and NL Agency, a public organization at arm's length from the Ministry of Finance. It seeks to overcome financial and legal barriers that obstruct the installation of solar panels on residential rental property — both individual homes and condominiums (Atrivé, 2012). The participating housing corporations collectively own approximately 25 percent of all housing corporation—owned rental units in the Netherlands (totaling approximately 2.4 million units).

By participating in the program rule-takers commit to sharing knowledge and experience on retrofitting their rental property, with a focus on the installation of solar panels. It set further collective targets of installing solar panels on ten thousand houses and two hundred housing blocks and condominiums by 2013, and a total of thirty thousand housing units by 2014. Progress is monitored by the consultancy firm; noncompliance is not penalized.

website (in Dutch only): www.zonnighuren.nl

Funds Provision Programs (Chapter 6)

1200 Buildings (Melbourne, Australia, 2010)

This is a voluntary program developed and implemented by the Melbourne City Council in 2010 in collaboration with one national bank, a major fund manager, and property owners (City of Melbourne, 2010). The Melbourne City Council administers the program. It encourages and supports building owners, managers, and facility managers to improve building energy and water efficiency and to reduce landfill waste. In particular, the program aims to accelerate the retrofitting of commercial buildings in Melbourne's central business district and has set a target of retrofitting of two-thirds of this building stock by 2020 (City of Melbourne, 2010; da Silva, 2011). A crucial part of the program is environmental upgrade financing, an approach to financially supporting property owners who are unable to source funds for retrofits elsewhere.

Under the program individual property owners commit to a minimum reduction of energy consumption of their office buildings of 38 percent in a letter to the mayor of Melbourne, outlining the retrofits they will undertake to achieve this aim. Neither the current Building Code of Australia nor other Australian mandatory requirements set performance requirements for existing buildings. As such the program asks for considerable beyond compliance behavior of its rule-takers. In return the

City of Melbourne provides these property owners with funds to retrofit their buildings and recovers these from the property owners through a statutory charge linked to rates collection. The city has entered into an agreement with banks to acquire the funds it provides to the property owners. The city monitors and enforces compliance with the program as part of its broader building code enforcement regime. Through the program the City of Melbourne further seeks to provide property owners with information on how to retrofit their buildings, particularly through a publicly accessible website, and it also aims to create a community of - rule-takers capable of benefiting from each other's experiences. Rule-takers in the program may use the promotional "1200 Buildings" logo to showcase their leading practice.

website: www.1200buildings.com.au

Additional Credit for Energy Efficient Homes ("Tijdelijke Regeling Hypothecair Krediet"; The Netherlands, 2012)

This program constitutes a temporary softening of home mortgage regulation by the Dutch minister of finance for the period 2012 to 2018. It allows mortgage suppliers to issue higher mortgages to lenders who want to improve the energy efficiency of their houses. In 2012 they were allowed to lend up to 6 percent more than the value of the house at the time of transaction (with a maximum of eight thousand euros), in 2013 up to 5 percent (to a maximum of seven thousand euros), and so on, until the temporary program is phased out in 2019. A specific temporary rule allows mortgage suppliers to lend up to twenty-five thousand euros more than the value of the house at the time of transaction to lenders for mortgagees who seek to make their planned house energy neutral (Dutch Ministry of Finance, 2012).

An evaluation of the program in 2015 indicates that its availability is not widely realized by consumers, and that mortgage suppliers are hesitant to apply for it. Suppliers argue that technical upgrades do not guarantee energy saving by consumers (such savings would reduce their energy costs and allow them to repay their higher mortgages) because consumer behavior can radically affect energy use (BuildingBusiness, 2015).

No website

Amsterdam Investment Fund (Amsterdam, The Netherlands, 2011)

This is a revolving-loan fund implemented by the Amsterdam City Council in 2011 — renamed "Amsterdam Energy Fund" over the course of the research project. It was established to fund projects that contribute beneficially to Amsterdam's economic competitiveness, social health, and urban sustainability. Within the €137 million fund a proportion (€70 million) is earmarked for projects that contribute to the sustainability goals of the city of Amsterdam, which include a 40 percent reduction of 1990 carbon emissions by 2025 , and a 70 percent reduction by 2040 (City of Amsterdam, 2011). The management and administration of the fund are outsourced to private sector fund managers.

The fund is divided into two parts: 20 percent is invested to yield "societal return," and 80 percent is invested to yield financial return. The former part is managed by the city of Amsterdam; the latter (the Amsterdam Climate and Energy Fund) by professional private sector fund managers — the Amsterdam Economic Board. Rule-takers seeking to obtain funding from the investment component propose to the board a project in one of seven clusters: agriculture and food; creative industries; financial and business sciences; ICT and e-science; life sciences and health; logistics, manufacturing; tourism and conventions; and horticulture. Proposals have to meet four basic requirements and at least two of seven additional criteria. The basic requirements are that the project is to be completed within fifteen years, that it will generate a minimum return on investment of 7 percent, and that it uses between €0.5 million and €5 million. Of the seven optional requirements, the project should achieve at least 1 percent greater economic growth than the European average; contribute to attracting international organizations to Amsterdam; or create at least an average number of jobs compared to the rest of Europe. The most promising proposals are funded. Compliance is monitored by private sector fund managers.

> website Amsterdam Energy Fund (in Dutch only): www
> .amsterdam.nl/wonen-leefomgeving/energie/amsterdams/
> Performance data (in Dutch only): www.amsterdam.nl/wonen-
> leefomgeving/energie/amsterdams/amsterdams
> website Amsterdam Climate and Energy Fund: www.akef.nl/en

Billion Dollar Green Challenge (United States, 2011)

This revolving-loan fund framework was implemented in 2011 by the Sustainable Endowments Institute, a project within the Rockefeller Foundation, and a number of partner organizations, mostly education and environment nonprofits. It encourages colleges, universities, and other nonprofit institutions to invest a total of U.S.$1 billion in self-managed revolving loan funds to finance energy efficiency improvements of educational facilities (Sustainable Endowments Institute, 2011).

The challenge does not supply or manage funds; rather, it provides support to establish such funds. Rule-takers of the challenge are supported with guidelines to help them to set up their own revolving-loan fund, with case studies provided from other rule-takers on how to improve energy efficiency, computer software to track returns on their own investments, and peer review of the efficiency of investments from other rule-takers (Bornstein, 2015).

website: www.greenbillion.org

Building Innovation Fund (South Australia, Australia, 2008–2012)

This competitive funding program was developed and implemented by the Government of South Australia in 2008 and concluded in 2012. A fund of AU$2 million was established to demonstrate innovative ways to reduce the carbon footprint and resource consumption of existing commercial buildings (Government of South Australia, 2012).

Rule-takers seeking to obtain funding would propose a solution to improve the urban sustainability of property they owned by lodging a fully developed construction or retrofitting plan. The proposals were then evaluated by a jury consisting of Government of South Australia representatives, City of Adelaide representatives, academics, and representatives of the property industry. The most promising proposals in terms of resource consumption and waste reductions would be awarded grant funding. Grant funding was considerable when compared to construction and retrofitting costs. A total of eleven projects were awarded, including the installation of a living wall system, in which plant-covered wall improved the thermal efficiency of a building, funded AU$214,000; and the installation of a solar façade made up of translucent photovoltaic cells, funded AU$240,000.[3] The program's rules did not specify minimum criteria for its rule-takers to meet — note that the Australian Building Code and other mandatory requirements for urban sustainability do not apply to existing buildings in Australia. It was expected that the competitive aspect of the program would incentivize rule-takers to propose projects with far-reaching levels of environmental sustainability. Compliance with the program was monitored and enforced by the state government, and partly relied on building code enforcement of construction work by the City of Adelaide building authority.

website: www.sa.gov.au/topics/water-energy-and-environment/
climate-change/tackling-climate-change/what-organisations-
business-and-industry-can-do/building-innovation-fund

E+ Green Building (Boston, 2011)

This sustainable building demonstration program aims to showcase the feasibility of sustainable building development in Boston, create best practices that can be used as models for future practice, provide affordable housing opportunities, raise public awareness for sustainable building development and use, and reinvigorate neighborhoods in Boston. Introduced in 2011, it is administered by the City of Boston government.

Among other projects, E^+ Green runs design competitions. In 2011 the program challenged designers and project developers to propose a building design for three highly sought-after inner-Boston development sites. Rule-takers had to propose designs that achieved at least LEED Platinum certification — the highest certification tier — and that were energy positive ("E^+"): that is, the buildings must generate more energy than they consume. The winning designs were awarded the development sites (City of Boston, 2013a, 2013b). A total of fourteen designs were submitted, from which three were selected for development.

website: www.epositiveboston.org

Energy Efficient Mortgage Program (United States, 1995)

This mortgage program was implemented by the United States Federal Housing Administration in 1995. It recognizes that homeowners can reduce their utility expenses through energy retrofits or upgrades of their houses,and allows those who seek to do so to top up their approved mortgage. The agency does not provide loans, but insures the supplementary mortgages that lending institutions supply (U.S. Department of Housing and Urban Development, 1995).

The mortgage can be used to make energy efficient improvements to new or existing homes. Homeowners are allowed additional mortgages that are less than the expected savings from building retrofits or energy upgrades. Maximum mortgage limits are set to 5 percent of the property, although exemptions apply. Although it is one of the longest-running building energy efficiency mortgage programs in the United States, it is not popular among homeowners (ACEEE, 2013; Kats et al., 2012).

No website

Environmental Upgrade Agreements (Sydney, Australia, 2011)

This government—property owner network was developed and implemented by the Sydney City Council in 2011 (New South Wales

Government, 2012). The program is inspired by and resembles the earlier-discussed 1200 Buildings program in Melbourne (described previously).

> website: www.cityofsydney.nsw.gov.au/business/business-sup port/greening-your-business/environmental-upgrade-finance

Property Assessed Clean Energy (PACE; United States, 2008)

PACE was developed and implemented in 2008 by the nonprofit organization PACE*Now*. It is a tripartite financing program that helps property owners to access long-term loans for energy retrofits and upgrades. Loans are sought from local governments and repaid through a property tax. Local governments issue bonds to obtain funds that can be lent to property owners. PACE requires state and local governments to pass laws that enable PACE financing (PACE Now, 2013) — the program is comparable to the environmental upgrade agreements in Australia (including 1200 Buildings), discussed previously.

PACE initially applied to commercial and residential property, but as a result of the subprime mortgage crisis the United States mortgage authorities, the Federal National Mortgage Association ("Fannie Mae") and the Federal Home Loan Mortgage Corporation ("Freddie Mac"), refused to finance mortgages under PACE (Bird & Hernandez, 2012; J. Kirkpatrick & Bennear, 2014; Sichtermann, 2011). By the beginning of 2015, PACE-enabling legislation was enacted in thirty states, with thirteen states establishing active commercial programs in thirty-four cities. It included some twenty-five thousand residential property projects and three hundred commercial properties. For this study the local implementation of PACE was observed in San Francisco (GreenFinance SF) and Sacramento (Clean Energy Sacramento).

> website: www.pacenow.org
> Performance data: www.pacenow.org/pace-data
> Application in San Francisco: www.greenfinancesf.org
> Application in Sacramento: www.ygrene.us/ca/sacramento

Small Business Improvement Fund (Chicago, United States, 2000)

The Small Business Improvement Fund provides funds to small businesses in the city of Chicago for building improvements. It was introduced in 2000 by the City of Chicago government and is managed and administered by SomerCor, a nonprofit development firm. It does not set requirements concerning the type of building improvements as long these are permanent. However, it does prefer building upgrades that improve urban sustainability, such as energy related investments in lighting, heating, ventilation, and air-conditioning upgrades. Specifications outline funding eligibility and quantity. Those seeking funds are required to pay the initial costs of building and then obtain reimbursement from the grant through SomerCor (SomerCor, 2014).

The fund is replenished through tax increment financing (TIF), a method that uses future tax gains for subsidizing current improvements. Such financing allocates a part of tax revenue from a specific part of the city — a TIF district — for building upgrades within that district; funds for a specific applicant derive from tax revenue collected from that applicant's local TIF district. When there are more applicants than available funds can accommodate, the City of Chicago holds a public lottery to allocate financing.

> website: www.somercor.com/sbif
> Performance data: www.cityofchicago.org/city/en/depts/dcd/supp_info/small_business_improvementfundsbif.html

Sustainable Development Grant (Brisbane, Australia, 2007–2010)

This competitive funding program was developed and implemented by the Brisbane City Council in 2007 and terminated in 2011. The program aimed to improve the urban sustainability of major office development projects. A system of criteria that assigned scored grades defining the sustainability performance of grant applicants' developments was introduced. The criteria were above and beyond those of the Building Code of Australia. If a threshold score was reached, the applicant would receive a grant. Higher scores corresponded with greater levels of sustainability and would attract larger financial grants. The minimum score to be achieved corresponded with a 4-Star rating under Green Star (discussed previously). In particular, it aimed to reward best practice within the Brisbane office market (Allens, 2007; Gold Coast City Council, 2008).

Assessment of projects was carried out by the Brisbane City Council. Funds would not be released to rule-takers before they had obtained Green Star certification of their building project. In the first two years of the program AU$10 million grant funding was available. Grant funding awarded related to gross floor area of a development project. As a result of the 2011 flood damage, Brisbane City Council determined that funding for these grants was to be redirected to Brisbane's flood recovery effort.

> website: No longer accessible

Certification and Classification Programs in India, Malaysia, and Singapore (Chapter 8)

Eco-Housing Certification Program (Pune, India, 2004)

This certification and classification program for housing development was instigated and implemented by the Pune Municipal Corporation — the building authority in Pune — in 2004, in collaboration with the United States Agency for International Development (USAID), the University of Pune, the University of Ahmedabad, the International Institute for Energy Conservation (IIEC), and the Energy Resource Institute (TERI). It is administered by a joint-certification body comprising the IIEC and both universities involved. The program acknowledges urban sustainability credentials of new housing development projects and considers on-site planning, environmental architecture, energy conservation and management, efficient building materials, water conservation and management, and solid waste management (IIEC, 2009).

As with other labeling-based programs, the Eco-Housing Certification Program specifies a set of criteria a building or development project has to meet in order to be certified. Some criteria are mandatory; others are optional. Mandatory criteria for energy and water consumption often require rule-takers to comply with the voluntary National Building Code (see Appendix A) and other applicable government regulation, while optional requirements set more ambitious targets. Since India's National Building Code is voluntary, these requirements ask for considerable "beyond compliance" behavior of rule-takers. Compliance is monitored and enforced by the joint-certification body prior to, during, and post construction. Certificates are issued for a period of five years, after which renewal of certification has to be sought (Darko et al., 2013). The more criteria that are met, the higher the level of certification: five levels of certification are awarded, represented by stars. The lowest level (1 star) requires that at least all mandatory criteria are met, and higher levels of certification require meeting optional criteria (IIEC, 2009). Once a project is certified, its developer or owner can use the star rating for marketing purposes. To incentivize participation in the program the Pune Municipal Corporation gives rule-takers a 50 percent rebate on the fees related to obtaining building permission, and a 25 percent rebate on the fees related to construction work inspections (Sonawane Sawant, 2009).

website: www.ecohousing.in
Performance data: www.ecohousing.in/List%20of%20Eco%20-
%20Housing%20Projects%20With%20Ratings.php

Eco-Office (Singapore, 2002)

This certification and classification program was implemented in 2002 by the Singapore Environment Council — an NGO independent of, but financially supported by the Singapore government — and City Developments Limited, one of Singapore's major property developers. It seeks to inform office tenants on how they can improve their energy performance and reduce their water and paper consumption. It certifies office tenants for meeting specific criteria, most of these relating to office tenant behavior (Singapore Environment Council, 2012, 2013). It actively markets itself as a means for office tenants to reduce operational costs.

Contrary to most certification and classification programs studied in this book, Eco-Office builds on benchmarking. It requires its rule-takers to meet a specified standard and does not rate or label them in a specific performance class (for terminology see Chapter 4). In short, the Eco-Office certificate awarded to rule-takers indicates that they meet this benchmark: it does not define their performance relative to other rule-takers. Mandatory building codes, planning legislation, and other statutory urban sustainability criteria do not relate to office tenants. The benchmark set in Eco-Office seeks to improve office tenants' behavior by 10 percent as compared to conventional behavior. Assessments occur in two stages: first an applicant carries out a self-assessment — if this indicates compliance with Eco-Office criteria, then it can apply for an assessment by a third party assessor. If this third party assessor confirms compliance, the Singapore Environment Council issues a certificate, subject to biannual renewal (Singapore Environment Council, 2011). These can be used by their holder for promotional activities.

website: www.sec.org.sg/ecooffice

Green Building Index (Malaysia, 2009)

This certification and classification program was developed and implemented in 2009 by the Malaysian Green Building Confederation, a nonprofit organization with strong ties to the property and construction sectors. It resembles labeling programs such as BREEAM, LEED, and Green Star. The Malaysian Green Building Confederation, however, decided not to adopt any of these international programs as it felt these did not account for Malaysia's equatorial climate, its environmental and developmental context, or its cultural and social needs. The Green Building Index acknowledges urban sustainability credentials of residential and commercial buildings and townships. It is predominantly used for commercial property.

As with the other labeling programs studied, it builds on a set of criteria a building has to meet in order to be certified in a specific class: energy efficiency, indoor environmental quality, sustainable site planning and management, material and resources, water efficiency, and innovation. A similar classification scale is used to that for LEED: "Certified," "Silver," "Gold," and "Platinum." All criteria are optional, thereby deviating from other labeling programs studied, which include both compulsory and optional requirements. Since Malaysia does not have mandatory requirements for sustainable building development, all requirements as a matter of circumstance require "beyond compliance" behavior. Some requirements are relatively ambitious. For instance, two credits are awarded if a landscape design does not require any potable water for irrigation. However, other requirements are lenient: a considerable number of credits (five) are awarded if a building generates 2 percent of the total electricity it consumes. At least fifty credits are needed for the classification "Certified" (GBI, 2009). Assessment of development projects is carried out by a Green Building Index Certifier, that is, by the program's administrators. A final certificate is issued one year after a building is completed, and certificates are subject to a three-year reassessment cycle (GBI, 2013). Once a project is certified under the Green Building Index, property developers and owners may use the program's logo and level of certification for promotion.

> website: www.greenbuildingindex.org
> Performance data: www.greenbuildingindex.org/organisation-certified-buildings-Summary.html

GreenLabel (Singapore, 1992)

This certification and classification program was developed by the Singapore Environmental Council — an NGO independent from, but financially supported by the Singapore government — and the Ministry of the Environment and Water Resources. It seeks to endorse a wide range of consumer and construction products and services that decrease conventional levels of undesirable impacts on the natural environment. The program relates to the Global Ecolabelling Network, a nonprofit association of third party environmental performance labeling organizations founded in 1994 to improve, promote, and develop the certification of environmental sustainability credentials of products and services.

Comparable to Eco-Office, another program administered by the Singapore Environmental Council (see earlier discussion), this program builds on benchmarking. It requires products and services to meet a specified benchmark and does not rate or label them in a specific performance class (see Chapter 4 for terminology). Although this program falls outside the scope of the other classification and benchmarking programs included in this book, it was selected because the Singapore Green Mark scheme awards credits to the use of GreenLabel products. With the rapid export of Green Mark (see later discussion; Chapter 8) by the Building and Construction Authority of Singapore, it provides Singapore-based and international manufacturers of construction goods and services that hold GreenLabel certification, an international competitive advantage over those that do not. However, this book does not pursue this specific issue.

website: www.sec.org.sg/sgls

Green Mark (Singapore, 2005)

This certification and classification program was developed by the Singapore Building Construction Authority. It was launched in 2005 and builds on international examples such as BREEAM, LEED, and Green Star. Green Mark seeks to increase the visibility of the sustainability credentials of buildings, building blocks, and city districts, including energy and water consumption, impact on the natural environment, and indoor environmental quality (BCA, 2012). Green Mark is an example of labeling: a series of criteria have to be met in order to be certified. Meeting these standards results in the award of credits. Credits are awarded in various categories — energy and water consumption, impact on the natural environment, indoor environmental quality — which are then combined in a total score. The more credits awarded, the higher the class of certification.

Green Mark awards certificates in four classes: Certified, Gold, Gold Plus, and Platinum. The criteria set under Green Mark relate directly to mandatory construction regulation in Singapore: as of 2008 a Green Mark classification of at least Gold is mandatory for all new development larger than two thousand square meters — because of a general practice in Singapore to build high-rise buildings, this requirement de facto implies that all new construction is mandated to meet Gold classification criteria. As of 2013, a Green Mark classification of at least Gold is also mandatory for commercial property retrofits larger than fifteen thousand meters. Assessment of projects is carried out by a Building Construction Authority assessor. Certificates are awarded to completed building or city development projects, and certification is subject to periodic renewal — reassessment is required every three years to maintain an awarded Green Mark class. The Singapore Government aspires to have 80 percent of all existing and new buildings certified under Green Mark and meeting at least the lowest "Certified" class by 2030 (BCA, 2012). Financial and informational incentives are in place to meet this goal. Once a project is certified under Green Mark, property developers and owners may use the Green Mark logo and level of certification for promotion.

> website: www.greenmark.sg
> Overview of projects: www.greenmark.sg/building_directory.php

Green Township (Malaysia, 2009)

This certification and classification program was developed and implemented in 2009 by the Malaysian Institute of Planners and the Government of Malaysia. As an example of benchmarking, it seeks to improve the urban sustainability performance of new and existing urban development in Malaysia, particularly at township level (Rosly, 2011).

In order to be certified, a building or city development project needs to demonstrate at least 10 percent less energy and water consumption than the set baseline. The program is applied only in Putrajaya — the federal administrative center of Malaysia — and Cyberjaya — the technology hub of Malaysia — but is developed for larger application throughout Malaysia. It builds on a set of guidelines that assist town planners and local governments in building and redeveloping townships with higher than conventional levels of urban sustainability. The program relies on the United Nations' Common Carbon Metrics Protocol, an instrument used to measure the carbon emissions of development projects (UNEP, 2010). At the time of research the program's administrators were in the midst of adapting criteria from the UN Protocol to the Malaysian context. Over the four years of study (2012–2015), however, not much progress appears to have been made. The Green Township website (in the following) has not been updated since 2010, and no cities other than Putrajaya and Cyberjaya appear to participate in the program.

> website: www.bcis.greentownship.my/index.php

GRIHA (Green Rating for Integrated Habitat Assessment (India, 2007)

This certification and classification program was developed and implemented in 2007 by the Energy and Resource Institute (TERI), an independent, not-for-profit research institute closely connected with the

Government of India, in collaboration with the Ministry of New and Renewable Energy of the Government of India. The program is administered by TERI. It acknowledges urban sustainability credentials of new development projects larger than twenty-five hundred square meters, giving close consideration to on-site selection and site planning, conservation and efficient resource use, building operation and maintenance, and construction innovation (Ministry of New and Renewable Energy, 2012).

The program structure is firmly founded on other labeling-based programs for improved urban sustainability such as LEED and Green Star. It consists of thirty-four criteria, of which four have to be met to achieve certification. Different classes of certification indicate how many criteria have been met, on a scale from 1 to 5 stars. A high class of certification corresponds to a high level of sustainability of a building or a city development project. The criteria that rule-takers are expected to meet in part relate to compliance with the voluntary National Building Code (see Appendix A), other applicable government regulation, and international codes (M. Evans et al., 2009). GRIHA certification relates to the design, construction, and use of a building or city development and is subject to periodic renewal: certification is valid for five years only (Ministry of New and Renewable Energy, 2012). Once a project is certified its developer or owner can use the GRIHA Star rating for marketing purposes.

website: www.grihaindia.org
Performance data: www.grihaindia.org/#&Library

LEED-India (India, 2001)

This certification and classification program was developed by the Indian Green Building Council (IGBC) and implemented in 2001. The IBGC is a nonprofit organization established by the Confederation of Indian Industry, an association of Indian businesses. It aims to facilitate the transition of India's built environment toward higher levels of urban sustainability and seeks global leadership by India in this area by 2025. The program adapts the United States—founded LEED program (discussed earlier). The IGBC has licensed the framework of LEED from the United States Green Building Council. Adaptations were made to suit local climate and industry characteristics. It is mainly applied to commercial property (IGBC, 2013).

Building on the framework of LEED-India, the IGBC has developed a range of related certification and classification programs for homes, factory buildings, schools, and townships. These were areas that LEED-India did not cover. As of 2015, the IGBC had fully switched to its own IGBC certification and classification programs and was in the process of phasing out LEED-India certification by 2018.[4]

> website: www.igbc.in[5]
> Performance data: www.gbci.org/GBCICertifiedProjectList.aspx

LCCFA (Low-Carbon Cities Framework and Assessment System, Malaysia, 2011)

This certification and classification program was developed by the Government of Malaysia and implemented in 2011. It acknowledges the urban sustainability credentials of cities, townships, and neighborhoods, paying particular attention to carbon emission reductions. The program allows for certification of new and existing cities and settlements. It is an example of labeling-based certification (KeTTHA, 2011). The LCCFA differs from the other programs studied in that it seeks to achieve its goals through implementation and oversight by local authorities. These are expected to commit to the program, recruit stakeholders, set carbon emission reduction targets, and develop and implement policies to achieve those targets.

Comparable to other labeling-based programs, the LCCFA builds on a set of criteria a city, township, or part thereof has to meet in order to be certified. Requirements relate to urban environment, urban transport, urban infrastructure, and buildings: the more criteria that are met, the higher the class of certification awarded. The LCCFA awards six classes of certification. A carbon emission calculator has been introduced to support local governments in keeping track of their performance, and in self-assessing their compliance with the program.

Program website no longer available

Appendix C Application of QCA in This Book and an Additional fsQCA

In the Chapter 1 I briefly explained my choice for QCA. Although QCA is gaining traction as a data analysis method and research approach in the social sciences, it will be novel to some readers. For them I present a slightly more extensive discussion in this appendix of why I have chosen to apply QCA in this study and how I have applied it. At the same time, readers with a good understanding of QCA may feel that the earlier discussion lacks some depth. For them I include a more extensive discussion in this appendix and apply fsQCA (fuzzy set) to a part of the data as a means to assess the robustness of the earlier presented csQCA (crisp set) findings (cf. Skaaning, 2011). This fsQCA is intended to help in understanding what factors are common to the programs that demonstrate promising performance in terms of attracting rule-takers (comparable to the first csQCA described in Chapter 7).

QCA was introduced by the social scientist Charles Ragin as a middle path between quantitative and qualitative social research (Ragin, 1987). QCA is grounded in set theory, a branch of mathematical logic that allows researchers to study in detail how causal conditions contribute to a particular outcome. Since the mid-1990s it has rapidly developed into an accepted research method for the type of study presented in this book and has been applied in hundreds of studies in the policy sciences in particular (Rihoux, 2013; Rihoux & Ragin, 2009). An example of this is the 2013 special issue of *Policy and Society* on "Innovative Methods for Policy Analysis: QCA and Fuzzy Sets" (Policy and Society, 2013).

Particularly the introduction of fsQCA has encouraged use of the method by a range of scholars from various backgrounds studying issues such as governance networks within a country (Verweij, Klijn, Edelenbos, & Van Buuren, 2013), job security regulations in Western democracies (Emmenegger, 2011), and organizational configurations (Fiss, 2011). The fundamentals and background of the method are explained and documented in a series of textbooks (Goertz & Mahony, 2012; Ragin, 2008; Rihoux & Ragin, 2009; Schneider & Wagemann, 2012).

These handbooks are useful further references for those unfamiliar with the foundations of the method.

The handbooks provide guidelines for QCA practice (Ragin, 2008, see in particular the "practical appendices"; Rihoux & Ragin, 2009, chapter 5; Schneider & Wagemann, 2012, chapter 11), which I have followed closely in conducting the analyses discussed in this book. One of the fundamental points for QCA practice is for the researcher to provide as much transparency in the analysis as possible. This is what I seek to provide by means of this appendix. I follow the "flowchart" of Jerry Mendel and Mohammad Korjani (2013) who, supported by Charles Ragin, have mathematically summarized QCA as a collection of thirteen steps. I do, however, take the liberty of using the jargon from the handbooks — as opposed to the mathematical jargon introduced by Mendel and Korjani — in order to clarify and reduce the steps to ten stages. In addition to Mendel and Korjani's steps regarding *how* the QCA analysis is carried out, it is, of course, of importance to consider *why* QCA was chosen in the first place. While researchers often support their choice for QCA with a practical motivation — for example, claiming they have a medium number of cases that are likely to allow for systematic cross-case analysis, but not for sophisticated statistical analysis — QCA is ideally chosen for a theoretical motivation (Schneider & Wagemann, 2012). I have added a step that recognizes motivations for choosing QCA, which is the issue I begin with in what follows.

Step 1: Why Apply QCA in This Study?

Earlier empirical studies have found that voluntary programs with similar designs such as pay-per-plastic-bag fees (Ackerman, 1997), organic food labeling (Thøgersen, 2010), building assessment certification and classification (K. M. Fowler & Rauch, 2006b), and revolving-loan funds (Boyd, 2013) elicit different outcomes depending on how their design conditions interact with contextual conditions (e.g., existing legislation, economic circumstances; Borck & Coglianese, 2009). Moreover, some studies indicate that a single design, such as a building certification and classification program, implemented in a number of similar contexts — for example, comparable national, geographical, or cultural conditions — may nevertheless result in different outcomes as a result of the role of governmental actors in these programs (K. M. Fowler & Rauch, 2006b).

This all indicates that the outcomes of voluntary programs are likely to be caused by different interacting conditions (that is, conjunctural causation), that different configurations of interacting conditions may cause a similar outcome (equifinality), and that the presence of a configuration of interacting conditions in the causal role of the outcome is of limited help in explaining the inverse situation. In other words, the causal role of the absence of the condition in the nonoccurrence of the outcome does not inversely equate with the presence of that condition: this amounts to what is termed "data asymmetry."

QCA is chosen as a data analysis methodology because it assists researchers in "unraveling causally complex patterns in terms of equifinality, conjunctural causation, and asymmetry" (Schneider & Wagemann, 2012, 8). QCA differs from other data analysis methods in its focus:

The key issue [for QCA] is not which variable is the strongest (i.e., has the biggest net effect) but how different conditions combine and whether there is only one combination or several different combinations of conditions (causal recipes) of generating the same outcome. (Ragin, 2008, 114)

QCA helps to trace patterns of association between these conditions in a highly systemized manner: it enables systematic comparison between empirical observations (cross-case) while allowing for in-depth, within-case understanding of individual observations (Rihoux & Ragin, 2009).

I have chosen crisp set QCA (csQCA) for reasons discussed in the Chapter 1, but in this appendix I will apply fuzzy set QCA (fsQCA) as a robustness test of one of the analyses presented in Chapter 7 (cf. Skaaning, 2011). Where csQCA is primarily a binary technique, fsQCA allows for more precise delineation of the qualitative differences in the empirical data by accounting for multiple relations — the degree of presence or absence of a condition or outcome in the cases under analysis. I will explain this particular issue in greater depth under Step 4.

Step 2: Selection of Outcome of Interest and Cases to Study

In Chapters 1 and 3 I explain the outcomes that are of interest to the research project. The operationalization of these outcomes is further explained later. The selection of cases — all real-world instances of voluntary programs — is also explained in Chapter 1.

Step 3: Select *k* Causal Conditions

In Chapter 3 I discuss a set of seven design conditions that constitute the theoretical model of my QCA analyses.

Step 4: Calibration of Set-Membership Scores for Outcomes and Conditions

The strength of fsQCA as compared to csQCA is that it enables relatively accurate delineation of qualitative differences in the units of observation. In other words, it allows the researcher to differentiate among qualitative categories of observations, and to compare sets of observations of a particular category with sets of observations of other categories. Established QCA practice requires the researcher to be clear about this calibration. In particular, the researcher needs to explain the two extremes of the observed data (that is, maximum and minimum parameters in a category), and the crossover point of the data (that is, the stage at which the data are considered to have maximum ambiguity — when they are as much within a determined category as they are external to it) (Ragin, 2008; Rihoux & Ragin, 2009; Schneider & Wagemann, 2012). In Chapter 7 I explain the calibration of data for the csQCA analyses. For the fsQCA analysis that I conduct in this appendix I have calibrated the data using a four-category qualitative scale, as represented in Table C.1. For the various outcomes and conditions the extremes and crossover points in the data are set as follows:

1. Observed outcome

    Attracting rule-takers. I have operationalized this outcome by considering the quantum of participants a voluntary program has attracted. Full membership is set at 15 percent of prospective participants or more (see Chapter 7 for motivation) and the crossover point is set at 10 percent of prospective participants. Thus, the more in than out category reflects 10–14 percent. Full nonmembership represents 0–4 percent of prospective rule-takers, and more out than in represents 5–9 percent.

Table C.1 *Verbal Description of Membership Scores of the Data in Qualitative Categories*

The Observation Is	Fuzzy Set Value
Full membership (i.e., in the highest stage observed)	1.00
More in than out	0.67
More out than in	0.33
Full nonmembership (i.e., in the lowest stage observed)	0.00

Improving rule-taker behavior. I have operationalized this outcome by considering the results of actions taken by rule-takers. Full membership is set at 20 percent improvement or more (see again Chapter 7 for motivation). The crossover point is set at 10 percent improvement. More in than out reflects 10–19 percent improvement. Full nonmembership represents 0–4 percent improvement, and more out than in represents 5–9 percent improvement.

2. Conditions

Stringency of rules. Full membership is defined by circumstances in which participants are required to perform significantly beyond the requirements of public law and regulation, for example, to achieve double the statutory requirement, or to show high-level performance in an area that is not yet addressed through statutory regulation. More in than out means that participants are required to perform well beyond the requirements of public law and regulation, for instance, to achieve more than the statutory requirement, or to show unspecified performance in an area that is not yet addressed through statutory regulation. More out than in indicates that participants are required to perform just beyond the requirements of public law and regulation. Full nonmembership defines a full absence of criteria. The crossover point of this condition is set at criteria that only require performance that is marginally better than required by law and regulation — where possible I have used a crossover point of 10 percent.

Stringency of enforcement. Full membership represents strict enforcement; for instance, enforcement is carried out by governmental actors, the enforcement process is documented, and a certificate or other form of compliance evidence is issued at the end of the process. More in than out defines medium enforcement; for instance, enforcement is undertaken by governmental actors, but there is no clear documented trail of such enforcement actions. More out than in represents weak enforcement, for example, reliance on self-enforcement by participants. Full nonmembership defines no enforcement. The crossover point is set at the reliance on enforcement documentation supplied by participants, such as enforced self-regulation.

Financial rewards. The qualitative categories for direct financial gain, including cost savings, that participants may obtain from joining a voluntary program are constructed by combining data on "promised" gains (that is, how prospective gains are marketed by the administrators of these voluntary programs) and "evidenced" gains (that is, how realized gains are marketed by administrators and participants of these voluntary programs). Full membership represents a marketed high certainty of achieving substantial financial gains based on evidence when participating. More in than out membership defines a marketed promised certainty of gains supplemented with evidence. More out than in describes a marketed promise of gains when participating, but without evidence. Full nonmembership represents a full absence of a marketing of gains. The crossover point is the marketing of promised high certainty of gains, but without evidence to support this promise.

Nonmonetary rewards. I followed the preceding line of reasoning. Thus, full membership represents a marketed high certainty of achieving substantial nonmonetary gain when participating based on evidence; full nonmembership represents a full absence of marketing of nonmonetary gains; and the crossover point is the marketing of promised high certainty of nonmonetary gain, but without evidence to support this promise.

Leadership rewards. To construct a fuzzy set for this condition I considered how administrators of voluntary programs reward and market leadership. Full membership represents concentration on national or global leadership combined with marketing of leading practice or awarding of leading practice through, for instance, yearly awards ceremonies. More in than out defines emphasis on regional or local leadership combined with marketing or awarding of such leadership. More out than in depicts attention centering primarily on leadership in the marketing of a voluntary program, but an absence of marketing or rewarding actual leadership by participants. Full nonmembership represents full absence of a concern with leadership in the marketing of a voluntary program. The crossover point of this condition is the marketing of best practice as opposed to local, national, or international leadership.

Local government as rule-maker. To construct a fuzzy set for this condition I have considered how local governments are involved in the voluntary programs. Full membership represents sole governmental involvement in initiating and administrating a voluntary program. More in than out defines sole governmental involvement in initiating a voluntary program. More out than in depicts equal involvement in the establishment of voluntary programs of governmental and nongovernmental actors. Full non-membership defines the absence of government involvement. The crossover point of this condition is set at the dominance of governmental involvement in this role.

Diffusion network. Full membership represents a diffusion network that makes it highly likely that a prospective rule-taker is frequently exposed to a voluntary program, for example, a relatively small group of frequently interacting prospective rule-takers combined with an authoritative industry body supporting the program. More in than out defines a network that makes it likely that a prospective rule-taker is frequently exposed to a voluntary program, for example, a relatively small group of frequently interacting prospective rule-takers, or an authoritative industry body supporting the program, but not a combination of both. More out than in indicates a network that makes it unlikely that a prospective rule-taker is frequently exposed to a voluntary program, for example, a relatively large group of noninteracting prospective rule-takers or a nonauthoritative industry body supporting the program. Full nonmembership represents a diffusion network that makes it highly unlikely that a prospective rule-taker is frequently exposed to a voluntary program — this network is considered absent. The crossover point is set at the improbability of being frequently exposed to a voluntary program.

Step 5: Create a Raw Data Matrix

Now that the various qualitative differences of the outcomes and conditions have been distinguished, the data can be transformed into a raw data matrix. Table 7.2 in Chapter 7 presents the raw data matrix for csQCA; Table C.2 provides the raw data matrix for the fsQCA conducted in this appendix.

Step 6: Analysis of Necessary Conditions

Following established QCA practice the data are first analyzed for necessary conditions before exposing them to more complex analysis in order to identify configurations of sufficient conditions (Rihoux & Ragin, 2009, chapter 5, box 8.1; Schneider & Wagemann, 2012, chapter 11). For a condition to be necessary to cause the outcome, the membership scores of the outcome need to be a perfect subset of the membership

Table C.2 Raw Data Matrix for fsQCA in Appendix C

Program name	Conditions						Outcomes		
	Rules	Enforcement	Financial Rewards	Nonfinancial Rewards	Leadership Rewards	Local Government as Rule-Maker	Diffusion Network	Attracting Rule-Takers	Improved Rule-Taker Behaviour
1200 Buildings	1.00	0.67	1.00	0.33	0.67	1.00	0.00	0.00	?
Additional credit for energy efficient homes	0.67	0.33	1.00	0.00	0.00	0.00	0.00	0.00	?
Amsterdam Investment Fund	0.33	0.67	0.67	0.00	0.67	1.00	0.00	0.00	?
Better Buildings Challenge	0.67	0.67	1.00	0.67	0.67	0.33	0.00	0.00	0
Better Buildings Partnership	1.00	0.67	1.00	0.67	1.00	0.67	1.00	1.00	1
Billion Dollar Green Challenge	0.33	0.33	0.67	0.67	0.67	0.00	0.00	0.00	1
BREEAM-NL (commercial)	0.33	1.00	0.67	0.33	0.33	0.00	1.00	1.00	1
Building Innovation Fund	0.33	0.33	0.67	0.33	1.00	1.00	0.33	0.00	1
Chicago Green Office Challenge	0.67	0.67	0.33	0.67	0.67	0.67	0.00	0.00	0.33
CitySwitch Green Office	1.00	0.33	0.33	1.00	1.00	1.00	0.33	0.33	0.67
E+ Green Building	1.00	0.67	0.33	0.00	1.00	1.00	0.00	0.00	1

Program									
Energy Efficient Mortgage	0.33	0.67	1.00	0.00	0.00	0.00	0.00	0.00	?
Energy Leap	1.00	0.33	0.33	0.67	0.33	0.33	0.00	?	?
Energy Star Building	0.67	1.00	0.67	0.00	0.33	0.00	0.00	0.00	1
Energy Star for Homes	0.67	1.00	0.67	0.00	0.00	0.00	0.00	0.33	1
EnviroDevelopment	1.00	1.00	0.67	0.00	0.33	0.00	0.33	0.33	1
Environmental Upgrade Agreements	0.67	0.33	1.00	0.33	0.00	1.00	0.33	0.00	?
Green Deals	0.67	0.33	0.67	0.33	1.00	0.00	0.00	?	?
Green Star (offices)	0.33	1.00	1.00	0.00	1.00	0.00	1.00	1.00	1
LEED (commercial)	0.33	0.67	0.67	0.33	0.67	0.00	0.33	0.00	1
NABERS (offices)	0.33	1.00	0.67	0.00	0.33	0.33	1.00	1.00	1
PACE	0.67	0.67	1.00	0.33	0.67	1.00	0.00	0.00	1
Retrofit Chicago (major office buildings)	0.67	0.33	0.33	0.00	1.00	1.00	1.00	0.33	0.67
Small Business Improvement Fund	0.67	0.33	1.00	0.33	0.00	1.00	0.00	0.00	0.33
Zonnig Huren	1.00	0.67	0.67	0.67	0.33	0.00	0.67	0.00	1
Sustainable Development Grant	1.00	0.67	1.00	0.00	0.33	1.00	0.00	0.00	1

Notes: Codes: See Table C1. ? = no (reliable) data
Source: Appendix B (Voluntary Program Snapshots)

Table C.3 *Necessary Conditions for Attracting Rule-Takers (fsQCA)*

Conditions	Consistency Score	Coverage Score
Stringent rules	0.62 *(0.25)*	0.21 *(0.06)*
Stringent enforcement	0.94 *(1.00)*	0.32 *(0.24)*
Assured financial rewards	0.88 *(1.00)*	0.26 *(0.20)*
Nonfinancial rewards	0.25 *(0.25)*	0.20 *(0.17)*
Leadership rewards	0.68 *(0.50)*	0.29 *(0.15)*
Local government involvement	0.31 *(0.25)*	0.14 *(0.08)*
Positive impact of diffusion network	0.94 *(1.00)*	0.68 *(0.67)*

Note: Numbers in brackets represent the scores based on csQCA data (see Table 7.3)

scores of the condition. Tables 7.3, 7.6, 7.8, and 7.11 in Chapter 7 present the results of the analysis for necessary conditions for the csQCAs. Table C.3 presents the results of the analysis for necessary conditions for attracting rule-takers applied to fsQCA data.

For necessary conditions two issues are of importance: consistency and coverage. *Consistency* indicates how strongly the condition relates to the outcome. In other words, if a hypothesized relation between a condition and an outcome is not consistent (where the advisory cutoff point of consistency is a score of 0.90), the hypothesized relation cannot be supported by the data as being necessary (Rihoux & Ragin, 2009, 45). *Coverage* indicates how relevant the condition is to causing the outcome. Coverage is only assessed for conditions that meet the consistency test. Here it is important to distinguish between relevant and trivial necessary conditions. In other words, if a consistent relation only covers a small number of cases (it has a low coverage score, such as the condition "assured financial gain"), it can be considered to be trivial in causing the outcome (see also Schneider & Wagemann, 2012, chapter 9). Another way to distinguish between relevant and necessary conditions is to assess whether or not the data are skewed toward conditions that have high scores for both the condition and the outcome. This suggests that such conditions may pass the test for both necessity and sufficiency and is likely to be a trivial necessary condition in achieving this outcome (Schneider & Wagemann, 2012, 232–237).

In comparing the findings of Table C.3 with those of Table 7.3 it becomes clear that there are only minor changes in the test for necessity between the fsQCA and csQCA calibrated data sets. Table C.3 indicates that two conditions pass the consistency test: the conditions "stringent enforcement" and "positive impact of diffusion network"; and the condition "assured financial rewards" almost passes the consistency test. However, both "stringent enforcement" and "assured financial rewards" have low coverage scores, indicating that they are likely to be trivial necessary conditions. This follows the earlier analysis for necessary conditions.

Step 7: Analysis of Sufficient Conditions (1): Create a Truth Table

Having studied the data for necessary conditions, the next step is to examine the data for sufficient conditions. For a condition or for a configuration of conditions to be sufficient to cause the outcome, the fuzzy set membership scores of the condition or the configuration of conditions need to constitute a perfect subset of the membership scores of the outcome. The analysis of configurations of sufficient conditions for the outcomes under scrutiny follows three substeps. The first substep is to create a truth table. Table C.4 provides the truth table for the analysis of sufficient conditions for the outcome "attracting rule-takers" (this table relates to Table 7.4 in Chapter 7). The truth table is created using the software FS/QCA (version 2.5).

The truth table is a data matrix with 2^k rows that represents all possible configurations of conditions that are logically possible. Note that the truth table reports data using the crossover points set; that is, 1 indicates more in than out of the set (including full membership), and 0 indicates more out than within the set (including full nonmembership). Thus, with the seven conditions here the number of logically possible configurations is 128: that is, 2^7. The empirical observations are included in this table. As the truth table indicates, out of 128 logically possible configurations 19 were empirically observed (rows 1–19). The different rows can be understood as ideal types (Schneider & Wagemann, 2012, chapter 7). The number column (No.) indicates how many cases fit best in this ideal type (that is, when a case has membership in the configuration of the fuzzy sets for the conditions of at least 0.5). The row "Outcome" indicates whether for a configuration of conditions the outcome was observed or not (1 indicates it is; 0 indicates it was not). Because some observations of configurations of conditions may be observed in different cases, some rows in the truth table may refer to many cases (for instance, row 8) while other rows refer only to a few cases or just one case (e.g., rows 1 and 12). It is normal that the truth table also contains rows of possible combinations without empirical observations (here, e.g., these are rows 20–128).

In the second substep the truth table is logically minimized on the basis of two conditions. First, the researcher sets a threshold for "logical

Table C.4 *Truth Table for Attracting Rule-Takers (fsQCA)*

	Conditions							Outcome	
Row	Rules	Enforcement	Financial Rewards	Nonfinancial Rewards	Leadership Rewards	Local Government as Rule-Maker	Diffusion Network	Frequency	Raw Consistency
1	0	1	1	0	0	0	1	2	0.80
2	0	1	1	0	1	0	1	1	0.80
3	1	1	1	1	1	1	1	1	0.75
4	1	0	0	0	1	1	1	1	0.67
5	1	0	0	1	1	1	0	1	0.25
6	1	1	0	1	1	1	0	1	0.25
7	1	1	1	1	0	0	1	1	0.25
8	1	1	1	0	0	0	0	3	0.15
9	0	1	1	0	0	0	0	1	0.11
10	1	0	1	0	0	1	0	2	0.00
11	1	1	1	0	1	1	0	2	0.00
12	0	0	1	0	1	0	0	1	0.00
13	0	0	1	1	1	0	0	1	0.00
14	0	1	1	0	1	0	0	1	0.00
15	0	1	1	0	1	1	0	1	0.00
16	1	0	0	0	0	0	0	1	0.00
17	1	1	0	0	1	1	0	1	0.00
18	1	1	1	0	0	1	0	1	0.00
19	1	1	1	1	1	0	0	1	0.00

Rows 20–128: logical remainders

Note: The table and symbols are explained in the text that follows

remainders." Logical remainders are those configurations of conditions that "lack enough empirical evidence to be subjected to a test of sufficiency" (Schneider & Wagemann, 2012, 152). It depends on the size of the research project (that is, the number of cases included) when determining what is to be considered as "enough empirical evidence." Most often a threshold of one observation (thus at least one case) is used, but for larger numbers of cases a higher threshold can be applied (Ragin, 2008; Schneider & Wagemann, 2012). Following this practice I have specified a threshold of at least one observation. Second, the researcher has to set a "consistency threshold for distinguishing [configurations of conditions] that are subsets of the outcome from those that are not" (Ragin, 2008, 143). In other words, how well do the configurations of conditions fit the outcome? This is what the "raw consistency" score in the truth table indicates. As discussed under Step 6, the higher the score the better the fit. Ragin (2008) advises a consistency score of at least 0.75, which I have followed — four cases meet this threshold. In FS/QCA, cases that met the consistency threshold were labeled 1 in the outcome column, and those that did not were labeled 0 (cf., Ragin, 2008, 144).

Step 8: Analysis of Sufficient Conditions (2): Dealing with Logical Remainders and Choice of Solution Term

Having carried out this minimization of the truth table, a standard analysis can be run in FS/QCA 2.5 (the third substep). This standard analysis is best understood as the identification of

the combinations of attributes [i.e., configurations of necessary conditions] associated with the outcome of interest using Boolean algebra and algorithms that allow logical reduction of numerous, complex causal [configurations of] conditions into a reduced set of configurations that lead to the outcome. (Fiss, 2011, 402)

Normally, a standard analysis results in a solution that consists of a number of "paths" or "solutions" (combinations of sufficient conditions) that lead to the outcome.

The standard analysis produces three types of logically reduced configurations of conditions that are sufficient for the outcome under scrutiny: a complex solution, an intermediate solution, and a parsimonious solution. The complex solution is exclusively based on the empirical information at hand. The complex solution can, however, be further simplified by using counterfactuals for the logical remainders. Distinction is made between "easy counterfactuals" and "difficult

Table C.5 *Assumed Causal Direction of Conditions for the Outcome Attracting Rule-Takers*

Condition	Assumed Causal Direction	Source
Rules	Unclear	(Potoski & Prakash, 2009)
Enforcement	Unclear	(Potoski & Prakash, 2009)
Financial rewards	The higher the rewards, the more attractive a voluntary program is to prospective rule-takers	(Borck & Coglianese, 2009; Potoski & Prakash, 2009)
Nonfinancial rewards	The higher the rewards, the more attractive a voluntary program is to prospective rule-takers	(Borck & Coglianese, 2009; Potoski & Prakash, 2009)
Leadership rewards	The higher the rewards, the more attractive a voluntary program is to prospective rule-takers	(Borck & Coglianese, 2009; Potoski & Prakash, 2009)
Local government involvement	Local government involvement as rule-maker makes a voluntary program attractive to prospective rule-takers	(B. Evans et al., 2005)
Impact of diffusion network	A network that frequently exposes a prospective rule-taker to the program, has strong players supporting the program, or both has a positive impact on attracting rule-takers	(Moore, 2002; E. M. Rogers, 1995)

counterfactuals" (this is explained by Fiss, 2011). Easy counterfactuals are based on the theoretical assumptions (or other substantive knowledge by the researcher): for this study these are the assumptions identified in Chapter 3. Table C.5 summaries the assumed causal direction for each condition.

The inclusion of easy counterfactuals in the standard analysis leads to an intermediate solution. The parsimonious solution (that is, the simplest solution) results from using difficult counterfactuals. Applying difficult counterfactuals is the inverse of applying easy counterfactuals. That is, assumptions are made about the outcome of a configuration if the counterfactual condition is redundant. This is a more complicated and hazardous undertaking, since typical expectations are that conditions are present, and not absent. Note, however, that a parsimonious solution may look "simpler" than an intermediate or complex solution, but in fact provides less categorical delineation. There also is a risk that parsimonious solutions may be "unrealistically simplistic" (Ragin, 2008, 175).

Following conventional QCA practice I present only the intermediate solutions in this book. Please note that for the complex causal direction of the conditions "rules" and "enforcement" I only use the observed data — that is, for these two conditions I do not rely on counterfactuals in the simplification process.

Step 9: Presentation of Results

After carrying out the standard analysis, results can be presented in various forms. I have chosen a fairly common tabulated form — see Tables 7.5, 7.9, 7.10, and 7.12 for the data calibrated for csQCA. Table C.6 presents the intermediate solutions for the outcome "attracting rule-takers" based on the data calibrated for fsQCA.

Table C.6 adopts a straightforward notation and presentation of causal configurations ("paths") that are sufficient to cause the outcome of interest (attracting rule-takers) — uppercase script indicates the condition is present, and lowercase script indicates the condition is absent in a causal configuration. It indicates that two configurations are related to attracting at least 15 percent of the pool of prospective rule-takers (path RT.1' and path RT.2'). The solution coverage (0.63) is moderate (Ragin, 2008), and it indicates that the solution relates favorably to the outcome observed (see Schneider & Wagemann, 2012, section 5.3). The solution consistency (0.77) is high and indicates that the solution is of high empirical importance in reaching the outcome. The solution

Table C.6 *Intermediate Solution for Attracting Rule-Takers (fsQCA)*

Solution	Formula	Coverage		Consistency	Programs
		Raw	Unique		
Path RT.1'	rule*ENF*FIN*NETW	0.44	0.44	1.00	BREEAM-NL, Green Star, NABERS
Path RT.2'	ENF*FIN* NON- FIN*LEAD*LG*NETW	0.20	0.20	1.00	Better Buildings Partnership
Solution coverage: 0.63					
Solution consistency: 0.77					

Note: Uppercase indicates the condition is present; lowercase indicates the condition is absent
Abbreviations: Rule = rules (sustainable building requirements); Enf = enforcement of rules; Fin = assured financial rewards for rule-takers; Non-fin = nonfinancial rewards for rule-takers (e.g., information); Lead = possibility to showcase leadership in the construction or property sector for rule-takers; LG = local government as rule-maker; Netw = positive impact of diffusion network; * = logical AND

for the analysis for sufficient conditions is the same for the data set calibrated for csQCA and fsQCA (compare with Table 7.5). The only difference pertains to the slightly lower consistency and coverage scores in the fsQCA. This is a result of the more nuanced calibration used for the fsQCA (see further Skaaning, 2011).

Step 10: Testing Robustness and Interpreting Results

Of course, csQCA and fsQCA analyses are but means to ends, and not ends in themselves. Critical to interpretation is the process of returning to the data collected and assessing whether the solutions and paths uncovered reflect the empirical reality of the data collected. This may be understood as a fundamental robustness test in QCA (Rihoux & Ragin, 2009). I do so in the "Significant Finding" section in Chapter 7. Alternative robustness tests involve the application of slightly varying calibrations or an increase in the frequency threshold for the number of cases to include in the analysis for sufficient conditions (Skaaning, 2011). I have done the former by calibrating my data for both csQCA and fsQCA and by conducting analyses for necessary and sufficient conditions. These analyses resulted in highly similar results. However, increasing the frequency threshold is of little avail to a medium-n study such as the one I present here. It requires the exclusion of cases from the analyses, which in my study would result in too few cases for a meaningful application of QCA (see also Skaaning, 2011). A final robustness test is to use the data obtained and assess different theoretical models through QCA (Schneider & Wagemann, 2012). This approach constitutes the core of my study, as discussed in the Chapter 1. The first theoretical model I applied was based on conditions identified by the club theory perspective. I then used a theoretical model that combined conditions identified by the club theory perspective with the local government perspective. I finally used a model that combined conditions identified by the club theory perspective, the local government perspective, and the diffusion network perspective (see Chapter 3).

Assured by the outcomes of these robustness tests, I can turn to the final step of interpreting the findings of the various analyses. I do so in Chapters 7 and 9.

Appendix D Interviews

This final appendix provides some additional insight into the interview data collected, coded, and analyzed.

Interviewees

Interviewees were traced through Internet searches and through social-network Websites, particularly LinkedIn. This resulted in a pool of 116 interviewees with various backgrounds for the programs studied in Australia, the Netherlands, and the United States and a pool of 97 interviewees for the programs studied in India, Malaysia, and Singapore. Table D.1 and Table D.2 provide an overview of the interviewees.

The interviews were recorded, and based on the recording and notes taken during the interviews a summary report was drafted that was sent back to the interviewees for validation. The interviewees were often aware of and involved in more than one voluntary program. It is expected that this partly helped to overcome a sampling bias of administrators and participants who were overly enthusiastic about their own case (Sanderson, 2002). Interviews lasted approximately one hour each and were generally conducted at the interviewee's work location. A number of interviewees were consulted by telephone or email during the writing of this book for follow-up interviews to clarify specific issues.

Interview Questions

Interviews were guided by a semistructured questionnaire that made allowances for additional questions. The guiding questions were:

Table D.1 *Overview of Interviewees and Their Backgrounds (Australia, Netherlands, United States)*

Interviewee Background	Government	Nongovernment
Policymaker	22	3
Administrator	17	27
Architect, engineer, adviser	5	21
Contractor, developer		7
Property owner		4
Other		10
Total	**44**	72

Table D.2 *Overview of Interviewees and Their Backgrounds (India, Malaysia, Singapore)*

Interviewee Background	Government	Nongovernment
Policy maker	7	
Administrator	14	15
Architect, engineer, adviser		21
Contractor, developer		10
Property owner		6
Other		24
Total	**21**	76

1. Why was [case X] developed and implemented?
   a. Have any program alternatives been considered when the program was developed?
   b. Have nonstate stakeholders expressed what they are willing to change (as considered from the previous/existing governance setting)?
   c. Have nonstate stakeholders expressed what they are willing to accept to change (as considered from the previous/existing governance setting)?
   d. Was [case X] developed in response to a sudden political problem (i.e., a problem that received considerable public and media attention)?
   e. Should I understand [case x] (when it was originally developed) as a "prototype" to be tested before rolling it out more broadly; or, as a program open to adaptation and change based on lessons learned during implementation?

2. Who was involved in the development and implementation of [case X]?
   a. Were/are any parties underrepresented in the development of the program?
   b. Were/are any parties overrepresented in the development of the program?
   c. How was consensus about the program achieved?
   d. To what extent were/are parties satisfied with the program?
   e. What role did/does the government play in the development and implementation of the program?

3. Why do [individuals/organizations] participate in the case?
   a. Does [case x] result in financial gain to participants (e.g., it gives them a market advantage)?
   b. Does [case x] provide regulatory/legal relief to participants? If so, is this a major reason for participation?
   c. Any other motivations for participation?

4. What are the outcomes of [case X]?
   a. How many [individuals/organizations] participate in the program?
   b. How many buildings were [built/retrofitted] under the program?
   c. To what extent do nonparticipants know about the program?

5. To what extent may [case X] be considered a success/failure?
   a. In terms of participants?
   b. In terms of buildings [built/retrofitted]?
   c. In terms of achieving actual carbon reductions?
   d. In terms of cost-effectiveness?
   e. In other terms?

6. What are the main characteristics of [case X] related to this success/failure?
   a. Rules (clearness, adaptability, flexibility)?
   b. Enforcement and monitoring?
   c. Sanctions (peer pressure, financial incentives, legal measures)?
   d. Rewards (access to information, access to government, public recognition, financial gain)?
   e. Other?

7. What are the main lessons learned from developing and implementing [case X]?
   a. What mechanism for learning/drawing lessons is implemented?
   b. Are lessons recorded and stored?

    c. Are lessons disseminated among participants? How?

    d. Are these lessons shared with the other [participants/administrators]?

    e. Have any negative outcomes been identified so far?

    f. If so, have these been reported? Have these been communicated? How?

    g. Has [case x] been adapted based on past lessons learned?

8. Representativeness

    a. To what extent are current lessons representative of an even wider implementation of [case x] in [region/country]? And nationwide/ abroad?

    b. Has [case x] received considerable funding when developed and implemented?

9. Achieving sustainable development

    a. To what extent has [case x] as an alternative policy program paved the way to achieving a more sustainable built environment (by changing the behavior of individuals/organizations)?

    b. What barriers, if any, has [case x] raised for implementing policy programs that aim to achieve a more sustainable built environment?

10. Other issues discussed?

    a. Main lessons learned ...

    b. What would be done differently ...

    c. Good example/best practice ...

    d. Failure example/worst practice ...

    e. Other relevant issues ...

Data Coding

The interview data were processed by means of a systematic coding scheme and qualitative data analysis software (Atlas.ti). The coding was carried out in three rounds, from roughly coding parts of interviews in which, for instance, interviewees discussed the outcomes of a program, to fine-grained coding within earlier-identified codes when, for instance, interviewees discussed whether an arrangement was considered effective because it had resulted in carbon reduction. Using this approach, the data were systematically explored, enabling insight into the "repetitiveness" and "rarity" of experiences shared by the interviewees. Table D.3 provides an overview of codes used.

Table D.3 *Overview of Codes for Data Analysis*

Primary Codes	Secondary Codes	Tertiary Codes
Context conditions	Country	Australia
		India
		Malaysia
		Netherlands
		Other country
		Singapore
		United States
	Economic circumstances	Global Financial Crisis
	Existing legislation	Lenient
		Stringent
	Societal pressure	
Development motivations	Affirmative	Cheaper than formal regulation
		Cost savings
		Green consumers
		Green financing
		Job creation
		Overcoming legal barriers
		Overcoming split incentives
		Showcasing good practice
		Showcasing leadership
		Sufficiency
	Negative	Hindering competitors
		Industry capture
		Prevent future regulation
		Societal pressure
		Worker pressure
Development process	Collaboration/participation	
	Consensus building	
	Context based	
	Deliberation/discussion/ dialogue	
	Devolved decision making	
	Heterarchy	
	Ongoing learning and readjustment	
Mandatory vs. voluntary		Mandatory is needed
		Mandating voluntary programs
Role of government	Assembling	
	Facilitating	
	Guarding	
	Supporting	Launching customer/ consumer

Table D.3 (*cont.*)

Primary Codes	Secondary Codes	Tertiary Codes
Participation motivations	Affirmative	Altruism
		Cost savings (general)
		Energy cost savings
		Financial gain (general)
		Green consumers
		Green financing
		Regulatory relief
		Showcasing good practice
		Showcasing leadership
		Sufficiency
	Negative	Liability and legitimacy
		Peer pressure
		Poor past performance
		Reputational harm
		Societal pressure
Program design	Certification and classification	Benchmarking
		Labeling
		Rating
	Enforcement and monitoring	Administered monitoring
		Government monitoring
		Self-monitoring
		Third party monitoring
	Existing buildings	
	Flexibility	
	Funds	
	Knowledge	
	Rules	Lenient
		Stringent
	Residential property	
	Rewards	Information
		Interaction with government
		Financial gain
		Public recognition
	Sanctioning	Financial penalty
		Reputational penalty (shaming)
		Warning
	Target and result orientation	
	Transparency	
	Other design category	
Program outcome	Attracting rule-takers	
	Changing rule-takers' behavior	
	Effective/efficient	Best practice
		Changed norm
		Lessons learned

Table D.3 (*cont.*)

Primary Codes	Secondary Codes	Tertiary Codes
		Physical results (buildings; energy)
		Reducing CO_2 emissions
		Success factor
		Spillover effects
	Not effective/efficient	Failure factor

Notes

Moving Forward, Moving Sideways

1 Foucault probably meant crabs and not crawfish for his metaphor. Crabs are among the few animals that indeed advance sideways. As anyone who has ever observed crawfish knows, they move forward — they can move backward much faster than they can forward, however, but that would make for an entirely different metaphor.

2 Particularly challenging is reporting on an in-depth medium-n study in peer-reviewed journals. Take the research for this book. If I use only 100 words to summarize each voluntary program studied in a table (name, year of implementation, brief description, performance, website address for further information for the reader to follow up on), I need 3,500 words. With many journals having word limits between five and eight thousand words, that does not leave much space for discussing general patterns and unique observations. To give you an idea of how much information fits into 100 words, this footnote is exactly 100 words.

3 Of course, there are a number of edited volumes on voluntary programs and other innovative forms of governance that analyze and discuss a considerable number of real-world programs each (DeLeon & Rivera, 2010; Morgenstern & Pizer, 2007; Potoski & Prakash, 2009; Ronit, 2012). While I am inspired by these edited volumes and am very positive about the insight they provide on voluntary programs and their performance, my criticism is that they draw conclusions based on *ex post* comparative research and not *ex ante* — designed comparative research. In other words, the examples in these works were not studied with similar questions in mind or built on a comparable research template. Thus, although these edited volumes at first glance compare apples with apples, they actually compare apples with oranges (research design X and its conclusions of one study with research design Y and its conclusion of another study). The conclusions drawn from them should be considered in that light — a fact that may in part explain why the club theory perspective is unable to capture the variance in voluntary program performance observed in this book.

1 Why Focus on Voluntary Programs for Sustainable Buildings and Cities?

1 That qualitative comparative analysis is capable of making visible and analyzing such asymmetry has been assumed before, but has not often been empirically observed (Schneider & Wagemann, 2012).

2 Ray Pawson and Nick Tilly use the term program "mechanism" where I use program "design" (Pawson, 2013; Pawson & Tilley, 1997).

3 A full overview is available from www.jeroenvanderheijden.net/research_cur rent_VENI.html (January 4, 2016).

4 Of course, there are relevant differences among these three countries also. For example, Australia and the United States have a federal system while the Netherlands does not; the Netherlands is subject to a higher governing body in the area of environmental governance (the European Union), while Australia and the United States are not. However, literature on voluntary programs does not point to such differences as relevant for voluntary program performance (see, e.g., Auld, 2014). The contextual conditions considered relevant for explaining program performance are built on the current state of the art in voluntary program studies (see Chapter 3). These are conditions that are considered sufficiently constant in Australia, the Netherlands, and the United States. In addition, the comparative synthesis chapter (Chapter 7) seeks to understand what combinations of conditions explain various forms of program performance. These combinations do not cluster along country contexts. This indicates that, for the purpose of this study, potential differences in the contextual conditions of this set of countries appear not to have a strong influence on the performance of the programs studied.

5 Regression analysis may be applied to a similar end; Vis (2012) and Warren and colleagues (2013) contrast QCA with regression analysis, highlighting the strengths and weaknesses of both approaches.

2 The Sustainable Building Challenge

1 Statistics on global building and city-related resource consumption and waste production cited here are, to the best of my knowledge, the most accurate data currently available. Country differences exist: see Appendix A. There is considerable noise in global data available on urbanization, the resources consumption and carbon emissions that can be allocated to buildings and cities, and the built-up space globally. This is, of course, not surprising. Many countries do not possess administrative systems capable of keeping track of such data, or might have incentives to skew data. For the purposes of this book exact figures are often not in issue because significance is mainly perceptible in the qualitative challenges and opportunities of voluntary programs. Whether the built environment requires 30-something or 40-something percent of all energy consumed (see, e.g., differences between ICCP, 2007 and ICCP, 2014), the overarching message is clear: buildings and cities require a large

share of global resource consumption, contribute significantly to global carbon emissions, and present enormous potential for improvement.

2 Buildings and cities produce a wide range of greenhouse gases, but predominantly carbon. The percentage reported here excludes carbon emissions produced by transport in, from, and to cities and that produced by industry in cities (Dodman, 2009; IPCC, 2014).

3 It could be argued that because birth rates per capita are much lower in urban than in rural contexts, future urbanization may actually result in a much lower world population than that forecast by the United Nations (P. Taylor, 2013). In addition, urban populations are likely better educated than rural populations, a possibility that might make urban populations more aware of a need to respond to response to environmental problems, including climate change (Dietz & O'Neill, 2013). Seen in this light, urbanization might represent a promisingl development in addressing environmental problems.

4 Building and city development is also a highly political issue — a topic that has traditionally received more scholarly attention than regulatory and governance issues of building and city development and use (Cheshire et al., 2014; Davidson & Martin, 2014; Davies & Imbroscio, 2009; Judd & Mendelson, 1973; D. Marshall, 1979). The latter topic appeared on the urban studies agenda in the late 1980s and early 1990s and has developed two related, but distinct theories: urban regime theory, which is most prominent in North America (Lauria, 1997; Mossberger & Stoker, 2001), and urban governance theory, which is most prominent in Europe (Kjaer, 2009; Pierre, 2011). I am inspired mostly by urban governance theory and the larger governance theorizing (Bell & Hindmoor, 2009; Bevir, 2011; Chhotray & Stoker, 2010; Levi-Faur, 2012).

5 Subsidies may also result in unequal distribution of wealth: those receiving subsidies normally have to pay a part of the initial costs of energy upgrades themselves, making subsidies unattractive for low-income households and small firms, but accessible for middle- and high-income households and large firms, which benefit from lower energy costs of these upgrades. This adds to reasons for having discontinued many early subsidy programs (Diaz Arias & van Beers, 2013; Glemarec, 2012; Zetland & Gasson, 2013).

6 These taxes and other economic instruments for buildings and cities are also criticized for the valid interpretation that harmful behavior is allowed when it is paid for. Property owners and users may consider them as just one of the many costs of doing business (Harper, 2007; Sandel, 2012; Zarsky, 1997). In addition, these government-led instruments are likely to be as slow as building codes and planning legislation to be implemented and to secure results; they confront opposition when proposed because they impose an additional financial burden on individuals and firms and create enforcement problems when implemented (Chiroleu-Assouline & Fodha, 2014; Kallbekken, 2011).

7 Some interviewees have requested anonymity, and to prevent discriminating among them I do not refer to any by name. I refer to their function and, where relevant, the type of organization they work for. Throughout the book — and all other publications that have resulted from this research project — each interviewee is identified by the same number.

8 Compare this with "fast-moving" consumer goods such as cell phones: it will be difficult for governments to require citizens to modify the cell phones they currently own, but if energy efficiency requirements are set for future cell phones it takes only two years for the vast majority of users to meet these requirements because of the high turnover rate of cell phones (Geyer & CDoctori Blass, 2010).

9 In other areas behavioral interventions are considered perfectly normal. Road safety, for example, is mainly regulated through mandatory speed limits.

10 Data from www.transitionnetwork.org (June 14, 2015). However, regarding criticism of the effectiveness of the Transition Town initiative, see Seyfang (2009).

11 The Forest Stewardship Council is an international not-for-profit organization that promotes responsible management of the world's forests. It has developed and implemented a voluntary certification system to certify forest management and products.

3 A World of Voluntary Programs

1 Governance here is understood as an intended activity undertaken by one or more actors seeking to shape, regulate, or attempt to control human behavior in order to achieve a desired collective end (Dean, 2009; Foucault, 2009; Lemke, 2002). Although this is an almost all-inclusive and slippery concept it has provided scholars with broad scope to study the agency and instrumentality involved in shaping, regulating, and controlling human behavior and the contextual study of their outcomes (Chhotray & Stoker, 2010; Kjaer, 2011; Kohler-Koch & Rittberger, 2006).

2 See, for instance, the discussions on the environmental Kuznets curve, an economic model that conceptualizes environmental degradation as increasing with economic growth until an average level of wealth or per capita income, after which environmental degradation decreases (Choumert et al., 2013; Dinda, 2004; Farhani, Mrizak, Chaibi, & Rault, 2014).

3 Agenda 21 supported the use of voluntary programs also.

4 In the realist evaluation terminology of Ray Pawson and Nick Tilley the diffusion network would be considered a context condition (Pawson, 2013; Pawson & Tilley, 1997). See further Chapter 1.

5 A variety of terminology has been proposed for the individual groups. This book follows Everett Rogers's (1995) classic work in this area, *Diffusion of Innovations*, but uses the term "leaders" instead of "innovators." Rogers uses these terms interchangeably in his work.

6 These are the people whom I met at the various business and trade conferences on sustainable buildings and city development that I visited as part of the research project. They are also likely to constitute the majority of rule-takers interviewed for this project.

7 For an overview of comparable examples in the United States, see www.dsireusa .org (April 5, 2015).

8 Ecofinance fits a larger category of economic governance instruments (EGIs). EGIs comprise fiscal instruments (including emission trading and taxes),

charge systems (e.g., user fees and pollution levies), and liability systems (including environmental insurance and legal liabilities) (Ali & Yano, 2004; Castellucci & Markandya, 2012; Panayotou, 1998).

9 The propositions also support the application of counterfactuals in the QCA analyses in Chapter 7. In short, the propositions define the assumed causal relation between conditions and outcomes (Ragin, 2008; Rihoux & Ragin, 2009; Schneider & Wagemann, 2012).

4 Certification and Classification

1 Data from www.BREEAM.org (July 5, 2015).
2 Data from www.breeam.nl (July 3, 2015).
3 Data from www.USGBC.org and www.BREEAM.org (July 7, 2015).
4 Data from www.cencus.gov and www.eia.gov (July 7, 2015).
5 All additional data in this section derive from www.nabers.gov.au (July 8, 2015).
6 Data from www.energystar.gov and www.census.gov (July 6, 2015).
7 Data from www.envirodevelopment.com.au, www.hia.com.au and www.abs .com.au (July 6, 2015).
8 This further muddles their transparency. Wooden products certified by the Forest Stewardship Council and flooring material certified under the "Carpet and Rug Institute Green Label Program" are typical examples. The use of these certified products in construction yields LEED credits — and thus higher levels of classification. But what is known about these organizations? The Forest Stewardship Council is an internationally acclaimed organization and its accreditation processes have been well documented and scrutinized (Cashore et al., 2004). The Carpet and Rug Institute, on the other hand, is less well known, less well studied, and less transparent. What is known is that the carpet industry has lobbied fiercely to see its own interests served over environmental considerations in programs such as LEED (McDonough, 2004; Perinotto, 2014b). Policy makers thus need to consider these issues before mandating LEED and comparable programs in their jurisdictions.
9 In part because many member states do not enforce this legislation (see van der Heijden & Van Bueren, 2013).
10 Data from www.propertyoz.com.au (July 9, 2015).

5 Urban Governance Networks

1 www.zonnighuren.nl (March 25, 2015) – my translation.
2 www.cityswitch.net.au/News/TabId/97/ArtMID/491/ArticleID/10311/City Switch-signatories-celebrate-record-achievements.aspx (March 29, 2015).
3 The 650 CitySwitch participants (tenants) correspond with more than 2.3 million square meters of office area, or 6 percent of the total office area of Australia in 2014 (40 million square meters). Energy consumption of offices in Australia for the base year 2011 was 35PJ (35 petajoules) (additional data from, COAG, 2012a). Under a situation of equal uptake of CitySwitch throughout

the Australian office market the offices of the 2014 participants consumed some 2PJ in 2011 (5.75 percent of 35PJ) — the 75-GWh, or 0.27-PJ energy savings, correspond with 13 percent of 2 PJ. The assumption of "equal uptake" can be challenged, however. CitySwitch tenants on average own or rent more energy efficient buildings than nonparticipants, and the total energy consumption of their 2011 buildings was therefore likely lower than 2PJ. The average CitySwitch tenant's NABERS rating of 3.9 stars indicates they occupy approximately 15 percent more energy efficient buildings than nonparticipants (see further Chapter 4 and Appendix A). Corrected for this difference, CitySwitch participants' 2014 energy savings as of 2011 were 16 percent.

4 The 0.27 PJ savings of 2014 are 0.78 percent of the 35 PJ total energy consumption in 2011 (see previous note). As an aside: the 2011 Australian census counted a little more than 8 million inhabited residential units in Australia (houses and other dwellings). The 12,712 houses reported by the CitySwitch administration make up 0.16 percent of these; data from: www.abs.goc.au/census (March 29, 2015).

5 See www.delta-institute.org/2015/06/tally-is-in-chicago-green-office-challenge-announces-winners/ (July 20, 2015).

6 Additional data from www.eia.gov (July 21, 2015).

7 Source www.rvo.nl/onderwerpen/duurzaam-ondernemen/groene-economie/green-deal# (July 22, 2015 — my translation).

8 See www.ondernemendgroen.nl (July 22, 2015).

9 See www.sydneybetterbuildings.com.au (July 24, 2015).

10 For more information: www.cityofsydney.nsw.gov.au/vision/towards-2030/sustainability/carbon-reduction/trigeneration (March 30, 2015).

11 Which again raises questions as to whether reported performance can be attributed to Retrofit Chicago, or whether retrofits would also have been carried out without the program in place (Lydersen, 2012; NRDC, 2014).

12 See www.betterbuildingssolutioncenter.energy.gov/partners-news (July 30, 2015).

6 Innovative Climate Financing

1 PACE initially applied to commercial and residential property, but as a result of the subprime mortgage crisis of 2008 the U.S. mortgage authorities (Fannie Mae and Freddie Mac) refused to finance mortgages under PACE (Bird & Hernandez, 2012; J. Kirkpatrick & Bennear, 2014; Sichtermann, 2011).

2 Combined data from www.architectureanddesign.com.au/news/bpn/wesley-house-sustainable-mission-accomplished and www.architectus.com.au/sites/default/files/sa-com-Wesley%20House%20HR_0.pdf (February 25, 2015).

3 The project is documented at: www.epositiveboston.org/?page_id=1665 (August 6, 2015). Keep in mind, though, that this relates to "as designed" certification and not "in operation" certification. See the critique of "as designed" certification in Chapter 4.

4 Data from www.architects.org (August 6, 2015).

5 Revolving loan funds are applied in Australia as well, but only in the area of land management (Mortimer, 2003).

6 Combined data from www.amsterdam.nl/wonen-leefomgeving/energie/amster dams/amsterdams and www.akef.nl/investeringen (April 14, 2015).

7 See www.cityclimateleadershipawards.com/2014-project-amsterdam-invest ment-fund (April 14, 2015).

8 A related program, the Better Building Accelerators program within the Better Buildings Initiative (discussed in Chapter 5), also addresses the U.S. university sector, but requires a commitment of 20 percent improvement of energy efficiency (White House, 2011a).

9 It had generated another U.S.$950 million for residential property. Data from www.pacenow.org (August 10, 2015).

10 See www.pacenow.org (August 10, 2015).

11 See www.cityclimateleadershipawards.com/melbourne-sustainable-buildings-program (April 15, 2015).

12 See www.melbourne.vic.gov.au/1200buildings/CurrentSignatories/Pages/Cur rentSignatories.aspx (April 15, 2015). By 2015, some participating property owners had already completed building retrofits, indicating that energy effi-ciency improvements of more than 50 percent are possible in a range of building types throughout the Melbourne central business district.

13 See www.melbourne.vic.gov.au/1200buildings/Pages/GoodForBusiness.aspx (August 10, 2015).

14 See www.c40.org/awards (August 11, 2015).

15 See www.c40.org/profiles/2014-amsterdam (August 11, 2015).

16 See, for example, www.amsterdamsmartcity.com/news/detail/id/268/slug/the-city-of-amsterdam-wins-climate-leadership-award (August 11, 2015).

17 Data from www.data.cityofchicago.org/Community-Economic-Development/ Small-Business-Improvement-Fund-SBIF-Grant-Agreeme/jp7n-tgmf#expand (August 12, 2015).

18 Data from www.nces.ed.gov (August 12, 2015).

19 Data from www.akef.nl/folio/mixed-portfolio-item/ (August 13, 2015). The Amsterdam Investment Fund expects that the installment of solar panels at the cost of €1.6 million will result in a carbon reduction of fifteen thousand tons over their twenty-year technical life span. At the time of awarding the project one ton of carbon was traded for less than €30 under the European Emissions Trading Scheme (ETS). It appears that no politician critical of the fund has done the math to argue that the fund is not allocating its money effectively: the €1.6 million could also have been used to buy emission permits representing more than fifty-five thousand tons of carbon — close to four times the yield of retrofitting the flagship soccer stadium (carbon price from Neslen, 2015).

7 Separating the Wheat from the Chaff

1 Setting numerical performance benchmarks introduces its own hazards, and some will likely disagree with the benchmarks I introduce — as being either too lenient or too strict. These benchmarks are set only to reduce data set

complexity, and to contrast the more promising voluntary programs with the less promising ones — these benchmarks are not normative descriptors of how voluntary programs ought to perform.

2 Understanding that this benchmark may discriminate against the younger programs studied, the benchmark for those younger than five years is set at 0.5 percent per year, which corresponds with the median yearly rule-taker attraction rate of all programs studied, and with the category of "leaders" in the diffusion of innovations literature. For each subsequent year 2.5 percent uptake is added to the benchmark; all programs older than ten years are assessed against the 15 percent uptake benchmark. Close scrutiny has determined that none of the programs studied is a borderline case.

3 Each analysis is concluded with brief mention of the most notable observations. In these I stay close to the findings from the analyses; in the concluding section of this chapter I interpret the findings in light of the broader study.

4 As a matter of certitude in this decision I also conducted analysis for sufficient conditions without using "rules" and "enforcement" as counterfactuals, as done for the earlier analyses for sufficient conditions. The outcome is only marginally different from the one presented, while the main findings are comparable.

5 Again, to establish a measure of certainty regarding this choice I also conducted analyses for sufficient conditions, including the programs that set lenient rules. The full solution, paths, coverage, and consistency scores are identical for both analyses. In sum, this specific data set regarding shirking (based on the theoretical template applied) also explains why rule-takers exhibit only marginal or no improvement of their behavior. However, this finding may not hold true for other data sets or other theoretical templates.

6 About 80 percent of all Australians live in the country's twenty largest cities, and about 40 percent of all Australians live in Sydney and Melbourne alone. Data from www.abs.gov.au (August 31, 2015).

8 Voluntary Programs for Sustainable Cities Elsewhere

1 But as I have explained in Chapter 4, the "promising results" marketed by program administrators of LEED and Green Star are part of a leadership delusion. While these programs have resulted in impressive best practice in terms of sustainable building development, their relative impact is marginal (see further Chapter 7).

2 Association of Southeast Asian Nations, a political and economic organization of Southeast Asian countries formed in 1947.

3 Data from www.igbc.in and www.ecohousing.in (October 6, 2015).

4 For documented date, see www.urbannewsdigest.in/green-cities/ (October 6, 2015).

5 Data from www.grihaindia.org (October 6, 2015).

6 Data from www.commonfloor.com/nyati-environ-pune/povp-8zjxq8 (August 28, 2015).

7 Data from www.gbig.org/places/752 (January 11, 2016).

8 See further www.breeam.com/newsdetails.jsp?id=955 (January 11, 2016).

9 Because a typical development project in Singapore is a high-rise building or a block of high-rise buildings, this requirement implies that in practice all new construction work in Singapore has to achieve "Gold" class certification. Compared to the few new construction projects that are exempted from the requirement to be Green Mark—certified, a "certified" project is at least 10 percent more energy efficient (BCA, 2010).

10 Data from www.sec.org.sg/web/files/resource/1395384403.pdf (January 11, 2016).

11 Data from www.singstat.gov.sg (January 11, 2016).

12 Data from www.nabers.gov.au/public/WebPages/Home.aspx (January 13, 2016). I combine the 5-Star and 6-Star NABERS ratings here as both indicate more than 20 percent improvement compared to mandatory requirements in Australia.

9 Beyond the Leadership Delusion

1 As highlighted in Chapter 1, this observation goes back to Karl Popper's (2002 [1935]) observation that the empirical sciences are concerned with one-sided falsification of statements, and that no symmetrical relationships can be assumed from one-sided falsification. Nassim Taleb (2007) refers to this as the "problem of silent evidence" — that focusing solely on successful examples results in an inaccurate, one-sided perspective of what explains success; in addition, it often remains unknown how many examples have failed, since it is far more difficult to obtain data on failed and terminated policy programs than for successful, ongoing programs.

2 Voluntary programs for sustainable buildings often cannot exclusively target a small number of very large producers (as, for instance, the Forest Stewardship Council can) or a small number of very large consumers (as, for instance, the International Air Transport Association can). While not a demonstrable conclusion of this study, it might be easier for some other sectors to capture the vast pool of resource consumption or carbon emissions by attracting the relatively small number of largest players in the sector.

3 One could argue that there is a "small head" in the property sector: governments own and use a large proportion of buildings. In Australia, the Netherlands, and the United States governments have already committed to voluntary programs, often through sustainable procurement criteria or by otherwise mandating that the building space they use complies with requirements in voluntary certification and classification programs such as Green Star, BREEAM-NL, and LEED (Colliers International, 2013; DTZ Zadelhoff, 2013; Knight Frank, 2014). The problem, however, is that this "small head" is already captured, thus only reinforcing concerns about the difficulty of capturing the very, very long tail.

4 See, for example, Transparency International's *Corruption Perception Index*, available from www.transparency.org (November 20, 2015).

5 Data from www.search.proquest.com (August 31, 2015).

6 It is of relevance here to note the current preponderance of urban governance books advocating mandatory regimes, such as Benjamin Barber's (2013)

If Mayors Ruled the World. Barber appeals for interventionist mayoral governance but is careful to sell this message as unconventional top-down government activism (see also Goldsmith & Crawford, 2014).

7 This title is inspired by a book by Arild Vatn (2005, 426).

8 Think of the water and energy intensive but nevertheless LEED-certified
casinos in the Nevada desert (Alter, 2008; USA Today, 2013), or the
Platinum-rated hotels and other sustainable buildings overlooking the slums
in Mumbai that I was shown when studying voluntary programs in India.

Appendix A Country Snapshots

1 Population 24 million, 2015; unless referenced otherwise, population data and
country and city statistics throughout this appendix are obtained from the
World Bank Databank: www.data.worldbank.org/ (August 31, 2015); and the
United Nations World Urbanization Prospects, the 2014 revision: www.esa.un
.org/unpd/wup/ (August 31, 2015).

2 A relatively low number when compared to the Netherlands or the United
States. This is due to the vast amounts of carbon emissions produced in
the Australian mining and industrial sectors. Data from www.environment.gov
.au/climate-change/greenhouse-gas-measurement/tracking-emissions (April 25,
2015).

3 Australians are among the world's largest carbon emitters: 17 metric tons
per capita in 2014 — on average Europeans emitted 8.6 metric tons per capita,
and citizens of India 1.7. For this book, however, total per capita emissions are
of limited relevance; where possible I present per capita carbon emissions
resulting from the construction, maintenance, and use of buildings (for
Australia: 23 percent of 17 metric tons equals 3.9 metric tons per capita —
data: see note 1). I am skeptical of the accuracy of publicly available per capita
emissions data — that is why I round up numbers considerably and frequently
use the word "approximately." Other than for India and Malaysia, for which
no locatable building-related per capita carbon emissions data exist, I include
these figures as approximations of the relative and qualitative differences
among the nations studied.

4 What follows is a simplified representation of how sustainable building is
governed in Australia. It is not the intention of the current book to offer a
comprehensive overview of urban planning and the processes underlying the
development of building codes in Australia or elsewhere. I address the main
instruments as they relate to governing sustainable buildings only. For introductory further reading, see Susan Thompson and Paul Magninn's (2012)
Planning Australia; for extensive discussion of environmental policy in Australia,
(see Australian Government, 2014; Dovers, 2002; Hamilton, 2006; Harding,
2006; Parliament of Australia, 2013; Saul et al., 2012; Staples, 2009).

5 Additional statistical data on India are obtained from the 2011 Census Data
India: www.censusindia.gov.in (August 31, 2015).

6 This includes overall population growth and increased urbanization. Urbanization in India is expected to occur predominantly in existing cities. Projections for 2030 are that India will have fifty-five cities with populations between

1 and 4 million (up from thirty-three in 2008), and thirteen cities with populations larger than 4 million (up from nine in 2008), including six megacities with populations of 10 million or more — projected populations of Delhi and Mumbai (by 2030) alone are larger than the combined populations of Australia and the Netherlands.

7 That said, it is difficult to speak of "one" urban India because at local scale considerable differences exist: the urban population in the state of Maharashtra (of which Mumbai is the capital) is projected to rise from 53 percent in 2010 to 67 percent in 2030; and in the state of Andhra Pradesh (of which Hyderabad is the capital) from 28 percent in 2010 to 46 percent by 2030 (McKinsey, 2010; UN, 2014). These differing rates of urbanization likely necessitate varying governance approaches. Added to this are complications of regional disparity, income inequality, and associated disparities in standards of living, which further hinder the governance of sustainable buildings (Sen, 2013).

8 In 2014, the per capita carbon emissions of India were 1.7 metric tons (data: see note 1). The construction, maintenance, and use of buildings and cities (transport excluded) account for 47 percent of energy consumption (M. Evans et al., 2009). Unfortunately, available data do not allow comparison between India's per capita building related carbon emissions and that of the other countries.

9 Corruption is a popular theme in the "insiders" literature on government in India (Jalan, 2012; Subramanian, 2009; Vittal, 2012).

10 Based on interview data — see Chapters 4–6.

11 Additional statistical data on Malaysia are obtained from the Department of Statistics Malaysia: www.statistics.gov.my (August 31, 2015).

12 Data from www.esa.un.org/wpp/unpp/p2k0data.asp (April 28, 2015).

13 Approximately half of all Malaysians (47 percent) live in the country's twenty largest cities and urban areas. On average, these have a population density of 560 people per square kilometer, with the city of Kuala Lumpur and the districts of North-East Penang Island and Petaling indicating very high population densities of 6,900 people per square kilometer, 4,300 people per square kilometer, and 3,600 people per square kilometer, respectively. While these three cities all have large population densities, they are the exeption and not the rule in Malaysia. Other urban areas are less densely populated, with extensive sub- and periurban sprawl (LESTARI, 1998).

14 In 2014, per capita carbon emissions in Malaysia were 7.7 metric tons (data: see note 1). These are considerably higher than in any other ASEAN country, except Brunei. Transport is the major contributor to Malaysia's carbon emissions, assumed to account for more than 40 percent of all emissions. The maintenance and use of buildings account for about 15 percent of Malaysia's energy consumption, and approximately 50 percent of its electricity consumption (see also Zaid & Graham, 2013). I have not been able to locate trustworthy data on per capita building and city related carbon emissions that allow for ranking Malaysia within the pool of countries studied (see also note 3).

15 As in India, urban Malaysia reflects its colonial past (LESTARI, 1998). Cities such as Kuala Lumpur, Georgetown, and Johor Bahru were developed as port

towns, while cities elsewhere in the country were outside the interest of the British rulers. After its independence in 1957, the Government of Malaysia faced considerable environmental problems, particularly resulting from large-scale deforestation and mining. Seeking to address these, environmental policies were first introduced in the late 1960s and have been gradually increasing in strength since. Sustainable building policies are largely a continuation of these (see also Hezri & Hasan, 2006).

16 See www.standardsmalaysia.gov.my (June 1, 2015).

17 On-site work also allows for a less-skilled labor force. This does not challenge or require those working in the construction industry to seek additional education. Were contractors to switch to prefabricated construction techniques, they would be unlikely to be able to source skilled labor domestically (Kamal et al., 2012; Shaffi et al., 2006).

18 Additional statistical data on the Netherlands are obtainable from the Statistics Netherlands databank: www.statline.cbs.nl/Statweb/default.aspx (August 31, 2015).

19 In 2014, the per capita carbon emissions of the Netherlands were eleven metric tons (data: see note 1).

20 Figures as at 2015: additional statistical data on Singapore were obtained from the Department of Statistics Singapore: www.singstat.gov.sg (August 31, 2015) and the association of Southeast Asian Nations (ASEAN): www.asean.org (August 31, 2015).

21 Data from International Energy Agency statistics: www.iea.org/statistics/ (August 31, 2015).

22 Approximately 25 percent of Singapore's carbon emissions can be attributed to the construction, maintenance, and use of buildings (National Climate Change Secretariat, 2012). In 2014, its total carbon emissions per capita were 2.7 metric tons (data: see note 1). Singapore's state-guided economic development (Huff, 1995) — sometimes described as a "limited democracy [that] has delivered an exceptional social and economic revolution" (Vasil, 2000, vi), or as illiberal and authoritarian but efficient (Rajah, 2012) — combined with a need for intensive land use and energy efficiency may explain Singapore's exceptionally low carbon emissions per capita.

23 The government has set a future sustainable building goal: 80 percent of all existing and new buildings are to be Green Mark—certified by 2030 (BCA, 2014a).

24 Public housing is developed and managed by the Housing Development Board, Singapore's public housing authority. It was established in 1960 and tasked with solving Singapore's housing crisis, in particular in providing healthy housing for the large majority of citizens then living in slums and squatter settlements. These high-rise building units are sold on ninety-nine-year leasing agreements (Fernandez, 2011).

25 However, see criticism of limited freedom of expression within Singaporean media and academia (Altback, 2001; Koh & Ling, 2004; Tierney & Lanford, 2014).

26 Population figure from 2015; additional statistical data on the United States were obtained from the United States' Census Bureau: www.census.gov (August 31, 2015).

27 In 2015, the per capita carbon emissions of the United States were 17.6 metric tons (data: see note 1).

28 What follows is a simplified representation of how planning and zoning are governed by local councils in the United States. State independence has spawned a wide variety of state-level approaches to governing the built environment. This is not a comprehensive overview: for further reading see Alexander Garvin's (2014) *The American City* (see also Andrews, 2006; Davenport, 2014; Dunlap & Mertig, 2013; Harrington, Morgenstern, & Sterner, 2004; Vig & Faure, 2004).

29 Again, a simplified representation follows (see also Bartlett et al., 2003; Halverson et al., 2009).

Appendix B Voluntary Program Snapshots

1 All Websites identified at the end of each case description were last accessed on August 31, 2015.

2 See further www.platform31.nl (August 12, 2015).

3 Data obtained from www.sa.gov.au/topics/water-energy-and-environment/climate-change/tackling-climate-change/what-organisations-business-and-industry-can-do/building-innovation-fund (February 25, 2015).

4 See www.igbc.in/igbc/redirectHtml.htm?redVal=showLeednosign (February 26, 2015).

5 The IGBC Websites provided information on LEED-India, but this information had been removed as of early 2015.

References

ABCB. (2010). *Energy Efficiency Provisions for BCA 201 0*, Vol. 2. Canberra: Australian Building Codes Board.

Abidin, N. (2010). Investigating the Awareness and Application of Sustainable Construction Concept by Malaysian Developers. *Habitat International, 34*(4), 421–426.

ACCC. (2011, September 2011). Continue to Beware of Scam Solar Offers. Retrieved from www.scamwatch.gov.au/content/index.phtml/itemId/876741.

ACEEE. (2013). *Energy Efficient Mortgage*. Washington, DC: Energy Efficient Mortgage.

Ackerman, F. (1997). *Why Do We Recycle?* Washington, DC: Island Press.

Agentschap NL. (2012). *Voortgangsrapportage Green Deals 20112*. Utrecht: Agentschap NL.

(2013). *Evaluatie zon PV-projecten bij woningcorporaties (Evaluation Solar Energy Production by Housing Corporations)*. The Hague: Agentschap NL.

AGO. (2006). *Scoping Study to Investigate Measures for Improving the Environmental Sustainability of Building Materials*. Melbourne: RMIT.

Aijaz, R. (2012). *Democracy and Urban Governance in India*. New Delhi: Academic Foundation New Delhi.

Albanese, A. (2013). Our Cities, Our Future. *Urban Policy and Research, 31*(3), 251–253.

Alberini, A., & Segerson, K. (2002). Assessing Voluntary Programs to Improve Environmental Quality. *Environmental and Resource Economics, 22*(1–2), 157–184.

Albertini, E. (2013). Does Environmental Management Improve Financial Performance? *Organisation & Environment, 26*(4), 431–457.

Alcott, B. (2005). Jevons' Paradox. *Ecological Economics, 54*(1), 9–21.

Ali, P., & Yano, K. (2004). *Eco-Finance: The Legal Design and Regulation of Market-Based Environmental Instruments*. The Hague: Kluwer.

Aliento, W. (2014, January 23, 2014). Retrofits: How Melbourne Can Encourage Private Interests to Engage with Public Ones. Retrieved from www.thefifthestate.com.au/property/commercial/retrofits-how-melbourne-can-encourage-private-interests-to-engage-with-public-ones/58407.

Allen, F., Barth, J., & Yago, G. (2012). *Fixing the Housing Market*. Philadelphia: Wharton School.

Allens. (2007, March 28, 2007). Client Update: Brisbane City Council Introduces Grants for "Green" Office Buildings. Retrieved from www.allens.com.au/pubs/env/cuenvmar07.htm.

Altback, P. (2001). Academic Freedom: International Realities and Challenges. *Higher Education, 41*(1–2), 205–219.

Alter, J. (2008, January 2, 2013). Slate on "Decidedly Dupable" LEED. Retrieved from www.treehugger.com/sustainable-product-design/slate-on-decidedly-dupable-leed.html.

Ameli, N., & Brandt, N. (2015). *What Impedes Household Investment in Energy Efficiency and Renewable Energy?* Paris: OECD.

Amsterdam City Council. (2013). *Evaluatie Amsterdams Investerings Fonds (AIF)*. Amsterdam: Gemeente Amsterdam.

Andrews, R. N. L. (2006). *Managing the Environment, Managing Ourselves: A History of American Environmental Policy*. New Haven, CT: Yale University Press.

Ansell, C., & Bartenberger, M. (2016). Varieties of Experimentatlism. *Ecological Economics, 130*, 64–73.

Ansell, C., & Gash, A. (2008). Collaborative Governance in Theory and Practice. *Journal of Public Administration Research and Theory, 18*(4), 543–571.

APEC/USAID. (2013). *APEC Building Codes, Regulations and Standards*. Singapore: Asia Pacific Economic Cooperation Secretariat/United States Agency for International Development.

Arimura, T., Hibiki, A., & Katayama, H. (2008). Is a Voluntary Approach an Effective Environmental Policy Instrument? *Journal of Environmental Economics and Management, 55*(3), 281–295.

Armstrong, K., & Kilpatrick, C. (2007). Law, Governance, or New Governance? The Changing Open Method of Coordination. *Columbia Journal of European Law, 13*(3), 649–678.

Arora, S., & Cason, T. N. (1995). An Experiment in Voluntary Environmental Regulation: Participation in EPA's 33–50 Program. *Journal of Environmental Economics and Management, 28*(3), 271–286.

ASBEC. (2008). *The Second Plank: Building a Low-Carbon Economy with Energy Efficient Buildings*. Sydney: Australian Sustainable Built Environment Council.

Athens, L. (2009). *Building an Emerald City*. Washington, DC: Island Press.

Atrivé. (2012). *Businessplannen voor uitrol zonne-energie in de corporatiesector (Business Plans for Renewable Solar Energy in the Housing Corporation Sector)*. Houten: Atrivé.

Auld, G. (2014). *Constructing Private Governance*. New Haven, CT: Yale University Press.

Aust, P. (2015). Shining Cities on the Hill? The Global City, Climate Change, and International Law. *European Journal of International Law, 26*(1), 255–278.

Australian Government. (2010). *Australia to 2050*. Canberra: Austrlaian Government.

(2012). Solar Credits for Small Generation Units. Retrieved from www.climatechange.gov.au/reducing-carbon/renewable-energy/renewable-energy-target/small-scale-renewable-energy-systems/solar-credits-small-generation-units.

(2013). *Sustainable Procurement Guide*. Canberra: Commonwealth of Australia.

(2014). Repealing the Carbon Tax. Retrieved from www.environment.gov.au/climate-change/repealing-carbon-tax.

Australian Parliament. (2011). *Clean Energy Bill 2011*. Canberra: The Parliament of the Commonwealth of Australia.

Backstrand, K., Khan, J., Kronsell, A., & Lovbrand, E. (2010). *Environmental Politics and Deliberative Democracy: Examining the Promises of New Forms of Governance*. Cheltenham, UK: Edward Elgar.

Bai, X., Roberts, B., & Chen, J. (2010). Urban Sustainability Experiments in Asia. *Environmental Science & Policy*, *13*(4), 312–325.

Bailey, I. (2007). Market Environmentalism, New Environmental Policy Instruments, and Climate Policy in the United Kingdom and Germany. *Annals of the Association of American Geographers*, *97*(3), 530–550.

(2008). Industry Environmental Agreements and Climate Policy. *Journal of Environmental Policy and Planning*, *10*(2), 153–173.

Baker, T., Cook, I., McCann, E., Temenos, C., & Ward, K. (2016). Policies on the Move: The Transatlantic Travels of Tax Increment Financing. *Annals of the Association of American Geographers*, *106*(2), 459–469: doi: 10.1080/00045608.2015.1113111

Baldwin, R., Cave, M., & Lodge, M. (2011). *Understanding Regulation: Theory, Strategy and Practice* , 2nd ed. Oxford: Oxford University Press.

Bals, C., Warner, K., & Butzengeiger, S. (2006). Insuring the Uninsurable: Design Options for a Climate Change Funding Mechanism. *Climate Policy*, *6*(6), 637–647.

Bannister, P. (2012). NABERS: Lessons from 12 Years of Performance Based Ratings in Australia. Paper presented at the Twelfth International Conference for Enhanced Building Operations, Manchester.

Barber, B. (2013). *If Mayors Ruled the World*. New Haven, CT: Yale University Press.

Bari, A. M., Begum, R. A., Jaafar, A. H., Abidin, R., & Pereira, J. J. (2010). Future Trend of Energy Demand and Supply and Its Impacts on CO2 Emission in Malaysia. Paper presented at the 2nd International Conference on Human Habitat Transformation and Environmental Change, Kuala Lumpur.

Baron, D. P., & Diermeier, D. (2007). Strategic Activism and Nonmarket Strategy. *Journal of Economics and Management Strategy*, *16*, 599–634.

Barras, R. (2009). *Building Cycles: Growth and Instability*. Chichester, UK: Wiley-Blackwell.

Barry, A., Osborne, T., & Rose, N. S. (1993). *Liberalism, Neo-Liberalism and Governmentality*. London: Routledge.

Bartle, I., & Vass, P. (2007). Self-Regulation within the Regulatory State. *Public Administration*, *85*(4), 885–905.

Bartlett, R., Halverson, M., & Shankle, D. (2003). *Understanding Building Energy Codes and Standards*. Washington, DC: U.S. Department of Energy.

Bartley, T. (2003). Certifying Forests and Factories. *Politics & Society*, *31*(3), 433–464.

Baughn, C., Bodie, N., & McIntosh, J. (2007). Corporate Social and Environmental Responsibility in Asian Countries and Other Geographical

Regions. *Corporate Social Responsibility and Environmental Management,* *14*(4), 189–205.

BCA. (2010). *Media Release: Building and Construction Authority Clinches Prestigious Award from the Aspen Institute and Sets Higher Green Mark Standards for New Buildings.* Singapore: Building and Construction Authority of Singapore.

(2011). *BCA Green Mark Reaches Out to Existing Residential Buildings.* Singapore: Building and Construction Authority of Singapore.

(2012). *BCA Green Mark: Certification Standards for New Buildings.* Version 4.1. Singapore: Building and Construction Authority.

(2013a). *BCA Green Mark for New Non-Residential Buildings.* Version NRB/4.1. Singapore: Building Construction Authority of Singapore.

(2013b). *Green Office Trend on the Rise.* Singapore: Building and Construction Authority of Singapore.

(2013c). *Singapore: Leading the Way for Green Buildings in the Tropics.* Singapore: Building and Construction Authority of Singapore.

(2014a). *3rd Green Building Masterplan.* Singapore: Building Construction Authority of Singapore.

(2014b). *More Building Projects Achieving Higher BCA Green Mark Standards.* Singapore: Building and Construction Authority of Singapore.

(2014c). *New BCA Incentive to Drive Green Building Retrofits and Practices under 3rd Green Building Masterplan.* Singapore: Building and Construction Authority of Singapore.

Beatley, T. (2009). *Green Urbanism Down Under.* Washington, DC: Island Press.

Beaufoy, H. (1993). The Green Office in Britain: A Critical Analysis. *Journal of Design History,* 6(3), 200–207.

Beerepoot, M., & Beerepoot, N. (2007). Government Regulation as an Impetus for Innovation. *Energy Policy,* 35, 4812–4825.

Bekkers, R., & Wiepking, P. (2010). A Literature Review of Empirical Studies of Philanthropy. *Nonprofit and Voluntary Sector Quarterly,* *40*(5), 924–973.

Bell, S., & Hindmoor, A. (2009). *Rethinking Governance.* Cambridge: Cambridge University Press.

Belzer, D., Mosey, G., Plympton, P., & Dagher, L. (2007). *Home Performance with Energy Star: Utility Bill Analysis on Homes Participating in Austin Energy's Program* Denver: National Renewable Energy Laboratory.

Berg-Schlosser, D. (2012). *Mixed Methods in Comparative Politics.* New York: Palgrave.

Berghoef, N., & Dodds, R. (2013). Determinants of Interest in Eco-Labelling in the Ontario Wine Industry. *Journal of Cleaner Production,* 52, 263–271.

Bergoeing, R., Loayza, N., & Piquillem, F. (2010). *Why Are Developing Countries So Slow in Adopting New Technologies?* Washington, DC: World Bank.

Berliner, D., & Prakash, A. (2014). The United Nations Global Compact: An Institutionalist Perspective. *Journal of Business Ethics,* *122*(2), 27–223.

(2015). "Bluewashing" the Firm? Voluntary Regulations, Program Design, and Member Compliance with the United Nations Global Compact. *Policy Studies Journal,* *43*(1), 115–138.

Bernstein, S., & Hannah, E. (2008). Non-State Global Standard Setting and the WTO: Legitimacy and the Need for Regulatory Space. *Journal of International Economic Law*, *11*(3), 575–608.

Betsill, M., & Bulkeley, H. (2006). Cities and the Multilevel Governance of Global Climate Change. *Global Governance*, *12*(2), 141–159.

Better Buildings Partnership. (2013). *Better Buildings Partnership: Annual Report 2012–2013*. Sydney: City of Sydney.

(2015). *Better Buildings Partnership: Annual Report 2013–2014*. Sydney: City of Sydney.

Bevir, M. (2011). *The SAGE Handbook of Governance*. London: Sage.

Biermann, F. (2008). Earth Systems Governance. In O. Young, L. King, & H. Schroeder (Eds.), *Institutions and Environmental Change* (pp. 277–301). Cambridge, MA: MIT Press.

Bird, S., & Hernandez, D. (2012). Policy Options for the Split Incentive. *Energy Policy*, *48*, 506–514.

Blackman, A., Uribe, E., van Hoof, B., & Lyon, T. P. (2013). Voluntary Environmental Agreements in Developing Countries: The Colombian Experience. *Policy Sciences*, *46*(3), 335–385.

Blanco, H., & Mazmanian, D. (2014). The Sustainable City. In D. Mazmanian & H. Blanco (Eds.), *Elgar Companion to Sustainable Cities* (pp. 1–11). Cheltenham, UK: Edward Elgar.

Bloom, B., Nobe, M., & Nobe, M. (2011). Valuing Green Home Designs: A Study of Energy Star Homes. *Journal of Sustainable Real Estate*, *3*(1), 109–126.

Blundell, L. (2014). *The Tenants and Landlords Guide to Happiness*. Sydney: Fifth Estate/Better Buildings Partnership.

Bond, S. (2011). Barriers and Drivers to Green Buildings in Australia and New Zealand. *Journal of Property Investment & Finance*, *29*(4/5), 494–509.

Boonstra, W. (2013, 6 November 2013). Gemeente Amsterdam erkent falen investeringsfonds (Amsterdam municipal government acknowledges failure of Amsterdam Energy Fund). *Binnenlands Bestuur*. Retrieved from www.binnenlandsbestuur.nl/financien/nieuws/gemeente-amsterdam-erkent-falen-investeringsfonds.9159271.lynkx.

Borck, J., & Coglianese, C. (2009). Voluntary Environmental Programs: Assessing Their Effectiveness. *Annual Review of Environmental Resources*, *34*, 305–324.

Borck, J., Coglianese, C., & Nash, J. (2008). Environmental Leadership Programs. *Ecology Law Quarterly*, *35*(4), 771–834.

Bornstein, D. (2015, February 6, 2015). Investing in Energy Efficiency Pays Off. *New York Times*. Retrieved from http://opinionator.blogs.nytimes.com/2015/02/06/investing-in-energy-efficiency-pays-off/

Borzel, T. (2001). Europeanization and Territorial Institutional Change. In M. Green Cowles, J. Caporaso, & T. Risse (Eds.), *Transforming Europe* (pp. 137–158). New York: Cornell University Press.

BouwendNederland. (2012). *De Bouw in 2020*. Zoetermeer: BouwendNederland.

Boyd, S. (2013). Financing and Managing Energy Projects through Revolving Loan Funds. *Sustainability*, 6(6), 345–352.

Brady, H. E., & Collier, D. (Eds.). (2004). *Rethinking Social Inquiry*. Lanham. MD: Rowman & Littlefield.

Braithwaite, J., & Drahos, P. (2000). *Global Business Regulation*. Cambridge and New York: Cambridge University Press.

BRE. (2011). *BREEAM New Construction: Non-Domestic Buildings*. Garston: BRE International.

——— (2013). Our History. Retrieved from www.bre.co.uk/page.jsp?id=1712.

BREEAM. (2014). Green Buildings Pay. *PropertyEU Magazine*, 8(October), 97–104.

Breen, J. (1908). *De verordeningen op het bouwen te Amsterdam, voor de negentiende eeuw*. Amsterdam: Ten Brink en De Vries.

Briscoe, F., & Safford, S. (2008). The Nixon-in-China Effect. *Administrative Science Quarterly.*, 53(3), 460–491.

Brouhle, K., & Ramirez Harrington, D. (2014). The Role of Environmental Management Systems in the Candian Voluntary Climate and Challenge Registry. *Journal of Environmental Planning and Management*, 57(8), 1145–1168.

Brounen, D., & Kok, N. (2011). On the Economics of Energy Labels in the Housing Market. *Journal of Environmental Economics and Management*, 62(2), 166–179.

Brown, M. (2010). A Tale of Three Buildings: Certifying the Virtue in the New Moral Ecology. *American Ethnologist*, 37(4), 741–752.

Brown, M. A., & Sovacool, B. (2011). Barriers to the Diffusion of Climate-Friendly Technologies. *International Journal of Technology Transfer and Commercialisation*, 10(1), 43–62.

Brunn, S., Hays-Mitchell, M., & Zeigler, D. (Eds.). (2012). *Cities of the World*. Lanham, MD: Rowman & Littlefield.

BuildingBusiness. (2015, March 6, 2015). Regeling extra hypotheek moet meer bekendheid krijgen (Additional Energy Efficiency Mortgage Not Well Known). Retrieved from www.buildingbusiness.nl/news/2801/15/Regeling-extra-hypotheek-moet-meer-bekendheid-krijgen/.

Bulkeley, H., & Betsill, M. (2003). *Cities and Climate Change*. London: Routledge.

Bulkeley, H., Carmin, J., Castan Broto, V., Edwards, G., & Fuller, S. (2013). Climate Justice and Global Cities. *Global Environmental Change*, 23(5), 914–925.

Bulkeley, H., Castan Broto, V., & Edwards, G. (2015). *An Urban Politics of Climate Change*. Abingdon, UK: Routledge.

C40 Cities. (2014). *Advancing Climate Ambition: Cities as Partners in Global Climate Action*. New York: C40 Cities.

Cabinet Office. (2011). *Behaviour Change and Energy Use*. London: Cabinet Office.

CAP. (2012). *Performance Audit on Jawaharlal Nehru National Urban Renewal Mission. Report No. - 15 of 2012–13*. New Delhi: Comptroller and Auditor General of India.

Cardwell, D. (2013, June 21, 2013). Tax Programs to Finance Clean Energy Catch On. *New York Times*. Retrieved from www.nytimes.com/2013/06/22/business/energy-environment/tax-programs-to-finance-clean-energy-catch-on.html?_r=0.

Carraro, C., & Leveque, F. (Eds.). (1999). *Volunary Apporaches in Environmental Policy*. Dordrecht: Kluwer Academic.

Carroll, A., & Shabana, K. (2010). The Business Case for Corporate Social Responsibility. *International Journal of Management Reviews*, 2(1), 85–105.

Casals, X. (2006). Analysis of Building Energy Regulation and Certification in Europe. *Energy and Buildings*, 38(3), 381–392.

Cashore, B., Auld, G., & Newsom, D. (2004). *Governing through Markets*. New Haven, CT: Yale University Press.

Castellucci, L., & Markandya, A. (2012). *Environmental Taxes and Fiscal Reform*. Houndsmill, UK: Palgrave Macmillan.

CBS. (2010). *Bevolkinsprognose 2009–2060*. The Hague: Centraal Bureau voor de Statistiek.

CDP. (2014). *India 200 Climate Change Report 2014*. New Delhi: CDP India.

CEC. (2008). *Green Building in North America*. Quebec: Commission for Environmental Cooperation.

Chan, E., Qian, Q., & Lam, P. (2009). The Market for Green Building in Developed Asian Cities. *Energy Policy*, 37(8), 3061–3070.

Chandler, A. (September 17, 2012). Builders Embrace Green Star Message. Sydney: Australian Financial Review.

Charles II. (1667 [1819]). *An Act for Rebuilding the Citty of London: Statutes of the Realm*. Vol. 5. *1628–80*. London: British Parliament.

Cheatham, C. (2009). New York City Backs Off Retrofit Requirement. Retrieved from www.greenbuildinglawupdate.com/2009/12/articles/codes-and-regulations/new-york-city-backs-off-retrofit-requirement/.

Cheshire, P., Nathan, M., & Overman, H. (2014). *Urban Economics and Urban Policy*. Cheltenham, UK: Edward Elgar.

Chhotray, V., & Stoker, G. (2010). *Governance Theory and Practice*. Houndsmills, UK: Palgrave.

Chiarella, D. (2005). *The History of Urban Planning and Cities*. Raleigh, NC: Lulu.

Chiroleu-Assouline, M., & Fodha, M. (2014). From Regressive Pollution Taxes to Progressive Environmental Tax Reforms. *European Economic Review*, 69(July), 126–142.

Chou, B., Hammer, B., & Levine, L. (2014). *Using State Revolving Funds to Build Climate-Resilient Communities*. New York: National Resource Defence Council.

Choucri, N. (1991). A Partnership with Nature. *Construction Business Review*, 1(2), 37–41.

Choumert, J., Combes Motel, P., & Dakpo, H. (2013). Is the Environmental Kuznets Curve for Deforestation a Threatened Theory? A Meta-Analysis of the Literature. *Ecological Economics*, 90(1), 19–28.

Cialdini, R. (2009). *Influence: The Power of Persuasion*. New York: William Morrow.

CIE. (2007). *Capitalising on the Building Sector's Potential to Lessen the Costs of a Broad Based GHG Emissions Cut.* Canberra: Centre for International Economics.

Cillo, P. (2005). Fostering Market Knowledge Use in Innovation: The Role of Internal Brokers. *European Management Journal, 23*(4), 404–412.

Cities Alliance. (2008). *Cities Alliance Annual Report 2008.* Brussels: Cities Alliance.

City Mayors. (2007). The Largest Cities in the World by Land Area, Population and Density. Retrieved from www.citymayors.com/statistics/largest-cities-density-125.html.

City of Amsterdam. (2011). *Structurrvisie Amsterdam* (Vision for the City of Amsterdam). Amsterdam: City of Amsterdam.

City of Boston. (2013a). E+ Green Building Program. Retrieved from www.epositiveboston.org/.

(2013b). *E+ Green Communities Program: Fact Sheet.* Boston: City of Boston.

City of Brisbane. (2009). *Growing a Green Heart Together.* Brisbane: City of Brisbane.

City of Chicago. (2011). *Chicago Climate Action Plan.* Chicago: City of Chicago.

(2014). *Building Energy Benchmarking Report.* Chicago: City of Chicago.

City of Melbourne. (2008). *Future Melbourne.* Melbourne: City of Melbourne.

(2010). *1200 Buildings. Advice sheet.* Melbourne: City of Melbourne.

(2013). *1200 Buildings Melbourne Retrofit Survey 2013.* Melbourne: City of Melbourne.

City of New York. (2005). *Local Laws of the City of New York. No. 86.* New York: City of New York.

City of Sydney. (2008). *Sustainable Sydney 2030: The Vision.* Sydney: City of Sydney.

(2011). *Sustainable Sydney 2030.* Sydney: City of Sydney.

CitySwitch. (2013). *2012 Progress Report.* Sydney: CitySwitch.

(2014a). *2013 Progress Report.* Sydney: CitySwitch.

(2014b). CitySwith Green Office. Retrieved from www.cityswitch.net.au/Home.aspx.

(2015). *Progress Report 2014.* Sydney: CitySwitch.

Cluett, R., & Amann, J. (2014). *Residential Deep Energy Retrofits.* Washington, DC: American Council for an Energy-Efficient Economy.

COAG. (2011). *Review of Capital City Strategic Planning System.* Sydney: Council of Australian Governments.

(2012a). *Baseline Energy Consumption and Greenhouse Gas Emissions.* Canberra: Council of Australian Governments.

(2012b). *Review of Capital City Strategic Planning Systems.* Sydney: COAG Reform Council.

Coglianese, C., & Nash, J. (2014). Performance Track's Postmortem. *Harvard Environmental Law Review, 38*(1), 2–87.

Coiacetto, E., & Bryant, L. (2014). How Does Access to Development Finance Shape Our Cities? *Urban Policy and Research, 32*(3), 305–321.

Cole, R., & Valdebenito, M. J. (2013). The Importation of Building Environmental Certification Systems. *Building Research & Information, 41*(6), 662–676.

Colliers International. (2013). *Leading the Charge*. Sydney: Colliers International.

Connors, P., & McDonald, P. (2010). Transitioning Communities: Community, Participation and the Transition Town Movement. *Community Development Journal*, 46(4), 558–572.

Corbett, C., & Muthulingam, S. (2007). Adoption of Voluntary Environmental Standards: The Role of Signaling and Intrinsic Benefits in the Diffusion of the LEED Green Building Standards. Unpublished manuscript.

Cork, S. (2010). *Resilience and Transformation*. Collingwood, VIC: CSIRO.

Cram, C. (2015, January 7, 2015). Why Singapore Is Building a New Indian City 10 Times Its Own Size. Retrieved from www.theguardian.com/public-leaders-network/2015/jan/07/singapore-building-india-city-andhra-pradesh.

Croci, E. (2005). *The Handbook of Environmental Voluntary Agreements*. Dordrecht: Springer.

da Silva, M. (2011). Melbourne City Council to Broker Green Retrofits. *Ethical Investor*, 97(June), 14–15.

Dale, O. J. (1999). *Urban Planning in Singapore*. Oxford: Oxford University Press.

Darko, E., Nagrath, K., Niaizi, Z., Scott, A., Varsha, D., & Vijaya Lakshmi, K. (2013). *Green Building: Case Study*. London: Overseas Development Institute.

Darnall, N., & Carmin, J. (2005). Greener and Cleaner? The Signaling Accuracy of U.S. Voluntary Environmental Programs. *Policy Sciences*, 38(2–3), 71–90.

Darnall, N., & Sides, S. (2008). Assessing the Performance of Voluntary Environmental Programs: Does Certification Matter? *Policy Studies Journal*, 36(1), 95–117.

Dasgupta, S., Mody, A., Roy, S., & Wheeler, D. (2001). Environmental Regulation and Development: A Cross-Country Empirical Analysis. *Oxford Development Studies*, 29(2), 173–187.

Dashwood, H. (2012). *The Rise of Global Corporate Social Responsibility*. Cambridge: Cabridge University Press.

Davenport, C. (2014, November 26). Obama Builds Environmental Legacy with 1970 Law. *New York Times*, p. A1. Retrieved from www.nytimes.com/2014/11/27/us/without-passing-a-single-law-obama-crafts-bold-enviornmental-policy.html?_r=0.

Davidson, M., & Martin, D. (2014). *Urban Politics*. London: Sage.

Davies, J., & Imbroscio, D. (2009). *Theories of Urban Politics*. London: Sage.

De Almeida, A., Fonseca, P., Schlomann, B., & Feilberg, N. (2011). Characterization of the Household Electricity Consumption in the EU, Potential Energy Savings and Specific Policy Recommendations. *Energy and Buildings*, 43(8), 1884–1894.

De Burca, G. (2010). New Governance and Experimentalism. *Wisconsin Law Review*, 227, 227–238.

De Búrca, G., & Scott, J. (2006). *New Governance and Constitutionalism in Europe and The US*. Oxford: Hart.

de Vries, F., Nentjes, A., & Odam, N. (2012). Voluntary Environmental Agreements: Lessons on Effectiveness, Efficiency and Spillover Potential. *International Review of Environmental and Resource Economics*, 6(2), 119–152.

Dean, M. (2009). *Governmentality*. Los Angeles: Sage.

DeLeon, P., & Rivera, J. (Eds.). (2010). *Voluntary Environmental Programs.* Plymouth: Lexington Books.

DeLeon, P., Rivera, J., & Manderino, L. (2010). Voluntary Environmental Programs: An Introduction. In P. DeLeon & J. Rivera (Eds.), *Voluntary Environmental Programs* (pp. 1–10). Plymouth: Lexington Books.

Della Porta, D., & Keating, M. (Eds.). (2008). *Approches and Methodologies in the Social Sciences.* Cambridge: Cambridge University Press.

Delmas, M. A., & Terlaak, A. K. (2001). A Framework for Analyzing Environmental Voluntary Agreements. *California Management Review, 43*(3), 44–62.

Deloitte. (2013). *Building Our Nation's Resilience to Natural Disasters.* Sydney: Deloitte Access Economics.

Den Hond, F., & De Bakker, F. G. A. (2007). Ideologically Motivated Activism:. *Academy of Management Review, 32*(3), 901–924.

Deng, Y., Li, Z., & Quigley, J. (2012). Economic Returns to Energy-Efficient Investments in the Housing Market: Evidence from Singapore. *Regional Science and Urban Economics, 42*(3), 506–515.

Department of Industry. (2014). *Nationwide House Energy Rating Scheme (NatHERS): Administrative and Governance Arrangements.* Canberra: Australian Government, Department of Industry.

DGBC. (2014a). *BREEAM-NL Magazine*, Vol. 2. Rotterdam: Dutch Green Building Council.

(2014b). *BREEAM-NL Nieuwbouw en Renovatie 2014: Versie 1.01 (BREEAM-NL for New Development and Retrofits).* Rotterdam: Dutch Green Building Council.

(2015, 12 March 2015). *Nieuwbouw statistieken* (Statistics for New Development). Retrieved from www.breeam.nl/projecten/statistieken/nieuwbouw.

Diamond, H., & Noonan, P. (1996). *Land Use in America.* Washington, DC: Island Press.

Diaz Arias, A., & van Beers, C. (2013). Energy Subsidies, Structure of Electricity Prices and Technological Change of Energy Use. *Energy Economics, 40*(November), 495–502.

Dibden, J., & Cocklin, C. (2010). Re-Mapping Regulatory Space: The New Governance of Australian Dairying. *Geoforum Geoforum, 41*(3), 410–422.

Dietz, R., & O'Neill, D. (2013). *Enough Is Enough: Building a Sustainable Economy in a World of Finite Resources.* Abingdon, UK: Routledge.

Dinda, S. (2004). Environmental Kuznets Curve Hypothesis. *Ecological Economics, 49*(4), 431–455.

District of Columbia Department of the Environment. (2012). *Green Building Report.* Washington, DC: District of Columbia Department of the Environment.

Dixon, T., Keeping, M., & Roberts, C. (2008). Facing the Future: Energy Performance Certificates and Commercial Property. *Journal of Property Investment & Finance, 26*(1), 96–100.

Dodman, D. (2009). Blaming Cities for Climate Change? *Environment and Urbanization, 21*(1), 185–201.

Domask, J. (2003). From Boycotts to Global Partnerships. In J. P. Doh & H. Teegen (Eds.), *Globalisation and NGOs* (pp. 157–186). Westport, CT: Praeger.

Dovers, S. (2002). Sustainability: Reviewing Australia's Progress, 1992–2002. *International Journal of Environmental Studies, 59*(5), 559–571.

Downey, L., & Hawkins, B. (2008). Race, Income, and Environmental Inequality in the United States. *Sociological Perspectives, 51*(4), 759–781.

Dryzek, J. (2005). *The Politics of the Earth*, 2nd ed. Oxford: Oxford Universtity Press.

DTZ Zadelhoff. (2013). *Nederland compleet: Kantoren- en bedrijfsruimtemarkt* (Report on the Office and Commercial Property Market in the Netherlands). Amsterdam: DTZ Zadelhof.

Dunlap, R., & Mertig, A. (Eds.). (2013). *American Environmentalism*. Abingdon, UK: Routledge.

Dutch Ministry of Finance. (2012). *Tijdelijke regeling hypothecair krediet: FM/ 2012/1887 M* (Temporary Rule for Additional Energy Efficiency Mortgage). the Hague: Dutch Ministry of Finance.

Dwars, O. (2013). Haastige spoed is zelden goed! Ook bij extra financiering energiezuinige woningen (Critical Blog Post on Temporary Rule for Additional Energy Efficiency Mortgage). Retrieved from www.bouwendnederland.nl/nieuws/33884/column–haastige-spoed-is-zelden-goed-ook-bij-extra-financiering-energiezuinige-woningen.

Eames, M., Dixon, T., May, T., & Hunt, M. (2013). City Futures: Exploring Urban Retrofit and Sustainable Transitions. *Building Research & Information, 41*(5), 504–516.

EC. (2009). *Directive 2009/125/EC*. Brussels: European Parliament.

(2010). *Directive 2010/31EU (EPBD - Recast)*. Brussels: European Parliament.

(2013). *Financial Support for Energy Efficiency in Buildings*. In *Report SWD (2013) 143 final*. Brussels: European Commission.

EDF, & IETA. (2013). *The World's Carbon Markets*. Geneva: Environmental Defense Fund and International Emissions Trading Association.

EEA. (2008). *Effectiveness of Environmental Taxes and Charges for Managing Sand, Gravel and Rock Extraction in Selected EU Countries*. Copenhagen: European Environment Agency.

Eichholtz, P., Kok, N., & Quigley, J. (2010). Doing Well by Doing Good? *American Economic Review, 100*, 2492–2509.

Emmenegger, P. (2011). Job Security Regulations in Western Democracies: A Fuzzy Set Analysis. *European Journal of Political Research, 50*(3), 336–364.

Energy Efficiency Council. (2010). *City of Melbourne Set to Become a Green Global Leader* Melbourne: Energy Efficiency Council.

Energy Matters. (2013). Feed-In Tariff for Grid-Connected Solar Power Systems. Retrieved from www.energymatters.com.au/government-rebates/feedintariff.php.

Engeli, I., & Rothmayr, C. (Eds.). (2014). *Comparative Policy Studies*. Houndsmills, UK: Palgrave Macmillan.

EnviroDevelopment. (2010). *EnviroDevelopment: National Technical Standards*. Version 2. Brisbane: EnviroDevelopment.

(2014). *Envirodevelopment: Annual Statement for the Year Ended 2013*. Brisbane: EnviroDevelopment.

(no date). *EnviroDevelopment: Fact Sheets*. Brisbane: EnviroDevelopment.

Environomist. (2014). *China Carbon Market Research Report*. Beijing: Environomist.

EPA. (1994). *EPA's Financial Management Status Report and Five-Year Plan*. Washington, DC: U.S. Environmental Protection Agency.

(1997). *Risk Reduction through Voluntary Programs*. Washington, DC: U.S. Environmental Protection Agency.

(2013, 3 August 2013). Tribal Green Building Codes: Codes, Standards, Rating Systems and Labeling Programs. Retrieved from www.epa.gov/region9/greenbuilding/codes/standards.html.

Essig, S., Ward, S., Steiner, M., Friedman, D., Geisz, J., Stradins, P., & Young, D. (2015). Progress Towards a 30% Efficient GaInP/Si Tandem Solar Cell. *Energy Procedia, 77*(August), 464–469.

Esty, D. C., & Chertow, M. R. (1997). Thinking Ecologically: An Introduction. In M. R. Chertow & D. C. Esty (Eds.), *Thinking Ecologically: The Next Generation of Environmental Policy* (pp. 1–16). New Haven, CT: Yale University Press.

Evans, B., Joas, M., Sundback, S., & Thobald, K. (2005). *Governing Sustainable Cities*. London: Earthscan.

Evans, J., Karvonen, A., & Raven, R. (Eds.). (2016). *The Experimental City*. London: Routledge.

Evans, M., Halverson, M., Delgado, A., & Yu, S. (2014). Building Energy Code Compliance in Developing Countries. *ACEEE Summer Study on Energy Efficiency in Buildings, 8*(1), 61–74.

Evans, M., Shui, B., & Somasundaram, S. (2009). *Country Report on Building Energy Codes in India*. Washington, DC: U.S. Department of Energy.

Farhani, S., Mrizak, S., Chaibi, A., & Rault, C. (2014). The Environmental Kuznets Curve and Sustainability. *Energy Policy, 70*(August), 189–198.

Feddersen, T. J., & Gilligan, T. J. (2001). Saint and Markets: Activists and the Supply of Credence Goods. *Journal of Economics and Management Strategy, 10*(1), 149–171.

Federal Housing Administration. (2011). *Annual Management Report: Fiscal Year 2011*. Washington, DC: U.S. Department of Housing and Urban Development.

(2012). *Annual Management Report: Fiscal Year 2012*. Washington, DC: U.S. Department of Housing and Urban Development.

(2013). *Annual Management Report: Fiscal Year 2013*. Washington, DC: U.S. Department of Housing and Urban Development.

(2014). *Annual Management Report: Fiscal Year 2014*. Washington, DC: U.S. Department of Housing and Urban Development.

Fernandez, W. (2011). *Our Homes: 50 Years of Housing a Nation*. Singapore: Housing and Development Board.

Fiorino, D. (2009). Green Clubs: A New Tool for Government? In M. Potoski & A. Prakash (Eds.), *Voluntary Programs* (pp. 209–229). Cambridge, MA: MIT Press.

References

301

(2014). Sustainable Cities and Governance: What Are the Connections? In D. Mazmanian & H. Blanco (Eds.), *Elgar Companion to Sustainable Cities* (pp. 413–433). Cheltenham, UK: Edward Elgar.

Fiss, P. (2011). Building Better Causal Theories: A Fuzzy Set Approach to Typologies in Organisation Research. *Academy of Management Journal, 52*(2), 393–420.

Florida, R., & Davison, D. (2001). Why Do Firms Adopt Advanced Environmental Practices (And Do They Make a Difference)? In C. Coglianese & J. Nash (Eds.), *Going Private: Environmental Management Systems and the New Policy Agenda* (pp. 82–104). Washington, DC: Resources for the Future.

Flyvbjerg, B. (2015). *Making Social Science Matter*, 17th ed. Cambridge: Cambridge University Press.

Fong, W. K. (2013, 29 April 2013). Lessons Learned from Low-Carbon City Planning in Malaysia. Retrieved from www.wri.org/blog/2013/04/lessons-learned-low-carbon-city-planning-malaysia.

Foucault, M. (2009). *The Birth of Biopolitics*. New York: Picador.

Fowler, E. (1995). *Building Cities That Work*. Quebec City: McGill-Queen's University Press.

Fowler, K. M., & Rauch, E. M. (2006a). Sustainable Building Rating Systems. Retrieved from Washington, DC, U.S. Department of Energy www.pnl.gov/main/publications/external/technical_reports/PNNL-15858.pdf.

(2006b). *Sustainable Building Rating Systems: Summary*. Richland, WA: Pacific Northwest National Laboratory.

Fransen, L., & Burgoon, B. (2014). Privatizing or Socializing Corporate Responsibility. *Business and Society, 53*(4), 583–619.

Frondel, M., Ritter, N., & Schmidt, C. (2008). Germany's Solar Cell Promotion. *Energy Policy, 36*(11), 4198–4204.

Frondel, M., & Schmidt, C. (2005). Evaluating Environmental Programs. *Ecological Economics, 55*(4), 515–526.

Gallucci, M. (2015, January 13, 2015). Pressure Mounts on India to Tackle Greenhouse Gas Emissions ahead of 2015 Climate Change Talks in Paris. *International Business Rimes*. Retrieved from www.ibtimes.com/pressure-mounts-india-tackle-greenhouse-gas-emissions-ahead-2015-climate-change-talks-1782296.

Gamerschlag, R., Möller, K., & Verbeeten, F. (2011). Determinants of Voluntary CSR Disclosure. *Review of Managerial Science, 5*(2–3), 233–262.

Garvin, A. (2014). *The American City: What Works and What Doesn't*. New York: Mc GrawHill.

GBCA. (2012). *A Decade in Green Building*. Sydney: Green Building Council of Australia.

(2013a). *Evolution: A Year in Green Building*. Sydney: Green Building Council of Australia.

(2013b). *The Value of Green Star*. Sydney: Green Building Council of Australia.

(2013c). *Valuing Green: How Green Buildings Affect Property Values and Getting the Valuation Method Right*. Sydney: Green Building Council of Australia.

(2014). *Green Star - Design & as Built: Caclulation Guidelines*. Syndey: Green Building Council of Australia.

(2015). *Introducing Green Star: Inspiring Innovation, Encouraging Environmental Leadership, Building a Sustainable Future*. Syndey: Green Building Council of Australia.

(no date). *Green Star - Performance: Eligibility criteria*. Syndey: Green Building Council of Australia.

GBI. (2009). *GBI Assessment Criteria for Non-Residential New Construction*. Kuala Lumpur: GreenBuildingIndex SDN BHD.

(2013). *Green Building Index*. Kuala Lumpur: Green Building Index SDN BHD.

GBPN. (2013). *A Comparative Analysis of Building Energy Efficiency Policy for New Buildings*. Paris: Global Buildings Performance Network.

Gemeente Oldenzaal. (2014). *Milieuprogramma 2014* (Municipal Environmental Policy Program). Oldenzaal: Gemeente Oldenzaal.

Genest, F. (1924). Building Laws in Ancient Rome. *Lawyer and Banker and Southern Bench and Bar Review*, *17*(5), 301–331.

Genschel, P. (1997). The Dynamics of Inertia: Institutional Persistence and Change in Telecommunications and Health Care. *Governance*, *10*(1), 43–66.

Georgiadou, M., Hacking, T., & Guthrie, P. (2012). A Conceptual Framework for Future-Proofing the Energy Performance of Buildings. *Energy Policy*, *47*(August), 145–155.

Geyer, R., & CDoctori Blass, V. (2010). The Economics of Cell Phone Reuse and Recycling. *International Journal of Advanced Manufacturing Technology*, *47*(5–8), 515–525.

Gibson, R. (1999a). Questions about a Gift Horse. In R. Gibson (Ed.), *Voluntary Initiatives* (pp. 3–12). Peterborough, Canada: Broadview Press.

(1999b). Voluntary Initiatives, Regulations and Beyond. In R. Gibson (Ed.), *Voluntary Initiatives* (pp. 239–257). Peterborough, Canada: Broadview Press.

(Ed.) (1999c). *Voluntary Initiatives: The New Politics of Corporate Greening*. Toronto: Broadview Press.

Giddens, A. (2009). *The Politics of Climate Change*. Cambridge: Polity Press.

Gifford, H. (2009). A Better Way to Rate Green Buildings. *Northeast Sun*, *27*(1), 19–27.

Gladwell, M. (2000). *The Tipping Point*. New York: Black Bay Books.

Gleeson, B., Darbas, T., & Lawson, S. (2004). Governance, Sustainability and Recent Australian Metropolitan Strategies. *Urban Policy and Research*, *22*(4), 345–366.

Glemarec, Y. (2012). Financing Off-Grid Sustainable Energy Access for the Poor. *Energy Policy*, *47*(S1), 87–93.

Global Cities Covenant on Climate. (2013). *The Mexico City Pact: Second Annual Report 2012*. Mexico City: Global Cities Covenant on Climate.

Global Commission on the Economy and Climate. (2014). *The New Climate Economy: Better Growth, Better Climate*. Washington, DC: World Resources Institute.

Goertz, G., & Mahony, J. (2012). *A Tale of Two Cultures*. Princeton, NJ: Princeton University Press.

Gold Coast City Council. (2008). *Adopted Report of the Sustainable City Future Committee Meeting Held Tuesday 20 May 2008 at 2:00 Pm* City of Gold Coast: Gold Coast City Council.

Goldsmith, S., & Crawford, S. (2014). *The Responsive City: Engaging Communities through Data-Smart Governance.* San Francisco: John Wiley & Sons.

Goldstein, N. J., Cialdini, R., & Griskevicius, V. (2008). A Room with a Viewpoint: Using Social Norms to Motivate Environmental Conservation in Hotels. *Journal of Consumer Research, 35*(3), 472–482.

Gollagher, M., & Hartz-Karp, J. (2013). The Role of Deliberative Collaborative Governance in Achieving Sustainable Cities. *Sustainability, 5*(6), 2343–2366.

Gonzalez, G. (2009). *Urban Sprawl, Global Warming, and the Empire of Capital.* Albany: State University of New York Press.

Government of India. (2001). *India National Report: Progress of Implementation of the Habit Agenda (1996–2000).* New Delhi: Government of India.

(2008). *National Mission on Sustainable Habitat.* New Delhi: Government of India.

(2013). *Rajiv Awas Yojana: Guidelines for Slum-Free City Planning.* New Delhi: Government of India.

Government Property Group. (2010). *National Green Leasing Policy.* Sydney: Ministrial Council on Energy.

Government of Singapore. (2013). *A Sustainable Population for a Dynamic Singapore: Population White Paper.* Singapore: Government of Singapore.

Government of SA. (2012). Building Innovation Fund. Retrieved from www.sa.gov.au/subject/Water,+energy+and+environment/Climate+change/Tackling+climate+change/What+organisations,+business+and+industry+can+do/Building+Innovation+Fund.

Green Deal Board. (2012). *Green Deal Board.* The Hague: Government of The Netherlands.

Green Globes. (2014). About Green Globes. Retrieved from www.greenglobes.com/about.asp.

Greene, D. (2011). Uncertainty, Loss Aversion, and Markets for Energy Efficiency. *Energy Economics, 33*(4), 608–616.

Greenhouse Office. (1999a). *Australian Commercial Building Sector Greenhouse Gas Emissions 1990–2010.* Canberra: Australian Greenhouse Office.

(1999b). *Australian Residential Building Sector Greenhouse Gas Emissions 1990–2010.* Canberra: Australian Greenhouse Office.

Greensense. (2013). *Out of Hours: The Easiest Way to Improve Your Building's Energy Efficiency.* Melbourne: Greensense.

Grimm, N. B., Faeth, S., Golubiewski, N., Redman, C., Wu, J., Bai, X., & Briggs, J. (2008). Global Change and the Ecology of Cities. *Science, 319* (5864), 756–760.

Gunningham, N. (2009). The New Collaborative Governance. *Journal of Law and Society, 36*(1), 145–166.

The Guardian. (2015, March 20, 2015). France Decrees New Rooftops Must Be Covered in Plants or Solar Panels. *The Guardian.* Retrieved from www.theguardian.com/world/2015/mar/20/france-decrees-new-rooftops-must-be-covered-in-plants-or-solar-panels.

Gunningham, N., Kagan, R. A., & Thornton, D. (2003). *Shades of Green*. Stanford, CA: Stanford University Press.

Hall, P., & Pfeiffer, U. (2013). *Urban Future 21: A Global Agenda for Twenty-First Century Cities*. New York: E&FN Spon.

Halverson, M., Shui, B., & Evans, M. (2009). *Country Report on Building Energy Codes in the United States*. Washington, DC: U.S. Department of Energy.

Hamilton, C. (2006). Ecologically Sustainable Development in a "Quarry" Economy. *Geographical Research, 44*(2), 183–203.

Hamilton-Hart, N. (2006). Singapore's Climate Change Policy. *Contemporary Souteast Asia, 28*(3), 363–384.

Hardie, M., & Manley, L. (2008). Exemplars of Successful Innovation Delivery by Small and Medium Construction Enterprises. In K. Brown, K. Hamoseon, P. S. Brandon, & J. Pillay (Eds.), *Clients Driving Construction Innovation*. (pp. 190–196). Brisbane: CRC Construction Innovation.

Harding, R. (2006). Ecologically Sustainable Development. *Desalination, 187*, 229–239.

Harper, C. (2007). Climate Change and Tax Policy. *Boston College International & Comparative Law Review, 30*, 411–460.

Harrington, W., Morgenstern, R., & Sterner, T. (Eds.). (2004). *Choosing Environmental Policy*. Washington, DC: Resources for the Future.

Hartman, R. (1988). Self-Selection Bias in the Evolution of Voluntary Energy Conservation Programs. *The Review of Economics and Statistics, 70*(3), 448–458.

Harvey, L. D. D. (2006). *A Handbook on Low-Energy Building and District Energy Systems*. London: James and James.

    (2013). *Energy Efficiency and the Demand for Energy Services*. Abingdon, UK: Routledge.

Hashim, N., Darus, Z., Salleh, E., Haw, L. C., & Rashid, A. (2008). Development of Rating System for Sustainable Building in Malaysia. Paper presented at the Environmental Problems and Development Conference 2008, Bucharest.

Hastings, K. (2013, December 14, 2013). Ratings Tool Crucial to Lifting Sustainability Standards. *Sydney Morning Herald*.

Haughton, G., & Hunter, C. (1994). *Sustainable Cities*. London: Jessica Kingsley.

Hay, C. (2001). The "Crisis" of Keynesianism and the Rise of Neo-Liberalism in Britain. In J. Campbell & O. Pedersen (Eds.), *The Rise of Neo-Liberalism and Institutional Analysis*. Princeton, NJ: Princeton University Press.

Hayden, A. (2014). *When Green Growth Is Not Enough*. Quebec: McGill-Queen's University Press.

Healthy Environs. (2015). *New Home Energy Efficiency Compliance Inspections*. Adelaide: State of South Australia.

Heiskanen, E., Johnson, M., Robinson, S., Vadovics, E., & Saastamoinen, M. (2010). Low-Carbon Communities as a Context for Individual Behavioural Change. *Energy Policy, 38*(12), 7586–7595.

Helm, D. (2012). *The Carbon Crunch*. New Haven, CT: Yale Universtity Press.

Héritier, A., & Eckert, S. (2008). New Modes of Governance in the Shadow of Hierarchy. *Journal of Public Policy, 28*(1), 113–138.

Hertier, A., & Lehmkuhl, D. (2008). The Shadow of Hierarchy and New Modes of Governance. *Journal of Public Policy, 28*(1), 1–17.

Hettige, H., Huq, M., Pargal, S., & Wheeler, D. (1996). Determinants of Pollution Abatement in Developing Countries. *World Development, 24*(12), 1891–1904.

Heyes, A. G., & Maxwell, J. W. (2004). Private vs. Public Regulation. *Journal of Environmental Economics and Management, 48*(2), 978–996.

Heymann, E. (2011). *ASEAN Auto Market*. Frankfurt: Deutsche Bank Research.

Hezri, A., & Hasan, M. (2006). Towards Sustainable Development? the Evolution of Environmental Policy in Malaysia. *Natural Resources Forum, 30*(1), 37–50.

Hodge, G. A. (2000). *Privatization: An International Review of Performance.* Boulder, CO: Westview Press.

Hoffman, A. J. (2015). *How Culture Shapes the Climate Change Debate*. Stanford, CA: Stanford University Press.

Hoffman, A. J., & Henn, R. (2009). Overcoming the Social Barriers to Green Building. *Organisation & Environment, 32*(4), 390–419.

Hoffmann, M. (2011). *Climate Governance at the Crossroads*. Oxford: Oxford University Press.

Holley, C., Gunningham, N., & Shearing, C. (2012). *The New Environmental Governance*. London: Routledge.

Hong, W., & Laurenzi, M. P. (2007). *Building Energy Efficiency: Why Green Buildings Are Key to Asia's Future*. Hong Kong: Asia Business Council.

Hoppe, T. (2009). *CO₂ reductie in de bestaande woningbouw* (Carbon Emission Reducations in the Residential Property Sector). Enschede: Universiteit Twente.

Hoppe, T., Bressers, J. T. A., & Lulofs, K. (2011). Local Government Influence on Energy Conservation Ambitions in Existing Housing Sites. *Energy Policy, 39*(2), 916–925.

Horne, R. (2009). Limits to Labels. *International Journal of Consumer Studies, 33*(2), 175–182.

Howarth, R. B., Hadda, B. M., & Paton, B. (2000). The Economics of Energy Efficiency: Insights from Voluntary Participation Programs. *Energy Policy, 28*(6–7), 477–486.

Howes, R., Skea, J., & Whelan, B. (Eds.). (1997). *Clean and Competitive? Motivating Environmental Performance in Industry*. London: Earthscan.

Hsueh, L. (2013). Beyond Regulations: Industry Voluntary Ban in Arsenic Use. *Journal of Environmental Management, 131*(3), 435–466.

Huff, W. G. (1995). The Developmental State, Government, and Singapore's Economic Development since 1960. *World Development, 23*(8), 1421–1438.

Hughes, M., & Macbeth, J. (2005). Can a Niche-Market Captive-Wildlife Facility Place a Low-Profile Region on the Tourism Map? An Example from Western Australia. *Tourism Geographies: An International Journal of Tourism Space, Place and Environment, 7*(4), 424–443.

Hungerford, H. R. (1996). The Development of Responsible Environmental Citizenship. *Journal of Interpretation Research, 1*(1), 25–37.

Hurley, B. (2010, August 13, 2010). Sustainable Building Gathers Pace. *Australian Financial Recview.*

Hwang, B.-G., & Tan, J. S. (2012). Green Building Project Management. *Sustainable Development, 20*(5), 335–349.

ICLEI. (2009). Five Lessons from the Chicago Green Office Challenge. Retrieved from www.icleiusa.org/blog/five-lessons-from-the-chicago-green-office-challenge.

    (2012). *Cities in a Post-2012 Climate Policy Framework.* Bonn: ICLEI.

Idris, N. H., & Ismail, Z. (2011). Framework Policy for Sustainable Construction in Malaysia. Paper presented at the IEEE symposium on Business, Engineering and Indusrtial Applications, Langkawl.

IEA. (2007). *Energy Efficiency in the North American Existing Building Stock.* Paris: International Energy Agency.

    (2008). *Energy Efficiency Requirements in Building Codes.* Paris: International Energy Agencay.

    (2009). *World Energy Outlook 2009.* Paris: International Energy Agency/OECD.

    (2013). *Modernising Building Energy Codes.* Paris: United Nations Development Programme.

IGBC. (2013). Indian Green Building Council. Retrieved from www.igbc.in/site/igbc/index.jsp.

    (2015). *Green Buildings of India.* Hyderabad: Green Building Council of India.

IIEC. (2009). *Eco-Housing Assessment Criteria.* Version II. Mumbai: International Institute for Energy Conservation.

IIHS. (2011). *Urban India: Evidence.* New Delhi: Indian Institute for Human Settlements.

Imbens, G., & Wooldridge, J. (2008). *Recent Developments in the Econometrics of Program Evaluation.* Cambridge: Natuinak Bureau of Economic Research.

Indvik, J., Foley, R., & Orlowski, M. (2013). *Green Revolving Funds.* Cambridge, MA: Sustainable Endowments Institute.

IPCC. (2007). *Contribution of Working Group III to the Fourth Assessment Report of the Intergovernmental Panel on Climate Change.* Cambridge: Cambridge University Press.

    (2014). *Climate Change 2014: Impacts, Adaptation, and Vulnerability.* Cambridge: Cambridge University Press.

IPSOS, & LEC. (2013). *Consumer Market Study on the Functioning of Voluntary Food Labelling Schemes for Consumers in the European Union EAHC/FWC/2012 86 04.* London: Ipsos and London Economics Consortium.

Irvine, H., Lazarevski, K., & Dolnicar, S. (2012). Strings Attached: New Public Management, Competitive Grant Funding and Social Capital. *Financial Accountability & Management, 25*(2), 225–252.

Ismael, S. (2009). Government Agencies and Public Services. In A. R. Baginda (Ed.), *Governing Malaysia* (pp. 141–164). Kuala Lumpur: Malaysian Strategic Research Centre.

Iwaro, J., & Mwasha, A. (2010). A Review of Building Energy Regulation and Policy for Energy Conservation in Developing Countries. *Energy Policy*, *38*(12), 7744–7755.

Iyer-Raniga, U., Moore, T., & Wasiluk, K. (2014). Residential Building Sustainability Rating Tools in Australia. *Environment Design Guide*, *80*(August), 1–14.

Jain, S. (2010). Special Issue on JNNURM. *Context*, *7*(2), 1–192.

Jalan, B. (2012). *Emerging India: Economics, Politics and Reforms*. New Delhi: Penguin.

James, G. (2009). *Australian Homes Are Biggest in the World*. Sydney: CommSec.

James, P. (2015). *Urban Sustainability in Theory and Practice*. London: Routledge.

Jawan, J. A. (2009). Federalism in Malaysia. In A. R. Baginda (Ed.), *Governing Malaysia* (pp. 91–111). Kuala Lumpur: Malaysian Strategic Research Centre.

Johanson, S. (2011, August 22, 2011). Australian Homes Still the World's Biggest. *The Sydney Morning Herald*.

Jordan, A., Wurzel, R., & Zito, A. (2005). The Rise of New Policy Instruments in Comparative Perspective. *Political Studies*, *53*(3), 477–496.

Judd, D., & Mendelson, R. (1973). *The Politics of Urban Planning*. Urbana: University of Illinois Press.

Junghans, L., & Dorsch, L. (2015). *Finding the Cinance: Financing Climate Compatible Development in Cities*. Berlin: Germanwatch.

Kahneman, D. (2011). *Thinking Fast and Slow*. New York: Farrar, Straus & Giroux.

Kajewski, S. (2001). *Industry Culture: A Need for Change*. Brisbane: Australian Cooperative Research Centre for Construction Innovation.

Kallbekken, S. (2011). Public Acceptance for Environmental Taxes. *Energy Policy*, *39*(5), 2966–2973.

Kamal, E., Haron, S., Ulang, N., & Baharum, F. (2012). The Critical Review on the Malaysian Construction Industry. *Journal of Economics and Sustainable Development*, *3*(13), 81–87.

Kamar, K., Hamid, Z. A., Ghani, M., Egbu, C., & Arif, M. (2010). Collaboration Initiative on Green Construction and Sustainability through Industrialized Buildings Systems (IBS) in the Malaysian Construction Industry. *International Journal of Sustainable Construction, Engineering & Technology*, *1*(1), 119–127.

Kane, G. (2014). *Accelerating Sustainability Using the 80/20 Rule*. Oxford: Do Sustainablity.

Kansas Committee on Energy and Environment. (2013). *House Bill No. 2366*. Kansas City: Kansas Committee on Energy and Environment.

Kats, G., Menkin, A., Dommu, J., & DeBold, M. (2012). *Energy Efficiency Financing: Models and Strategy*. Washington, DC: Capital E.

Katshiwagi, D. T. (2010). "Root of All Evils" Misunderstanding of Construction Industry Structure. In N. Ghafoori (Ed.), *Challenges, Opportunities and Solutions in Structural Engineering* (pp. 15–21). London: Taylor & Francis.

Kaygusuz, K. (2012). Energy for Sustainable Development: A Case of Developing Countries. *Renewable and Sustainable Energy Reviews*, *16*(2), 1116–1126.

Kein, A. T. T., Ofori, G., & Briffett, C. (1999). ISO 14000: Its Relevance to the Construction Industry of Singapore and Its Potential as the Next Industry Milestone. *Construction Management and Economics, 17*(4), 449–461.

Keller, K. (2012). Leading in the Wrong Direction: Addressing Concerns with Today's Green Building Policy. *Southern California Law Review, 85*(5), 1377–1412.

Kelly, K. (2013). National Urban Policy. *Urban Policy and Research, 31*(3), 257–259.

KeTTHA. (2011). *Low-Carbon Cities Framework and Assessment System.* Putrajaya: Kementerian Tenaga, Teknologi Hijau dan Air.

Khanna, M. (2007). The U.S. 33/50 Voluntary Program. In R. Morgenstern & W. Pizer (Eds.), *Reality Check* (pp. 15–42). Washington, DC: Resources for the Future.

Khanna, M., & Anton, W. R. Q. (2002). Corporate Environmental Management: Regulatory and Market-Based Incentives. *Land Economics, 78*(4), 539–558.

Khanna, M., & Damon, L. (1999). EPA's Voluntary 33–50 Program: Impact on Toxic Releases and Economic Performance of Firms. *Journal of Environmental Economics and Management, 37*(1), 1–25.

Kibert, C. T. (2008). *Sustainable Construction: Green Building Design and Delivery,* 2nd ed. Hoboken, NJ: Wiley & Sons.

Kickbusch, I., Hein, W., & Silberschmidt, G. (2010). Addressing Global Health Governance Challenges through a New Mechanism. *Journal of Law, Medicine and Ethics, 38*(3), 550–563.

Kim, E.-H., & Lyon, T. P. (2015). Greenwash vs. Brownwash. *Organisation Science, 26*(3), 705–723.

King, A. (1976). *Colonial Urban Development.* Abingdon, UK: Routledge.

King, A. A., & Lenox, M. J. (2000). Industry Self-Regulation without Sanctions: The Chemical Industry's Responsible Care Program. *Academy of Management Journal, 43*(4), 698–716.

King, B. G. (2008). A Political Mediation Model of Corporate Response to Social Movement Activism. *Administrative Science Quarterly., 53*(3), 395–421.

Kirkpatrick, C., & Parkers, D. (2004). Regulatory Impact Assessment and Regulatory Governance in Developing Countries. *Public Administration and Development, 24*(4), 333–344.

Kirkpatrick, J., & Bennear, L. (2014). Promoting Clean Energy Investment. *Journal of Environmental Economics and Management, 68*(2), 357–375.

Kishnani, N. (2013). Asia's Greening Challenge: Is the Green Building Becoming a Barrier to Sustainable Development? Paper presented at the Sustainable Buildings 2013, Quezon City, Manila Philippines.

Kjaer, A. M. (2009). Governance and the Urban Bureaucracy. In J. Davies & D. Imbroscio (Eds.), *Theories of Urban Politics* (pp. 137–125). London: Sage. (2011). Rhodes' Contribution to Governance Theory. *Public Administration, 89*(1), 101–113.

Klein Woolthuis, R. (2010). Sustainable Entrepreneurship in the Dutch Construction Industry. *Sustainability, 2*(February), 505–523.

Knight Frank. (2014). *India Real Estate Outlook*: Mumbai: Knight Frank.

Koehler, D. A. (2007). The Effectiveness of Voluntary Environmental Programs. *The Policy Studies Journal, 35*(4), 689–722.

Koh, G., & Ling, O. G. (2004). Relationship between State and Civil Society in Singapore. In L. H. Guan (Ed.), *Civil Society in Southeast Asia* (pp. 167–197). Singapore: ISEAS.

Kohler-Koch, B., & Rittberger, B. (2006). The "Governance Turn" in EU Studies. *Journal of Common Market Studies, 44*(s1), 27–49.

Kolstad, L. (2014). *Designing a Mortgage Process for Energy Efficiency*. Washington, DC: American Council for an Energy-Efficient Economy.

Kosters, M., & van der Heijden, J. (2015). From Mechanism to Virtue: Evaluating Nudge Theory. *Evaluation, 21*(3), 276–291.

KPMG. (2011). *Survey on Bribery and Corruption*. Mumbai: KPMG.

Krueger, R., & Gibbs, D. (Eds.). (2007). *The Sustainable Development Paradox*. New York: Guilford Press.

Kumar, S., & Managi, S. (2012). The Potential for LCE in India. In A. Srinivasan, F. H. Ling, & H. Mori (Eds.), *Clima Smart Development in Asia* (pp. 41–56). Abingdon, UK: Routledge.

Kunmar, A. (2013). Challenges and Issues in Mega City Planning in India. *International Journal of Scientific Engineering and Research, 1*(3), 128–132.

Kwatra, S., & Essig, C. (2014). *The Promise and Potential of Comprehensive Commercial Building Retrofit Programs*. Washington, DC: American Council for an Energy-Efficient Economy.

Kwink Groep. (2013). *Externe Audit Green Deal Aanpak*. The Hague: Kwink Group.

Lack, B. (2012, 9 January 2012). The Better Buildings Initiative. Retrieved from www.dailyenergyreport.com/the-better-buildings-initiative-why-companies-are-taking-the-challenge/.

Lafferty, W., & Eckerberg, K. (1998). *From the Earth Summit to Local Agenda 21*. London: Earthscan.

Lane, M. B., & Morrison, T. H. (2006). Public Interest or Private Agenda? A Meditation on the Role of NGOs in Environmental Policy and Management in Australia. *Journal of Rural Studies, 22*(2), 232–242.

Lauria, M. (Ed.) (1997). *Reconstructing Urban Regime Theory*. London: Sage.

Layder, D. (2006). *Understanding Social Theory*. London: Sage.

Lechtman, H., & Hobbs, L. (1986). Roman Concrete and the Roman Architectural Revolution. In E. Lense (Ed.), *High-Technology Ceramics*. Westerville, OH: The American Ceramic Society.

Lee, T., & Koski, C. (2012). Building Green: Local Political Leadership Addressing Climate Change. *Review of Policy Research, 29*(5), 605–624.

Lee, W. L., & Yik, F. W. H. (2004). Regulatory and Voluntary Approaches for Enhancing Building Energy Efficiency. *Progress in Energy and Combustion Science, 30*(5), 477–499.

Lefcoe, G. (2011). Competing for the Next Hundred Million Americans: The Uses and Abuses of Tax Increment Financing. *The Urban Lawyer, 43*(2), 427–482.

Lemke, T. (2002). Foucault, Governmentality, and Critique. *Rethinking Marxism: A Journal of Economics, Culture & Society, 14*(3), 49–64.

Lenox, M. J., & Nash, J. (2003). Industry Self-Regulation and Adverse Selection. *Bussiness Strategy and the Environment, 12*(6), 343–356.

Lepatner, B. (2008). *Broken Buildings, Busted Budgets: How to Fix America's Trillion-Dollar Construction Industry*. Chicago: University of Chicago Press.

LESTARI. (1998). *Urbanization and Environment in Malaysia*. Chiba: Institute of Developing Economies Japan External Trade Organisation.

Levi-Faur, D. (2006). Varieties of Regulatory Capitalism. *Governance, 19*(3), 363–366.

(2012). *The Oxford Handbook of Governance*. Oxford: Oxford University Press.

Levy, J. (2008). Case Studies: Types, Designs, and Logics of Inference. *Conflict Management and Peace Science, 25*(1), 1–18.

Li, X., Clarck, C., Jensen, K., & Yen, S. (2014). Will Consumers Follow Climate Leaders? *Environmental Economics and Policy Studies, 16*(1), 69–87.

Lijphart, A. (1971). Comparative Politics and the Comparative Method. *The American Political Science Review, 65*(3), 682–693.

Lillie, N., & Greer, I. (2007). Industrial Relations, Migration and Neo-Liberal Politics. *Politics and Society, 35*(4), 551–581.

Lim, S., & Prakash, A. (2014). Voluntary Regulations and Innovation: The Case of ISO 14001. *Public Administration Review, 74*(2), 233–244.

Lin-Heng, L., & Youngho, C. (2004). Singapore: National Energy Security and Regional Cooperation. In B. Barton, C. Redgwell, A. Ronne, & D. Zillman (Eds.), *Energy Security: Managing Risks in a Dynamic Legal and Regulatory Environment* (pp. 391–412). Oxford: Oxford University Press.

Liu, F., Meyer, A., & Hogan, H. (2010). *Mainstreaming Building Energy Efficiency Codes in Developing Countries*. New York: The World Bank.

Lloyd, G. (2013, 25 May 2013). Solar Price Rise to End Power Divide. Retrieved from www.theaustralian.com.au/national-affairs/solar-price-rise-to-end-power-divide/story-fn59niix-1226650277855#.

Loosemore, M. (2013). Impediments to Reform in the Australian Building and Construction Industry. *Australian Journal of Construction Economics and Building, 3*(2), 1–8.

(2014, February 26, 2014). Building Output Lift Needs More than IR Reform. *Financial Review*. Retrieved from www.afr.com/p/opinion/building_output_lift_needs_more_ULL53n3jfHLlmyubIGiuII.

Lopez, R. (2002). Segregation and Black/White Differences in Exposure to Air Toxics in 1990. *Environmental Health Perspectives, 110*(Suppl 2), 289–295.

Lovins, A. (2013). *Reinventing Fire*. White River Junction, VT: Chelsea Green.

Lubell, M. (2004). Collaborative Environmental Institutions: All Talk and No Action? *Journal of Policy Analysis and Management, 23*(3), 549–573.

Ludlam, S. (2013). Whether or Not Australia Needs a National Urban Policy. *Urban Policy and Research, 31*(3), 261–264.

Lydersen, K. (2012, 31 August 2012). Retrofit Chicago: Is Energy Efficiency Plan Worth the Hype? *Midwest Energy News*. Retrieved from www.midwestenergynews.com/2012/08/31/retrofit-chicago-is-energy-efficiency-plan-worth-the-hype/.

Lyon, T. P., & Maxwell, J. W. (2006). *Greenwash*. Ann Arbor, MI: Ross School of Business.

(2007). Environmental Public Voluntary Programs Reconsidered. *The Policy Studies Journal, 35*(4), 723–750.

Lyon, T. P., & Wren Montgomery, A. (2015). The Means and End of Greenwash. *Organisation & Environment, 28*(2), 223–249.

Ma, H., Shao, H., & Song, J. (2013). Modeling the Relative Roles of the Foehn Wind and Urban Expansion in the 2002 Beijing Heat Wave and Possible Mitigation by High Reflective Roofs. *Meteorology and Atmospheric Physics, October,* 1–10.

Macnintosh, A., & Wilkinson, D. (2011). Searching for Public Benefits in Solar Subsidies: A Case Study on the Australian Government's Residential Photovoltaic Rebate Program. *Energy Policy, 39*(6), 3199–3209.

MacVaugh, J., & Schiavone, F. (2010). Limits to the Diffusion of Innovation. *European Journal of Innovation Management, 13*(3), 197–221.

Mahadevia, D., Joshi, R., & Sharma, R. (2009). *Integrating the Urban Poor in Planning and Governance Systems, India.* New Delhi: Centre for Urban Equity/CEPT University.

Mahoney, J. (2000). Path Dependency in Historical Sociology. *Theory and Society, 23*(4), 507–548.

Makri, A. (2014, September 26, 2014). Urban Sustainability Research with a Local Flavour. Retrieved from www.scidev.net/global/cities/scidev-net-at-large/urban-sustainability-research.html.

Maller, C., & Horne, R. (2011). Living Lightly: How Does Climate Change Feature in Residential Home Improvements and What Are the Implications for Policy? *Urban Policy and Research, 29*(1), 59–72.

Markandey, K., & Reddy Anant, G. (2011). *Urban Growth Theories and Settlement Systems of India.* New Delhi: Concept.

Marshall, D. (1979). *Urban Policy Making.* London: Sage.

Marshall, G. (2014). *Don't Even Think about It: Why Our Brains Are Wired to Ignore Climate Change.* New York: Bloomsbury.

Martin, J. (2012, 16 July 2012). 3kW Solar PV Systems: Pricing, Output, and Returns. Retrieved from www.solarchoice.net.au/blog/3kw-solar-pv-systems-pricing-output-and-returns/.

Martine, G. (2011). Preparing for Sustainable Urban Growth in Developing Areas. In United Nations Department of Economic and Social Affairs (Ed.), *Population Distribution, Urbanization, Internal Migration and Development.* New York: United Nations.

Marx, A., & Wouters, J. (2014). *Competition and Cooperation in the Market of Voluntary Sustainability Standards.* Leuven: KU Leuven.

Maryland Energy Administration. (2012, 7 May 2012). Maryland Green Building Tax Credit Program. Retrieved from http://energy.maryland.gov/Business/greenbuild.html.

Masoso, O. T., & Grobler, L. J. (2010). The Dark Side of Occupants' Behaviour on Building Energy Use. *Energy and Buildings, 42*(2), 173–177.

Matisoff, D. (2013). Different Rays of Sunlight: Understanding Information Disclosure and Carbon Transparency. *Energy Policy, 55*(1), 579–592.

Matthews, J. (2012). Green Growth Strategies – Korean Initiatives. *Futures, 44*(8), 761–769.

(2015). *Greening of Capitalism*. Stanford, CA: Stanford University Press.

Mattoo, A., & Subramanian, A. (2013). *Greenprint: A New Approach to Cooperation on Climate Change*. Washington, DC: Centre for Global Development.

Maxwell, J. W., Lyon, T. P., & Hackett, S. C. (2000). Self-Regulation and Social Welfare. *Journal of Law and Economics, 43*(October), 583–618.

Mazmanian, D., & Blanco, H. (Eds.). (2014). *Elgar Companion to Sustainable Cities*. Cheltenham, UK: Edward Elgar.

Mazzucato, M. (2015). The Innovative State. *Foreign Affairs, 94*(1), 61–68.

McDonough, W. (2004). Principles, Practices and Sustainable Design. In E. Huge & S. Tuerk (Eds.), *Perspecta 35: Building Codes*. Cambridge, MA: MIT Press.

McGraw Hill. (2013). *World Green Building Trends*. New York: Mc Graw Hill Construction.

McIntosh, A., & Wilkinson, D. (2010). *The Australian Government's Solar PV Rebate Program: An Evaluation of Its Cost-Effectiveness and Fairness*. Canberra: The Australia Institute.

McKinsey. (2009a). *Modernising Building Energy Codes*. New York: McKinsey. (2009b). *Unlocking Energy Efficiency in the U.S. Economy*. New York: McKinsey.

(2010). *India's Urban Awakening: Building Inclusive Cities, Sustaining Economic Growth*. Mumbai: McKinsey Global Institute.

McLaughlin, K., Osborne, S., & Ferlie, E. (2002). *New Public Management: Current Trends and Future Prospects*. New York: Routledge.

McLoughlin, B., & Huxley, M. (Eds.). (1986). *Urban Planning in Australia*. Melbourne: Longman Cheshire.

McManus, P. (2005). *Vortex Cities to Sustainable Cities: Australia's Urban Challenge*. Sydney: UNSW Press.

Meijer, F., Itart, L., & Sunikka-Blank, M. (2009). Comparing European Residential Building Stocks. *Building Research & Information, 37*(5–6), 533–551.

Mendel, J., & Korjani, M. (2013). Theoretical Aspects of Fuzzy Set Qualitative Comparative Analysis. *Information Sciences, 237*(1), 137–161.

Meres, R., Sigmon, J., DeWein, M., Garett, K., & Brown, J. (2012). Successful Strategies for Improving Compliance with Building Energy Codes *2012 ACEEE Summer Study on Energy Efficiency in Buildings*, 4_275-274_288.

Merton, R. K. (1957). *Social Theory and Social Structure: Revised and Enlarged Version*. Glencoe: Free Press.

Meyer, M. (2010). The Rise of the Knowledge Broker. *Science Communication, 32*(1), 118–127.

Michaelowa, K., & Michaelowa, A. (2012). India as an Emerging Power in International Climate Negotiations. *Climate Policy, 12*(5), 575–590.

Mikler, J. (2009). *Greening the Car Industry*. Cheltenham, UK: Edward Elgar.

Milburn, O. (2015). *Urbanization in Early and Medieval China*. Seattle: University of Washington Press.

Ministry of Economic Affairs. (2013a). *Intentieverklaringen Green Deal (Signed Green Deals)*. The Hague: Dutch Ministry of Economic Affairs.

(2013b). *Voortgangsrapportage Green Deals 2013* (Progress Report Green Deals 2013). The Hague: Ministerie van Economische Zaken (Dutch Ministry of Economic Affairs).

Ministry of Infrastructure and the Environment. (2013). *The Netherlands First Biennial Report under the United Nations Framework Convention on Climate Change.* The Hague: Ministry of Infrastructure and the Environment.

Ministry of New and Renewable Energy. (2012). *The Little Book of GRIHA Rating.* New Delhi: Ministry of New and Renewable Energy.

Ministry of the Environment and Water Resources. (2014). *Sustainable Singapore Blueprint 2015.* Singapore: Ministry of the Environment and Water Resources/Ministry of National Development.

Moe, E. (2012). Vested Interests, Energy Efficiency and Renewables in Japan. *Energy Policy,* 40(1), 260–273.

Moon, S.-G., & Ko, K. (2013). Act in Good Faith? The Effectiveness of U.S. Voluntary Environmental Programs. *International Review of Public Administration,* 18(3), 163–184.

Moore, G. (2002). *Crossing the Chasm.* New York: HarperCollins.

Morgenstern, R., & Pizer, W. (Eds.). (2007). *Reality Check: The Nature and Performance of Voluntary Environmental Programs in the United States, Europe and Japan.* Washington, DC: RFF Press.

Mortimer, D. (2003). *The Landcare Revolving Loan Fund: A Development Report.* Canberra: Rural Industries Research and Development Corporation

Mosier, S., & Fisk, J. (2013). Can Local Voluntary Environmental Programs "Work"? *Environmental Management,* 51(5), 969–987.

Mossberger, K., & Stoker, G. (2001). The Evolution of Urban Regime Theory. *Urban Affairs Review,* 36(6), 810–835.

Mumbai First. (2014). *Newsletter January 2014.* Mumbai: Bombay First.

Mumovic, D., & Santamouris, M. (2013). *A Handbook of Sustainable Building Design and Engineering.* Abingdon, UK: Routledge.

Municipality of Amsterdam. (2003). *Stadsdeelblad, afdeling 1, 169.* Amsterdam: Stadsdeel Amsterdam-Centrum.

Municipality of De Bilt. (2010). *DuBo-Covenant.* De Bilt: Gemeente De Bilt.

Murphy, L. (2012). A Qualitative Evaluation of Policy Instruments Used to Improve Energy Performance of Existing Private Dwellings in the Netherlands. *Energy Policy,* 45(June), 459–468.

(2014). The Policy Instruments of European Front-Runners: Effective for Saving Energy in Existing Dwellings? *Energy Efficiency,* 7(2), 285–301.

Murthy, N. (2010). *A Better India, a Better World.* New Delhi: Penguin India.

NABERS. (2013). History. Retrieved from www.nabers.gov.au/public/ WebPages/ContentStandard.aspx?module=10&template=3&include= History.htm&side=EventTertiary.htm.

Nan, N., Zmud, R., & Yetgin, E. (2014). A Complex Adaptive Systems Perspective of Innovation Diffusion: An Integrated Theory and Validated Virtual Laboratory. *Computational and Mathematical Organisation Theory,* 20(1), 52–88.

Nath, P., & Behera, B. (2011). A Critical Review of Impact of and Adaptation to Climate Change in Developed and Developing Economies. *Environment, Development and Sustainability,* 13(1), 141–162.

National Climate Change Secretariat. (2012). *Climate Change and Singapore: Challenges. Opportunities. Partnerships.* Singapore: National Climate Change Secretariat.

NCBG. (2003). *NCBG's TIF Almanac.* Chicago: Neighborhood Capital Budget Group.

NeJaime, D. (2009). When New Governance Fails. *Ohio State Law Journal, 70*(2), 323–399.

Neslen, A. (2015, February 25, 2015). European Carbon Market Reform Set for 2019. Retrieved from www.theguardian.com/environment/2015/feb/24/european-carbon-emissions-trading-market-reform-set-for-2019.

Newell, G., MacFarlane, J., & Kok, N. (2011). *Building Better Returns.* Sydney: Australian Property Institute.

Newman, P. (2014). Rediscovering Compact Cities for Sustainability. In D. Mazmanian & H. Blanco (Eds.), *Elgar Comanion to Sustainable Cities: Strategies, Methods and Outlook* (pp. 15–31). Cheltenham, UK: Edward Elgar.

Newman, P., & Kenworthy, J. R. (1999). *Sustainability and Cities: Overcoming Automobile Dependence.* Washington, DC: Island Press.

Newsham, G., Mancini, S., & Birt, B. (2009). Do LEED-Certified Buildings Save Energy? Yes, but ... *Energy and Buildings, 41*(8), 897–905.

Nielsen. (2011). *Sustainable Efforts and Environmental Concerns around the World.* New York: Nielsen.

North Carolina General Assembly. (2008). *Senate Bill 1597/S.L. 2008–22.* Raleigh, NC: North Carolina General Assembly.

NRDC. (2014). *Retrofit Chicago: Commercial Buildings Initiative.* Chicago: Natural Resources Defence Council.

NSW Government. (2011a). *About the NABERS Program.* Sydney: New South Wales Government.

(2011b). *National Australian Built Environment Rating System.* Sydney: New South Wales Government.

(2012). *Environmental Upgrade Agreements: A New Way to Finance Building Upgrades.* Sydney: NSW Government.

NYC Buildings. (2013). *Local Law 87/09 Energy Audits & Retro-Commissioning.* New York: NYC Buildings..

OECD. (2003). *Voluntary Approaches for Environmental Policy.* Paris: OECD.

(2013). *Greening Household Behavior: Overview from the 2011 Survey.* Paris: OECD.

Osbaldiston, R., & Schott, J. P. (2012). Environmental Sustainability and Behavioral Science. *Environment and Behavior, 44*(2), 257–299.

Osborne, D., & Gaebler, T. (1992). *Reinventing Government.* Reading, MA: Addison-Wesley.

Özen, Ş., & Küskü, F. (2009). Corporate Environmental Citizenship Variation in Developing Countries. *Journal of Business Ethics, 89*(2), 297–313.

Paavola, S. (2004). Abduction as a Logic and Methodology of Discovery. *Foundations of Science, 9*(3), 267–283.

PACE Now. (2013). *Annual Report.* Pleasantville, NY: PACE Now.

(2015). *Annual Report 2014.* Pleasantville, NY: PACE Now.

Pacewicz, J. (2013). Tax Increment Financing, Economic Development Professionals and the Financialization of Urban Politics. *Socio-Economic Review, 11*(3), 413–440.

Pan, W., & Garmston, H. (2012). Compliance with Building Energy Regulations for New-Build Dwellings. *Energy, 48*(1), 11–22.

Panayotou, T. (1998). *Instruments of Change: Motivating and Financing Sustainable Development.* Abingdon, UK: Earthscan.

Papadopoulos, A. (2015). Resilience: the Ultimate Sustainability. Retrieved from www.buildingresilient.com/. Retrieved from www.buildingresilient.com/.

Parliament of Australia. (2013, December 2, 2013). Australian Climate Change Policy: A Chronology. Retrieved from www.aph.gov.au/About_Parliament/Parliamentary_Departments/Parliamentary_Library/pubs/rp/rp1314/ClimateChangeTimeline.

Pawson, R. (2013). *The Science of Evaluation.* London: Sage.

Pawson, R., & Tilley, N. (1997). *Realistic Evaluation.* London: Sage.

Payne, G., & Williams, M. (2005). Generalization in Qualitative Research. *Sociology, 39*(2), 295–314.

Pérez-Lombard, L., Ortiz, J., González, R., & Maestre, I. R. (2009). A Review of Benchmarking, Rating and Labelling Concepts within the Framework of Building Energy Certification Schemes. *Energy and Buildings, 41*(3), 272–278.

Pérez-Lombard, L., Ortiz, J., & Pout, C. (2008). A Review on Buildings Energy Consumption Information. *Energy and Buildings, 40*(3), 394–398.

Perinotto, T. (2010). Melbourne Finds Holy Grail to Funding Green Retrofits. Retrieved from www.thefifthestate.com.au/politics/government/melbourne-finds-holy-grail-to-funding-green-retrofits/16137.

(2014a). Melbourne 1200 Building Programs on HVAC 101. Retrieved from www.thefifthestate.com.au/innovation/energy/melbourne-1200-building-programs-on-hvac-101/62307.

(2014b). The Ratings Battle: How Industry Is Trying to Derail LEED. Retrieved from www.thefifthestate.com.au/politics/government/the-ratings-battle-how-industry-is-trying-to-derail-leed/61428.

Perkins, R., & Neumayer, E. (2010). Geographic Variations in the Early Diffusion of Corporate Voluntary Standards: Comparing ISO 14001 and the Global Compact. *Environment and Planning A, 42*(2), 347–365.

Peters-Stanley, M., & Hamilton, K. (2012). *Developing Dimensions: State of Voluntary Carbon Markets 2012.* New York: Bloomberg New Energy Finance.

Peters, B. G. (1998). *Comparative Politics.* Houndsmills, UK: Palgrave.

Peters, B. G., & Pierre, J. (2012). Urban Governance. In P. John, K. Mossberger, & S. Clarcke (Eds.), *The Oxford Handbook of Urban Politics* (pp. 72–84). Oxford: Oxford University Press.

Pheng, L. S., Liu, J. Y., & Wu, P. (2009). Sustainable Facilities: Institutional Compliance and the Sino-Singapore Tianjin Eco-City Project. *Facilities, 27*(9/10), 368–386.

Pianoo. (2015). *Milieucriteria voor het maatschappelijk verantwoord inkopen van Kantoorgebouwen huur en aankoop* (Sustainable Procurement Criteria for Offices). The Hague: Pianoo.

Pierre, J. (2011). *The Politics of Urban Governance.* Houndsmills, UK: Pallgrave Macmillan.

Pierson, P. (2004). *Politics in Time*. Princeton, NJ: Princeton University Press.

Pinto, M. (2008). Urban Governance in India — Spotlight on Mumbai. In I. S. A. Baud & J. de Wit (Eds.), *New Forms of Urban Governance in India* (pp. 37–64). New Delhi: SAGE.

Pitt & Sherry. (2014). *National Energy Efficient Building Project*. Melbourne: Pitt & Sherry/Swinburne University of Technology.

Pivo, G. (2010). Owner-Tenant Engagement in Sustainable Property Investing. *The Journal of Sustainable Real Estate, 2*(1), 183–199.

Platform 31. (2014). *Rapportage Energiesprong 2013* (Annual Report Energy Leap 2013). The Hague: Platform 31.

Policy and Society. (2013). Innovative Methods for Policy Analysis: QCA and Fuzzy Sets. *Policy and Society, 32*(4), 279–356.

Ponrahono, Z. B. (no date). A Theoretical Study on Malaysia Development Planning Mechanism and Its Institutional Process. University Putra Malaysia, Serdang.

Popper, K. (2002 [1935]). *The Logic of Scientific Discovery*. London: Routledge.

Portney, K., & Berry, J. (2013). Civil Society and Sustainable Cities. *Comparative Political Studies, 47*(3), 395–419.

Potoski, M., & Prakash, A. (2005). Covenants with Weak Swords: ISO 14001 and Facilities Environmental Performance. *Journal of Policy Analysis and Management, 24*(4), 745–769.

(2009). *Voluntary Programs: A Club Theory Perspective*. Cambridge, MA: MIT Press.

(2013a). Do Voluntary Programs Reduce Pollution? Examining ISO 14001's Effectiveness across Countries. *Policy Studies Journal, 41*(2), 273–294.

(2013b). Green Clubs: Collective Action and Voluntary Environmental Programs. *Annual Review of Political Science, 16*(1), 399–419.

Prakash, A., & Potoski, M. (2012). Voluntary Environmental Programs: A Comparative Perspective. *Journal of Policy Analysis and Management, 31*(1), 123–138.

Property Council of Australia. (2014). *Office Market Report*. Sydney: Property Council of Australia.

Qinghua, G. (1998). Yingzao Fashi: Twelfth-Century Chinese Building Manual. *Architectural History, 41*(1), 1–13.

Ragin, C. (1987). *The Comparative Method*. Berkeley: University of California Press.

(2008). *Redesigning Social Inquiry*. Chicago: Chicago University Press.

Ragin, C., & Davey, S. (2014). *fs/QCA (Version 2.5)*. Irvine, CA: University of California.

Rajah, J. (2012). *Authoritarian Rule of Law: Legislation, Discourse and Legitimacy in Singapore*. Cambridge: Cambridge University Press.

Redclift, M., & Sage, C. (1998). Global Environmental Change and Global Inequality: North/South Perspectives. *International Sociology, 13*(4), 499–516.

Reid, E. M., & Toffel, M. W. (2009). Responding to Public and Private Politics. *Strategic Management Journal, 30*(11), 1157–1178.

RESNET. (2014, June 17, 2014). What's Behind the Growing Popularity of HERS Index Scores? Retrieved from www.hersindex.com/growing-popularity-of-hers-index-scores.

Resolve. (2012). *Towards Sustainability: The Roles and Limitations of Certification.* Washington, DC: RESOLVE.

Retrofit Chicago. (2015). Two Years into the Program, Participants Reduce Energy Use by 7%. Retrieved from http://retrofitchicagocbi.org/our-media/entry/two-years-into-the-program-participants-reduce-energy-use-by-7.

Rhodes, R. A. W. (2007). Understanding Governance: Ten Years On. *Organisation Studies, 28*(8), 1243–1264.

Riazi, S., Skitmore, M., & Cheung, Y. (2011). *The Use of Supply Chain Management to Reduce Delays: Malaysian Public Sector Construction Projects.* Paper presented at the 6th Nordic Conference on Construction Economics and Organisation in Society, Copenhagen.

Rihoux, B. (2013). Qualitative Comparative Analysis (QCA), Anno 2013. *Swiss Political Science Review, 19*(2), 233–245.

Rihoux, B., & Ragin, C. (2009). *Configurational Comparative Analysis.* London: Sage.

Rivera, J., & de Leon, P. (2004). Is Greener Whiter? Voluntary Environmental Performance of Western Ski Areas. *The Policy Studies Journal, 32*(3), 417–437.

Robinson, J., & Cole, R. (2015). Theoretical Underpinnings of Regenerative Sustainability. *Building Research & Information, 43*(2), 133–143.

Rocky Mountains Institute (2016). *Reinventing Fire: China.* New York: Rocky Mountains Institute.

Roderick, Y., McEwan, D., Wheatley, C., & Alonso, C. (2009). *A Comparative Study of Building Energy Performance Assessment between LEED, BREEAM and Green Star Schemes.* Paper presented at the Building Simulation 2009, Glasgow.

Rogers, E., & Weber, E. (2010). Thinking Harder about Outcomes for Collaborative Governance Arrangements. *The American Review of Public Administration, 40*(5), 546–567.

Rogers, E. M. (1995). *Diffusion of Innovations.* New York: Free Press.

Rogers, E. M., Medina, U., Rivera, M., & Wiley, C. (2005). Complex Adaptive Systems and the Diffusion of Innovations. *Innovation Journal, 10*(3), 1–26.

Rong, F. (2010). Understanding Developing Country Stances on Post-2012 Climate Change Negotiations. *Energy Policy, 38*(8), 4582–4591.

Ronit, K. (Ed.) (2012). *Business and Climate Policy: The Potentials and Pitfalls of Private Voluntary Programs.* New York: United Nations University Press.

Rose, R. (2014). *Learning about Politics in Time and Space.* Wivenhoe Park, UK: ECPR Press.

Rosly, D. (2011). Green Township Policy Initiatives in Malaysia. *IMPAK, 2011*(3), 1–7.

Rotmans, J. (2010). *Transitieagenda voor Nederland (Transition Agenda for the Netherlands).* Rotterdam: Kennisnetwerk Systeeminnovaties en transities/ Erasmus University Rotterdam.

(2011, October 6, 2011). Green Deal is Groene Façade (Green Deals Are Merely Window Dressing). Retrieved from www.youtube.com/watch?v=62sqtlX5g7o.

Roy, A. (2009). Why India Cannot Plan Its Cities. *Planning Theory, 8*(1), 76–87.

Rusk, B., Mahfouz, T., & Jones, J. (2011). Electricity's "Disappearing Act": Understanding Energy Consumption and Phantom Loads. *Technological Directions, 71*(1), 22–25.

Sabel, C., Fung, A., Karkkainen, B., Cohen, J., & Rogers, J. (2000). *Beyond Backyard Environmentalism.* Boston: Beacon Press.

Sabel, C., & Zeitlin, J. (2011). Experimentalist Governance. In D. Levi-Faur (Ed.), *The Oxford Handbook of Governance* (pp. 169–185). Oxford: Oxford University Press.

Salop, S. C., & Scheffman, D. T. (1991). Raising Rivals' Costs. *The American Economic Review, 73*(2), 267–271.

Sandel, M. (2012). *What Money Can't Buy.* London: Penguin Books.

Sandercock, L. (1990). *Cities for Sale: Property, Politics and Urban Planning in Australia.* New Brunswick, NJ: Transaction.

Sanderson, I. (2002). Evaluation, Policy Learning and Evidence-Based Policy Making. *Public Administration, 80*(1), 1–22.

Satterthwaite, D. (2009). The Implications of Population Growth and Urbanization for Climate Change. *Environment and Urbanization, 21*(2), 545–567.

Saul, B., Sherwood, S., McAdam, J., Stephens, T., & Slezak, J. (Eds.). (2012). *Climate Change and Australia.* Sydney: The Federation Press.

Schindler, S. B. (2010). Following the Industry's LEED: Municipal Adoption of Private Green Building Standards. *Florida Law Review, 62*(2), 285–350.

Schmidt, T. M., & Fischlein, M. (2010). Rival Private Governance Networks. *Global Environmental Change, 20*(3), 511–522.

Schneider, C., & Wagemann, C. (2012). *Set-Theoritic Methods for the Social Sciences.* Cambridge: Cambridge University Press.

Scofield, J. (2009). Do LEED-Certified Buildings Save Energy? Not Really . . . *Energy and Buildings, 41*(12), 1386–1390.

(2013). Efficacy of LEED-Certification in Reducing Energy Consumption and Greenhouse Gas Emissions for Large New York City Office Buildings. *Energy and Buildings, 67,* 517–524.

Scott, J., & Sturm, S. (2006). Courts as Catalysts: Re-Thinking the Judical Role in New Governance. *Colombia Journal of European Law, 13*(2), 565–594.

Segerson, K., & Miceli, T. (1998). Voluntary Environmental Agreements: Good or Bad News for Environmental Protection? *Journal of Environmental Economics and Management, 36*(2), 109–130.

Sen, J. (2013). *Sustainable Urban Planning.* New Delhi: The Energy and Resource Institute.

Sengers, F., Raven, R., & Van Venrooij, A. (2010). From Riches to Rags: Biofuels, Media Discourses, and Resistance to Sustainable Energy Technologies. *Energy Policy, 38*(9), 5013–5027.

Seville, C. (May 24, 2011). How to Cheat at LEED for Homes. Retrieved from www.greenbuildingadvisor.com/blogs/dept/green-building-curmudgeon/how-cheat-leed-homes.

Seyfang, G. (2009). *Green Shoots of Sustainability*. Norwich, UK: University of East Anglia.

Shaffi, F., Ali, Z. A., & Othman, M. Z. (2006). *Achieving Sustainable Construction in the Developing Countries in Southeast Asia*. Paper presented at the 6th Asia-Pacific Structural Engineering and Construction Conference, Kuala Lumpur.

Shah, V., & Joshi, P. (2010). *Revisioning Mumbai: Conceiving a Manifesto for Sustainable Development*. Mumbai: The Asiatic Society of Mumbai.

Shamsuddin, S., Zakaria, R., Mohamed, S., & Mustaffar, M. (2012). *Drivers and Challenges of Industrialised Building System*. Paper presented at the Sustaining the World with Better Structures & Construction Practice, Surabaya.

Shavell, S. (2007). On Optimal Legal Change, Past Behaviour, and Grandfathering. *NBER Working Paper Series, Working Paper 13563*, 1–36.

Sheehy, B. (2011). Understanding CSR: An Emprical Study of Private Self-Regulation. *Monash Law Reciew, 38*(2), 103–127.

Short, J. (2013). Self-Regulation in the Regulatory Void. *The Annals of the American Academy of Political and Social Science, 649*(1), 22–34.

Short, J., & Toffel, M. W. (2010). Making Self-Regulation More than Merely Symbolic. *Administrative Science Quarterly, 55*(2), 361–396.

Shrestha, P., & Kulkarni, P. (2013). Factors Influencing Energy Consumption of Energy Star and Non—Energy Star Homes. *Journal of Management in Engineering, 29*(3), 269–278.

Shui, B., Evans, M., Lin, H., Jiang, W., Liu, B., Song, B., & Sosmasundaram, S. (2009). *Country Reports on Building Energy Codes in China*. Washington, DC: U.S. Department of Energy.

Sichtermann, J. (2011). Slowing the Pace of Recovery: Why Property Assessed Clean Energy Programs Risk Repeating the Mistakes of the Recent Foreclosure Crisis. *Valparaidso University Law Review, 46*, 263–309.

Silver, H., Scott, A., & Kazepov, Y. (2010). Participation in Urban Contention and Deliberation. *International Journal of Urban and Regional Research, 34*(3), 453–477.

Simpson, G., & Clifton, J. (2014). Picking Winners and Policy Uncertainty: Stakeholder Perceptions of Australia's Renewable Energy Target. *Renewable Energy, 67*(July), 128–135.

Singapore Environment Council. (2011, October 15, 2011). FAQ about Project Eco-Office. Retrieved from http://sec.org.sg/ecooffice/faq.php.

(2012). *Project: Eco-Office Turns 10*. Singapore: Singapore Environment Council.

(2013). Project ECO-Office. Retrieved from www.ecooffice.com.sg/web/index.php.

Skaaning, S.-E. (2011). Assessing the Robustness of Crisp-Set and Fuzzy-Set QCA Results. *Sociological Methods and Research, 40*(2), 391–408.

Smith, A. (2011). The Transition Town Network: A Review of Current Evolutions and Renaissance. *Social Movement Studies: Journal of Social, Cultural and Political Protest, 10*(1), 99–105.

Soeter, J. P. (2010). *Bouw- en Voorraadeconomie 1960–2025*. Delft: Delft University of Technology.

Solanki, P. S., Malella, V. S., & Zhou, C. (2013). An Investigation of Standby Energy Losses in Residential Sector. *International Journal of Energy and Environment, 4*(1), 117–126.

Solomon, J. (2008). Law and Governance in the 21st Century Regulatory State. *Texas Law Review, 86,* 819–856.

SomerCor. (2014). *City of Chicago Small Business Improvement Fund (SBIF): Grant Program Rules*. Chicago: SomerCor.

Sonawane Sawant, S. (2009, October 12, 2009). Cities in State to Emulate PMC's Eco-Housing Programme. *The Times of India*. Retrieved from http://timesofindia.indiatimes.com/city/pune/Cities-in-state-to-emulate-PMCs-eco-housing-programme/articleshow/5113599.cms.

Squires, G., & Lord, A. (2012). The Transfer of Tax Increment Financing (TIF) as an Urban Policy for Spatially Targeted Economic Development. *Land Use Policy, 29*(4), 871–826.

Srinivasan, A., Ling, F. H., & Mori, H. (2012). *Climate Smart Development in Asia*. Abingdon, UK: Routledge.

Standing Committee on Environment and Heritage. (2005). *Sustainable Cities*. Canberra: The Parliament of the Commonwealth of Australia.

Staples, J. (2009). Environment: "What Was Right Was Also Popular." In G. Bloustien, B. Comber, & A. Mackinnon (Eds.), *The Hawke Legacy* (pp. 152–166). Kent Town, Australia: Wakefield Press.

Steger, M., & Roy, R. (2010). *Neoliberalism: A Very Short Introduction*. Oxford: Oxford University Press.

Steinfeld, J., Bruce, A., & Watt, M. (2011). Peak Load Characteristics of Sydney Office Buildings and Policy Recommendations for Peak Load Reduction. *Energy and Buildings, 43*(9), 2179–2187.

Stellberg, S. (2013). *Assessment of Energy Efficiency Achievable from Improved Compliance with U.S. Building Energy Codes: 2013 – 2030*. Washington, DC: Institute for Market Transformation.

Stevenson, A. (2015, February 17, 2015). A High-End Property Collapse in Singapore. *New York Times*, p. B1.

Stewart, R. (2006). Instrument Choice. In D. Bodansky, J. Brunnée, & E. Hey (Eds.), *The Oxford Handbook of Environmental Law* (pp. 147–181). Oxford: Oxford University Press.

Subramanian, T. S. R. (2009). *GovernMint in India: An Inside View*. New Delhi: Rupa.

Sundaraj, G. (2007). The Way Forward: Construction Industry Master Plan 2006–2015. *Master Builders, 2007*(1st Quarter), 48–51.

Sunikka-Blank, M., & Galvin, R. (2012). Introducing the Prebound Effect. *Building Research & Information, 40*(3), 260–273.

Sunikka, M., & Boon, C. (2003). Environmental Policies and Efforts in Social Housing: The Netherlands. *Building Research & Information, 31*(1), 1–12.

Sustainable Endowments Institute. (2011). *The Billion Dollar Challenge: Save Energy, Grow Money*. Washington, DC: Sustainable Endowments Institute.

Swan, W., & Brown, P. (2013). *Retrofitting the Built Environment*. Oxford: John Wiley & Sons.

Taleb, N. N. (2007). *The Black Swan*. London: Penguin Books.

Tao, J. (2009). Thinking Inside the Box: How Theory Frames Urban Problems. *State & Local Government Review, 41*(3), 223–230.

Taylor, N., Jones, P., Searcy, J., & Miller, C. (2014). Evaluating Ten Years of Energy Performance of HERS-Rated Homes in Alachua County, Florida. *Energy Efficiency, 7*(4), 729–741.

Taylor, P. (2013). *Extraodrinary Cities*. Cheltenham, UK: Edward Elgar.

Teisman, G., van Buuren, A., & Gerrits, L. (2009). *Managing Complex Governance Systems*. London: Routledge.

TERI. (2009). *An Exploration of Sustainability in the Provision of Basic Urban Services in Indian Cities*. New Delhi: TERI Press.

Teulings, B. (2013). *Balanceren tussen maatschappelijk en financieel rendement* (Balancing Societal and Financial Results). Amsterdam: BartTeulings Programma-Management en Advies.

Thaler, R., & Sunstein, C. (2009). *Nudge*, revised ed. London: Penguin.

Thatcher, M., & Coen, D. (2008). Reshaping European Regulatory Space. *West European Politics, 31*(4), 806–836.

Thøgersen, J. (2010). Country Differences in Sustainable Consumption. *Journal of Macromarketing, 30*(2), 171–185.

Thompson, S., & Maginn, P. (2012). *Planning Australia*. Cambridge: Cambridge University Press.

Tierney, W., & Lanford, M. (2014). The Question of Academic Freedom. *Frontiers of Education in China, p*(1), 4–23.

Tigchelaar, C. (2012). *Achtergrondrapport bij herijking Convenanten energiebesparing gebouwde omgeving*. Petten: ECN.

Timmer, C. P. (2012). Behavioral Dimensions of Food Security. *PNAS, 109*(31), 12315–12320.

Todd, J. A., Pyke, C., & Tufts, R. (2013). Implications of Trends in LEED Usage. *Building Research & Information, 41*(4), 384–400.

Trubek, D., & Trubek, L. (2010). The World Turned Upside Down. *Wisconsin Law Review, 719*, 719–726.

Trubek, D., & Trubek, L. G. (2007). Narrowing the Gap? Law and New Approaches to Governance in the European Union. *The Columbia Journal of European Law, 13*(3), 539–564.

Turaga, R., Howarth, R. B., & Borsuk, M. (2010). Pro-Environmental Behavior: Rational Choice Meets Moral Motivation. *Annals of the New York Academy of Sciences, 1185*(1), 211–224.

Tweede Kamer der Staten Generaal. (2012). *Kamerstuk 33124*. The Hague: Sdu Uitgevers.

U.S. Department of Energy. (2014a, May 9, 2014). Better Buildings Challenge to Cut Energy Waste Grows by 1 Billion Square Feet. Retrieved from http://energy.gov/articles/better-buildings-challenge-cut-energy-waste-grows-1-billion-square-feet.

(2014b). *Better Buildings Challenge: Progress Update Spring 2014*. Washington, DC: U.S. Department of Energy.

(2014c). *Saving Energy and Money with Building Energy Codes in the United States*. Washington, DC: U.S. Department of Energy.

(2015). *Progress Report 2015*. Washington, DC: U.S. Department of Energy.

U.S. Department of Housing and Urban Development. (1995). *Mortage Letter 95–46*. Washington, DC: U. S. Department of Housing and Urban Development

UGC. (2014a). *Baby It's Cold Inside*. New York: Urban Green Council.

(2014b). GPRO. Retrieved from http://gpro.org/.

UN-HABITAT. (2013). *State of the World's Cities 2012/13*. New York: Routledge.

UN. (2012a). *Resilient People, Resilient Planet: A Future Worth Choosing*. New York: United Nation.

(2012b). *World Population Prospects: The 2012 Revision*. New York: United Nations.

(2014). *World Urbanization Prospects: The 2014 Revision*. New York: United Nations.

UNCED. (1992). *Agenda 21*. Rio de Janerio: United Nations.

UNDP. (2013a). *Addressing Urban Poverty, Inequality, and Vulnerability in a Warming World*. Bangkok: United Nations Development Programme.

(2013b). *Human Development Report 2013*. New York: United Nations Development Programme.

UNEP. (2003). *Sustainable Building and Construction: Facts and Figures*. Paris: United Nations Environment Programme.

(2007). *Buildings and Climate Change: Status, Challenges and Opportunities*. Paris: United Nation Environment Programme.

(2009). *Buildings and Climate Change: Summary for Decision Makers*. Paris: United Nation Environment Programme.

(2010). *Common Carbon Metric*. Copenhagen: UNEP SBCI.

United Nations. (2013). *Population Distribution, Urbanization, Internal Migration and Development*. New York: United Nations.

URA. (2014). *Mater Plan: Written Statement*. Singapore: Urban Renewal Agency.

Urban Green. (2013). *Building Resiliency Taskforce: Full Report. June 2013*. New York: Urban Green Council.

(1995). *Mortage Letter 95-46*. Washington, DC: U. S. Department of Housing and Urban Development.

US Energy Information Administration. (2013). *International Energy Outlook*. Washington, DC: US Energy Information Administration.

US EPA. (1993). *Introducing …The Green Lights Program*. Washington, DC: U.S. Environmental Protection Agency.

(1997). *Risk Reduction through Voluntary Programs*. Washington, DC: United States Environmental Protection Agency.

USA Today. (2013, June 13, 2013). In U.S. Building Industry, Is It Too Easy to Be Green? Retrieved from www.usatoday.com/story/news/nation/2012/10/24/green-building-leed-certification/1650517/.

USAID ECO-III Project. (2010). *Performance Based Rating and Energy Performance Benchmarking for Commercial Buildings in India*. New Delhi: USAID ECO-III Project.

USGBC. (2010). *LEED Reference Guide for Green Building Operations and Maintenance.* Washington, DC: US Green Building Council.
(2013a, April 16, 2013). Certified Project Directory. Retrieved from www.gbci.org/GBCICertifiedProjectList.aspx.
(2013b). Incentives and Financing. Retrieved from www.usgbc.org/advocacy/priorities/incentives-financing.
(2013c, May 3, 2013). Infographic: LEED in the World. Retrieved from www.usgbc.org/articles/infographic-leed-world.
(2013d). USGBC History. Retrieved from www.usgbc.org/about/history.
(2014). *U.S. Green Building Council and the Energy and Resources Institute.* Washington, DC: US Green Building Council.
Van Bueren, E., & Priemus, H. (2002). Institutional Barriers to Sustainable Construction. *Environment and Planning B, 29*(1), 75–86.
van der Heijden, J. (2012). Voluntary Environmental Governance Arrangements. *Environmental Policies, 21*(3), 486–509.
(2013a). Greening the Building Sector: Roles for Building Surveyors. *Journal of Building Survey, Appraisal & Valuation, 2*(1), 24–32.
(2013b). Is New Governance the Silver Bullet? Insights from the Australian Buildings Sector. *Urban Policy and Research, 31*(4), 453–471: doi:10.1080/08111146.2013.769156
(2013c). Looking Forward and Sideways: Trajectories of New Governance Theory. *Amsterdam Law School Research Paper, 2013*(04), 1–26.
(2013d). Voluntary Environmental Governance Arrangements in the Australian Building Sector. *Australian Journal of Political Science, 48*(3), 349–365: doi:10.1080/10361146.2013.821456
(2013e). Win-Win-Win: Promises of and Limitations to Voluntarily Greening the Building Sector. *Construction Infrastructure Architecture World,* 2013 (August–September), 80–85.
(2014a). *Governance for Urban Sustainability and Resilience.* Cheltenham, UK: Edward Elgar.
(2014b). Selecting Cases and Inferential Types in Comparative Public Policy Research. In I. Engeli & C. Rothmayr (Eds.), *Comparative Policy Studies: Conceptual and Methodological Challenges* (pp. 35–56). Basingstoke: Palgrave Macmillan.
(2014c). What Role Is There for the State in Contemporary Governance? Insights from the Dutch Building Sector. *Recht der Werkelijkheid, 35*(3), 12–31.
(2015a). Interacting State and Non-State Actors in Hybrid Settings of Public Service Delivery. *Administration & Society,* (47), 2, 99–121.
(2015b). On the Potential of Voluntary Environmental Programmes for the Built Environment: A Critical Analysis of LEED. *Journal of Housing and the Built Environment, 30*(4), 553–567.
(2015c). Regulatory Failures, Split-Incentives, Conflicting Interests and a Vicious Circle of Blame: The New Environmental Governance to the Rescue? *Journal of Environmental Planning and Management, 58*(6), 1034–1057.

(2015d). The Role of Government in Voluntary Environmental Programs: A Fuzzy Set Qualitative Comparative Analysis. *Public Administration, 93*(3), 576–592.

(2015e). Voluntary Programmes for Building Retrofits: Opportunities, Performance and Challenges. *Building Research & Information, 43*(2), 170–184.

(2015f). What "Works" in Environmental Policy-Design? Lessons from Experiments in the Australian and Dutch Building Sectors. *Journal of Environmental Policy & Planning, 17*(1), 44–64.

(2015g). What Roles Are There for Government in Voluntary Environmental Programs? *Environmental Policy and Governance, 25*(5), 303–315.

(2016a). Experimental Governance for Low-Carbon Buildings and Cities: Value and Limits of Local Action Networks. *Cities, 53*(April), 1–7.

(2016b). The New Governance for Low-Carbon Buildings: Mapping, Exploring, Interrogating. *Building Research & Information, 44*(5–6), 575–584.

(2016c). Opportunities and Risks of the "New Urban Governance" in India. *Environment and Development, 25*(3), 251–275.

(2017). Eco-Financing for Low-Carbon Buildings and Cities: Value and Limits. *Urban Studies.* Retrieved from http://journals.sagepub.com/doi/abs/10.1177/0042098016655056

van der Heijden, J., & De Jong, J. (2009). Towards a Better Understanding of Building Regulation. *Environment and Planning B, Planning & Design, 36*(6), 1038–1052.

van der Heijden, J., & Van Bueren, E. (2013). Regulating Sustainable Construction in Europe: An Inquiry into the European Commission's Harmonization Attempts. *International Journal of Law in the Built Environment, 5*(1), 5–20.

van der Heijden, J., Visscher, H., & Meijer, F. (2007). Problems in Enforcing Dutch Building Regulations. *Structural Survey, 24*(3/4), 319–329.

Van der Horst, T., & Vergragt, P. (2006). The Seven Characteristics of Successful Sustainable System Innovations. In P. Nieuwenhuis, P. Vergragt, & P. Wells (Eds.), *The Business of Sustainable Mobility* (pp. 125–141). Sheffield, UK: Greenleaf.

van der Ven, H. (2015). Correlates of Rigorous and Credible Transnational Governance: A Cross-Sectoral Analysis of Best Practice Compliance in Eco-Labeling. *Regulation & Governance, 9*(3), 279–293.

Van Eijk, G. (2010). *Unequal Networks, Spatial Segregation, Relationships and Inequality in the City.* Amsterdam: IOS Press.

van Rooijen, S., & van Wees, M. (2006). Green Electricity Policies in the Netherlands. *Energy Policy, 34*(1), 60–71.

van Straalen, J. J., de Winter, P. E., Coppens, E. G. C., & Vermande, H. M. (2007). *Historische achtergronden gestelde eisen in het Bouwbesluit 2003 en de Regeling Bouwbesluit 2003* (History of Dutch Building Codes and Regulation). Utrecht: TNO Bouw en Ondergrond.

van Zoelen, B. (2014, September 23, 2014). Omstreden Amsterdams fonds wint klimaatprijs (Highly Contested Energy Fund Wins Climate Award).

Het Parool. Retrieved from www.parool.nl/parool/nl/4/AMSTERDAM/article/detail/3753079/2014/09/23/Omstreden-Amsterdams-fonds-wint-klimaatprijs.dhtml.

Vandenbergh, M., Barkenbus, J., & Gilligan, J. (2008). Individual Carbon Emissions: The Low-Hanging Fruit. *UCLA Law Review, 55,* 1701–1758.

Varcoe, B. (1991). Proactive Premises Management. *Property Management, 9*(4), 364–372.

Vasil, R. (2000). *Governing Singapore: A History of National Development and Democracy.* Singapore: Institute of Southeast Asian Studies.

Vatn, A. (2005). *Institutions and the Environment.* Cheltenham, UK: Edward Elgar.

Vedela, S. C., Bilolokar, R., Jaiswal, A., Connolly, M., & Deol, B. (2014). *Building Efficient Cities: Strengthening the Indian Real Estate Market through Codes and Incentives.* New York/Hyderabad: Natural Resources Defence Council/Administrative Staff College of India.

Venugopal, M., Srivastava, A., & Polycarp, C. (2012). *Public Financing Instruments to Leverage Private Capital for Climate-Relevant Investment.* Washington, DC: World Resources Institute.

Verweij, S., Klijn, E.-H., Edelenbos, J., & Van Buuren, A. (2013). What Makes Governance Networks Work? *Public Administration, 81*(4), 1035–1055.

Videras, J., & Alberini, A. (2000). The Appeal of Voluntary Environmental Programs. *Contemporary Economic Policy, 18*(4), 449–461.

Vig, N. J., & Faure, M. (Eds.). (2004). *Green Giants? Environmental Policies of the United States and the European Union.* Cambridge, MA: Massachusetts Institute of Technology.

Vinagre Diaz, J. J., Wilby, M. R., & Belén Rodríguez González, A. (2013). Setting up GHG-Based Energy Efficiency Targets in Buildings: The Ecolabel. *Energy Policy, 59*(C), 633–642.

Vis, B. (2012). The Comparatve Advantages of fsQCA and Regression Analysis for Moderately Large-N analyses. *Sociological Methods and Research, 41*(1), 168–198.

Vittal, N. (2012). *Ending Corruption? How to Clean Up India.* New Delhi: Viking.

Vogel, S. K. (1996). *Freer Markets, More Rules.* London: Cornell University Press.

Vreugdenhil, H., Slinger, J., Thissen, W., & Ker Rault, P. (2010). Pilot Projects in Water Management. *Ecology and Society, 15*(3), art. 13.

Vringer, K., van Middelkoop, M., & Hoogervorst, N. (2014). *Energie besparen gaat niet vanzelf. Evaluatie energiebesparingsbeleid voor de gebouwde omgeving* (Evaluation Building Energy Efficiency Policy). The Hague: Planbureau voor de Leefomgeving.

Wada, K., Akimotot, K., Sano, F., Oda, J., & Homma, T. (2012). Energy Efficiency Opportunities in the Residential Sector and Their Feasibility. *Energy, 48*(1), 5–10.

Walker, N., & de Búrca, G. (2007). Reconceiving Law and New Governance. *Colombia Journal of European Law, 13*(4), 519–537.

Wang, R. (2012). Adopting Local Climate Policies: What Have California Cities Done and Why? *Urban Affairs Review, 49*(4), 593–613.

Wang, X., Hawkings, C., & Berman, E. (2014). Financing Sustainability and Stakeholder Engagement: Evidence from U.S. Cities. *Urban Affairs Review*, *50*(6), 806–834.

Wang, X., Stern, R., Limaye, D., Mostert, W., & Zhang, Y. (2013). *Unlocking Commercial Financing for Clean Energy in East Asia*. Washington, DC: World Bank.

Warren, J., Wistow, J., & Bambra, C. (2013). Applying Qualitative Comparative Analysis (QCA) to Evaluate a Public Health Policy Initiative in the North East of England. *Policy and Society*, *32*(4), 289–301.

Weber, R. (2013). Tax Increment Financing in Theory and Practice. In S. White & Z. Kotval (Eds.), *Financing Economic Development in the 21st Century* (pp. 283–301). New York: Routledge.

Welch, E. W., Mazur, A., & Bretschneider, S. (2000). Voluntary Behavior by Electric Utilities. *Journal of Policy Analysis and Management*, *19*(3), 407–425.

Welford, R. (2005). Corporate Social Responsibility in Europe, North America and Asia. *Journal of Corporate Citizenship*, *17*(1), 33–52.

Wenren, J. (2012). *Ancient Chinese Encyclopedia of Technology*. Abingdon, UK: Routledge.

WGBC. (2013). *The Business Case for Green Building*. Toronto: World Green Building Council.

Wheeler, S. M., & Beatley, T. (2009). *The Sustainable Urban Development Reader*, 2nd ed. London: Routledge.

Whelan, R. (2012). *Submission: Recent Trends in and Preparedness for Extreme Weather Events Letter to Senate Standing Committees on Environment and Communications*. Sydney: Insurance Council of Australia.

The White House. (2011a). *Factsheet Better Buildings Initiative*. Washington, DC: The White House.

(2011b, December 2, 2011). We Can't Wait: President Obama Announces Nearly $4 Billion Investment in Energy Upgrades to Public and Private Buildings. Retrieved from www.whitehouse.gov/the-press-office/2011/12/02/we-cant-wait-president-obama-announces-nearly-4-billion-investment-energ.

(2013). *The President's Climate Action Plan*. Washington, DC: The White House.

Wilkinson, M. (2010). Three Concepts of Law. *Wisconsin Law Review*, *637*, 637–718.

Wong, J., Teh, P. S., Wang, V., & Chia, L. (2013). Solar Capability Building Programme for Public Housing. *Energy Procedia*, *33*(2013), 288–301.

Wong, T.-C. (2011). Eco-Cities in China. In T.-C. Wong & B. Yuen (Eds.), *Eco-City Planning* (pp. 131–150). Dordrecht: Springer.

Wong, T.-C., Yuen, B., & Goldblum, C. (Eds.). (2008). *Spatial Planning for a Sustainable Singapore*. New York: Springer.

Wood, S. (2003). Green Revolution or Greenwash? In Law Commission of Canada (Ed.), *New Perspectives on the Public–Private Divide* (pp. 123–165). Vancouver: UBC Press.

(2007). Voluntary Environmental Codes and Sustainability. In B. Richardson & S. Wood (Eds.), *Environmental Law for Sustainability* (pp. 229–276). Portland: Hart.

World Bank. (2011a). *Climate Change and the World Bank Group: The Challenge of Low-Carbon Development*. Washington, DC: The World Bank.

(2011b). *Supporting Efforts to Scale Capacity for Managing Urban Transformation*. New York: World Bank Institute.

World Water Council. (2007). *The Struggle for Water*. Marseille World Water Council.

Wurzel, R., Zito, A., & Jordan, A. (2013). *Environmental Governance in Europe*. Cheltenham, UK: Edward Elgar.

WVS. (2014). World Values Survey Wave 6. Retrieved from www.worldvaluessurvey.org/.

Yeow, C. T. (2010). National Green Technology Policy. *The Ingenieur*, *44*(December 2009–January 2010), 21–23.

Yu, D., & Hang, C. C. (2010). A Reflective Review of Disruptive Innovation Theory. *International Journal of Management Reviews*, *12*(4), 435–452.

Yudelson, J., & Meyer, U. (2013). *The World's Greenest Buildings*. Abingdon, UK: Routledge.

Yue, C. S. (2001). Singapore: Global City and Service Hub. In F.-C. Lo & P. Marcotullio (Eds.), *Globalization and the Sustainability of Cities in the Asia Pacific Region* (pp. 239–268). Tokyo: United Nations University Press.

Zaid, S., & Graham, P. (2013). GHG Emission of Low-Cost Housing in Malaysia Using UNEP-SBCI Common Carbon Metric. Retrieved from www.academia.edu/6572759/GHG_emission_of_low-cost_housing_in_Malaysia_using_UNEP-SBCI_Common_Carbon_Metric._Case_study_of_Kuala_Lumpur.

Zaid, S., Myeda, N. E., Mahyudding, N., & Sulaiman, R. (2014). Lack of Energy Efficiency Legislation in the Malaysian Building Sector Contributes to Malaysia's Growing GHG Emissions. Retrieved from www.e3s-conferences.org/articles/e3sconf/pdf/2014/02/e3sconf_etsdc2014_01029.pdf.

Zarsky, L. (1997). *Stuck in the Mud? Nation-States, Globalization and the Environment*. The Hague: Nautilus Institute.

Zetland, D., & Gasson, C. (2013). A Global Survey of Urban Water Tariffs: Are They Sustainable, Efficient and Fair? *International Journal of Water Resources Development*, *29*(3), 327–342.

Zimmerman, G. (2012). Department of Energy: Goal of Better Buildings Challenge Is to Cut Down on $60 Billion in Wasted Energy. Retrieved from www.facilitiesnet.com/energyefficiency/article/Department-of-Energy-Goal-of-Better-Buildings-Challenge-is-to-Cut-Down-on-60-Billion-in-Wasted-Energy-Facilities-Management-Energy-Efficiency-Feature–13269.

Zobel, T. (2013). ISO 14001 Certification in Manufacturing Firms. *Journal of Cleaner Production*, *43*(1), 37–44.

Index